Taming Sino-American Rivalry

T03555351

TAMING SINO-AMERICAN RIVALRY

FENG ZHANG
AND
RICHARD NED LEBOW

OXFORD
UNIVERSITY PRESS

Oxford University Press is a department of the University of Oxford. It furthers
the University's objective of excellence in research, scholarship, and education
by publishing worldwide. Oxford is a registered trade mark of Oxford University
Press in the UK and certain other countries.

Published in the United States of America by Oxford University Press
198 Madison Avenue, New York, NY 10016, United States of America.

Library of Congress Cataloging-in-Publication Data
Names: Zhang, Feng, 1980– author. | Lebow, Richard Ned, author.
Title: Taming Sino-American rivalry / Feng Zhang and Richard Ned Lebow.
Description: New York, NY : Oxford University Press, 2020. |
Includes bibliographical references and index.
Identifiers: LCCN 2019056327 (print) | LCCN 2019056328 (ebook) |
ISBN 9780197521946 (hardback) | ISBN 9780197521953 (paperback) |
ISBN 9780197521977 (epub) | ISBN 9780197521960 (updf) |
ISBN 9780197521984 (online)
Subjects: LCSH: United States—Foreign relations—China. |
China—Foreign relations—United States. |
Conflict management—United States. | Conflict management—China. |
National security—United States | National security—China.
Classification: LCC E183.8.C5 Z4218 2020 (print) | LCC E183.8.C5 (ebook) |
DDC 327.73051—dc23
LC record available at https://lccn.loc.gov/2019056327
LC ebook record available at https://lccn.loc.gov/2019056328

3 5 7 9 8 6 4 2

Paperback printed by LSC Communications, United States of America
Hardback printed by Bridgeport National Bindery, Inc., United States of America

To my loves, Shu Man and Zhang Han
—Feng Zhang

To Carol, Kate, Eli, David, and Andrew,
who add the icing to the cake of life
—Richard Ned Lebow

Contents

I

Thinking Differently about Conflict Management

COMPETITION BETWEEN AMERICA and China has intensified since 2009. Old tensions over the South China Sea, Taiwan, and North Korea continued to fester. China pressed ahead with its territorial claims in the South China Sea, deploying antiship and antiaircraft missiles and forces and a long-range bomber on islands it built. The US military ratcheted up its sea and air patrols, sailing warships close to Chinese-held islands and flying B-52 bombers over them. Beijing froze high-level contact with the pro-independence government in Taiwan, weaned away its diplomatic allies, and began "island-encircling" patrols.[1] In response, the Donald Trump administration and Congress tightened US ties with Taiwan. A new Taiwan Travel Act was passed, four arms sales were approved in less than three years, and warships were dispatched through the Taiwan Strait to stare down Beijing.[2] On the Korean Peninsula, Trump accused China of thwarting the progress of denuclearization.[3]

New disputes over trade, technology, and political interference shot to the top of the American agenda. By September 2019 Trump had imposed tariffs on $361 billion in Chinese imports, bringing average tariffs on Chinese imports to 21.2 percent, up from only 3.1 percent when he took office.[4] In August 2019 he claimed authority to order American businesses to leave China.[5] His administration, led by the Justice Department and intelligence agencies, began indicting Chinese technology firms such as Huawei and arresting Chinese personnel on espionage and other charges, even outside of US territory for extradition to the United States.[6] American scholars and commentators, meanwhile, supplied ammunition to the administration by accentuating the gravity of technological competition and the urgency that the United States win it.[7]

In September 2018 Trump accused China—without evidence—of interfering in the coming US midterm congressional elections.[8] His officials, think tank analysts, and journalists alleged sustained and far-reaching Chinese efforts at influencing American voters.[9] The following month Vice President Mike Pence accused Beijing of "employing a whole-of-government approach, using political, economic, and military tools, as well as propaganda, to advance its influence and benefit its interest in the United States." "China," he insisted, "wants nothing less than to push the United States of America from the Western Pacific and attempt to prevent us from coming to the aid of our allies."[10]

Competition and rivalry replaced engagement and cooperation. This about-face met little opposition within the US Congress or among the media and intellectuals. Few public discussions portrayed China in a positive light. Most depicted it as an aggressive, illiberal, and authoritarian power bent on challenging America in Asia and around the world.[11] The few who called for smart engagement aimed at reducing tension were ridiculed for their supposed naiveté.[12] Accommodating China was equated with rewarding bad behavior.[13] Frustration over China was so intense that many applauded Trump for no other reason than his rhetorical pounding of China.[14] In February 2019 a task force of leading American experts warned that tensions had risen to levels "unprecedented in the past forty years of U.S.-China relations."[15]

Chinese leaders and analysts watched Washington's anti-China frenzy with increasing alarm. Many were stupefied by the rapid downturn of the relationship and worried about where it would lead.[16] The Ministry of Finance organized a think-tank alliance across China's major research institutes to grapple with the new, increasingly hostile political reality.[17] For many influential Chinese, American initiatives and rhetoric have produced a parallel reaction: the belief that Washington is unprepared to accept peacefully China's rise as a great power.

Rivalry between America and China has serious consequences for regional and international order. These two countries command the world's largest economies, strongest militaries, and most advanced technological bases. A military clash between these titans would be calamitous for them and the world.

This book explains why Sino-American competition has intensified since the Barack Obama administration and, more important, how leaders in both countries can develop a constructive strategic framework to ease competition, manage conflict, and reach an accommodation without giving up any of their meaningful goals.

America and China have every reason to live in harmony and benefit themselves and the world by doing so. No territorial disputes divide them the way they did many other great power rivalries that led to war. Neither country seeks to conquer the other or invade its formal allies. They disagree on many substantive issues, but none whose effects cannot be addressed or softened, or even resolved, by diplomacy. Yet in both countries more and more officials and pundits think that the two most powerful countries of the twenty-first century are on a collision course. Why is this so, and what can be done about it?

We contend that there are two underlying causes of conflict. First, Chinese and American leaders and peoples seek self-esteem, and do so in large part through their country's standing in the world; therefore Sino-American competition is more a clash of egos than of interests.[18] The symbolic nature of the competition makes it more, rather than less, difficult to resolve. Max Weber observed in the context of Franco-German relations, "Nations will sacrifice their interests, but never their honor."[19] It is now apparent to prominent historians of the period that World War I was more about honor than about security or material interests.[20] It was also a major driver of the Cold War, and perhaps the major driver after the 1975 Helsinki Accords recognized the European postwar territorial status quo.[21]

Classical realists such as Hans Morgenthau understood that there was no such thing as "the" national interest, only different and competing formulations. Conceptions of national interest are all subjective and at best serve as a guide for foreign policy. They are often shaped by ideology that has little to do with real interests. There are invariably difficult trade-offs to make between or among important goals. And very few leaders can conduct foreign policy without being hobbled by domestic constraints.[22] Formulating coherent conceptions of national interest is not an easy task, and we examine the difficulties American and Chinese leaders have had in this regard. We contend that there is no fundamental conflict of interests between the two nations, and when such conflict of interests does arise it is often attributable to unenlightened understandings of mutual interests and less than shrewd ways of advancing them.

The second principal cause of conflict is the faulty conceptions leaders and intellectuals in both countries use to understand one another's motives and foreign policies. These conceptions are rooted in history, confirmed tautologically, and make the other country more rather than less threatening. A prime example on the American side is power transition theory, which encourages the belief, some argue the near certainty, that rising powers always challenge dominant powers for leadership of international society and that this is the major cause of great power wars. But there is absolutely no evidence in support of power transition theory—quite the reverse. The history of the past five hundred years reveals that dominant powers routinely accommodate rising ones and that the latter seek recognition and accommodation, not dominance achieved by war.[23]

Policies based on so-called historical lessons generate Sino-American tensions, just as they did Soviet-American tensions during the Cold War. Deterrence was the principal offender in the Cold War and threatens to become so in Sino-American relations. Both the USSR and the United States were convinced that they had to display resolve or be perceived as weak. Deterrence in the form of arms buildups, forward deployments, and threatening rhetoric became a principal cause of war-threatening crises between the United States and the Soviet Union and between the United States and China.[24] It has the potential to do so again in the Pacific.

As our take on deterrence suggests, our book is at odds with the conventional wisdom in China and America about how to manage their relationship. We challenge many of the principal strategies the two countries have pursued, not only the way in which they have been applied. We argue that some of these strategies are based on superficial learning and false historical lessons. Our critique lays the foundation for an alternative set of conceptions we think more appropriate to Sino-American relations, and whose application would make it possible for both nations to buttress their self-esteem in less confrontational ways.

We are dubious about realist and liberal approaches to Sino-American relations. Chapter 2 provides a detailed critique of these paradigms. Analyzing foreign policy in terms of power and relative power is always inadequate, no matter how these concepts are conceived and measured. Considerations of power are never more than an enabling condition and instrumentality. This is not to dismiss their importance; the rise of China is itself a reflection of power as a critical enabling condition. Classical realists like Morgenthau understood that power is a starting point—but by no means the end point—of any serious analysis of international affairs. Morgenthau believed that successful foreign policy depended more on the quality of diplomacy than on military and other capabilities and had to be tempered by ethical considerations. Contemporary realists who start with power and infer foreign policy goals from it conduct their analysis the wrong way around.[25]

Liberals have long been optimistic about the ability of the so-called liberal international order to accommodate peacefully China's rise.[26] This expectation has become increasingly shaky by virtue of China's trajectory under President Xi Jinping. Without any good remedy to reboot cooperation, liberals now fear that the divergence between China and America in terms of political and economic development models may ineluctably lead to tension and conflict.

We recognize the challenges in managing the American-Chinese relationship but are not as pessimistic about the prospect of a cooperative relationship as are many realists and liberals. We believe there are many reasons for cautious optimism, all the more so if leaders and their advisors recognize the counterproductive results of some of their previous strategies and formulate more realistic understandings of each other. Chapters 3 and 4 foreground the most important of these mistakes. Chapter 5 through 7 explore how some of these strategies and others might be used effectively and, of equal importance, how they might be combined as part of a holistic approach to conflict management and resolution.

Our analysis of mistakes focuses on the recent past, from 2009 to 2019. In the case of the United States, this period covers the Obama and Trump administrations. The former was the last "normal" era of government and foreign policy, and its approach to China is indicative of the assumptions and goals of what might be called the national security establishment. The Trump administration is a radical departure and atypical of the kinds of policies that would have been pursued by any other Republican or Democratic president. We cannot ignore the history of these two administrations because they have profoundly affected how the Chinese think about America, but we should recognize Trump's policies as significantly deviant. Our critique will accordingly address both administrations and their policies but focus more on Obama's. The successes and failures of Sino-American relations during his eight years in office are likely to create an illustrative framework to which Trump's successors will return.

Chapter 3 argues that the most glaring American mistake is the reluctance to develop a productive strategy for transforming the relationship with China into one that is stable and cooperative. The Obama administration developed no distinct China strategy and was in fact averse to developing such a strategy. It chose to embed largely reactive China policies within a regional strategy of the pivot or rebalance to Asia. The rebalance strategy relegated China to a management issue and damaged the relationship by deepening strategic mistrust and exacerbating Chinese assertiveness. Under Trump relations deteriorated further, but not as the result of any coordinated American strategy. Rather it was due to Trump's trade war and the opportunism of his senior officials.

Chapter 4 identifies three critical junctures and examines Chinese mistakes at each. In 2009, President Obama's first year in office, China failed to fully reciprocate his positive signaling for a cooperative relationship. The second juncture came in February 2012, when Vice President Xi's visit to Washington ignited high-level diplomacy for building what Xi referred to as "a new model of major-country relationship."[27] But this diplomacy, promising at the start, was defeated by faulty implementation on the Chinese side. After 2014 the relationship became bogged down in worsening mistrust and rising tensions, especially in maritime Asia.

Our analysis of Sino-American relations during the Obama years yields an important finding: neither country managed to develop a holistic strategy for easing their intensifying competition. How, then, can such a strategy be developed? Recent scholarly works offer useful suggestions. James Steinberg and Michael E. O'Hanlon argue that a well-crafted strategy needs to combine reassurance and resolve, and they identify a number of tools toward this end.[28] Tom Christensen's argument is similar, although critical of the concept of reassurance. His preferred strategy is a combination of engagement and deterrence.[29] Lyle Goldstein offers a model of "cooperation spirals" whereby America and China take consecutive and sequential steps toward building greater confidence and trust that will eventually result in a stable relationship.[30] Amitai Etzioni suggests actions America can take to reach accommodation with China.[31]

We share the spirit of these works. Growing competition is creating risks for conflict, compelling all concerned scholars and analysts to propose remedies to prevent it. But our approach is different. We do not recommend a fixed set of policies. Rather, drawing on theoretical advances in international relations over the past half-century and historical lessons since the two world wars and the Cold War, we offer a holistic framework for conflict management and resolution based on the three pillars of deterrence, reassurance, and diplomacy. In principle, this framework should be applicable to any great power relationship in modern international relations. Its application, as in the case of Sino-American relations, is highly context-dependent.

Chapter 5 assesses the relevance and risks of deterrence in conflict management. Deterrence aims to prevent an adversary from resorting to force by manipulating its cost calculus. It is appropriate when directed against states whose leaders harbor aggressive intentions. Yet even then the success rate of general and immediate deterrence is low. We demonstrate the downside of deterrence and the psychological and political reasons why the use of threats, especially credible ones, often provokes the kind of behavior they are intended to prevent.

Deterrence is currently foundational to American and Chinese security policy, although more so in America's case than in China's. We characterize the American strategy as one of hegemonic deterrence and the Chinese approach as active defense. These strategies together can produce tit-for-tat buildups and displays of resolve that encourage, and then confirm, each side's worst-case assumptions of the other. We have no illusion that either country will abandon deterrence as a principal security strategy. We suggest, however, that it would be in their mutual interest to reduce the intensity of deterrence and create room for the more constructive strategies of reassurance and diplomacy.

Reassurance seeks to ease competition and induce accommodation by reducing the fear, misunderstanding, and insecurity that can be responsible for escalation and war. Chapter 6 identifies six forms of reassurance that have contributed to ameliorating past conflicts: reciprocity, irrevocable commitment, self-restraint, norms of competition, limited security regimes, and trade-offs. We provide historical examples to illustrate the distinct functions and advantages of these strategies, as well as the risks and conditions for their effective implementation.

Reassurance has played a major role historically in facilitating accommodation between America and China. The best example is the rapprochement initiated by Richard Nixon and Henry Kissinger in the 1970s and greeted positively by Mao Zedong and Zhou Enlai. Reassurance combined with diplomacy reset the relationship in dramatic fashion. Does it have the potential to do so again? We select four major areas of tension in the relationship—Taiwan, North Korea, Asian maritime disputes, and the American alliance system in Asia—to examine this question, and find that all six forms of reassurance would be relevant and useful.

American-Chinese rivalry is probably inevitable. But there is no reason for it to take forms that threaten economic intercourse and good political relations between the countries. Cooperation and accommodation can be achieved through sophisticated strategies of reassurance. Toward these ends policymakers must take full advantage of diplomacy—the third generic strategy of conflict management and resolution. Chapter 7 examines the conditions for successful diplomacy. It requires leaders committed to accommodation who are imaginative and flexible in their thinking and have domestic political freedom to maneuver. They must break free from conceptions of their adversary that have shaped prior policies, find ways of testing the water before committing themselves to initiatives that would be costly if unsuccessful, and devise careful plans for their implementation. Diplomats, like political leaders, need sufficient latitude to exercise initiative and apply their expertise in pursuit of leader-sponsored initiatives. Incentives and catalysts, or crises, can be useful to leaders and diplomats alike when they generate urgency and lead to the recognition that threat-based strategies such as war and deterrence are counterproductive.

Numerous observers of the international scene argue that the key strategic challenge in Asia is peaceful accommodation between China and its rising ambitions and the United States and its commitment to maintain international leadership.[32] We think this a feasible goal under two conditions. China must adopt some version of its traditional concept of *wangdao*, something akin to the Greek concept of *hēgemonia*. It is a form of regional leadership based on receiving honor in return for providing security and economic benefits. And the United States must recognize that China's rise to power does not have to constitute a threat to its security and economic interests; it might actually advance those interests if it took the form of *wangdao*. The United States in turn would be well advised to give up its fruitless and costly search for hegemony and to adopt something closer to *hēgemonia*.

Several caveats are in order. Conflict management is no silver bullet. Even the most sophisticated and best-coordinated strategies can fail, and for multiple reasons. Target leaders can be obtuse to signals, miscalculate the costs and risks of cooperation or competition, subordinate avoidance or resolution to other foreign and domestic goals, or correctly conclude that continued competition is in their national or political interest. Leaders attempting to reduce tensions can miscalculate the effects of their initiatives on key foreign or domestic constituencies. Many conflicts are simply not ready for serious amelioration, let alone resolution, because leaders do not have sufficient authority or control over their governments or armed forces, fear losing control if they appear weak or compromising, or believe the risks and costs of any move toward peace greater than those of enduring the status quo. We believe good prospects for Sino-American relations will present themselves in the future, but timing and overcoming domestic and organizational constraints will still be essential.

Strategies of conflict management take time to produce positive effects. General deterrence aims to discourage an adversary in the long term from considering the use of force a viable option, and immediate deterrence aims to prevent a specific use of force when a challenge appears likely or imminent. Ideally the two strategies work together to prevent challenges but also to convince adversarial leaders that the military option is fruitless and that their national and political interests are best served by some kind of accommodation. When successful, deterrence can not only forestall armed conflict but can also provide an incentive for adversaries to seek accommodation. Reassurance and diplomacy also take time but have the potential to produce more rapid results.

This empirical reality further highlights the importance of context. The most sophisticated and cleverly applied strategy of conflict management can fail when adversarial leaders are unreceptive or fearful of the consequences of grasping the olive branch. Less sophisticated and cleverly applied strategies can succeed when leaders are well disposed to accommodation. Ripeness is a concept used to describe the latter situation and is often applied in a circular manner. Conflicts that are resolved are thought to have been ripe for resolution, and conflicts that are not ripe remain unresolved. We avoid this circularity by stipulating the conditions that facilitate or hinder conflict management and resolution. Most, but not all, are beyond the direct control of adversaries or third parties. Efforts at conflict resolution when there is little chance of success may make subsequent efforts more difficult, as may be true in several Middle Eastern conflicts.

We distinguish conflict management from conflict resolution. "Conflict management" is a general term applied to efforts to keep strategic competition contained. This can mean preventing military escalation (e.g., the use of armed force or development, the deployment of new weapons, or the forward deployment of existing weapons) or political escalation that extends existing competition to new regions or participants. Our goal with respect to the Sino-American relationship is conflict management in the short term but conflict resolution in the longer run. Both goals contribute to the ultimate objective of taming American-Chinese rivalry.

Our final point is a conceptual one. We reject realist and liberal approaches that assume a privileged analytical perspective, and one moreover with predictive potential. Any theoretical perspective is merely a starting point for a narrative that folds in context. Theories are frames of reference for organizing inquiry into questions and problems and subsequent narratives that purport to explain events or make admittedly uncertain forecasts about the future. This assumption informs our approach to conflict management. We do not provide rigid guidelines about how these theories should be combined or which areas of tension should be addressed first. Leaders can assess the relative importance of contentious issues and decide the order in which they should be addressed. There is no general rule because behavior and outcomes are determined by agents acting in context.

2

Imagining the Worst, Hoping for the Best

THE RESURGENCE OF China has become a matter of growing concern for American policymakers and academics. Policy memos, newspaper articles, and academic journals describe China as an emerging behemoth. Analysts disagree about the consequences of this rise. Realists generally portray China as a revisionist power intent on dominating Asia and changing the rules of the global economy to its own benefit at others' expense. Before President Xi Jinping came to power in 2012, liberals depicted Chinese leaders as focused primarily on economic development and increasingly tamed and constrained by virtue of their country's growing dependence on foreign markets and investment. Now they cast China in a darker light, criticizing its slide toward political repression, economic mercantilism, and international competition. Liberals remain skeptical about the realist prognosis of a future conflict between China and America. But they are increasingly disillusioned by China's trajectory under Xi. Believing that China is diverging from, rather than converging with, America in terms of political liberty and economic openness, they no longer see it as a genuine partner.

We challenge these realist and liberal interpretations. Driven by their ideological assumptions they amplify some aspects of Chinese behavior but overlook others. They fail to capture the complexity and nuance of Chinese policy. They all but ignore Chinese culture and history and how they might influence Chinese policy thinking. And they use evidence selectively. Some of the most widely quoted newspaper columnists and, alas, the occasional scholar offer quotes and figures that can be interpreted to support their positions and ignore those that cannot.

American assertions of hegemony, statements by elected officials and scholars that war with a rising China is a real possibility, and efforts to build an anti-Chinese coalition of Pacific Rim states have become matters of increasing concern in China. Chinese analysts differ among themselves as to how China should respond to a militarily ever more powerful and aggressive America. The hardliners of the People's Liberation Army assert that China should intensify its military modernization program to reduce America's military superiority in the Western Pacific, deterring it from intervening in local contingencies such as the Taiwan Strait. Moderates in the civilian foreign policy establishments urge caution but also complain bitterly about America's "hegemonic mindset" and its damage to strategic trust between the two countries.

Powerful forces in both countries consider themselves on the defensive in the face of the assumed aggressive intentions of the other. Many analysts in both countries use worst case analyses and cherry-pick facts to support their claims. Unfortunately both countries have frequently behaved in ways that make it easier for those who propagate Cassandra-like visions of future conflict, if not war. The United States has invaded Afghanistan and Iraq, arms Taiwan, deploys ships and aircraft in provocative ways off China's coasts, and spends more on its military than the next ten largest military powers. China in turn crushes internal dissent, rules Tibet and Xinjiang in a heavy-handed manner, fails to restrain North Korea's nuclear weapons program, and makes far-reaching offshore territorial and maritime claims, increasingly backed by military efforts to intimidate its neighbors.

On the American side, the dominant analytical lens is power transition theory, which asserts that war is all but inevitable between a rising, would-be dominant power and an existing, if declining, one. Its proponents contend that this has always happened in the past and is something akin to a law of history. There is absolutely no historical evidence for power transition theory, and we will debunk its claims in due course. It is so sharply at odds with history that one cannot help but conclude that at least some of the policymakers, academics, and journalists who flog it should know better. They use it to justify their claims to a gullible and frightened public that war is likely, if not inevitable, and that the United States should maintain, if not increase, its military efforts to balance China's in the Pacific.

There are diverse discourses in China. Until President Donald Trump took office in January 2017, the dominant discourse depicted the United States as simultaneously engaging and balancing China. The moderates focused on the US strategy of engagement and appreciated its contribution to China's integration into international society. In the face of the Trump administration's penchant for disengagement and competition, however, this view was increasingly marginalized. Gaining steady currency was the hawkish interpretation, long flogged by a vocal minority of hardliners, that America's so-called strategy of balancing China was in fact a smokescreen for containment. To China the implication is obvious enough: it must develop robust military capabilities and strategic options to confront it. Whatever their policy persuasions, most Chinese observers, including the moderates, believe that there is a structural contradiction inherent in Sino-American relations, in the sense that China's interests as a rising power are bound to come into conflict with America's interests as the dominant established power. In such thinking they are much influenced by American international relations theories, notably realist and power transition theories. These theories reinforce pessimism in both countries and feed arguments about the utility of coercive strategies for competition and conflict. We argue that such theories are intellectually dubious and dangerous for policy.

Yet all is not as dark as it may appear on the analytical front. There is impressive work on Chinese politics and foreign policy by knowledgeable Western scholars who are fairer in their use of evidence and more cautious in their judgments. The same is true in China, where well-trained scholars of the United States and its foreign policy produce nuanced studies. Alas, nuance does not count for much in the policy world. People want simple answers, and there are many politicians, journalists, and scholars who are quite willing to provide them. In both countries there is more to gain from posing as tough and uncompromising than pliant and accommodating, even when it may clearly be in the national interest. Depictions of the other as a grasping and overreaching enemy resonate among American and Chinese publics, in contrast to efforts to understand the world from the other's point of view. The former all but drowns out the latter.

Making sense of China today is somewhat easier than trying to understand the Soviet Union during the Cold War. That country was characterized by extreme secrecy, official publications that rarely, if ever, deviated from the party line, and analysts and scholars for the most part unwilling to express their own views. China is a more open society by comparison. Its newspapers are responsive to its leadership but publish a surprising range of opinions, as do various Chinese ministries, organizations, and businesses. As all scholars who deal with their Chinese counterparts know, they can be quite outspoken at scholarly gatherings, and more so in private. The Chinese make available far more data about their economy than did the Soviets. This provides Western analysts with useful information about such matters as the frequency of violent protests in rural China, the Chinese military budget and debates over force structures, Chinese energy shortages, and, of particular interest to us, the views of Chinese analysts about American foreign policy goals. While these should not be viewed naively, they do provide us with more insight than is often admitted by American international relations scholars who commonly ignore them.

This information does not allow us to resolve the question of what China wants. One reason for this is the diversity of views on these subjects within the country. Consider the problem in reverse: Chinese analysts attempt to fathom

America's goals. Their answers would depend on which segment of American opinion they listened to, and even then any smart observer would know that American foreign policy reflects not only presidential goals and congressional pressures and constraints but also unpredictable compromises with relevant bureaucracies. While China is not a pluralist country in the same sense as is the United States, its policies reflect input from diverse internal sources and different understandings of international constraints and opportunities. The best analysts in either country can identify trends and construct narrative forecasts that they believe will be more likely to occur than others—but in full recognition that events at home or abroad can bring about significant and unanticipated shifts in policy. The events of September 11, 2001, had this effect for the United States, as have other political and economic shocks for both countries. Certainty is out of the question, and for this reason so is prediction. Cautious judgments and forecasting—with the expectation of updating and revision—are the best we can provide.

With these caveats in mind, we offer a critique of the realist and liberal positions on China. Any argument advanced with near certainty, as is so often the case with these analyses, can be regarded as hyperbole. Even more serious accounts by area specialists run into difficulties when they interpret Chinese goals and policies in terms of paradigms of largely American origin. Realist and liberal scholars assume that their respective paradigms are based on universal principles that apply with equal force to all regions and cultures of the world. The only analyses we should take seriously are those based on careful empirical work that use credible sources, including Chinese sources, and that interpret data in terms of Chinese understandings of the issues in question.

American Analysts and Chinese Power

Many prominent American realists write with certainty about China's ambitions. They depict China as the inheritor of the Japanese mantle, as a threatening, rising challenger to American hegemony, the difference being that its economy will soon overtake that of the United States. Realists and many liberals interpret current Chinese policies as narrowly self-interested and inconsistent with any broader global interest in stability. China, they assert, not only fails to provide public goods, as the United States has supposedly done through its leadership, but creates tensions by challenging its neighbors in their territorial disputes and by competing with the United States for Asian dominance. They also criticize China for causing serious economic problems. In the 2000s the complaints included its unwavering focus on exports and growth and its largely unconvertible currency that was unfairly pegged to the US dollar. Since Xi came to power, the broadside has shifted to "unfair trade practices," including government subsidies to state-owned enterprises, restricted market access, cyber theft, intellectual property violations, and forced technology transfers. Aaron L. Friedberg, in his persistent attempts to hammer home what appears to him to be China's hegemonic ambitions, has long been the standard-bearer of the realist approach. He also presents Chinese authoritarianism as an ideological challenge to American liberalism.[1] He represents the fusion of an increasingly prominent realist-liberal consensus on competing with and confronting China.

The most anguished realists are "offensive realists," led by John Mearsheimer and Christopher Layne. Drawing on power transition theory, they argue that a rising China will assert itself—by war, if necessary—and demand a change to the rules of the system.[2] Offensive realists ignore any countervailing evidence by insisting that the present is no guide to future behavior because calculations and goals will shift once the opportunity for hegemony presents itself.[3] Journalists and politicians who aim to influence a wider audience propagate offensive realism in its most alarmist form.[4] Power transition has become more or less the conventional wisdom in the policy community, where it is the dominant frame of reference for assessing the possible consequences of China's rapid rise to great power status.[5] It is an article of faith among neoconservatives such as former deputy secretary of defense Paul Wolfowitz, who insists that "in the case of China . . . the obvious and disturbing analogy is the position of Germany, a country that felt it had been denied its 'place in the sun,' that believed it had been mistreated by other powers, and that was determined to regain its rightful place by nationalistic assertiveness."[6] It is also embraced by moderates such as former deputy assistant secretary of state Susan Shirk, who asserts, as if it were fact, "History teaches us that rising powers are likely to provoke war."[7]

The most prominent recent use—and misuse—of power transition theory to understand Sino-American relations is Graham Allison's thesis of the "Thucydides trap." The trap, according to Allison, is suggested in the ancient Greek historian Thucydides's famous observation that "it was the rise of Athens and the fear that this instilled in Sparta that made war inevitable."[8] It is supposed to be "the natural, inevitable discombobulation that occurs when a rising power threatens to displace a ruling power," as happened between Athens and Sparta and between Germany and Britain.[9] Based on this reading of history, Allison contends, war between America and China "is more likely than not," although he is quick to add that it is not inevitable.[10] Yet, as Richard Ned Lebow has argued, it was not the changing power balance that led to war between Sparta and Athens. Sparta feared not Athenian power but the threat to its own leadership status and sense of self-worth: Sparta chose war for reasons of identity, not security.[11] Other historical cases that Allison marshals are equally problematic.

Take the Anglo-German rivalry, which Allison reckons to be the dominant cause of the First World War. This rivalry was in fact only one—and not always the most important—factor in an intricate and multilateral process that led to that war.[12] The Thucydides trap, while it draws our attention to Sino-American tensions, misreads a big part of history and misidentifies causes of conflict.

Allison aside, there are serious problems with long-standing academic theories of power transition. Two prominent formulations see war as the most likely outcome but disagree about who initiates it. Kenneth Organski and Jacek Kugler contend that the dominant nation and its supporters are generally unwilling to grant rising powers more than a small part of the advantages they derive from the status quo. Those rising powers accordingly become increasingly dissatisfied and go to war against the dominant powers to impose orders more favorable to them. War is most likely, of longest duration and greatest magnitude, when a dissatisfied challenger enters into approximate parity with the dominant state. Order is most secure when all the great powers are satisfied with the structure of the system.[13]

Robert Gilpin focuses on the decline of dominant powers.[14] In ordering and defending the system, dominant states inevitably make cumulative commitments that come to exceed their capabilities. Imperial overreach "creates challenges for the dominant states and opportunities for the rising states of the system." The latter aspire to remake "the rules governing the international system, the spheres of influence, and most important of all, the international distribution of territory."[15] Dominant states see preventive war as the most attractive means of eliminating this threat. It is not the only strategy available. They can reduce their commitments or possibly reduce their costs through further expansion. Dominant powers can also ally with states who have an interest in defending the status quo, seek rapprochements with less threatening states, or appease challengers by making concessions to them.[16]

Benjamin Valentino and Ned Lebow demonstrate that there is no historical evidence to support power transition theory.[17] They constructed a data set of great power wars from 1648 to 2018 that reveals that rising powers hardly ever attack great powers, or vice versa. Historically, rising powers are accommodated and rewarded, and power transitions are the result of wars, not the cause of them. Power transition theory also errs in thinking that there is a hegemonic power capable of imposing its preferences regionally or globally. Since 1648 no power has been in a position to impose its preferences on a regional, let alone an international system and dictate the rules of war and peace. Power transitions involving leading powers are rare and are not the result of gradual differences in economic growth rates, as power transition theories expect. The only examples of such transitions are Russia overtaking France and the United States overtaking Russia in the late nineteenth century, neither of which involved war.

Leading states often aspire to the status of a dominant power. They are not content with their position and advantages and attempt to gain more power through further conquests. By means of their augmented power, they impose their preferences on others. Habsburg Spain, France under Louis XIV and Napoleon, Wilhelmine and Nazi Germany, and arguably the United States in the post–Cold War era are cases in point. None of these states was seriously threatened by rising powers or coalitions of great powers. They went to war because they thought they were powerful enough to become more powerful still. Perceptions of strength, not of weakness and threat, are the precondition and incentive for many, if not most, superpower wars.

Lebow uses an expanded data set to offer a more general analysis of interstate war in *Why Nations Fight*.[18] His evidence indicates a pattern of conflict that is the reverse of that predicted by power transition theories. Great power wars arise in the absence of hegemony, not because of it. These wars lead to power transitions and peace settlements that often impose new orders by virtue of a consensus among the leading powers. These orders are never dictated by a single power but by a coalition of them, and they endure as long as a consensus holds among the major powers responsible for upholding them.

With two notable exceptions, leading powers have avoided the intentional challenges of other great powers or rising powers. They generally prefer to make war against smaller, third parties and once great but now seriously declining great powers, although they have frequently been drawn into war with other great powers when these smaller wars escalate. Rising powers devote a high proportion of their income to their armed forces and wage frequent wars of expansion. When they were rising, Prussia, Russia, Germany, and Japan generally avoided attacking leading powers, their preference being once again for warring against smaller third parties and once great but declining powers. As a rising power the United States also conformed to this pattern, attacking Mexico and Spain.[19] Recent research offers strong support for these findings.[20]

Equally striking, and in sharp contrast to power transition theories, is the general failure of leaders and the media to distinguish the general from the military power balance. There has been much discussion among US policymakers and in the media about the rising power of China and concern that it could challenge the United States in the not too distant future. Since its 2011 annual report on China's military power, the US Department of Defense has been warning that the People's Liberation Army is developing key power projection capabilities that include submarines, advanced fighter aircraft, imposing ballistic and cruise missiles, and broad naval capabilities that include aircraft carriers.[21] These capabilities, it fears, will "degrade core U.S. military-technological advantages."[22] As in the Cold War, the Defense Department has strong budget incentives to greatly inflate a would-be adversary's military capabilities and intentions.

Independent analysts contend that China's military power does not reflect its latent power and that this is largely a matter of choice. China's defense expenditures, while rising rapidly in the past several years, have remained well below those of the United States in absolute terms and less than half the percentage of its gross domestic product (GDP). China's material capabilities have not given it the power to restructure the international system in its favor, let alone challenge a great power like the United States. The evidence is plentiful. Telling testimony comes from Tai Ming Cheung, director of a US Department of Defense–sponsored project on Chinese military technology at the University of California–San Diego. In a 2013 lecture in Paris, Cheung suggested that Chinese efforts to develop key "disruptive" and "component" military technologies had generally been unsuccessful. China is in no position to challenge the United States globally and will probably have to buy military technology from Russia to shore up its position in the short to medium term. This, Cheung suggested, is evidence of failure given the decline of Russia's capacities in military technological innovation.[23] More recently Michael Beckley has argued that, far from overtaking America, China is in fact struggling to keep up and will probably fall further behind in the coming decades.[24] In a similar vein, Stephen G. Brooks finds five "structural barriers" that will make it harder for China to rise than was the case for all past rising powers.[25] China's leaders are pinning their hopes on developing their capacities in the longer term. They will face evident and significant obstacles to doing so, including a slowing economy, social discontent, political corruption, and an aging population.

Should war occur between the United States and China, it will not be as a result of a power transition. The greater risk is that conflict will arise from the misperception that such a transition is imminent. Power transition theory could be made self-fulfilling and generate its own corroboration where history has hitherto failed to oblige.[26] Power transition is not unique in this potential. Realism more generally may have become to some degree self-fulfilling. Security discourses in China and elsewhere in Asia—much more than in Europe—tend to take realism's fundamental propositions as verities. It would be ironic if US-China relations deteriorated because each power had based its expectations on how the other would behave on theories that lack any empirical support. One Chinese scholar warns that his country "has spent a lot of time learning from rising powers like Russia, Japan, and Germany, so as to avoid the mistakes of past rising powers. The United States should spend time learning how previous dominant powers dealt with rising powers [peacefully]."[27]

It is worth adding that we are far from alone in our criticism of offensive realism and power transition theory. Take just two articles published in the summer of 2019. Jonathan Kirshner, an American international relations scholar, avers that these theories "are fundamentally flawed in their analytical approach and dangerous in their policy advice."[28] Shivshankar Menon, a former national security advisor of India, observes that they reflect "a bleak and limited view, drawing solely on analogies from Western experience and strategic culture."[29] And as we shall see, most Chinese scholars throw doubts on these theories.

More moderate defensive realists like Charles Glaser suggest that the prospects for hegemonic war may be reduced by mutual defensive postures that have the goal of forestalling exaggerated threat perception and overreaction by one or both countries. Glaser nevertheless employs a questionable historical comparison between the US-China relationship and the Cold War relations of the United States and the Soviet Union. On the basis of this comparison he argues that China's rise can be peaceful but that this outcome is far from guaranteed. Contrary to offensive realists, he does not believe that basic pressures generated by the international system will force the United States and China into conflict. Nuclear weapons, separation by the Pacific Ocean, and reasonably good political relations should enable both countries to maintain high levels of security and avoid military policies that severely strain their relationship. Washington's political need to protect its allies in Northeast Asia complicates matters somewhat, but there are strong grounds, Glaser insists, for believing that the United States can continue to maintain its nuclear umbrella over Japan and South Korea without unduly provoking China.[30]

Liberals, not surprisingly, respond favorably to Glaser's underlying optimism, although they often disagree with his argument. Geoffrey Garrett objects to Glaser's historical comparison on the grounds that close economic relations and interdependence between the United States and China make any comparison with the Soviet Union deeply problematic.[31] Liberal expectations of good relations rest on several reinforcing assumptions. Economic development will further enlarge the rapidly growing Chinese middle class, which, sooner or later, will insist on political inclusion through democratic reforms. In keeping with the democratic peace thesis, a democratic China will be a peaceful China.[32] Liberals contend that even in the absence of democratic reforms, economic interdependence will blunt any Chinese propensity toward aggression.[33]

Liberals have long characterized the existing international order as one of economic and political openness that can peacefully accommodate China's rise. The United States and other leading powers are expected to incorporate China into this order in a manner that facilitates its economic development. Rational Chinese leaders will prefer accommodation to the risks inherent in any struggle to overturn the system and establish an order more to its own liking.[34]

As noted, liberals' increasing disillusionment with the authoritarian turn of Xi's China has dented their earlier optimism.[35] Kurt M. Campbell and Ely Ratner, two former Obama administration officials, lament that the United States has failed to transform China's internal development and external behavior by deepening the two countries' commercial, diplomatic, and cultural ties.[36] American elites have again come to the realization that US power cannot really mold China to America's liking.

The presumption that global engagement and rising prosperity would drive Chinese convergence with Western values is highly problematic. It results from a blindness to history and a failure of imagination and is at odds with actual US engagement policy toward China. Economic interdependence by no means guarantees accommodation or even peace, as the First World War so painfully demonstrated. Long before Xi, Chinese leaders had insisted on the uniqueness of China's history, culture, and model of political and social development. It is unrealistic, to say the least, to expect China to converge on the Western liberal democratic and capitalist model simply by virtue of its closer contact with the West. American policymakers from the Nixon through Obama administrations did not attach priority to democratizing China in their engagement policies. They held it out as a pleasant possibility. But they neither posited systemic political liberalization or democratization as inexorable nor applied much pressure to bring them about.[37] Many, anticipating the long timeframe of China's modernization, have expected China to "become more prosperous, stable, and secure, and more deeply enmeshed in the rules-based order."[38] Engagement has not failed as much as its critics allege.

A common flaw of realist and liberal theories is that they do not attempt to understand Chinese foreign policy goals and means with reference to Chinese culture and history. We suggest that such reference is a starting point critical to any serious analysis. The relevant history includes the past seventy years (from 1949) of the People's Republic of China (PRC), and also its imperial history. Contemporary understandings of the successes, failures, and traditions of communist and imperial China are the crucible in which contemporary policies are forged. Just like their American counterparts, Chinese analysts and leaders regularly think in terms of historical analogies and use them to formulate and mobilize support for policies. Different Chinese narratives about the past encourage different framings of security and economic issues that are at odds with those nested in the realist or liberal paradigms.

Understanding Chinese history and culture is by no means easy—not even for the Chinese themselves. When American analysts venture into Chinese history and culture for clues about contemporary strategy, they sometimes produce astonishingly slanted readings. Michael Pillsbury's 2015 book on "China's

secret strategy to replace America as the global superpower"—which he refers
to as "the hundred-year marathon"—is a case in point.[39] Pillsbury comes close
to arguing that China's entire strategy is based on the Thirty-Six Stratagems, an
ancient Chinese strategic folklore, thus assuming a seamless transmission of strategic ideas across millennia. He argues that China's hawks, who have supposedly
been advising their leaders to avenge a century of humiliation and replace the
United States as the dominant world power, represent the real strategic mainstream in Beijing. Pillsbury is engulfed in Chinese military analysts with whom
he has interacted for decades. His background in the US intelligence and defense
establishments inclines him to cite anonymous Chinese defectors to support his
contention of a hidden Chinese strategy. These sources are, however, unverifi-
able, and the defectors—as they often do—may have misled their US handlers to
court their favor. A great deal of other evidence presented by Pillsbury is equally
problematic and has been demolished by Alastair Iain Johnston in a devastating review of the book.[40] Yet it is precisely views such as Pillsbury's that are now
influencing policy in Washington; President Trump publicly referred to Pillsbury
as "the leading authority on China."[41] We counsel a more balanced approach to
considering the full range of Chinese views while carefully assessing their relative
policy importance.

Chinese Analysts and the United States

Many Chinese analysts, scholars, and journalists challenge realist and liberal
interpretations. During the presidency of Hu Jintao (2003–12), Zheng Bijian, a
prominent scholar-official and advisor to President Hu, insisted that China could
"peacefully rise to great power status" through what he called "the developmental
path." He maintained that China would not follow the path of Germany in the
decades before the First World War or those of Germany and Japan leading up to
the Second World War, when these countries violently plundered resources and
sought world or regional hegemony. Neither would China follow the superpowers vying for domination during the Cold War. Instead China would transcend
ideological differences to strive for peace, development, and cooperation globally.[42] In this line of thinking, China can be dissatisfied with the status quo and
advocate change without seeking to destabilize the system.

Shi Yinhong, an international relations scholar at Beijing's Renmin University,
made a similar point at the end of 2007. China did not need to dance to the West's
tune, but risked alienating other countries, including those in the developing
world, if it refused to become a "responsible stakeholder."[43] "Responsible stakeholder" was a concept coined by the George W. Bush administration to exhort
China to help safeguard the existing international order. Although it was not

formally accepted in Beijing, official Chinese views leaned toward it. In March 2008 Foreign Minister Yang Jiechi argued that China should take on more international responsibility, but in an à la carte way that served its own interests.[44] We must be careful to take such statements at face value, but they do indicate that China can be a dissatisfied yet responsible power.

After Trump's inauguration in January 2017 the future of international order absorbed scholarly and policy discussions. American worries about China's challenge to the existing order were exacerbated by agony over Trump's crude rhetorical and substantive responses. Chinese scholars concluded that Trump's America was a more serious and wilder challenger than Xi's China. Beijing does not seek to upend the current order but wants to revise parts of it considered unjust or injurious. Shiping Tang notes China's struggle between two positions: "modifying by leading" and "modifying by working together with others." Beijing, he insists, wants "only piecemeal modification of the existing order," not a fundamental transformation.[45] Suisheng Zhao contends that China is dissatisfied not with fundamental rules of the current order but with its status in the order hierarchy. He calls China "a revisionist stakeholder."[46] Wu Xinbo argues that China seeks a "liberal partnership" composed of an open economic order, a relatively more equal political order, and a cooperative security order.[47]

There is a widespread perception that since the final three years of Hu's presidency, and especially since the beginning of Xi's, Chinese foreign policy has taken a dramatic turn, from responsibility to assertiveness,[48] and that, as Trump's America abdicated international leadership, China may have been doubling down to fill the vacuum. This view is too simplistic. Chinese assertiveness, while undeniable in certain areas, is not uniform across the board.[49] Nor is it necessarily a bad thing, since assertiveness can also be constructive, as reflected in China's recent approaches toward the North Korean nuclear program and climate change.[50] Yan Xuetong, a distinguished international relations scholar at Tsinghua University, argues that China has transformed its international strategy from "keeping a low profile" to "striving for achievement" since Xi came to power.[51] This insightful observation should not be read as an unreserved endorsement of Xi's policy. In fact Yan's purpose is to demonstrate the value of his "moral realism" by arguing that Chinese foreign policy should have a more prominent moral component.[52] He believes in neither unbridled Chinese assertiveness nor a new Sino-American cold war. Beijing has no clear plan for filling the international leadership vacuum vacated by America. Quite the contrary: "caution, not assertiveness or aggressiveness, will be the order of the day in Beijing's foreign policy in the coming years."[53]

Caution is the overwhelming response Chinese scholars promote in the face of surging American assertiveness. They are fully cognizant of the unsettling transformation of America's China strategy brought about by the Trump administration. Yuan Peng, president of the influential China Institutes of Contemporary International Relations in Beijing, a think tank affiliated with the powerful Ministry of State Security, observes that Sino-American relations have entered a new phase of "strategic stalemate," with China largely on the defensive. Yet he does not advocate a future strategy of strategic offense when Beijing achieves a better position. He maintains that China's strategy is always focused on developing itself—an internally generated motive—rather than on contending with America for world leadership.[54]

Nor did respected Chinese analysts promote a strategy of confronting the Trump administration in the short term. They treated Trump with a combination of bewilderment, scorn, and trepidation. Shi Yinhong called Trump "a cruel strategist and an astute tactician." He recommended making concessions in the trade war, in part to placate Trump but, more important, to spur stalled domestic reforms for the sake of China's own development and to salvage globalization by addressing the legitimate concerns of Western countries now engulfed in populism.[55] Many other analysts concurred. Chu Shulong of Tsinghua University suggested that China should keep seeking a stable and cooperative relationship with America. Tactical competition should not lead to strategic confrontation, and there was no need for tit-for-tat reprisal in the trade war.[56] Trump was rash and the hawks surrounding him reckless, but China should not stoop to their level; instead it must maintain a firm grip on the bottom line of preventing Sino-American relations from escalating into a full-blown confrontation.[57] Chinese policy during the first two years of the Trump administration, which Evan S. Medeiros characterizes as marked by moderation, calibration, and proportionality, had corresponded closely to such thinking.[58]

Chinese analysts decry American elites' emerging consensus that Xi's China is now competing with America for regional hegemony or global leadership as an epic misjudgment of China's strategic intentions.[59] In the main they attribute this consensus to America's loss of strategic confidence and its "status anxiety" since the Obama years.[60] But some of them are also aware of China's own faults, and they plead for a strategic introspection that can minimize outside misapprehension. They are especially critical of the propagandistic and triumphalist rhetoric of the nationalistic media and some government officials and analysts.[61] They implore Washington to reduce misperception, misjudgment, and miscalculation and meet China halfway. While China needs to play a more constructive part in Sino-American relations and in international order more generally, America needs to adjust to a new world in which it is no longer as dominant as before.[62] The central problem in the American approach to China, they contend, is its hegemonic hauteur. Curb that and adopt a more accommodating attitude, and Sino-American competition may take on a benign character.[63] Chinese analysts have grudgingly accepted competition as the new default of the relationship, but they earnestly hope to forestall it from degenerating into confrontation.[64]

Rejecting hegemony as China's goal, Chinese scholars see much less risk of a new Sino-American cold war than American analysts do.[65] The Sino-American relationship today is markedly different from the old US-Soviet relationship, and the United States cannot contain China in the way it had contained the Soviet Union. Conditions conductive to a benign sort of competition still exist, among them China's own strategic culture that eschews unbridled rivalry and confrontation.[66] Niu Jun, a prominent Peking University scholar, is among the most pessimistic. He contends that the structural tensions in Sino-American relations are now so intractable that the relationship has reached a historic turning point from engagement to rivalry—and probably is on a path of no return. Yet even he holds that the possibility of a new cold war depends on the intensity of ideological competition between the two countries.[67] For now, China has little appetite for an ideological rivalry. Facing the new reality of competition, China hopes to steer it in a stable or even benign direction.[68] Thus Foreign Minister Wang Yi remarked in March 2018 that China and America may compete, but as partners rather than rivals.[69]

Many Chinese scholars are unimpressed by Allison's thesis of the Thucydides trap. They point out that such a trap was by no means intended by Thucydides but is rather an arbitrary conceit imposed by scholars motivated by contemporary concerns. Scholars need to avoid the mistake of misreading and abusing history. Policymakers need to learn appropriate historical lessons and act sensibly in new contexts.[70] Allison and his followers misattribute the cause of the Peloponnesian War to the rise of Athenian power. Their focus on power transition blinds them to the critical importance of political strategy. Chinese analysts warn that Beijing must place political strategy—not power transition—front and center in managing conflict with the United States. They are hopeful that innovation and improvement in political strategy will eventually succeed in breaking any "trap" and steering the relationship on a more stable and cooperative course.[71] Even those analysts who are attracted to the Thucydides trap insist on China's ability to avoid it.[72]

Chinese Concepts and Perspectives

Chinese analysts' refusal to be drawn into the American discourse of hegemonic competition, a new cold war, and the Thucydides trap underscores the importance of understanding Chinese concepts and perspectives derived from Chinese history and culture. Western conceptions, notably hegemony and balance of power, are largely alien to China. If they bear a resemblance to precedents in

Chinese history, they are not conceptualized or understood in the same way as in Western international relations theory. Present-day Chinese officials and scholars understand them only because they are familiar with relevant Western literature. In order to fathom China's motives, priorities, goals, and indeed behavior, we need to apply concepts that are indigenous to the Chinese political vocabulary.

At the heart of traditional Chinese thinking is the distinction between power and influence. Imperial China established a clientelist relationship, or tribute system, with its developed neighbors. In its relations with its Confucian neighbors—Korea, Vietnam, Japan, and the Ryukyus—and further afield through intermittent trade and exploration China sought honor in the form of recognition of its cultural supremacy and centrality. In return it provided practical security and economic rewards. Lesser states often referred to China as the "cultural efflorescence" or the "domain of manifest civility," based on its closer approximation of Confucian ideals. The tribute system found institutional representation in investiture, a diplomatic protocol by which a state sent envoys to China to accept explicitly their subordinate status. Subsequent embassies were required to reaffirm the relationship, exchange information, and arrange for trade and cultural exchanges. Tributary states had to adopt the Chinese calendar in all communications with the emperor.[73] These forms of obeisance were acknowledgments of Chinese cultural superiority, not political overlordship.[74]

China had no desire to impose its vision on the world but was interested in stable and productive relations with its neighbors. At its best the tribute system embodied the Chinese principle of *wangdao,* or humane authority, and is surprisingly similar to the ancient Greek understanding of *hēgemonia*. It worked to the advantage of both parties: the strong gained honor, while the weak gained protection and trade advantages. Of equal importance, this arrangement encouraged China in accord with its self-image and honorific status.[75] Here too the ancient Greek and Chinese systems were similar, as honor brought with it a set of rules that imposed self-constraint.

History, of course, offers examples in which the practices of China and its neighbors deviated from the *wangdao* ideal. Chinese rulers did not always have humane motives in mind, nor did its neighbors always accept Chinese cultural supremacy and political centrality. Instrumental rationality was far from absent in traditional East Asian international relations. Nevertheless, as Feng Zhang has argued, *wangdao* as embodied by the tribute system achieved sufficient empirical significance for it to be taken seriously as both a reality and an ideal.[76]

David Kang argues that this clientelist arrangement accounts for the glaring discrepancy in the frequency of war between the European and East Asian regional systems. From 1368 to 1841—that is, from the institutionalization of the tribute system to the Sino-British Opium War—there were only two wars involving China, Korea, and Japan. These episodes aside, the three countries maintained peaceful and even friendly relations, which became more stable as they each became more powerful. The key to peace was the unquestioned dominance of China, in cultural as well as economic and military domains, and its reluctance to expand territorially at the expense of its civilized neighbors. Other states accepted China's primacy and sought to benefit from it culturally and economically. Korean, Vietnamese, and Japanese elites copied Chinese institutional, linguistic, and cultural practices, which in turn facilitated closer and more productive relations with China.[77]

Present-day Chinese leaders—and many of their domestic critics—appear to envisage a similar role for their country. Indications come from how Beijing has sought to structure its relationship with its smaller neighbors, especially those in Southeast Asia.[78] If China seeks regional leadership of this kind, its foreign policy goals and American economic and security interests appear as fully compatible as they were, albeit for different reasons, between the United States and Britain in the nineteenth century.

In imperial times there were two neighbors that could not be integrated into a clientelist relationship: the nomads of Inner Asia and the Japanese. The nomads were unprepared to accept such a relationship, and the Chinese tried to manage them through a combination of carrots and sticks. They were to some degree dependent on the nomads, as they supplied the army with horses, while nomads depended on China for various finished goods. Both sides used violence to coerce the other into making political and economic concessions, but the nomads also periodically conducted raids to get goods and women for free. Historically the balance of power swung back and forth between the two groups, with China succumbing on two occasions to conquest by nomadic peoples.[79]

Japan posed a different problem. It rejected a clientelist relationship because it wanted to claim an equal status with China or even supplant China as the center of the universe. Elsewhere Lebow has argued that Japan's deeply ambivalent relationship with China—characterized by equal doses of admiration and resentment—reveals the insecurity of the late cultural developer.[80] Such countries are keen to excel and copy much of the culture and technology of leading powers while proclaiming their superiority. This is another way in which Japan was like Germany. Over the centuries Japanese leaders struggled to make the minimum accommodations to China that would allow a profitable trade. In the late nineteenth century, when Japan was militarily strong, it sought to supplant China as the leading regional power by force.[81]

The 2000s offer a mixed record of *hēgemonia*'s role in Chinese foreign policy. On the one hand, from the late 1990s to around 2008, Beijing sought accommodations with all of its neighbors. They in turn sought to develop good relations with China, especially in the economic domain. This reciprocal accommodation muted regional balancing against the phenomenal growth of Chinese power.[82] On the other hand, since 2009 China has become more assertive in protecting its territorial and maritime interests, especially in the East and South China seas. *Hēgemonia* in the form of general reassurance gives way to conditional reassurance coupled with limited coercion against a small group of countries, notably the Philippines and Japan.[83]

Such strategic adjustments point to the importance of sovereignty and territorial conflicts in China's foreign relations. In almost every case where it shares a frontier with another country, it has been a contested one. This abiding problem is the inheritance of colonialism, where lines were drawn on maps by administrators and never really demarcated. Beginning with India in the 1960s, Chinese leaders sought to overcome these conflicts with a policy of concession. In return for territorial settlements that invariably favored the other country, China demanded recognition, any halt to the support or de facto sanctuary of armed opponents of its government, and the right of hot pursuit if they launched attacks across the Chinese border. This approach has led to the settlement of seventeen of China's twenty-three territorial disputes, with China usually receiving less than 50 percent of the contested land. For various reasons, but primarily due to bad intelligence and nationalist outbidding in Parliament, the Indians spurned all offers of compromise and provoked a disastrous war with China in 1962. After decisively defeating the Indian army on two fronts, Chinese forces withdrew for the most part to their prewar positions.[84]

Beijing has adhered scrupulously to its border treaties, and relations with almost all of its neighbors have improved. Exceptions are India on the land border and its maritime neighbors in the East and South China seas, most notably Japan, the Philippines, and Vietnam. Tension with Japan was prompted by the Japanese government's decision in 2012 to purchase the disputed Diaoyu/Senkaku Islands. Japan's attempt to consolidate its claims of sovereignty over them, fully supported by Prime Minister Shinzo Abe, who assumed office in December 2012, is in abrogation of the postwar Cairo Declaration of 1943 and the Potsdam Agreement of 1945, and thus of international law. In China nationalist opinion and local authorities fanned the issue; for Japan it became a vehicle in a regional power struggle.[85] So far there has been more oratory and probing than actual conflict. It is nevertheless a troubling situation because the nationalism and confrontational instincts of both countries, coupled with their festering historical dispute, may compel their governments to overreact.

Taiwan remains a major flashpoint, and Tibet and Xinjiang irritants, between China and the West. The vast majority of Chinese consider these territories part of China and therefore a domestic question. There is widespread resentment against India and the West for what is seen as interference in Chinese affairs and infringement of Chinese sovereignty. From the Western perspective, China has run roughshod over the civil and cultural rights of Tibetans, Uighurs, and other minorities in western China. Its policy of populating these areas with Chinese settlers, reminiscent of Josef Stalin's policies in the Baltics, Karelia, Crimea, and parts of the Caucasus, is deeply offensive to indigenous residents. These policies provoke internal unrest; in an era of rising tensions, they also stand in the way of good relations with the West, not least because they make it more difficult for Western governments to build domestic coalitions in favor of a positive China policy.

Sino-American rapprochement in the 1970s and the end of the Cold War have partially defused the Taiwanese conflict. China remains committed to national unification as a matter of principle and has pledged to go to war if Taiwan should ever declare its independence. China's political elite believes that Taiwanese independence would disrupt their country's social stability, national unity, and great power aspirations. Once again there are grounds for cautious optimism. Although the Taiwanese independence movement remains a potent political force, cross-Strait economic integration has achieved a solid foundation. Bilateral trade in 2014 approached US$200 billion, and the stock value of Taiwan investment in the PRC is estimated to exceed US$150 billion. Taiwan's exports to the PRC account for roughly 40 percent of the island's total exports. Meanwhile, as much as 80 percent of Taiwan's outbound foreign direct investment flows to the PRC.[86] Tourist exchanges have increased, and over two million Taiwanese business people and their families have homes on the mainland. Time is on Beijing's side, and its government is in no rush to force unification. If China suffers an economic decline, if Taiwan declares its independence, or if Taipei and Washington double down on their security ties by, say, stationing American troops in Taiwan, a clash could occur in the Straits that could draw in the United States and put the two most powerful nations in the world on a collision course.[87]

China professes an international strategy of peaceful development. It has now sustained a nearly forty-year peace in its foreign relations since 1980. Before 1980 its few resorts to force—in Korea in 1950, Tibet in 1950, and along the Indian frontier in 1962—were arguably defensive in nature or associated with national unification. Only the war with Vietnam in 1979 lends itself to another narrative.[88] Following the Chinese communist takeover in 1949, the United States was seen as the linear descendant of Japan—a predatory power encouraged by China's division and relative weakness to encroach militarily on its territory. This understanding was clear in internal Chinese descriptions of the United States on the eve of the Korean War and an important reason why the communists felt compelled to intervene.[89] The United States is no longer regarded in this way by most influential Chinese, nor is present-day Japan. However, neither country fits the traditional Chinese understanding of how clients should behave. They do not expect this kind of conformity from the United States and have no category in which to fit powerful and sophisticated states they consider "barbarian." The arrival of European powers in China in the nineteenth century created a similar problem. Meaningful accommodation accordingly requires changes in the understanding that elites have of one another and the working out of some mutually acceptable framework for their relations.

Another useful metric for assessing Chinese intentions is China's adherence to global norms. Rosemary Foot and Andrew Walter have conducted an exhaustive comparative evaluation of China and the United States in this regard. They considered norms regarding the use of force, macroeconomic policy, nuclear nonproliferation, climate change, and financial regulation.[90] In recent decades, they find, China has moved from a position of generally low behavioral consistency toward gradually higher levels in all categories.[91] In no domain, however, is its adherence comparable to the highest levels of compliance by some states. A case in point is Beijing's failure to value the denuclearization of North Korea and Iran over its parochial interests regarding both states, although its signals regarding the former suggest that its view may be changing under its new leadership.[92] Where Chinese compliance is high, as with respect to the Kyoto Protocol, it often involves low costs. There are some instances of Chinese compliance involving high costs.[93] The principal exception, Foot and Walter argue, is in the area of macroeconomic policy surveillance, where compliance with norms has declined from previously moderate levels as domestic constraints have increased. In other economic areas, compliance has risen as domestic reformers used norm compliance as a strategic means of modernizing China's financial system.[94]

The apparent confidence and assertiveness of Xi's China gives the impression that Beijing is now violating international norms and rules at will. American policymakers fear China's revisionist challenge to the rules-based order. But this discourse of Chinese revisionism tells at most only half the story and is thus misleading.[95] It is based on the myth of a singular US-dominated liberal order and misses the considerable diversity in China's policies toward international norms and institutions.[96] Sophisticated American analysts recognize that China's approach to the global and regional order is not a binary one of acceptance vis-à-vis revision: Beijing rejects some rules, accepts others, and seeks to rewrite others still. This is a multifaceted approach that defies simplistic or monolithic characterizations. Even in the South China Sea, where Beijing is seen to have strongly challenged parts of the prevailing rules, it often opts for ambiguity rather than attempting to completely overturn the existing rules.[97]

The Chinese case looks more interesting still when compared with the United States. Washington remains a principal center of norm innovation, but its record of compliance is quite mixed. It has repeatedly chosen to use force unilaterally, overlooks proliferation by friendly states, and spurns pleas from the International Monetary Fund to reduce its deficits. In recent years it has withdrawn commitments to implement financial and climate agreements that it helped to shape. The US position on compliance overall has been characterized by selectivity and inconsistency; support for the Montreal Protocol and the stonewalling of the Kyoto Protocol are cases in point. In both countries compliance falters when it encounters strong domestic opposition for economic or ideological reasons. Overall, however, Chinese compliance has been rising, in contrast to the behavior of the United States.[98]

The Trump administration took willful liberty to tear up major international agreements. Notable casualties included the Trans-Pacific Partnership, the Paris climate accord, the Iran nuclear deal, and the Intermediate-Range Nuclear Forces Treaty. This dealt a further blow to the US record of compliance with international norms, raising widespread anxiety that America, not China, had become a principal threat to the rules-based order. Small wonder that Wang Jisi, a distinguished Peking University scholar, bemoaned, "It has become harder and harder for foreign-policy makers in China to discern what rules the Americans want themselves and others to abide by, what kind of world order they hope to maintain, and where Washington is on major international issues."[99] Since 2017 China's US watchers have found the country they have studied for years "increasingly unrecognizable and unpredictable."[100]

From Power to Goals and Motives

This overview drives home the inadequacy of analyzing foreign policy in terms of power and relative power, no matter how they are conceived and measured. It highlights the importance of the goals that political elites seek and the ends they consider appropriate to them. These elites determine how states acquire and use power, rooted in historical and cultural lessons. Even so, they do not dictate policy. Foreign policy consists of initiatives, responses, and adjustments made in regard to the initiatives, responses, and adjustments of others and the perceived consequences of one's own behavior. Beijing's evolving policy must be analyzed in this broader interactive context.

Considerations of power are never more than an enabling condition and instrumentality. This is not to dismiss their importance; absent its clearly extraordinary economic development, China could not hope to play a key role on the world stage. Nor could this development have occurred without a centrally controlled military that unified and protected the country and its regime. Sophisticated realists like Hans Morgenthau and John Herz understood that power is a means to an end, not an end in itself. Modern-day realists who start with power and infer foreign policy goals from it conduct their analysis the wrong way around.

Foreign policy goals may not determine power, but as power is to some degree fungible, they help determine where resources are invested. Here too realist analyses that focus on China's threatening military miss the mark. Without going into detail about the order of battle and the trajectory of military spending, certain facts seem incontestable. China has used some of its wealth to upgrade its military forces, but primarily to provide the capability to deal with sovereignty disputes, as regarding Taiwan and the islands in the East and South China seas, and to protect its expanding overseas trading interests.[101] The US military alleges that China is developing anti-access/area denial capabilities to thwart US power projection in the region, perhaps with the eventual aim of driving the United States out of East Asia and imposing a Chinese hegemony in the region. This is an exaggeration based on a self-serving mirror image of America's hegemonic strategy, and one that this book will take great lengths to critique.

China's recent military modernization efforts, especially the focus on naval and air power, are consistent with its stated goals of near-seas defense, especially the goals of protecting its territorial security, sovereignty, and maritime rights. In the South China Sea, China maintains some ambiguity in its positions for strategic and domestic political reasons.[102] This highlights the importance of understanding Chinese leaders' assessments of China's interests in the region and the motives behind their policies. Those interests determine how China will invest its resources and deploy its capabilities.

China's strategic programs are also minimal. Only in recent years has it begun to upgrade its nuclear deterrence force, which now includes road-mobile intercontinental ballistic missiles (ICBMs), improved nuclear-powered ballistic-missile submarines, and multiple independently targetable reentry vehicles (MIRVs)–capable silo-based ICBMs, as well as the ongoing development of hypersonic-glide vehicles and MIRV-capable mobile ICBMs. Nevertheless it has stuck to the long-standing policy of maintaining a "lean and effective" deterrent capability.[103] As of January 2018 its nuclear stockpile includes roughly 280 warheads, and only forty to fifty of its ICBMs are capable of targeting the continental United States.[104]

By contrast, the United States has undertaken significant strategic upgrading since the end of the Cold War. It maintains a stockpile of roughly 6,550 warheads as of February 2018. Several hundreds of its land-based ICBMs can hit China, in addition to a range of sea- and air-based missiles and warheads. Trident I missiles were replaced with Trident IIIs with a GPS navigation system and larger warheads. Greater accuracy and larger warheads make them more deadly to Chinese missile silos. Three warheads targeted on each Chinese silo have a 99 percent chance of destroying all of them while killing fewer than six thousand Chinese, with hardly any fallout.[105] If China decides to escalate nuclear competition, out of fearing losing an effective second-strike deterrent, it will most likely result from US provocations in entrenching its nuclear superiority. The Trump administration's 2018 "Nuclear Posture Review," which called for a significant modernization of its nuclear forces, was an ominous step that would likely elicit a Chinese response to upgrade its own nuclear forces.[106]

Chinese defense spending grew at double-digit annual rates between 1989 and 2015. Since 2016, however, it has declined to a single-digit rate of around 7 to 8 percent. Foreign estimates of Chinese defense spending in 2006 ranged from US$31 billion to US$90 billion, with US$44 billion probably the most accurate figure. By comparison, the United States spent US$518 billion in 2004 dollars, Russia US$63 billion, and the United Kingdom US$38 billion in 2003. By 2016 these figures stood at US$611 billion for the United States, US$215 billion for China, US$69.2 billion for Russia, and US$48.3 billion for the United Kingdom.[107] China spends a higher proportion of its GDP on the military than many developed countries, at an average of 2 percent between 2008 and 2012. Still, this is a mere fraction of the 4.7 percent spent by the United States in the same period.[108] In 2016 China spent 1.9 percent of its GDP on the military, in contrast to the US figure of 3.3 percent.[109] Judging from this comparatively low proportion, China is far from engaging in an arms race with America.

China's military modernization is accelerating rapidly but still has a long way to go. The much-hyped naval buildup offers a telling example. Its first aircraft carrier, commissioned into the Chinese navy in 2012, is a remodeled Soviet-era Kuznetsov-class carrier, lacking the requisite slingshot technology to launch technologically advanced fighter planes. The second indigenously built carrier, launched in April 2017, also derives from the old Soviet model and will not become operational until 2020.[110] Although a mature carrier force—up to five more carriers are planned—will eventually give China power projection capabilities dwarfing those of its smaller Asian neighbors, the current carriers are more a symbol of national power and a training instrument than a combat platform. The carrier force is hardly the only area where China lags far behind the United States. In a series of studies, the most recent one published in 2019, Stephen Brooks and William Wohlforth contend that in every key dimension of military power, the United States still enjoys an overwhelming advantage.[111]

The figures of Chinese military spending are debatable, as are Chinese military capabilities more generally. What is indisputable, however, is the fallacy of trying to reason from capabilities to intentions. If any more evidence for this truth is required, one need only look back on attempts to do this with regard to the Soviet Union. Faulty conceptions played a large role in intensifying US-Soviet competition during the Cold War. A constructive US-China relationship in the twenty-first century would require a different, and productive, set of strategic conceptions.

Toward a New Approach

Beginning with the 2009–17 presidency of Barack Obama, strategic competition has become an increasingly major feature of Sino-American relations. It increases the possibility of a military conflict. This recognition is not a nod to realist interpretations. We do not see war as likely, let alone inevitable, and attribute tensions to reasons having nothing to do with the balance of power. We highlight leaders' faulty conceptions about interests, goals, and the means to achieve them, their struggles to coordinate and implement policy, bureaucratic rivalry, and other domestic political dynamics in inhibiting the development of a productive strategy for conflict management in both countries. We also stress policymakers' cognitive, motivational, and psychological frames of reference and the domestic process of formulating and implementing policy. These are the more immediate and empirically traceable causes of foreign policy change.

We recognize the challenges in managing the Sino-American relationship but are not as pessimistic about the prospect of a cooperative relationship as are many realists and liberals. This book takes an integrated series of steps to develop a holistic approach to conflict management and reduction. The approach rests on three strategic pillars: deterrence, reassurance, and diplomacy. Deterrence, although a deeply flawed strategy, nevertheless holds an important place in the relationship, and in international relations more generally. It is appropriately directed against states whose leaders harbor aggressive intentions, although those practicing deterrence must do so with finesse and recognition that the success rate of general and immediate deterrence is low. Threat-based strategies are only one response to international conflict. Of equal importance are reassurance and diplomacy aimed at reducing or finessing substantive differences. We describe these strategies and identify their associated mechanisms, how they are expected to work, and the conditions in which they are most appropriate.

Regardless of how international conflicts begin, they are usually characterized over time by hostility, conflicts of interest, and misunderstandings. The critical question is not the choice of a particular strategy—as they are often all relevant—but rather how they are combined, staged, and integrated into a sophisticated approach to conflict management tailored to the conflict in question. Managing Sino-American conflict would demand such a holistic approach. But first we must explain why their competition has intensified since the Obama years. Chapters 2 and 3 seek to answer this question by examining American and Chinese policy mistakes, respectively.

3

American Mistakes

IN NOVEMBER 2009, just as President Barack Obama was about to embark on his first visit to China, he declared, "The United States does not seek to contain China. . . . The rise of a strong, prosperous China can be a source of strength for the community of nations."[1] His administration's China policy appeared to get off to a good start. His Asia team wanted to expand areas of cooperation with China while managing the two countries' differences. Yet eight years later the perception was widespread in both Washington and Beijing that the relationship had deteriorated significantly, especially in strategic domains. What went wrong?

In this chapter we examine the policy mistakes that the Obama administration made in managing the relationship. Chapter 3 performs a similar assessment of Chinese policy mistakes. The Obama administration developed no distinct China strategy and was in fact averse to developing such a strategy. It chose to embed largely reactive China policies within a regional strategy of the so-called "pivot" or "rebalance" to the Asia-Pacific region. While China was relegated to a management issue, the rebalance strategy damaged the US-China relationship by deepening strategic mistrust between the two countries and agitating China to seek strategic adventures in Asia.

Some US officials and analysts argue that the rebalance carried a mixed message of reassurance and resolve toward China. They relish the fact that Chinese reactions were not hysterical or aggressive.[2] In particular, Beijing refrained from taking a tit-for-tat confrontational approach toward the military component of the rebalance. But such cool-headedness did not signify Chinese indifference or inaction. In assessing China's response as restrained, US observers underestimated the novelty and consequences of China's multifaceted response. Far from seeing the rebalance as a benign reassurance about building a constructive relationship with China, Chinese elites considered it a major strategic challenge that must be met with a determined yet patient response.

Some Chinese commentators were tempted to criticize the rebalance as America's latest attempt to contain China. Indeed plenty of nationalistic and hardline voices inside China decried America's entire post–Cold War policy toward China as nothing less than a Cold War–style containment. Sophisticated analysts recognized that containing China, in the same way that Washington sought to contain the Soviet Union during the Cold War, was not the US intention and was in any case foolhardy and infeasible. But they almost universally regarded hedging against and competing with China as a dominant motivation of the rebalance.[3] Some found it offensive that the Obama administration adopted a global strategy of retrenchment to make way for an assertive Asia-Pacific regional strategy of rebalance in order to concentrate on dealing with China's rise and reinvigorating America's regional hegemony.[4] If the administration's global strategy was restrained, its Asia-Pacific regional strategy was not.

We begin with a discussion of America's traditional grand strategy of liberal hegemony in Asia. The Obama administration's Asian rebalance strategy was in fact based on that long-standing pursuit of hegemony and betrayed its refusal to reconsider that traditional strategy in the face of China's rise. The chapter documents American policy mistakes associated with the rebalance strategy. In the military domain, the rebalance amounted to a doubling down of an already robust US presence in the region and thus aggravated China's sense of insecurity. In the diplomatic domain, America's significantly enhanced relations with critical Asian states increased China's suspicion of a US-led encirclement. High-profile US interventions in China's territorial and maritime disputes with its neighbors produced the counterproductive effect of steeling its resolve and exacerbating its assertiveness. In the economic domain, the Obama administration framed the Trans-Pacific Partnership (TPP) free trade agreement as a geopolitical competition with China over Asian leadership, thus further raising Chinese suspicion of US intentions. In the political domain, Washington's refusal to engage China over core interests suggested its lack of genuine respect for a rising China under the rule of the Chinese Communist Party (CCP). The Obama administration did not bear all the blame for the deterioration of the relationship under its watch. Its assertive Asian rebalance strategy nevertheless deprived it of a chance to establish a new strategic framework for US-China relations and contributed to new tensions and problems that might have been averted with a more productive China strategy.

Two caveats are in order. First, our critiques of American and Chinese mistakes in this chapter and the next may inhibit a full discussion of the interactive dynamics of the relationship. We will draw attention to such interactions where necessary. Second, our critiques should not imply that there was no improvement or progress in the relationship during the Obama years. Most notably the two countries reached a landmark agreement on tackling climate change. This was a crucial joint contribution to the successful negotiation of the Paris Agreement in December 2015. They cooperated on reaching a nuclear nonproliferation accord with Iran. Their navies coordinated antipiracy operations off the Gulf of Aden. Less notable but significant for their strategic relations, they avoided military conflict and crises despite intensifying competition in the Asia-Pacific. The two militaries began to build multifaceted and multilayered dialogues and crisis management mechanisms.[5] In 2014 they agreed to the Code for Unplanned Encounters at Sea, a protocol designed to maximize safety and reduce escalation when vessels meet at sea. In the same year they signed two memoranda of understanding, with a new annex added to each in 2015. Indeed despite periodic tensions, the Sino-American military relationship during the Obama years were the most wide-ranging and stable since the 1989 Tiananmen Square crackdown.[6] This record looks vastly superior to what transpired in the first three years of the Trump administration. In hindsight America and China had lost a critical opportunity to rectify the relationship during the Obama years. Had they developed a productive strategy for conflict management, the relationship would have looked healthier today.

The Pursuit of Hegemony

Many scholars agree that since the end of the Second World War, and especially since the end of the Cold War, the United States has pursued an ambitious global strategy of liberal hegemony. According to Barry Posen:

> The strategy is hegemonic because it builds on the great power advantage of the United States relative to all other major powers and intends to preserve as much of that advantage as possible through a range of actions, including a sustained investment in military power whose aim is to so overwhelm potential challengers that they will not even try to compete, much less fight. . . . It is liberal because it aims to defend and promote a range of values associated with Western society in general and U.S. society in particular—including democratic governance within nation-states, individual rights, free markets, a free press, and the rule of law.[7]

When it comes to the Asia-Pacific region, numerous US officials, analysts, and scholars assert that preventing the rise of a dominating hegemon has been a fixed goal of US policy for well over a century. Such a goal would presumably make the region safe for American pursuits like trade promotion, faith advocacy, democracy support, and territorial security.[8] For American policymakers, however, keeping Asia safe from a hostile hegemon requires making the region safe for America's own hegemony. A dramatic example came in 1992, when a draft Defense Planning Guidance prepared by the US Department of Defense asserted, "Our strategy must now refocus on precluding the emergence of any potential future global competitor." And in East Asia the United States strove to maintain its status "as a military power of the first magnitude" and act "as a balancing force and prevent emergence of a vacuum or a regional hegemon."[9]

There is now an eerie convergence between the policy goal of American hegemony and some academic international relations theories about the optimal US strategy toward the Asia-Pacific. Across the realist-liberal divide in international relations, prominent scholars have called for a hegemonic US strategy toward Asia. The neorealist John Mearsheimer asserts that the central aim of American foreign policy is to be the hegemon in the Western Hemisphere and to have no rival hegemon in either Europe or Northeast Asia. He argues that the United States should stop "engaging" China and begin to "contain" it in order to prevent its rise as a peer competitor.[10]

On the other side of the theoretical divide, the liberal G. John Ikenberry is a leading protagonist of American liberal hegemony. He argues that the United States has created a "liberal hegemonic order" built around multilateral institutions, alliances, strategic partners, and client states on the basis of strategic understandings and hegemonic bargains. The United States provided "services" to other states through the provision of security and its commitments to stability and open markets. Ikenberry declares that "in the fifty years following World War II, this American-led liberal hegemonic order has been remarkably successful."[11]

This is a controversial claim. Michael Mastanduno argues that the United States has maintained only an incomplete hegemony in the Asian security order.[12] Simon Reich and Richard Ned Lebow have authored a more fundamental attack on hegemony. They maintain that American hegemony was only partial (restricted largely to the Western hemisphere) and short-lived and that American efforts to establish a hegemonic order (e.g., in Vietnam, Afghanistan, and Iraq) have been a primary source of disorder in the international system since the end of the Cold War.[13] The United States has promulgated and then wallowed mindlessly and parochially in messianism and in such self-infatuated characterizations as "exceptionalism" and "indispensability." It has bullied other countries in a self-defeating manner and reneged on its own liberal trading rules. And it has often been unable to impose solutions consistent with hegemony and remained studiously distant from genocide in Cambodia and Rwanda and from catastrophic civil war in Congo.

In any case, in contemporary Asia-Pacific, America's strategy of liberal hegemony is a major source of friction and tension in its relations with China. Almost
all of the major policy mistakes that the US side has made in this relationship
since the end of the Cold War—and indeed during the Cold War period as
well—can be traced ultimately to the pursuit of this grand strategy. And despite
the many differences between the Trump and Obama administrations, the
Trump administration pressed ahead with the drive for hegemony, albeit a sort of
illiberal hegemony. Trump still sought to retain America's material primacy, but
he chose to forgo the export of democracy and abstain from multilateral trade
agreements. The American search for hegemony—a major source of conflict in
Sino-American relations—has shown no signs of abating. Thus the US foreign
policy establishment continues to avoid the fundamental question of whether US
hegemony of any kind is sustainable.[14]

Rebalance to the Asia-Pacific

During the first two years of President Obama's first term in office (2009–11),
his administration developed no coherent or distinct strategy toward China. The
overarching goal of its China policy was to foster a relationship marked primarily
by cooperation rather than confrontation.[15] That goal was strategic in the sense
that it clarified the nature of America's China policy. But the administration had
neither formed a clear strategic plan about how to achieve that goal nor engaged
in serious rethinking about how that goal might be reconciled with the long-
standing US strategy of liberal hegemony.

Jeffrey A. Bader, the senior director for East Asian Affairs on the National
Security Council during this period, reveals in his memoirs that the administration made policy choices largely on the basis of a series of tactical decisions.[16] It
wanted to pursue a fine-tuned approach that avoided reliance "solely on military
muscle, economic blandishments, and pressure and sanctions on human rights"
on the one hand and "a policy of indulgence and accommodation of assertive
Chinese conduct, or indifference to its internal evolution" on the other hand.[17]
But as critics point out, "not too hot, not too cold makes for good porridge, but
is not a clear guideline for foreign policy."[18]

The incentive to produce a distinct China strategy was further reduced after
2011, when the Obama administration began to focus on developing a region-
wide, rather than China-focused, Asian strategy. China became an element in
and an implicit target of this strategy, but not in itself an object of strategy. In
October 2011 Secretary of State Hillary Clinton announced a "pivot" to the
Asia-Pacific region in a prominent article published in *Foreign Policy*, reaffirming
America's strong commitment to continued regional leadership.[19] One month

later, in a speech to the Australian Parliament, President Obama echoed this "pivot" message by declaring, "The United States is a Pacific power, and we are here to stay."[20] In January 2012 the US Department of Defense released a strategic blueprint for the Joint Force in 2020, announcing, "*We will of necessity rebalance toward the Asia-Pacific region.*"[21] By that point, the "pivot" or "rebalance" toward the Asia-Pacific had become the Obama administration's settled Asian strategy.

According to Kurt M. Campbell, assistant secretary of state for East Asian and Pacific affairs during Obama's first term in office and the chief architect behind the pivot, this strategy was to fulfill America's "traditional post–World War II role in the region, keeping credible its alliance commitments, and sustaining Asia's 'operating system' (the complex legal, security, and practical arrangements that have underscored four decades of prosperity and security)."[22] It is a comprehensive and integrative strategy that includes "bolstering traditional alliances, forging new partnerships, engaging regional institutions, diversifying military forces, defending democratic values, embracing economic statecraft, and developing a truly multifaceted and comprehensive approach to an increasingly assertive and capable China."[23]

In her article Clinton declared that "a thriving America is good for China and a thriving China is good for America."[24] Obama affirmed that the United States welcomed the rise of a peaceful and prosperous China.[25] Similarly Campbell argued that "the Pivot is primarily about increasing ties to Asia, not containing China."[26] Toward China the strategy is "perhaps best understood as a mixture of reassurance and resolve that underscore elements of cooperation and competition respectively."[27] He claimed that "building a constructive and productive relationship with China has been an important part of the Pivot ever since it was first announced." In his view, "China's official response to the Pivot was no knee-jerk reaction driven by concern over US intentions but instead a reasonable and measured decision to wait and see how US policy would evolve."[28]

Campbell seems to argue that the rebalance strategy has been a success overall, even in the area of China policy. We evaluate this argument as part of our assessment of the Obama administration's China policy, since the administration chose to embed China policy within the larger regional strategy of the rebalance rather than developing a distinct China strategy of its own. We further assess the efficacy of the strategy as a mixed approach of both reassurance and resolve toward China and its impact on the overall US-China relationship. Our argument is that the rebalance was in fact harmful to the relationship, both because it deprived the Obama administration of an opportunity to develop a productive China strategy and because it undermined strategic trust between the two countries and exacerbated Chinese assertiveness.

Aggravating Chinese Insecurities

For all the multifaceted nature of the rebalance strategy, the most alarming to Beijing was no doubt its military component. In addition to existing deployments of 50,000 troops in East Asia, the Obama administration planned to move 60 percent of naval and air forces to the Asia-Pacific, including the latest and most advanced weapons systems in the US arsenal. The administration planned to deploy 2,500 marines to Australia and rotate troops through five military bases in the Philippines. It also enhanced existing defense relationships with Singapore and signed new defense agreements with Vietnam and India. These moves amounted to a doubling down of an already robust—and to China, threatening—military presence in the region.

Yuan Peng, a senior analyst at the prestigious China Institutes of Contemporary International Relations in Beijing, contended that these moves were threatening China's near-sea defense system over the waters between the Chinese coast and the so-called First Island Chain, running from Japan to the Philippines and Indonesian islands, and were casting a long shadow over the China-US military relationship. Moreover America's increasingly frequent bilateral and multilateral military exercises around China's periphery aggravated China's regional security environment.[29]

Campbell claims that China's response to the rebalance was not driven by concern over US intentions. Yet Fu Ying, a high-profile former vice foreign minister, pointed out that the "intentions of the U.S. military alliances in the Asia-Pacific remain a particular source of concern for China," especially after the "pivot."[30] More ominously, the rebalance actually bolstered Chinese hardliners' assertion about a hegemonic United States bent on containing China and keeping it down.[31] To some, the rebalance was but the latest manifestation of America's "Cold War mentality" that had only served to raise tension.[32]

Yuan's and Fu's assessments of the military component of the rebalance represented the mainstream view among Chinese analysts and officials. US military strategy under the rebalance reconfirmed the long-held Chinese belief that the United States sought absolute military advantage over China, even during the current period of China's military modernization. Two specific policies of the Obama administration, one of its own making and the other inherited from a long-term pattern, further exacerbated Chinese frustrations.

From the Air-Sea Battle to the Third Offset Strategy

In September 2009 the chiefs of the US Navy and Air Force signed a classified memorandum on developing a new operational concept called the air-sea Battle

(ASB). The concept was endorsed by the 2010 Quadrennial Defense Review. Secretary of Defense Robert Gates tasked the air force and navy to develop "a new joint air-sea battle concept for defeating adversaries across the range of military operations, including adversaries equipped with sophisticated anti-access and area denial capabilities."[33] In late 2011 Secretary of Defense Leon Panetta formed the new Multi-Service Office to Advance Air-Sea Battle.[34] Meanwhile the Pentagon was developing a more overarching Joint Operational Access Concept (JOAC) able to nest specific concepts such as the ASB, in response to what it saw as emerging anti-access and area-denial (A2/AD) security challenges.[35] In January 2015 the Pentagon changed the name of the air-sea battle, which had become controversial, into the new Joint Concept for Access and Maneuver in the Global Commons (JAM-GC).

According to American military planners, ASB/JAM-GC is focused on the rising challenge of the global proliferation of A2/AD capabilities to the US military's freedom of access to the global commons.[36] The chiefs of the US Navy and Air Force wrote in a coauthored article that the purpose of the ASB was to "ensure that U.S. forces remain able to project power on behalf of American interests worldwide" by improving integration of air, land, naval, space, and cyberspace forces. If America's freedom of action and its ability to project military power in strategically significant regions are threatened, so the thinking goes, this "could erode the credibility of U.S. security commitments to partners and allies, and with it their political stability and economic prosperity."[37]

The US government was careful to emphasize that ASB/JAM-GC was driven not by any one particular country or geopolitical scenario but rather by the trend of the proliferation of A2/AD capabilities throughout the world. It was nevertheless directed at only a handful of countries—and above all, China.[38] A senior navy official declared, "[It] is all about convincing the Chinese that we will win this competition."[39] Clearly ASB/JAM-GC is a hegemonic concept bent on preserving America's military advantage over China.

ASB/JAM-GC and the larger concept of JOAC seek to offset what the Pentagon perceives as China's rapidly growing A2/AD capabilities and their challenges to US power projection in the Western Pacific. But the operational requirements behind these concepts are highly offensive. Just in order to gain access to the Western Pacific theater they require attacking, even preemptively, Chinese defenses in full depth rather than rolling back those defenses from the maritime perimeter within the First Island Chain. In other words, the US military would need to penetrate into the depth of Chinese defenses on the mainland "by striking at critical hostile elements, such as logistics and command and control nodes, long-range firing units, and strategic and operational reserves."[40]

The consequences of striking deep into China's sovereign territory, as critics of these concepts point out, could escalate beyond a conventional conflict between the United States and China into a nuclear war if China perceives US conventional strikes into its mainland targets as a first strike to disarm its nuclear deterrent.[41] Indeed the US military recognizes that the highly offensive operational requirements behind ASB/JAM-GC and JOAC may not receive national policy support because of the extraordinary military and political risks associated with them.[42] The high stakes raised by the offensive aspects of these concepts are also making US allies nervous. If some of the US strikes against mainland Chinese targets are launched from allied bases, as is likely, this will draw those allied countries into a war with China.[43] Fear of such dangerous confrontation helps to explain these countries' reticence about ASB/JAM-GC since the concept first appeared in 2009.

In peacetime ASB/JAM-GC will almost guarantee an intense US-China arms race in both conventional and nuclear, cyber, and space domains, as China will be provoked to develop a counterstrategy. Already the US military is increasing costly investments in capabilities and doctrines in this area. Alongside the implementation of the JOAC doctrine, it is committed to sustaining its undersea capabilities, developing a new stealth bomber, improving missile defense, and enhancing the resilience and effectiveness of space-based capabilities.[44] The US military's determination to preserve its superiority will in all likelihood be met by a strong Chinese determination to reduce that superiority. The result will be greater strategic instability in the US-China relationship.

ASB/JAM-GC and JOAC are operational concepts, not strategy per se. Alongside these concepts, however, the Pentagon has also been trying to develop a military strategy for the same purpose of countering the A2/AD challenge. In September 2014 Secretary of Defense Chuck Hagel announced the crafting of a new game-changing strategy akin to President Dwight Eisenhower's New Look strategy in the 1950s and Secretary of Defense Harold Brown's Offset Strategy in the 1970s. This Third Offset Strategy, as it is now known, seeks to exploit US capability advantages to restore and maintain US global power projection capability. In particular it emphasizes leveraging US "core competencies" in unmanned systems and automation, extended-range and low-observable air operations, undersea warfare, and complex system engineering and integration in order to project power differently.[45]

Like ASB/JAM-GC, the Third Offset Strategy is targeted at China in particular. And in requiring the identification and destruction of high-value targets regardless of where they are located or how they are defended,[46] it is also a doctrine of striking deep into Chinese territory, with all the same risks of military escalation and political breakdown associated with ASB/JAM-GC. Moreover the historical precedents in US offset strategies are not encouraging. The first offset strategy, in the form of Eisenhower's New Look, relied on nuclear weapons to make up for the shortfall of men and equipment to face the Warsaw Pact in Europe. But this explicit reliance on nuclear strategy exacerbated the American-Soviet arms race, encouraged both France and Britain to develop their own nuclear force, and eventually provoked a backlash that led to heavy reinvestment in conventional arms in Europe.[47] Were the Third Offset Strategy to be implemented in its current fashion, it would likely trigger a US-China arms race across all domains; compel key US allies such as Japan, South Korea, and Australia to increase military spending in order to keep pace with US military innovations; exacerbate tension between China's and America's regional allies and partners; and undermine regional peace and stability.

Persistent through all of the Obama administration's new military thinking—from the air-sea battle to the Third Offset Strategy—is a remarkable obsession with unchallenged global military superiority and a striking reluctance to accept any significant erosion of its military edge in the Western Pacific as a result of China's rise. Yet leading officials and analysts have all recognized that the brief interval of America's unimpeded global access since the end of the Cold War is a historical anomaly. The rise of other countries' so-called A2/AD capabilities—deliberately framed by the Pentagon in especially threatening ways—merely signals a return to normalcy.[48] Rather than accepting this new reality, strategists present it in terms of a bleak choice between acquiescence in a new world order wherein the United States is no longer a global military hegemon or the old order whereby the US military exploited and often abused its advantages.[49] The almost obsessive concern with China's A2/AD capabilities is ultimately tied to the US pursuit of Asian hegemony. Aaron Friedberg represents the prevailing American thinking: "Because they [China's A2/AD capabilities] challenge Washington's ability, and perhaps its willingness, to project power in the region, the continuing growth of these forces could call American security guarantees into question, weakening the alliances on which they rest and eventually undermining the United States' place as the preponderant Asia-Pacific power."[50]

But it is not at all clear that A2/AD—a Pentagon lexicon that is nowhere to be found in original Chinese discourses—is China's settled military strategy toward the United States. Examining Chinese sources, M. Taylor Fravel and Christopher P. Twomey show that China's strategy, at least for now, does not seek to push the United States out of the Asian littoral.[51] The fundamental problem is this: if America cannot modify its fixation with military hegemony, it is bound to face a tense relationship with China, whose modernizing military force is naturally reducing its military superiority.

Close-in Military Surveillance

New US military thinking such as ASB/JAM-GC, JOAC, and the Third Offset Strategy are worrying Chinese military planners over long-term competition. On a day-to-day basis they are more frustrated with a seemingly mundane issue: US close-in airborne electronic surveillance of Chinese military targets along China's coastline and in the hinterland. Yet if there is one urgent military issue to be resolved and one that will greatly contribute to improving strategic trust between the two militaries, this is it.

For years the United States has been conducting such surveillance with very high frequency. Some reports suggest there have been more than four hundred reconnaissance missions per year, an average of over one per day.[52] According to a Chinese scholar based at Peking University, the US military has been flying more than ninety surveillance missions over China each month, an average of over three per day. Other public sources put the number for the year 2014 at 1,200, up from 260 in 2009.[53] Moreover many of these missions have flown not just over China's two-hundred-nautical-mile exclusive economic zones (EEZs) beyond its twelve-nautical-mile territorial sea, but have actually transgressed into China's sovereign airspace, over militarily sensitive (and thus valuable) inland regions such as Xinjiang and Gansu provinces in China's west. At the moment the PLA has few options to prevent these flights apart from forced interceptions. This is one area where the PLA is feeling humiliated by the US military on a daily basis and is hard put to explain its impotence to the top leadership. According to this scholar, the PLA's assertive actions in the South China Sea over the past decade— including land reclamation and island building in the Spratly Islands—are in part driven by its frustration with US surveillance. They want to create trouble for the US military in other areas.[54]

US surveillance of China is not only generating combustible grievances inside the PLA but can lead to unsafe encounters. The PLA routinely intercepts and monitors US missions. About one-third of these missions prompt the Chinese to scramble their aircraft,[55] setting the stage for incidents and crises. In fact this happened on April 1, 2001, when a US EP-3 surveillance plane collided with an intercepting Chinese F-8 fighter over the South China Sea. The US pilot survived the near-fatal accident and made an emergency landing at the PLA's Lingshui airfield on Hainan Island. The Chinese F-8 fighter crashed and its pilot was presumed dead.

Because the collision took place some 70 miles (104 kilometers) to the southeast of China's Hainan Island, it was an incident over China's EEZ. The United States maintained that the EP-3 plane was flying over "international waters" and thus was entitled to freedom of navigation and overflight. China, on the other hand, did not acknowledge the US term "international waters" and asserted that foreign military activities within its EEZ were subject to its laws and regulations.

International legal opinions as well as state practices are divided over the legality of military activities inside the EEZ. The major international treaty in this area, the United Nations Convention on the Law of the Sea (UNCLOS), is somewhat ambiguous on this point. Article 58 of UNCLOS stipulates that all states enjoy freedom of navigation and overflight in the EEZ, but it also requires that states shall have due regard to the rights and duties of the coastal state and shall comply with the laws and regulations adopted by the coastal state.[56]

Essentially the division is between those maritime powers hoping to internationalize the EEZ without much concern for the jurisdiction of coastal states and those coastal states intent on territorializing the EEZ in order to strengthen control over their EEZs. The United States has taken an internationalization approach by conflating the EEZ with the high seas. It uses its own concept of international waters to refer to all waters seaward of the territorial sea where the ships and aircraft of all states enjoy the high-seas freedom of navigation and overflight. But this concept is neither acknowledged nor addressed in UNCLOS.[57] China tends to take a territorialization approach to the EEZ and stresses the rights and jurisdiction of coastal states. Its disputation of the right of the United States to conduct military activities in its EEZ does not command wide international support. It is not groundless, however, especially when several other regional countries, including India, Malaysia, and Thailand, share its position on military activities in the EEZ.[58]

Many US officials and scholars claim that international law is on their side and that military activities, including surveillance and reconnaissance inside other countries' EEZs, are legal under UNCLOS. They tend to focus on legal and operational technicalities and address disputes on a case-by-case basis. Thus, with respect to the 2001 collision incident, the US side argued that international law allowed the freedom of overflight over China's EEZ. Such reconnaissance flights were standard and routine for the US military and had been conducted not just off the coast of China but around the world.[59] Moreover, treating the collision as an isolated event and a pure accident, they pointed to the PLA pilot's fatal error in judgment as the direct cause of the collision.[60] Secretary of State Colin Powell declared, "We did not do anything wrong,"[61] and the US military swiftly resumed such flights after the resolution of the crisis.

Yet even if all the technical arguments are on the US side, they still do not address China's most pressing concerns. Rather than treating the collision incident as a stand-alone case, China took a political and contextual approach to the whole issue of US surveillance by putting the incident in a larger strategic context. As leading Chinese experts point out, China regards US surveillance as an indication of hostile intentions and as a threat to its national security.[62] The longtime pattern of US intelligence gathering and intimidation in the air and on the sea may even be traced back to the humiliating gunboat diplomacy Western powers conducted along China's coast in the late nineteenth century.[63] The 2001 collision, from this perspective, was merely one of the many consequences of a long-term US policy and could not be seen as an isolated incident insulated from broader strategic patterns in US-China relations.

Airborne surveillance flights have indeed been a standard US military practice since at least the Second World War. Such missions were valuable during the Cold War when intelligence-gathering satellites were not yet available. They remain useful today because airborne missions can obtain imagery and signals intelligence in areas that are not consistently covered by satellites. US electronic surveillance missions against China aim to seek as detailed and up-to-date an understanding as possible of the existence, locations, numbers, and technical characteristics of the radar and other electronically transmitting military systems of the PLA. Clearly such intelligence is valuable to the US military in times of both peace and war.[64] But for China, it is simply another manifestation of the US hegemonic strategy of preserving military superiority without due regard for Chinese concerns. It is not surprising, then, that the PLA is deeply mistrustful of US strategic intentions.

Exacerbating Chinese Assertiveness

Under the rebalance the United States has significantly enhanced its diplomatic and strategic relations with crucial Asia-Pacific countries, including both its traditional allies and new security partners. In Northeast Asia the April 2015 upgrade of the Guidelines for US-Japan Defense Cooperation represented the latest in a series of enhancements since the 1997 revision of the Defense Guidelines, enabling the two countries to cooperate more closely on maritime security and regional stability.[65] But it was in Southeast Asia that the rebalance received the most attention. The Obama administration opened new ties with Myanmar, elevated relations with Vietnam, forged a new strategic partnership with Indonesia, and strengthened an already excellent relationship with Singapore. The traditional alliance with the Philippines received a significant boost with the conclusion of an Enhanced Defense Cooperation Agreement that gave the United States access to multiple bases on Philippine soil. President Obama also upgraded the relationship with the Association of Southeast Asian Nations (ASEAN) by acceding to the ASEAN Treaty of Amity and Cooperation, joining the East Asia Summit, and hosting, for the first time, a US-ASEAN summit on American soil in February 2016.[66]

Chinese officials and scholars criticized the rebalance for intensifying diplomatic and strategic pressure on China. In particular they argued that the rebalance contributed to tensions between China and its neighbors in territorial and maritime disputes. In July 2010 Secretary of State Clinton announced at the ASEAN Regional Forum in Hanoi that the United States had a national interest in the peaceful resolution of disputes in the South China Sea, welcomed a multilateral solution, and would be willing to facilitate multilateral talks.[67] She reasoned, based on a worst-case assumption, that "if nobody's there to push back to create a balance, then they're [the Chinese] going to have a chokehold on the sea lanes and also on the countries that border the South China Sea."[68] But her intervention risked escalating territorial disputes between China and its neighbors to a geopolitical rivalry between the United States and China, thus considerably raising the strategic stakes.[69] Since October 2015 the US Navy has begun to conduct so-called Freedom of Navigation Operations near Chinese-held features in the South China Sea.[70] Clinton affirmed the application of the US-Japan security treaty to the Diaoyu/Senkaku Islands in the East China Sea, which are under dispute between China and Japan. President Obama reaffirmed this pledge in 2014, as did James Mattis, President Trump's first secretary of defense, in 2017.[71]

American officials claimed that the rebalance did not change the US position of taking no sides in the sovereignty disputes between China and its neighbors. They averred that interventions in the East and South China Sea disputes were simply meant to fulfill its alliance obligations or maintain a rules-based order. Chinese elites, however, contended that Washington was fanning the flames of dispute to preserve its maritime dominance by constraining and countering China's expanding naval and maritime activities in the Western Pacific. Rather than helping to calm tensions and facilitate a peaceful solution to the disputes, Washington was turning these disputes into a battlefield for Sino-American strategic rivalry.[72] But by raising the strategic stakes, Washington increased its own strategic burden as its regional allies exploited the rebalance to challenge China and test America's security commitments, trapping it in a precarious strategic quandary.

Moreover Chinese elites argued that American interventions significantly complicated the management and resolution of these disputes by encouraging regional states' risk-taking behavior. Fu Ying argued, "Some U.S. allies in the region have made claims on China's sovereign territory and infringed on Chinese maritime rights, hoping that by cozying up to Washington, they could involve the United States in their disputes with Beijing. This is a dangerous path, reminiscent of the 'bloc politics' of the Cold War."[73]

Believing that some countries were counting on the US rebalance to enhance their interests and make demands on China's sovereignty and maritime rights,

Chinese analysts concluded that China must respond with sufficient resolve to protect its own interests and beat back these countries' provocations.[74] Failure to do so would not only inflate regional countries' ambitions at the cost of China's interests but also embolden the United States to capitalize on their provocations to enhance the efficacy of the rebalance strategy. Following this logic, it is not difficult to see that the rebalance—especially the US desire to make credible its commitments to its allies in the face of China's rise—actually contributed to a greater Chinese resolve to face down perceived provocations from regional countries, especially when these countries were Japan, the Philippines, and other US allies. Thus, in mounting strategic pressure on China, the rebalance stiffened China's resolve to counter that pressure in response, producing a competition over strategic resolve fraught with risks of miscalculation and misjudgment.

Chinese analysts highlighted that those countries involved in territorial and maritime disputes with China were either US allies (Japan and the Philippines) or newly emerging security partners of the United States (India and Vietnam). For them, this could not be a mere coincidence. They believed too that the United States, adopting a nominally neutral position, was in fact supporting and encouraging these countries' positions and policies against China. American policy toward Asian territorial and maritime disputes, halfway between principled neutrality and de facto bias, motivated by its concern with strategic credibility, was emboldening regional countries to challenge Chinese interests. The resulting provocations and incidents brought diplomatic and security pressure on China, at times even the pressure of war.[75] It was in this sense that China criticized the rebalance for damaging its interests and eroding trust between Beijing and Washington.

We do not accept these claims at face value. They are self-serving in overlooking the Chinese side of the story, including China's increasing maritime assertiveness since 2009.[76] Like the United States, China also raised the strategic stakes, most notably by land reclamation and island building in the South China Sea since late 2013. The deterioration of Sino-American relations in maritime Asia is a story of bilateral and regional strategic interactions, not simply unilateral mistakes from one side. (We will explain the Chinese mistakes and discuss interaction dynamics in Chapter 4.) The Chinese argument also misses the fact that Washington did try to rein in its allies to prevent them from using US protection to provoke conflict with China. A few exceptional and bold scholars, such as the widely respected Wang Jisi, hold a more balanced view of US policy.[77]

Nevertheless the sense that Washington was the "behind-the-scene black hand" and "trouble-maker" behind China's recent disputes with its neighbors was widespread in Beijing.[78] And it is clear that the rebalance, through Chinese perceptions and misperceptions and in conjunction with other contextual factors, aggravated negative Chinese reactions and damaged the overall China-US relationship. It is fair to ask, as many Chinese elites do, whether Washington would be able to handle the delicate task of deterring Chinese assertiveness and preventing provocations from its allies at the same time.

The rebalance did not cause Chinese assertiveness by itself. As the next chapter will show, Chinese assertiveness was well in place prior to the rebalance. Nevertheless the geopolitical setting it created served to exacerbate China's already fermenting assertive inclinations and prompted its strategic adventurism. China's island building in the South China Sea, examined in the next chapter, was probably an indirect consequence. The irony of the rebalance, Robert Ross observes, is that it was meant to check a rising China but instead "sparked its combativeness and damaged its faith in cooperation."[79] In seeking resolution to Asian maritime disputes, the Obama administration should have made it clear that it was supporting all bilateral and multilateral diplomatic negotiations conducted by the claimants and other interested parties. The maintenance of an active US military presence should not have overshadowed regional diplomatic efforts. Freedom of Navigation Operations conducted in a highly politicized manner only served to signal a US intention to contain China or take sides in the disputes.[80]

Heightening Economic Competition

Economic interactions are supposed to create positive-sum outcomes even if a degree of competition exists between nations. The Obama administration, however, almost made the TPP free trade agreement into a zero-sum geopolitical struggle with China over Asian leadership and rule-making in the global economy. Signed by twelve Asia-Pacific countries in February 2016,[81] the TPP was the largest and most ambitious free trade agreement undertaken by the United States. Significant economic advantages of the TPP include eliminating trade barriers; encouraging market-oriented reforms in member states; creating higher standards on a range of issues, including labor, the environment, and intellectual property; and establishing new trade rules and disciplines.[82]

Rather than emphasizing those economic benefits, however, US officials and analysts elevated the TPP as the economic centerpiece of the Obama administration's rebalance strategy. They hyped it as the litmus test of America's credibility and leadership in Asia. Campbell goes so far as to claim that the TPP was "the true sine qua non" of the rebalance.[83] Thus an economic initiative came to acquire an outsized geopolitical role. Along the way, American thinking about the TPP narrowed considerably from economic mutual benefit to zero-sum geopolitical competition. One prominent commentator likened the failure of the US Congress to ratify the TPP to the American version of a Brexit from the

Pacific region, a colossal strategic mistake that would supposedly herald the end of US leadership in Asia.[84] Believing that "the TPP is ultimately more important as a geostrategic, rule-setting initiative than simply as a trade pact," another influential analyst warned that "a failure to bring the TPP to fruition would deliver a punishing blow to U.S. standing and credibility."[85] Secretary of Defense Ashton Carter bluntly declared, "Passing the TPP is as important to me as another aircraft carrier."[86]

President Obama seemed to buy this argument. In an article for the *Washington Post* in May 2016, he described the TPP in highly competitive and—to many Chinese observers—hegemonic terms. He noted that sixteen Asia-Pacific countries, including China, were negotiating the Regional Comprehensive Economic Partnership (RCEP). He asserted that this trade pact under China's leadership "would carve up some of the fastest-growing markets in the world at our expense, putting American jobs, businesses and goods at risk." The TPP, in contrast, "puts American workers first and makes sure we write the rules of the road in the 21st century." "The United States, not countries like China," he reiterated, "should write them." And "other countries should play by the rules that America and our partners set, and not the other way around."[87]

Yet if the ultimate goal of the TPP was to advance a wider Asia-Pacific free trade area,[88] it was in perfect harmony with China's trade agenda, whose stated goal was also to create such an Asian free trade zone. If American and Chinese goals were not only compatible but in fact identical, it made little sense to juxtapose the TPP and RCEP as rival trade pacts. True, the TPP and RCEP differed in terms of the breadth and depth of trade liberalization; America wanted a "high quality" agreement that would address what it saw as the failures of the existing multilateral trade rules embodied by the World Trade Organization. But that hardly undermined the common goal of advancing free trade. The two pacts overlapped significantly in membership, as seven TPP countries were also negotiating the RCEP. Rather than seeing the TPP and RCEP as rival trade pacts, they could be more constructively seen as mutually reinforcing pathways to the ultimate goal of establishing an Asia-Pacific free trade area. Rather than applying zero-sum geopolitical thinking pitting US leadership against a putative Chinese challenge, policymakers would serve the region better by coordinating and integrating the two pacts in the common interests of all countries involved. And the constructive approach to economic cooperation was to write the new rules together rather than excluding particular countries for geopolitical purposes.

For those who view economic relations in geopolitical terms, there is a dramatic lesson from an embarrassing blunder of the Obama administration's economic policy toward China. In October 2014 China proposed to establish the Asian Infrastructure Investment Bank as part of its effort to increase its regional economic and financial influence. An alarmist Obama administration lobbied its allies not to join. The obstruction backfired spectacularly when the United Kingdom became the first US ally to announce its decision to join the bank in March 2015, followed by all major US allies except Japan. US officials were suspicious of China's efforts to establish international institutions that could challenge the US-centered Bretton Woods institutions such as the World Bank and the International Monetary Fund. They accused Britain of a "constant accommodation" of China.[89] Yet most US analysts and former officials now consider the hostile US response to the Asian Infrastructure Investment Bank a mistake. Campbell, for example, recognizes that establishing a rules-based order will at times require engaging with, rather than avoiding, Chinese-led programs and institutions. Rejecting the Bank deprived Washington of an opportunity to shape the organization from within.[90] Accommodating China's reasonable and legitimate interests is a necessary requirement for achieving a healthy US-China relationship and for buttressing a rules-based order.

In framing the TPP as a geopolitical contest with China for Asian leadership, the Obama administration was trying to sell it to a skeptical Congress and domestic audience where popular backlash against free trade and globalization was on the rise. Nevertheless, targeting China in such competitive terms, in an area most conducive to making a persuasive case for mutual benefit, could not but create negative Chinese perceptions of US intentions and was thus detrimental to the relationship. Unsurprisingly, Chinese elites criticized Washington for strategically manipulating the TPP to disrupt the existing tempo of East Asian economic integration and to challenge China's regional economic strategy.[91]

Occasionally US officials appeared open-minded about the prospect of China joining the TPP, as did National Security Advisor Susan Rice in a speech in November 2013.[92] They may have intended the TPP to raise the bar for liberalization standards and thereby place greater pressure on China to further reform its economic system.[93] The Chinese government erred in not taking a more positive attitude toward the TPP. But such motivation and the sporadic invitations for China to join the TPP from the US side were drowned by the dominant discourse about the geopolitical significance of the TPP in a competitive US-China struggle for leadership in Asia. With even an economic initiative portrayed as a geopolitical struggle, the Obama administration had to squarely face the Chinese criticism that the rebalance amounted to a thinly veiled containment strategy against China. That said, nothing Obama did in the economic realm came close to the willfullness of Trump, who on his first day in office withdrew the United States from the TPP.[94] The Obama administration's full-throttled advocacy came to naught.

Snubbing the Chinese Desire for Respect

During President Obama's visit to China in November 2009, the two countries painstakingly negotiated a joint statement holding that "respecting each other's core interests is extremely important to ensure steady progress in U.S.-China relations."[95] In April 2010 President Hu Jintao told President Obama, "China and the United States should respect each other's core interests and major concerns. This is the key to the healthy and stable development of bilateral ties."[96] In February 2012, during a visit to the United States, Vice President Xi Jinping proposed building a new model of a major country relationship between China and the United States. In June 2013, during a famous "shirtsleeves" summit with President Obama at the Sunnylands estate in California, President Xi outlined three key components of such a relationship: no conflict and no confrontation, mutual respect, and win-win cooperation.[97]

Underlying all these initiatives was China's search for respect from the United States, especially its expectation of US respect for what it referred to as its "core interests and major concerns." Yet apart from the November 2009 joint statement, the Obama administration consistently refused to accept China's call for respecting each other's core interests. One exception was the speech by Deputy Secretary of State James Steinberg in September 2009, in which he emphasized the need for "strategic reassurance" in US-China relations. He also insisted that the two countries "must each take specific steps to address and allay each other's concerns."[98] But his speech did not go through interagency clearance,[99] and the idea of strategic reassurance disappeared from official thinking after Steinberg left the State Department in March 2011.

The Americans' snub of China's plea for mutual respect of each other's core interests frustrated Chinese elites. It was taken as another example of America's "hegemonic mindset" and its unwillingness to place the relationship on an equal footing. For China, core interests include, first, its political system and stability, especially the leadership of the CCP; second, sovereignty, territorial integrity, and national unity over Taiwan, Tibet, and Xinjiang; and third, sustainable economic and social development.[100] Chinese leaders fretted about US arms sales to Taiwan, US support of the Dalai Lama, its relations with separatists in Xinjiang, and its periodic call for political freedom inside China and active promotion of democracy worldwide. For them, America's lack of genuine respect for a rising China under CCP rule was clear.[101]

The United States disputed China's definition of its "core interests." They were seen to run counter to existing American policies or to violate venerable American values and principles. American political ideology makes it very hard for the US government to support the CCP's authoritarian one-party rule in

China. Washington seeks to promote political liberalization and democratization in China, although not as a matter of priority. It also disagrees with Beijing's sovereignty claims to Taiwan, the Diaoyu/Senkaku Islands in the East China Sea, and the islands and waters of the South China Sea.[102]

Thomas Christensen provides a scholarly rationale for rejecting China's call for mutual respect of each other's core interests. He argues that this concept mainly serves to raise unrealistic Chinese expectations of fundamental changes in US policy. As a result, "the *pursuit of mutual interests*, not mutual respect for allegedly distinct sets of national core interests, should be the centerpiece of the relationship."[103]

Christensen's logic seems to be that because the United States and China are going to differ on issues related to China's core interests such as Taiwan and CCP legitimacy, it is futile for Beijing to insist on US respect for such interests and more useful to instead work on mutual interests such as nonproliferation and counterterrorism. But such reasoning, reflecting a common US reluctance to change long-standing policies in the face of changing realities, may be taken by the Chinese side as another example of an American hegemonic mindset expecting Chinese compliance while offering little compromise in return.

Christensen is particularly critical of what he refers to as China's horse-trading view of cooperation; that is, China would reciprocate US policies that respect China's core interests by respecting US core interests and cooperating with Washington over mutual interests.[104] He is correct that the pursuit of US-China mutual interests is a worthy goal and that the cooperation that Washington seeks from China is also in China's interests. But he overlooks the priority and political origins of core interests in Chinese thinking.

For China, mutual interests offer the basis for China-US cooperation, but US attitudes toward China's core interests reflect the degree of American respect for China's standing as a rising power and are thus politically more significant. As Wang Jisi points out, China's principle of mutual respect requires Washington to "respect China's form of nationhood and its political system," namely its political order based on CCP leadership. For Beijing, respect for core interests, ostensibly a foreign policy principle, is in fact "driven from its desire to maintain domestic order and stability."[105] Bilahari Kausikan, a veteran Singaporean diplomat, observes that CCP rule "is an existential issue for the Chinese leadership, against which all other issues are of secondary importance."[106] Christensen's "horse-trading" interpretation of Chinese views does not fully capture China's domestically oriented concerns. If Washington is seen to undermine—or at least not fully support—China's domestic order, it will be very difficult to put the China-US relationship on a secure and lasting foundation. As Wang warns, "only by respecting China's fundamental political institutions and domestic order can Washington persuade Beijing to reciprocate by refraining from challenging American supremacy and the current international order."[107]

American values emanating from political liberalism and the Protestant religion—dressed with universalist pretentions—are a significant obstacle to achieving political equality between the two countries. But it is not insurmountable, even though overcoming it may take a long time. As noted in Chapter 2, the American government from Nixon to Obama did not make democratization a top goal of its China policy, nor did the Trump administration in its first three years (2017–19). America's broad agenda of worldwide democracy promotion since the 1990s has been a failure.[108] Many American elites have realized that "the US has put too much faith in its power to shape China's trajectory."[109] The American attempt to liberalize China—and much elsewhere—has foundered.[110] Two former Obama administration officials have called for a return to humility; neither seeking to isolate and weaken China nor trying to transform China for the better, they suggest, should be the lodestar of US strategy in Asia.[111] This advice—that Washington should focus more on the limits of its own power and base its China policy on more realistic expectations—is worth taking seriously.[112]

The Chinese concept of mutual respect for each other's core interests speaks to the question of equality and fairness in the China-US relationship and is bound up with Beijing's quest for national dignity and international standing. Some American observers recognize that Beijing has earned the right to be treated as an equal and that American leaders should be less condescending toward Beijing.[113] The Obama administration's failure to appreciate this, and its lingering patronizing habit, impeded a genuine accommodation between the two countries. The administration could have disagreed with Beijing's definition of core interests while still engaging in a candid dialogue on what might constitute China's "legitimate core interests." But by giving it short shrift, the administration missed an opportunity to shape the relationship in a more sustainable and productive direction. Its China policy was then left without a credible reassuring message, apart from the rhetorical assurance that the United States welcomed a rising China. As a result, in Chinese eyes, Obama's China policy was all "resolve" as carried by the rebalance strategy and no "reassurance" because of its snub of China's desire for respect.

The Failure of Conflict Management

We are now in a position to evaluate the Obama administration's China policy on the basis of our assessment of its rebalance strategy. Both Clinton and Campbell, the main architects of the rebalance, tried to argue that it would enhance America's relationship with the Asia-Pacific region as a whole, including both

China and other regional countries. In her 2011 article Clinton declared, "We will continue to embed our relationship with China in a broader regional framework of security alliances, economic networks, and social connections."[114] Echoing Clinton, Campbell argued that "embedding China policy . . . within a larger Asia policy framework" would enable the United States to "more consequentially shape the contours of China's rise."[115] But all failed to address the contradiction between America's China policy and its policy toward the larger Asian region. Campbell adamantly maintained that the United States should "move away from the kind of 'China first' or 'G-2' approach that has often dominated US policy toward Asia."[116] But in going to the other extreme of embedding China strategy in a larger regional framework, the rebalance deprived the administration of any distinctive China strategy at all. Max Baucus, Obama's last ambassador to China, bemoaned the ad hoc nature of America's China policy and its "lack of strategic vision."[117]

The Obama administration relegated China policy to a management issue. Its goal was simply to "preserve key national interests where necessary while sustaining a workable and sustainable relationship with China whenever possible."[118] But "sustaining a workable relationship" with China was hardly an adequate strategy for dealing with the world's biggest rising power. There was no sense of urgency in finding a strategy for containing competition and promoting cooperation. Chinese elites pointed out that rather than a coherent strategy, the Obama administration's China policy was a hodgepodge of reactive and ad hoc decisions, reflecting a contradictory, disorderly, and confusing assortment of engagement, containment, balancing, competition, and cooperation.[119]

The rebalance's convoluted strategic design was plain to Chinese as well as American analysts. Da Wei, a leading US foreign policy expert at the China Institutes of Contemporary International Relations, contended that the rebalance's goal of simultaneously enhancing relations with China and other Asia-Pacific countries was nearly impossible to achieve in practice. In fact the improvement of US relations with other Asian countries under the banner of the rebalance came at the expense of its relationship with China.[120] On the American side, Patrick Cronin noted that the rebalance "never achieved high-level clarity and coherence."[121]

If such conceptual malaise was the basis of Campbell's claim that the rebalance was a mixture of reassurance and resolve toward China, then this mixed approach failed. Chinese elites considered the rebalance threatening because for them it was all resolve and no reassurance. A prominent analyst alleged that the US approach of compromising Chinese interests while claiming to act only at regional countries' invitation was double-faced and damaging to its reputation.[122] The rebalance was strongly motivated by a US concern with the credibility of its strategic commitments in Asia, and thus should appear reassuring to its allies. Yet a Chinese Foreign Ministry official held that it could reassure neither China nor its allies, at least not in terms of the level of the Obama administration's strategic investment. And the "resolve" part of the strategy also failed, because apparent US resolve only steeled greater Chinese resolve, especially when Washington was seen to challenge China's regional standing in this era of growing Chinese power and confidence.[123]

Not only had the rebalance failed to shape China's rise; it had also triggered a series of indirect and unintended consequences by stimulating a vigorous Chinese strategy toward countries on its regional periphery.[124] The so-called Belt and Road Initiative and island building in the South China Sea, two of Beijing's most significant moves during the Obama administration, were indirect responses to the rebalance and measures to relieve its strategic pressures.[125] But they were interpreted by Washington as evidence of Chinese expansionism and its alleged intention to push America out of Asia.[126] Alarmed by Chinese assertiveness but overlooking the compounding effect of the rebalance, Washington became all the more keen to use the rebalance to check Chinese power. In this sense the rebalance made both countries worse off by agitating Chinese assertiveness and undermining mutual strategic trust. China and America increasingly saw each other as security threats and strategic competitors. This made cooperation on common security challenges less likely and the risk of misjudgments and miscalculations more acute.[127]

The rebalance was the continuation and latest manifestation of America's traditional strategy of liberal hegemony in Asia. Chinese critics were right to point out the contradiction between engaging China and entrenching US dominance in Asia. For many American strategists this was no contradiction at all, for they determined that one of the key purposes of engaging China was to dissuade it from seeking hegemony in Asia. The primary means to this end was to balance rising Chinese power by increasing the combined power of the United States and its allies and partners in the region. The United States should engage, not contain, China in order to channel Chinese power, facilitate cooperation, and prevent conflict, but it must also put a lid upon China's hegemonic ambitions. The Americans were happy to see cooperation with China under US hegemony but would not grant China an equal status and shared leadership in Asia.

Such a strategy of preserving American hegemony by preventing Chinese hegemony has been in place since the mid-2000s.[128] The Obama administration, in wanting only to sustain a workable relationship with China while upholding the long-standing principle of US leadership, unwittingly inherited the preceding Bush administration's China strategy. Chinese critics viewed the strategy as contradictory because America's pursuit of regional hegemony was at odds with its declaratory policy of welcoming China's rise. US officials saw no contradiction because the strategy was designed to shape China's rise in ways that would not challenge US hegemony. This mismatch between Chinese and American views about the coherence of US strategy helps to explain rising bilateral tension.

Yet some officials and analysts want to make the rebalance even more ambitious. Campbell argues that preventing hegemony is no longer enough to achieve American interests. He would add to the military and ideological foundations of liberal hegemony a new institutional component: a set of American-sanctioned rules, norms, and institutions that he refers to as "Asia's operating system."[129] He would also add to the traditional hub-and-spokes model of America's bilateral alliance system in Asia "a tire that links allies to one another without interfering with their strong ties to the US hub."[130]

If Washington follows Campbell's suggestion of taking a "network approach" to its Asian alliance system without finding a proper place for China in the evolving security order, Beijing is likely to feel further besieged and more uncompromising in safeguarding its perceived interests. Hardline voices decrying US containment will be on the rise, and Beijing will be more compelled to respond assertively and even aggressively. US-China relations during the first three years of the Trump administration manifested these hazards.

Respected American scholars recognize the dangers of such an approach. Christensen points out that even the exaggerated language about a pivot or rebalance could feed into Chinese conspiracy theories about alleged US containment and encirclement.[131] Ross argues that the rebalance "unnecessarily compounds Beijing's insecurities and will only feed China's aggressiveness, undermine regional stability, and decrease the possibility of cooperation between Beijing and Washington."[132] A new US-China modus vivendi is needed to transform their relationship, and that requires an effective strategy of conflict management and resolution.

Summary

Among all the various mistakes that the Obama administration made in its China policy, the most glaring was its reluctance and failure to develop a new productive strategy for transforming the relationship into a stable, equal, cooperative, and productive one. Wary of giving China too much weight, the administration chose to embed its China policy within a larger regional strategy of rebalance to the Asia-Pacific. From Washington's perspective, the rebalance demonstrated the credibility of American commitment to addressing security challenges, promoting economic prosperity, and safeguarding a rules-based regional order.

Chinese elites, however, concluded that the rebalance was a deliberate strategy of competition with, if not outright containment of, China and therefore constituted a major strategic challenge to be countered. The most sympathetic Chinese assessment considered the rebalance an attempt to balance China's rise and maintain US regional leadership.[133] America's characterization of balancing China's rise, however, was seen by China as a hegemonic attempt to entrench the inherent imbalance of the Asia-Pacific regional order as it was after the Second World War—that is, to maintain America's regional dominance.[134]

US officials and analysts admit as much when they argue that the goal of America's Asia policy should be to "prevent hegemony *and* bolster Asia's operating system."[135] But that goal is not compatible with building a constructive relationship with China as a rising Asian power. In the end the Obama administration was still captured by the traditional US grand strategy of liberal hegemony in Asia and saw no need to revise or transform it. The rebalance, based on that traditional pursuit of hegemony, challenged China's aspirations as a rising power, damaged the bilateral relationship, and complicated regional relations. Washington did not bear all the blame for the deterioration of the relationship, and we lay bare China's fair share of culpability in Chapter 4. But the rebalance strategy was at least partially responsible for deepening strategic mistrust, creating new security tensions, and reducing the incentive to achieve genuine cooperation. It was not a productive strategy of conflict management.

4

Chinese Mistakes

IF THE CARDINAL mistake of the Obama administration's China policy was the lack of a productive strategy for managing a relationship characterized by competition and cooperation, that was also the principal error of China's US policy. Just as contradictions between Obama's China and Asia policies damaged the US-China relationship, so contradictions between China's US and Asia policies undercut its goal of building a new relationship with Washington.

Under President Xi Jinping, China attempted to develop a strategy toward the United States by building what it referred to as "a new model of major-country relationship." All strategy involves identifying and ranking interests and goals and developing resources and means to protect them.[1] The "national interest" was probably the most important concept for Chinese policy thinking during this period; it was also the most difficult for policymakers to grasp, especially at a time when they perceived a rapid expansion of Chinese interests. Where to draw the line in the expansion of interests became a major strategic question.

Chinese foreign policy under Xi reflected a testing struggle to grapple with the elusive idea of China's national interest. Beijing never came to a clear, shrewd, and enlightened understanding of its national interest during the period under discussion. This is perhaps not surprising. Classical realists such as Hans Morgenthau understood that there was never such a thing as "the" national interest, but only different and competing formulations. All conceptions of national interest are subjective and at best serve as a guide for foreign policy—and even then only incompletely. Even if leaders have developed a foreign policy theory guided by some notion of national interest, very few of them will be able to conduct foreign policy without domestic constraints.[2]

China also fell short in implementing its policy of building a new model of relationship with the US. As in every country, Chinese foreign policy is made in response to day-to-day pressures and is subject to domestic and leadership politics, organizational and societal pressures, and psychological and motivational limitations. Its US policy during the Obama years (2009–16) was beset by a dysfunctional decision-making system dominated by parochial but powerful interest groups that focused on narrow, short-term gains rather than broad, long-term benefits. Nationalism, especially at the elite level, was also a driving force behind assertive policy. Faulty conceptions and domestic constraints arrested the potential of the "new model" policy toward the US.

We evaluate these Chinese mistakes in managing US policy by examining three critical junctures of the relationship during the Obama administration. In President Obama's first year in office (2009), Beijing failed to fully reciprocate Obama's positive signals for a cooperative relationship. This was partly because of Chinese elites' deep-rooted strategic distrust of Washington, and also because of their newly acquired belief, based on an emerging triumphalist nationalism, that China now possessed new power to get tough with America. The relationship experienced a dramatic downturn in 2010 as a result of Obama's returning normalcy to the relationship and China's uncompromising Asia policy.

The second juncture came in February 2012, when Vice President Xi's visit to Washington ignited high-level diplomacy for building a new model of major-country relationship, culminating in the famed June 2013 Obama-Xi summit at Sunnylands. On the US side, high officials responded positively, if not keenly, to the Chinese proposal by urging practical cooperation to bring it about. The most positive and constructive period of the relationship occurred between February 2012 and November 2013, galvanized above all by a high-level push for a new model diplomacy.

With the third juncture in late 2013 and early 2014, the relationship once again took a turn for the worse, and it did not recover during the rest of Obama's tenure. China's November 2013 announcement of an East China Sea Air Defense Identification Zone (ADIZ) raised regional apprehensions about Chinese revisionism. Its decision to reclaim land in the South China Sea was made no later than September 2013 and produced more serious consequences over the long run by setting in motion military competition. Its May 2014 deployment of an oil rig in the Paracels, sparking violent clashes with Vietnam, invited further criticism from the United States and Asian countries. In the same month, President Xi's "Asia for Asians" speech aroused US suspicion of a Chinese plot to push America out of Asia. The Obama administration began to selectively roll back Chinese advances. On the Chinese side, suspicions about the allegedly anti-China design of the administration's Asia rebalance strategy were also on the rise, spawning an instinct to counteract rather than cooperate.

The result was a deteriorating relationship with deepening strategic mistrust on both sides. In the final years of the Obama administration, both Obama and

Xi tried to stabilize the relationship and prevent strategic mistrust from spiraling out of control. Some notable achievements notwithstanding, their efforts failed to revive the "new model" diplomacy. The US side had lost interest, and the Chinese side did not know how to revitalize it. Compared with 2009, when the relationship started off on a positive note, the strategic aspects of the relationship had declined considerably by 2016.

Failure to Reciprocate Us Overtures

When President Obama took office in January 2009, his administration genuinely wanted to reduce the friction with China that had been common in the early years of previous administrations. He also wanted China's cooperation on a range of critical policy areas, including climate change, nuclear proliferation, and economic recovery. In speeches delivered during his November 2009 visit to Japan and China, Obama announced that the United States "[did] not seek to contain China" but would instead welcome China as a strong, prosperous, and successful member of the community of nations.[3] He described the US-China relationship as "positive, cooperative, and comprehensive" and called on China to play "a greater role on the world stage—a role in which a growing economy is joined by growing responsibilities."[4] Two months earlier, Deputy Secretary of State James B. Steinberg had proposed "strategic reassurance" as a new approach to managing US-China relations, by which both countries were to "take specific steps to address and allay each other's concerns."[5] To drive home the new cooperative spirit, Obama refrained from meeting with the Dalai Lama and did not approve arms sales to Taiwan—issues of great sensitivity to Beijing—during his first year in office. Meanwhile, as the financial crisis of 2008 and the long wars in the Middle East had weakened America's global standing, pundits began to suggest a "G2" relationship whereby the United States and China would jointly govern global affairs in a cooperative and coordinated fashion.[6]

Chinese leaders and elites welcomed the Obama administration's positive overtures and saw some significance in Steinberg's new approach of strategic reassurance. They were relieved that Sino-American relations at the beginning of the Obama administration would not resemble the acrimonious and crisis-ridden beginnings of the Bill Clinton and George W. Bush administrations. But for reasons explained in the next section, Beijing failed to reciprocate, let alone take up the charge of joining a G2. Instead American officials and analysts detected a new Chinese confidence bordering on arrogance. Even though Obama was the first US president to pay a state visit to China during his first year in office, Beijing did not receive his November 2009 visit with great enthusiasm. The Chinese government refused to televise nationally Obama's speech to college students and allowed only a short, stiff press conference between President Hu Jintao and Obama without question time.[7] One month later, during sharp exchanges between Chinese and American delegations at the United Nations Climate Change Conference in Copenhagen, a Chinese official at the vice-ministerial rank sought to criticize Obama even when Premier Wen Jiabao, who was leading the Chinese delegation, tried to restrain him.[8] China's cool and at times obstructionist behavior prompted American observers to conclude that Beijing read Obama's conciliatory stance as American weakness—and as an invitation for Beijing to push back.[9]

Disappointed, the Obama administration implemented rescheduled policy decisions that it knew would irk the Chinese. In January 2010 it announced a US$6 billion arms sales package to Taiwan. One month later Obama met with the Dalai Lama in the White House Map Room.[10] For the Chinese, Obama's return to these policies suggested that his restraint in 2009 was, at best, a tactical move to enlist Chinese cooperation, not a strategic change of long-standing US policy. At worst, Obama's overtures in 2009 and about-face in 2010 were interpreted as a coordinated strategy to trap, embarrass, and humiliate China.

Thus, just as the Obama administration became disappointed with China after a year of positive signaling, China became disillusioned with the Obama administration after 2010. Beijing reacted strongly to the Taiwan arms sales decision. It not only resorted to the usual countermeasure of suspending military exchanges between the two countries, but also, for the first time, threatened to impose sanctions on US companies involved in the arms sales.[11] Although such sanctions were never implemented, Beijing's harsher than usual rhetoric fed the domestic American narrative about "an assertive China."[12]

China's policies toward the Korean Peninsula and maritime Asia dealt a further blow to the relationship. These policies did not concern China-US relations at the bilateral level; they nevertheless had repercussions because of their impact on US interests in Asia. On the Korean Peninsula, China refused to accept an international commission's verdict that a North Korean submarine sank the South Korean naval ship *Cheonan* in March 2010. In November 2010 North Korea revealed the existence of a modern uranium centrifuge facility in Yongbyon. In the same month it shelled South Korea's Yeonpyeong Island, killing four military and civilian personnel and wounding several more. In all three instances China refrained from directly criticizing the North Korean government, giving the impression that it was taking Pyongyang's side and thus alienating the United States, South Korea, and Japan in the process.

Beijing's notably more assertive maritime policy after 2009 also created tension with Washington. In March 2009 Chinese ships interfered with the survey activities of the US navy ship *Impeccable* in China's exclusive economic zone off the coast of Hainan Island. In May China submitted two *notes verbales* to the

United Nations explaining its claims to the South China Sea. Both documents contained the "nine-dash line" or "U-shaped line" map, which encircled about 80 percent of the South China Sea, as the basis for China's sovereignty claims. The South China Sea began to embroil not only China and Southeast Asian claimant states, but also China and the United States. American press reports mistakenly suggested at this time that China had taken the South China Sea as a "core interest" on a par with Taiwan or Tibet.[13] Chinese officials did not characterize the South China Sea as a core interest, although they did highlight it to their US counterparts as a national priority.[14]

Taking notice of what it regarded as China's growing assertiveness in maritime Asia, the Obama administration began to develop a more active posture.[15] In July 2010 Secretary of State Hillary Clinton declared an American national interest in the South China Sea at the ASEAN Regional Forum meeting in Hanoi. This first attempt by the Obama administration at high-profile intervention into South China Sea disputes sparked a vehement response from Foreign Minister Yang Jiechi. Meanwhile, in the East China Sea, Beijing retaliated against Japan's arrest of a Chinese fishing boat captain and its crew near the disputed Diaoyu/Senkaku Islands in September 2010. It temporarily restricted rare-earth exports to Japan and demanded an apology and reparations.

Elite Triumphalism

Obama's overtures to China in 2009 may have created unrealistic expectations in Beijing about a truly accommodating policy from the new US administration. Its return to normalcy in handling sensitive issues such as arms sales to Taiwan and the Dalai Lama shattered these expectations and prompted unusually harsh responses from Beijing. But the abrupt downturn of the relationship in 2010 begs a deeper explanation than unfulfilled expectations.

One such explanation is the perennial Chinese distrust of US intentions. From the start, Chinese elites wondered whether Obama's cooperative gesture represented a fundamental change of policy or a mere tactical shift. Deeply suspicious of America's strategic intentions, many interpreted Obama's overtures as a feint to draw China into excessive global commitments that would exhaust its resources and derail its rise. Such distrust led easily to conspiracy theories about Washington trying to weaken China by embroiling it in unnecessary commitments in places like Iran, Afghanistan, and North Korea. It also created an unfortunate habit among Chinese elites to routinely interpret US moves on worst-case assumptions. Even Steinberg's strategic reassurance idea, which was criticized inside the United States as too accommodating to China,[16] was interpreted by some Chinese elites as a new plot to weaken China.

Chinese elites sensed that the Obama administration had not changed long-standing US strategy toward China; it was still the old mix of engagement and balancing. Declaratory and symbolic gestures during the administration's first year in office, in the expectation of Chinese reciprocity in supporting America in a series of substantive policy issues, struck some Chinese elites as too narrowly instrumental and not strategic enough.[17] They were correct that the Obama administration had no intention of modifying US strategy, as we argued in the preceding chapter. The administration's tactical finesse proved strategically counterproductive by creating and then dampening Chinese expectations. But China also made the mistake of seeking to take advantage of perceived American weakness to achieve quick breakthroughs in long-standing issues such as Taiwan arms sales and the Dalai Lama.[18] It also failed to take US attempts at strategic reassurance sufficiently seriously and thus missed an opportunity in strategic reciprocity and confidence building.

These misjudgments stemmed in no small part from the rise in China of a new triumphalist nationalism after 2008, with immediate foreign policy consequences in 2009 and beyond.[19] The triumph of the Beijing Olympics in 2008 and coping with the financial crisis gave Chinese elites confidence that China had finally moved beyond the so-called century of humiliation wrought by Western powers and Japan between the mid-nineteenth and mid-twentieth centuries.[20] Moreover the Sino-American power balance seemed to be shifting decisively in China's favor. China had sustained three decades of double-digit growth without a major economic crisis. In 2008 and 2009 the Chinese economy continued to grow at an annual rate of 10 percent. The United States, in contrast, was mired in a major recession because of a financial crisis of its own making.

Such triumphalism fed the view that Beijing was in no hurry to reciprocate US overtures in 2009. China's rising power had given it new leverage to deal with the United States in a more confident and assertive manner. It could more forcefully assert its interests in areas where it previously lacked leverage, such as American arms sales to Taiwan. Perhaps it was no longer necessary for China to accord the United States the same degree of respect and deference as before.[21]

This new triumphalist nationalism was much more pronounced at the elite than at the popular level. In fact China's popular nationalism has been in decline since around 2009.[22] It was elite nationalism among policymakers, bureaucrats, and pundits, not popular nationalism among ordinary citizens, that produced direct foreign policy consequences. Triumphalist elite nationalism was at least partially responsible for what Thomas Christensen describes as China's "ideological and acerbic" foreign policy in 2010.[23]

Triumphalism led to an overestimation of Chinese power, an exaggeration of American decline, and the misstep of giving short shrift to the Obama administration's new China thinking. These misjudgments produced China's tactical assertiveness on surface issues like Taiwan arms sales. But Beijing had not yet acquired a true strategic confidence. It was exhibiting a mixed foreign policy mindset that was simultaneously confident and yet defensive, assertive and yet sensitive.[24] Had China developed *strategic* assertiveness instead of tactical assertiveness—that is, the ability to move beyond politicized surface issues toward a deep strategic dialogue with Washington—the two countries might have been able to capitalize on the momentum of 2009 and carve out a more positive direction for their relationship.

This did not happen. China's newly activist Asia policy prompted a new assessment of China's strategic intentions in the United States and across the region and undermined US confidence in the emergence of a more powerful but also more cooperative China. In 2010 Beijing's protection of North Korea even in the face of Pyongyang's willful provocations increased US frustration with China as a security partner. China's expansion of maritime interests was, in one sense, a natural outgrowth of its rising power, and such expansion was not in itself illegitimate. But the approaches that Beijing took to expand its interests intensified disputes with its Asian neighbors, many of them US allies and security partners, and also directly affected American interests in Asia. China had the right to challenge hegemonic and unreasonable US interests; at the same time it needed to appreciate those aspects of US interests that were legitimate.

Not all of China's policies toward its neighboring countries in 2009–10 were assertive. The meme about "Chinese assertiveness" was overdramatized and not entirely fair. It failed to describe a range of areas wherein Chinese policy was not changing as much as had been alleged.[25] Yet while each of these policies might be accounted for in terms of its own dynamics, some had spillover effects on Sino-American relations and thus should not be treated in isolation. Chinese policymakers seemed oblivious to this interactive effect between its regional policy and its relations with the United States. Moreover "assertiveness" did capture China's emerging coercive diplomacy in maritime disputes.[26] During the Obama years, those Asian maritime tensions drove US-China competition. The Obama administration, having gone through a psychological transition from hopefulness to disillusionment with China, came to the conclusion in 2010 that the United States must sustain its traditional hegemony in East Asia in order to rein in China's rising power.[27] In less than a year this judgment helped produce the strategy of "pivot" or "rebalance" toward Asia, focusing on balancing Chinese power by deepening strategic cooperation with countries on China's periphery, as we examined in detail in the preceding chapter.

Strategic Malaise

During President Obama's November 2009 visit to China, the Chinese leadership conveyed clearly their desire for a cooperative, not a confrontational, relationship with the United States.[28] If cooperation was at the center of the Chinese conception of the relationship, then the process of bilateral strategic interaction and any tensions that might have arisen from it ought to have been managed mainly by diplomatic reassurance. This did not happen in 2010. If cooperation was the guiding principle, then Beijing ought to have thought carefully about how its activist regional policy might adversely affect it—and how reassurance supported by diplomacy might help to ease the impact. Although the Obama administration developed no new strategy toward China in its first two years, it signaled a strong desire to seek practical cooperation rather than deliberate confrontation with China. This goal was in harmony with the Chinese leadership's professed objective of seeking cooperation with the United States. But the two countries missed the opportunity to translate the harmony of goals into a convergence of action that could enhance strategic trust and elevate the relationship to a new level. During the first two years of the Obama administration, China was more responsible for this failure than the United States.

China's strategic malaise can in part be understood by looking at the background of a raging domestic debate about the necessity of changing Deng Xiaoping's strategic doctrine of keeping a low profile (*tao guang yang hui*) into a more assertive posture.[29] Deng laid down this maxim at the end of the 1980s during a time of domestic turmoil and geopolitical transformation that appeared highly threatening to the CCP regime. In his view, China should guard against Western attempts to destabilize CCP rule but eschew confrontation with the West so as to balance domestic politics and foreign relations to serve the larger goal of developing China's national strength. Twenty years on, as China had hoisted its power position vis-à-vis the West, many analysts began to argue that Deng's maxim had become obsolete. They asserted that China needed a bolder foreign policy, should no longer fear confrontation, and should vigorously protect national interests even at the expense of damaging relations with other countries.[30]

In 2009–10 the debate was inconclusive. A number of prominent scholars continued to highlight the practical significance of Deng's dictum, while acknowledging the need to adjust it for new geopolitical realities. China should employ more effective means to protect its national interest. But that did not mean becoming blindly hawkish or blithely exaggerating the role of coercion in resolving foreign policy disputes. Nor should protecting national interests mean downgrading the importance of shaping a favorable international environment. For scholars of a moderate persuasion, Deng's dictum embodied the spirit of modesty and prudence in foreign policy—a spirit that would never become obsolete.[31]

Partly because of the inconclusive nature of this strategic debate, and partly because of the factors discussed earlier, China's foreign strategy became discrete and confused. Beijing lost sophistication in its judgment about the international and regional environment, tended to overemphasize its national interest, and consequently failed to grasp appropriate strategic goals.[32] The result was damaged relations with the United States and Asian countries.

The Rise and Fall of "New Model" Diplomacy

By the end of 2010 Beijing had begun to realize the costs of its ineffectual approach to both the United States and its Asian neighbors. In December 2010 State Councilor Dai Bingguo, China's top-ranking foreign policy official, published a prominent article on "persisting with taking the path of peaceful development."[33] This article tried to reaffirm China's strategic intention as "peaceful development." It also lent support to moderates in domestic debates by highlighting the consistency between the modest and prudent spirit of Deng's dictum of keeping a low profile and China's current chosen strategy of peaceful development. Injecting an authoritative voice into the raging domestic debates about China's foreign policy direction, the article sanctioned the continuing relevance of Deng's maxim.

In January 2011, barely a month after the article's publication, President Hu undertook a carefully planned state visit to the United States. In a joint statement released after Hu's meeting with Obama, China was said to welcome "the United States as an Asia-Pacific nation that contributes to peace, stability and prosperity in the region." The United States, on the other hand, would welcome "a strong, prosperous, and successful China that plays a greater role in world affairs." Both sides resolved to "build a cooperative partnership based on mutual respect and mutual benefit."[34] Hu's visit stabilized bilateral ties and redefined the relationship as a cooperative partnership based on mutual respect and mutual benefit.

By the end of 2011 the Obama administration had unleashed its Asia rebalance strategy. Although many Chinese elites were suspicious of the strategy's true intent, the initial announcement of the rebalance did not visibly undermine the relationship. In February 2012, as the rebalance was under way, Vice President Xi visited the United States and proposed building a new type of cooperative partnership between the two countries.[35] The Obama administration responded positively, if not enthusiastically, to this idea. Less than one month after Xi's visit, Secretary of State Clinton delivered an important speech on China policy. Taking up Xi's proposal, she pledged to build a model in which the two countries could "strike a stable and mutually acceptable balance between cooperation and competition."[36] Riding on this positive momentum, the two countries decided to adopt "constructing a new model of Sino-US major country relationship" as the theme of the fourth round of the Strategic and Economic Dialogue, the highest-level consultation mechanism between the two countries, to be held in Beijing in May 2012. President Hu's speech focused almost exclusively on building this new type of relationship.[37]

The year 2013 saw breakthroughs in the two countries' thinking about such a relationship. On the US side, departing national security advisor Tom Donilon delivered a thoughtful speech in March on the future of America's Asia policy. He rejected the premise that a rising power and an established power were somehow destined for conflict, as implied by the so-called the Thucydides trap.[38] He suggested that the United States and China would be able to achieve a better outcome than either conflict or containment: "But it falls to both sides—the United States and China—to build a new model of relations between an existing power and an emerging one. Xi Jinping and President Obama have both endorsed this goal."[39]

One could not have expected a clearer endorsement of the Chinese proposal of building a new model of relationship from the US side. Equally significant, Donilon emphasized the importance of demonstrating practical cooperation for building such a model. He highlighted three areas: military-to-military dialogue, the economic relationship, and cybersecurity. As cybersecurity was rapidly becoming a pressing concern, he placed special emphasis on it.[40] In effect, Donilon had presented a checklist of possible pathways toward a new model of relationship. At this point the question was not whether Washington would accept the Chinese proposal and build such a model with China, but how the two countries should go about doing so.

On the Chinese side, the visit of Xi, now China's president, to California's Sunnylands retreat in June 2013 represented the climax of Beijing's diplomacy for building a new model of relationship with Washington. At his meetings with Obama, Xi summarized three central components of the model: no conflict and no confrontation, mutual respect, and win-win cooperation. No conflict and no confrontation would require China and the United States to make each other a partner rather than an adversary, by viewing each other's strategic intentions in an objective and rational manner. Dialogue and cooperation, not confrontation and conflict, should be used to address differences. Mutual respect called for respecting each other's choice of social system and development model, as well as core interests and major concerns. Rejecting zero-sum thinking, win-win cooperation urged each to consider the other side's interests while pursuing its own interests, so as to deepen the interlocking nature of their interests.[41] In less than a year, however, disquiet would grow on the American side regarding Xi's formulation of the new model. American officials would suspect a Chinese trick in beguiling the United States into accepting Chinese control of Taiwan, the legitimacy of CCP rule in China, and a Chinese sphere of influence in Asia. At Sunnylands, however, these apprehensions hardly surfaced.

US and Chinese officials deliberately designed the informal, shirtsleeve style of the Obama-Xi summit at Sunnylands to foster a relaxed atmosphere for the two leaders to conduct deep dialogue and build personal rapport and trust. By all accounts, the summit was highly successful in creating a new momentum for the relationship. Obama expressed a personal interest in the idea of a new model of relationship and wanted Xi to explain it. In the joint press conference following the summit, Obama gave better military-to-military communications as an example of how the two countries could advance such a model.[42]

While the Chinese side focused on fleshing out the conceptual underpinnings of a new model of relationship, the US side wanted to see concrete action. In a November 20, 2013, speech, Obama's new national security advisor Susan E. Rice declared, "When it comes to China, we seek to operationalize a new model of major power relations. That means managing inevitable competition while forging deeper cooperation on issues where our interests converge—in Asia and beyond. We both seek the denuclearization of the Korean Peninsula, a peaceful resolution to the Iranian nuclear issue, a stable and secure Afghanistan, and an end to conflict in Sudan."[43]

In addition Rice called for a closer alignment of the two countries' interests on major challenges, especially confronting the threat of North Korea's nuclear weapons program and managing the rise of maritime disputes in the East and South China seas.[44] From Donilon to Obama to Rice, Washington's response to Beijing's proposal of building a new model of relationship was positive and specific. US officials focused less on conceptual modalities than on practical cooperation to deliver policy outcomes. Following Rice's speech, Vice President Joseph Biden was scheduled to visit China in December 2013. His central task was to operationalize a new model of relationship through practical cooperation.[45]

Unfortunately Rice's speech proved to be the last time senior US officials spoke positively about the Chinese proposal. An abrupt turning point came on November 23, 2013, three days after Rice's speech, when China announced the creation of an East China Sea ADIZ. This sudden decision caused consternation in Washington, in addition to the affected countries of Japan and South Korea.[46]

During his December 4–5, 2013, trip to Beijing, Biden felt compelled to criticize China's decision for creating "significant apprehension in the region."[47] To his chagrin, and to the frustration of many Chinese elites who were expecting Biden's visit to further advance the new model diplomacy, the ADIZ decision eclipsed the spotlight of the visit and spoiled the original diplomatic agenda. In a joint press conference with President Xi, Biden still struck a hopeful note: "This new model of major country cooperation ultimately has to be based on trust and a positive notion about the motive of one another. The relationship that you and President Obama have established thus far is full of promise and real opportunity for us. If we get this relationship right, engender a new model, the possibilities are limitless."[48]

Dashing Biden's hope, the promise and opportunity were, at best, only partially realized. The concept of a new model of major-country relationship fell into disrepute on the US side. After 2014 senior US officials never again openly talked about it, even though some of the practical cooperation they achieved with China could be fit into its framework. We argued in the preceding chapter that one reason for the US rejection of the concept after 2014 was American reluctance to accept mutual respect of each other's core interests—the second component of the concept—as a guiding principle of the relationship: Washington may not agree with Beijing's definition of each other's core interests. This principle, however, was not the only reason behind the American rebuff.

Faulty Conception and Implementation

Some Chinese scholars argue that flaws in China's conceptualization and operationalization of the proposal for a new model of relationship foreshadowed its failure. Da Wei, a leading US foreign policy expert at the influential China Institutes of Contemporary International Relations in Beijing, pointed out that the Chinese side could not explain the concept in concrete and precise terms. He astutely observed that while the US side tended to approach the concept by trying to operationalize it into manageable policy issues, the Chinese side was prone to mesmerizing the Americans with grand visions of the future but without policy specifics to which the US side was looking. Needed was thus a common frame of reference that could lead to concrete policy action.[49]

Da was certainly correct that the concept was plagued by conceptual ambiguities and vagueness. Its first ingredient called for no conflict and no confrontation between the two countries, but in what areas and over what issues? Did it exclude all kinds of conflict, or did it really mean the avoidance of major wars? The second ingredient proposed mutual respect for each other's core interests. But China often failed to specify the content and boundary of its core interests.

The challenge was that in an era of rapidly expanding interests, it was difficult to make any determinative specification. Besides, China had not shown a deep appreciation of US interests in the Asia-Pacific region. In any case, defining US core interests that would have been acceptable to both sides would have been too hard. And assuming that Beijing and Washington could reach a reasonable agreement on their core interests, what would respecting these interests have entailed in concrete policy terms? The third component—win-win cooperation—was even more vacuous. More a general desire than a specific proposal, it failed to prioritize areas of cooperation or to describe steps to achieve such cooperation.

These conceptual problems were real. But they were not fatal and certainly did not preordain the failure of the proposal itself. When diplomacy for the new model was at its height in 2012 and 2013, China took the conceptual lead in framing principles, and the United States took the policy lead in seeking practical cooperation. This suggests that the US side was not too bothered by the conceptual inadequacy of the proposal. Indeed the Chinese idea of building a new model of Sino-American relationship that was distinct from past models of relationship between rising and established powers is intellectually interesting and important for policy. This kind of interaction holds genuine promise.

As Da shows, Xi's idea of building a new model of Sino-American relationship draws on a series of policy ideas that Chinese leaders have developed since the 1990s.[50] A common thread running through all of these ideas is a manifest distaste for zero-sum security competition and a concomitant strong conviction that China should reject this logic and avoid the disastrous past path of major wars between rising and established powers. A central target of the Chinese critique is the determinist realist logic of great power balancing and conflict, especially the offensive realist variant that still infects a prominent portion of the international relations scholarship in the West.[51] Xi has emphasized several times the need for China and the United States to avoid the Thucydides trap, including in a speech during his September 2015 state visit to the United States.[52] Foreign Minister Wang Yi stated that at the conceptual level, China's purpose of building a new model of relationship was to transcend "traditional international relations theory based on realism."[53] Coming from high officials, these remarks suggest a seriousness in Chinese attempts to seek a new way of conducting great power politics in the twenty-first century when, for the first time in almost two centuries, China is again becoming one such power.

By proposing a new model of relationship, the Xi leadership was trying to develop a new strategy toward the United States, one that would eschew the realist logic of zero-sum competition and instead build on a new constructive spirit of peace and cooperation. True, many details of the strategy had yet to be filled; China had a long-standing problem of issuing slogans or principles without

thinking through or developing institutional mechanisms by which these principles might be realized and actual progress advanced. But at least there was a
reasonably clear overarching goal and a general direction for the relationship to
move forward. Once the overall goal was agreed, both sides could gradually draw
a roadmap to achieve it. With deft diplomacy from both sides, disagreements
and disputes need not disrupt the overall trajectory. Unfortunately that trajectory was in fact disrupted by Beijing's policy choices, not so much at the bilateral
level directed toward the United States as at the regional level toward its Asian
neighbors, with ramifications for US interests in Asia. By 2014, when the practical cooperation that Washington was seeking was not forthcoming from Beijing
and when China took actions perceived as contradicting the stated intention of
achieving win-win cooperation, US attitudes changed and hardened.

The new model diplomacy was undermined above all by Chinese policies
in maritime Asia. The Obama administration began to feel China's new assertiveness in the South China Sea almost from the beginning, as demonstrated
by the *Impeccable* incident of March 2009. Beijing's more robust law enforce-
ment actions against Southeast Asian claimant states, particularly Vietnam and
the Philippines, also became a new concern. The Philippines, moreover, is a US
treaty ally demanding American security protection. In April–May 2012 a stand-
off at sea took place between China and the Philippines over Scarborough Shoal.
Claiming not to take sides in sovereignty disputes, Washington tried to broker
an agreement for the withdrawal of both sides' vessels from the area. The return
of Chinese vessels to control the shoal deepened American mistrust of China.[54]

Up to this point the Obama administration had not carved out a direct and
active role for itself in the South China Sea. Despite Secretary of State Clinton's
July 2010 assertion of a US national interest, American actions were limited to
urging China and its neighbors to resolve their disputes peacefully in accordance
with international law.[55] Although the administration was uncomfortable with
Chinese maritime assertiveness, many officials also recognized that part of this
assertiveness was a reaction to provocations from regional countries such as Japan
and the Philippines. But such reactive assertiveness could no longer explain three
major Chinese decisions in late 2013 and early 2014: the decision to create an
ADIZ for the East China Sea in November 2013, island building in the South
China Sea after September 2013, and the May 2014 deployment of an oil rig in
waters around the Paracel Islands considered by Vietnam to be within its own
exclusive economic zone.[56] In that last incident a violent clash between Chinese
and Vietnamese vessels prompted the US State Department to issue a strongly
worded statement criticizing the Chinese action for raising tensions and undermining peace and stability in the region.[57] Less significant but also worth noting, in December 2013 a Chinese warship cut across the bow of the US Navy

guided-missile cruiser USS *Cowpens*. The *Cowpens* was observing the first voyage of China's new aircraft carrier *Liaoning* in the South China Sea and only narrowly avoided a collision.[58]

These events led many in Washington to conclude that Chinese strategy was undergoing a decisive and challenging shift: away from reactive assertiveness in response to perceived provocations and toward a proactive and systematic effort to alter the strategic status quo in Asia. This belief attributed a more aggressive stance to China than was warranted, but it was not off the mark in capturing a critical adjustment in its strategic priorities. In October 2013 China held its first conference on diplomacy toward countries on its periphery. President Xi emphasized the need to strive for achievement in periphery diplomacy (*zhoubian waijiao*) so as to secure a favorable regional environment for China's development. Attended by representatives from the CCP, local and central government, the military, state-owned enterprises, and the diplomatic corps, this conference was a milestone in raising the profile of periphery diplomacy in the history of Chinese foreign policy. The distinguished Chinese scholar Yan Xuetong argues that the conference indicated a strategic shift in Chinese foreign policy, from "keeping a low profile" to "striving for achievement." In his view it put an end to the inconclusive debate about Deng's strategic dictum of keeping a low profile, discussed earlier, and ushered in a new era of a more activist regional strategy.[59] That the East China Sea ADIZ, South China Sea island building, and oil rig deployment all took place shortly after the conference appears to confirm such a strategic adjustment. Beijing considered itself simply trying to seize the initiative in maritime disputes and gain strategic advantages. But it is exactly that attempt to make gains in Asian maritime politics, understandable from the standpoint of China's new regional strategy of "striving for achievement," that came into conflict with its US policy of building a new model of relationship.

East China Sea ADIZ

The decision to create an ADIZ, a US invention from the early Cold War, for China's national defense was not a problem in itself.[60] The problem, rather, was its sudden nature and its expansive scope. To begin with, the announcement occurred without any prior warning or consultation with foreign governments. To be sure, all countries' ADIZ decisions are supposed to be unilateral. There is no international law governing ADIZ, only a set of norms. China was thus under no international legal obligation to consult with anybody. But the manner of its rollout created a particularly unfortunate problem for the new model diplomacy because, as noted, US officials, including President Obama, had singled out better military-to-military communications as a priority area to build a new model of relationship.

That said, US military policy provided the initial impetus for the Chinese ADIZ desire. According to Ji You, the ADIZ decision was the result of a serious study by the PLA, not an impromptu decision. The key objective was to protect China's national security by better handling pervasive US reconnaissance and surveillance activities along China's east coast. The PLA's combustible grievances against US intelligence operations along the Chinese coast, as examined in the preceding chapter, lay at the heart of the ADIZ decision. The decision was more about creating air-defense depth than about restating sovereignty claims.[61]

If so, the decision was strangely counterproductive. It damaged the new model diplomacy with the United States in three ways without measurably increasing China's strategic advantage in its territorial disputes with Japan over the Diaoyu/Senkaku Islands. First, geographically the Chinese ADIZ overlaps with the ADIZs of Japan and South Korea. The original announcement required that all aircraft, not just those intending to enter Chinese airspace, notify Chinese authorities. Ordinarily an ADIZ is designed to give coastal nations warning of aircraft approaching with the intent to enter the nation's territorial airspace. As demanded by China, however, a civilian jetliner traveling from Japan to Australia, with a route outside Chinese airspace but within the declared zone, would be expected to notify Chinese authorities in the same way as a plane with the intent to enter Chinese airspace. The claim that the PLA had the right not only to monitor the ADIZ but to take "emergency defensive measures" against aircraft not complying with Chinese demands created further worries among policymakers in Washington and Asian countries that the move might trigger incidents and crises.[62]

Second, the zone's coverage of the Diaoyu/Senkaku Islands had strategic implications not only for Japanese but also for US military flights in the East China Sea. Strictly following China's initial statement, Japanese and American planes heading toward the Diaoyu/Senkaku Islands also needed to notify Chinese authorities. That would have been an unacceptable restriction on the US military's freedom of maneuver. Thus, soon after the ADIZ announcement, the Pentagon flew two unarmed B-52s through the zone to contest the new strategic space that China was attempting to establish.

Third, although the creation of the zone apparently eroded Japan's uncontested administrative control over the disputed islands, that erosion also provided stronger arguments for the extension of the US-Japan security treaty over the islands. President Obama's clarification that the treaty applied to the islands, made during his visit to Japan in April 2014, was not unrelated to the ADIZ decision, even though US officials, including Secretary of State Clinton, had advanced that position as early as 2012.[63] Obama felt it necessary to declare explicitly that the United States opposed "unilateral attempts to undermine Japan's administration of these islands."[64] In part, at least, the Chinese decision had firmed up Washington's security commitment to Japan and its strategic resolve toward China.

The Chinese leadership must have anticipated opposition from Washington. Concern over US pushback and the possibility of increased midair incidents between Chinese and US aircraft underlay President Hu's reluctance to endorse an ADIZ announcement. In contrast, President Xi may have placed the defense needs of an ADIZ above considerations of overall Sino-American relations. Or he may have believed that, following his successful Sunnylands summit with Obama six months earlier, the momentum for building a new model of relationship would be strong enough to withstand a US backlash. If so, he miscalculated, as the Obama administration reacted strongly to the announcement. If Xi had tried to strike a delicate balance between deterring US surveillance flights and advancing the Sino-American relationship, he failed in this as well. Without deterring US flights, the ADIZ decision damaged the new model diplomacy that he had so successfully engineered at Sunnylands. Because of this decision, and because of Chinese policies in the South China Sea (discussed later), US officials began to see China as a revisionist power to be met with a tough response. Xi's endorsement of the PLA's military policy spoiled his strategic objective of building a new model of relationship with the United States. The PLA achieved its organizational interest of asserting China's strategic space—at the expense of China's relations with the United States and regional countries.

Ten days after the ADIZ announcement, Xi was in damage-control mode during his seven-hour-long meeting with Vice President Biden on December 4, 2013. He reassured Biden that China would not forcefully expel US spy planes from the zone, in effect granting Washington a continued right to surveillance flights along the Chinese coast. And in practice the PLA enforced the ADIZ mainly through electronic scans and radar surveillance rather than through aircraft engagement.[65] Biden was not placated. Publicly criticizing the decision, he told Xi that China would see a lot more B-52 flights through the zone.[66]

If Xi was not using the ADIZ to deter US intelligence operations, as the PLA had originally intended, what useful purpose had the decision served other than to ruin the new model diplomacy that was the hallmark of his US policy? It also turned out that the PLA did not enforce ADIZ rules over the Diaoyu/Senkaku Islands, as Xi did not want the PLA to fly over the area. Only once, on December 13, 2012, did China's State Oceanic Administration send its patrol aircraft over the islands' airspace, measured as extending twelve nautical miles out toward the sea.[67] Thus China gained no significant strategic advantage over Japan either. The

ADIZ decision gave China few gains but plenty of injuries, including a damaged relationship with the United States and rising apprehension across the East Asian region about Chinese revisionism.

South China Sea Island Building

If China's ADIZ decision in the East China Sea halted the momentum of the new model diplomacy with the United States, its actions in the South China Sea produced enduring strategic consequences for the relationship over the long run. China's massive land reclamation and island-building project in the Spratly Islands (and, to a lesser extent, in the Paracel Islands) was a game changer not just in Asian maritime politics but also in Sino-American relations.

According to the Pentagon (no such data are available from the Chinese side), from December 2013 to June 2015 China reclaimed more than 2,900 acres of land over seven Spratly reefs under its control. This was seventeen times more land reclaimed in twenty months than that of the other claimants—Vietnam, Malaysia, the Philippines, and Taiwan—combined over the past forty years, accounting for approximately 95 percent of all reclaimed land in the Spratly Islands.[68] By 2016 all seven reefs had been turned into islets. In particular, Beijing expanded Mischief Reef, Subi Reef, and Fiery Cross Reef to 5.6 square kilometers, 4 square kilometers, and 2.6 square kilometers, respectively, making them the largest islands in the South China Sea. In addition, each of these three islands are equipped with airstrips over three kilometers long, capable of handling both civilian and military aircraft.[69]

In June 2015 China began the second phase, of installing military as well as civilian facilities on the newly constructed islands. These include aircraft hangars that can accommodate all types of fighter-jets and shelters for surface-to-air missile (SAM) batteries at Mischief Reef, Subi Reef, and Fiery Cross Reef.[70] In April 2018 SAM and antiship missiles were deployed on these three reefs.[71] China also built point-defense capabilities, in the form of large anti-aircraft guns and close-in weapons systems, at each of its Spratly islands.[72] In addition to the Spratlys, Beijing undertook substantial upgrades of its military infrastructure in the Paracels to strengthen its surveillance and power project capabilities. Woody Island, the largest of the Paracels, now hosts an airstrip, hangars, and HQ-9 SAM batteries. H-6K, a long-range bomber with a combat radius of nearly 1,900 nautical miles, putting the entire South China Sea within range, landed there in May 2018.[73] Several other islands have protected harbors capable of hosting large numbers of naval and civilian vessels.[74] The largest islands in both the Spratlys and Paracels can now deploy advanced fighter aircraft as well as SAM and antiship cruise missiles.

These installations created suspicion and fear across the region that China was steadily militarizing its outposts, despite repeated denials. More significant for Sino-American relations, Washington began to perceive China's new islands as undermining its fundamental strategic interests in the Western Pacific. From the US perspective, China was trying to create a chain of air- and sea-capable military fortresses across the entire north (Paracels) and south (Spratlys) range of the South China Sea to enhance its power projection capabilities and to enforce its expansive but vague claims to sovereignty and maritime rights. David Shear, assistant secretary of defense for East Asia, contended in May 2015 that, with this kind of industrial-scale island building, "China's actions are not viewed solely in the context of territorial and maritime disputes; they are viewed as indicators of China's long-term strategic intentions."[75]

More than anything else, Chinese reclamation exacerbated already heightened US suspicion of Beijing's strategic intentions and was probably the single most important factor in intensifying China's strategic competition in maritime Asia. With the new islands, and also given China's accelerating military reform and modernization efforts, US elites believed that Beijing was consciously embarking on a strategic offensive to challenge US military superiority in the Western Pacific, beginning in the South China Sea. Such a worry prompted a debate inside the United States about the adequacy of its own Asian maritime strategy. In July 2015, for the first time in its history, the Pentagon published a maritime strategy for the Asia-Pacific region, criticizing China for "unilaterally altering the physical status quo in the region, thereby complicating diplomatic initiatives that could lower tensions."[76]

Since 2015 the United States has ratcheted up its military presence in the South China Sea in an effort to deter China's rising capabilities during peacetime and overwhelm them in the event of conflict. In addition the National Defense Authorization Act for 2016 authorized the establishment of a US$425 million Maritime Security Initiative over five years to help Southeast Asian nations build up their maritime capacities. Beginning in October 2015 the Obama administration conducted four FONOPs against Chinese-held features in both the Spratly and Paracel parts of the South China Sea to contest excessive Chinese maritime claims.[77] The Trump administration pressed ahead with FONOPs in a more frequent and assertive manner, inciting Chinese nationalistic outcries and heightening the sense of strategic competition between the two countries. In December 2018 Trump signed the Asia Reassurance Initiative Act, which authorized an annual appropriation of US$1.5 billion to support his Indo-Pacific strategy.[78] None of these policies, however, deterred China from fortifying its islands.

China has offered a variety of reasons for island building. It pledges to use the islands for maritime search and rescue, disaster prevention and mitigation, marine scientific research, meteorological observation, ecological environment conservation, navigation safety, and fishery production. It claims that the military facilities built on the islands are for necessary defensive needs only.[79] In private, Chinese officials also suggest that island building was in part a response to the Obama administration's strategy of Asia rebalance.[80] A majority of Chinese analysts support the move. They argue that international law did not prohibit China from building over maritime features under its control. Moreover China was simply following the reclamation and building activities that Vietnam, the Philippines, Malaysia, and other claimants have been undertaking since the 1970s.[81]

China has some legitimate grounds for island building, and the US interest of military superiority in Asia is by no means unassailable, as we argued in Chapter 3. With those islands and the new facilities, China has succeeded in extending its security perimeter more than a thousand kilometers southward and strengthened its capabilities in the South China Sea. But if the question is whether island building has served the purpose of building a new model of Sino-American relationship so enthusiastically promoted by President Xi, the answer is clearly no. Xi defines no conflict or confrontation as the first component of such a model, yet competition in the South China Sea clearly entails risks of military incidents and crises. A more serious long-term consequence is the further erosion of strategic trust between the two countries.

The argument that island building took place under the pressure of the US rebalance to Asia has some merit.[82] But it overlooks the fact that until the end of 2013, Sino-American diplomacy for building a new model of relationship was steaming ahead following a series of policy successes, including the Xi-Obama meeting at Sunnylands. We noted in Chapter 3 Chinese elites' increasing anxiety about the US rebalance. That sense of encirclement and insecurity was no doubt real, and it grew stronger after 2014. But in 2013 high-level diplomacy for a new model of relationship was still able to withstand the fallout from the rebalance. It was really after the East China Sea ADIZ and the South China Sea island-building decisions, both made at the end of 2013, that the United States soured on China's new model proposal. In Chapter 3 we criticized the US rebalance strategy for impairing the relationship. Now that this chapter has brought to light the two countries' interaction dynamics in 2012–13, it is clear that the rebalance, up to 2013, was not so damaging as to cripple China's new model diplomacy. China bore the primary responsibility for the deterioration of the relationship during those years.

Significantly, both decisions were prompted by the PLA rather than by civilian foreign policy establishments such as the Ministry of Foreign Affairs. In the case of island building, the Ministry was kept in the dark until it became an international issue.[83] The PLA failed to enhance communication with the US military—a first step urged by the Obama administration toward building a new model of relationship. It was also unwilling to allow interagency coordination within China's own decision-making apparatus. The PLA had its own organizational interests in pushing these decisions, which might enhance China's national interest in some way. But they were detrimental to Xi's new model diplomacy with the United States. These decisions illustrate complex problems in Chinese foreign policy thinking and making. For our purpose, they reveal once again how the contradiction between a strategy toward the United States and a strategy toward Asian regional issues, as well as the PLA's organizational interests and the lack of interagency coordination in the decision-making process, could derail the larger direction of Sino-American relations.

An additional element to the island-building decision suggests the realpolitik edge of Chinese strategic thinking. Some Chinese policymakers perceived the cerebral Obama as a weak and indecisive leader, as supposedly demonstrated by his refusal to enforce the red line over Syria. They gambled that America's preoccupation with the Middle East over conflicts in Syria, Iraq, and Afghanistan, and with Russia over Ukraine, would divert its attention from the South China Sea, thus giving China a more or less free hand in the region. Obama's "strategic patience"—which some Chinese elites interpreted as "strategic indecisiveness"—was seen to provide China with a rare window of opportunity to make rapid and irreversible gains in the South China Sea.[84] Such opportunism can indeed help to explain the scale and speed with which China executed reclamation. Short-term calculations had ridden roughshod over an enlightened understanding of long-term benefits.

Asia for Asians

In May 2014 Xi delivered a major speech to the Conference on Interaction and Confidence-Building Measures in Asia held in Shanghai. The speech was supposed to promote China's new "Asian security concept" about achieving common, comprehensive, cooperative, and sustainable security in Asia. But it also dwelt on Asians' ability to manage their own affairs: "Asian affairs must ultimately be dealt with by Asians. Asian problems must ultimately be addressed by Asians. Asian security must ultimately be maintained by Asians. Asians have the capacity and wisdom to realize Asian peace and stability through enhanced cooperation."[85]

For many US observers, these remarks sound like a clear signal of China's intention to exclude the United States from Asian affairs. They suspect that this could be the beginning of a Chinese Monroe Doctrine for China's Asian neighborhood, in the same manner in which the original Monroe Doctrine had worked for America's neighborhood in the Western Hemisphere during the 1820s. It is an ominous harbinger of China's attempt to dominate Asia, contradicting Beijing's declaratory policy of welcoming the United States as an Asia-Pacific nation.

Chinese officials and analysts criticize this interpretation as overly suspicious of China's strategic intention. They fault US observers for taking the remarks out of context. Immediately after these remarks, Xi also said that Asia is open and that Asian countries welcome other countries and organizations to play a constructive role in Asian affairs. But it is apparent that Beijing realized the mistake of including such remarks in the speech. Xi has never again said similar things, not, for example, in another speech to the Conference's foreign ministers' meeting in April 2016.[86]

Damage had nevertheless been done. Occurring six months after the East China Sea ADIZ and South China Sea island-building decisions, US elites could not but wonder whether these were part of a deliberate plot to enhance Chinese interests in Asia at the expense of US interests. If so, they could not help but see the proposal of building a new model of relationship as China's ruse for advancing Chinese interests by lowering America's guard. Such fear of a Chinese design to push the United States out of Asia and the conspiracy theory of the new model concept as a deliberate deception were overblown but perhaps understandable. Elsewhere the strengthening of China's relationship with Russia after the escalating confrontations between Moscow and Western governments over Ukraine also irked Washington. If China really did not have anti-US intentions, the contradictions in its declaratory policies toward the United States and the Asian region had done little to quell such suspicions. Again this illustrates Chinese policymakers' poor understanding of the spillover effects of its Asian policy on its US policy or, if such an understanding did exist, the presence of serious domestic constraints that prevented them from acting on it.

Strategic Mistrust

The final three years of Sino-American relations during the Obama administration (2014–16) were largely driven by the need to manage policy fallout from the previous five years. On the Chinese side, the preoccupation was with the intensified implementation of the US rebalance strategy; on the US side, China's maritime assertiveness and island building in the South China Sea.

In April 2014 Obama paid a high-profile visit to Japan, South Korea, Malaysia, and the Philippines.[87] In Japan and Malaysia he pressed the host governments to conclude negotiations over the Trans-Pacific Partnership that was in part conscious geo-economic statecraft aimed at China, as discussed in Chapter 3. More alarming to Beijing was Obama's extension of the US-Japan security treaty over disputed islands in the East China Sea. For the first time a sitting US president had declared that although America does not take sides in sovereignty disputes, it would defend Japan's administration of the islands. Moreover Obama offered his support for Prime Minister Shinzo Abe's move to reinterpret Japan's pacifist Constitution to allow the exercise of "collective self-defense" by the Japanese Self-Defense Forces. Beijing, embroiled in simmering hostility with Tokyo and suspicious of Japanese militarism, saw this as another unwelcome step in the strengthening of the US-Japan alliance.

In the Philippines Obama concluded the Enhanced Defense Cooperation Agreement, a ten-year deal that gave American military forces and assets expanded rotational access to five Philippines military bases. This represented a significant enhancement of military cooperation between the two allies since Washington relinquished its giant Subic Bay Naval Base and Clark Air Base in the early 1990s. During his speech to Filipino and US armed forces in Manila on April 29, 2014, Obama avowed that international law must be upheld, freedom of navigation must be preserved, and disputes must be resolved peacefully and not by intimidation or force—all pointed jabs at Chinese approaches to maritime disputes.[88]

America's Asian allies and partners generally welcomed Obama's reassurance of a US strategic commitment to Asia. China, in contrast, saw such a demonstration of US resolve as a reflection of the rebalance strategy's real goal of encircling China. Its siege mentality deepened.[89] By mid-2014, however, both Beijing and Washington realized that they needed to stabilize the relationship lest strategic distrust spiral out of control. They used the sixth round of the China-US Strategic and Economic Dialogue held in July 2014 as an opportunity to inject some positive momentum. President Xi again made building a new model of relationship the central theme of his speech at the opening ceremony. But Beijing clearly sensed that the project had gone awry; Xi's speech emphasized the importance of enhancing trust and avoiding misjudging each other's strategic intentions.[90] President Obama's November 2014 visit to Beijing provided another occasion for steering the relationship. Most notably the two countries produced a landmark joint statement on climate change, demonstrating major progress in their cooperation in this area.[91] Like the shirtsleeve summit at Sunnylands, Chinese officials designed an informal "night chat" by Xi and Obama inside Zhongnanhai, the Chinese leadership compound in Beijing, in the hope that the two leaders might be able to build personal trust.

Entering 2015 the relationship continued to be beset by maritime tensions. These were now focused more on Chinese reclamation in the South China Sea than on sovereignty and maritime disputes between China and its neighbors.

A new concern over a Chinese government-sponsored, cyber-enabled theft of confidential business information and proprietary technology from US companies rapidly rose to dominate the policy agenda. Already in May 2014 the US Justice Department had charged five members of the PLA with hacking US companies.[92] From the US perspective, such cyber theft of US trade secrets amounted to a new form of geo-economic tactics distinct from traditional security espionage. The Obama administration became so concerned that it threatened sanctions on the eve of Xi's scheduled September 2015 state visit to the United States.[93] Meanwhile old complaints about currency, intellectual property rights, market access, and political and civil freedom inside China also lingered.

As a result, President Xi spent much of his visit quelling US misgivings rather than advancing his cherished agenda of building a new model of relationship. He made remarkable concessions to most US demands, including those about cyber theft.[94] The concessions were even more impressive given that during the joint press conference, Obama almost went into a lecturing mode on cybersecurity and human rights issues, while Xi seemed uncomfortably defensive.[95] This revealed the great length that Xi would go to preserve his signature new model diplomacy and his strong personal commitment to a healthy Sino-American relationship. It also brought to light the brittle nature of the actual relationship. Two years earlier, in the June 2013 Sunnylands summit, Obama had shown a personal interest in Xi's idea of a new model of relationship. Now he failed to even mention it.

Xi's visit also produced a curious side effect on tensions in the South China Sea. During the joint press conference with Obama, Xi stated that China did not intend to pursue militarization in the Spratly Islands.[96] Yet US elites saw Chinese actions since 2015, as described earlier, as the opposite of that pledge. Perhaps China defined "militarization" differently from the United States. But that gap between words and deeds created an unfortunate impression among US officials of Chinese hypocrisy and contributed to the deepening of US distrust of Chinese intentions. Xi's nonmilitarization pledge was also controversial among Chinese elites (it was not publicly reported inside China), especially among PLA hawks for whom militarization was the raison d'être of island building. It appeared to have been a result of Xi's own improvisation rather than a premeditated plan.[97] Regardless, the pledge, and the failure to honor it with actions, once again damaged trust between the two countries.

During the final months of his administration in 2016, President Obama tried to stabilize the relationship with China by downplaying the strategic stakes in the South China Sea and restraining his generals from provocative rhetoric about an intensifying military competition with China. The task became harder after July 2016, when an international tribunal issued a ruling in an arbitration case initiated by the Philippines against China over their maritime disputes in the South

China Sea. The ruling overwhelmingly favored the Philippines and was hailed by international observers as a game changer in Asian maritime politics. China rejected it, setting off a new phase of legal and strategic contests not only with the Philippines and other Southeast Asian claimant states but also with a loose international coalition of states, including the United States, Australia, Japan, France, and Britain.[98] No amount of diplomatic finesse could obscure the competition between the two powers. Doubtless such competition further reduced Washington's appetite for building a new model of relationship with China.

Summary

A number of Chinese mistakes, in conjunction with those of the United States as analyzed in the preceding chapter, accounted for the deterioration of the Sino-American security relationship during the Obama years. The single most important flaw was the failure to develop a holistic strategy for managing increasing competition with the United States. To the extent that President Xi had conceived of a new model of relationship, it was motivated by the goal of achieving a mutually respectful and cooperative relationship. That was not a bad start, but China floundered in taking the critical next step of implementing the new model policy. It failed to achieve practical cooperation with the United States on the basis of an enlightened understanding of its national interest.

The rapid expansion of Chinese interests lay at the heart of its assertiveness in maritime Asia. An intriguing example is the controversy over whether China views the South China Sea as a core interest on a par with Taiwan or Tibet. The Chinese government has neither affirmed nor denied it. In his December 2010 article, State Councilor Dai defined China's core interests as the stability of the CCP-led political system; sovereignty, territorial integrity, and national unity; and sustainable economic and social development.[99] The breadth of this conception gave ample room for ambiguities and misrepresentations. Chinese officials to this day insist that China does not pursue interest maximization. What foreign observers criticize as Chinese assertiveness is simply China's efforts to safeguard its core interests and national honor.[100] To make such a defense more effective, Beijing needs to offer more precise and reasonable definitions of its core interests, as many Chinese scholars have urged.[101]

An expansive and crude definition of China's core interests can easily bring it into conflict with the United States. A domestic side effect is portraying America as always willfully harming Chinese interests, thus increasing assertive and even aggressive attitudes toward it.[102] Some expansion of Chinese interests as a rising power is legitimate, but Beijing must maintain a healthy appreciation of legitimate US interests in Asia too. As the Chinese scholar Wang Jisi observes, by approaching each other with empathy and open minds, China and the United States can begin to agree on common interests while at the same time acknowledging, respecting, and managing divergent interests.[103]

National interest aside, China's implementation of the new model policy was problematic. In American eyes, Chinese actions after November 2013— most notably creating the East China Sea ADIZ and building islands in the South China Sea—contradicted the stated goals of the policy. It appeared to American officials that China had itself violated two major principles of the new model: mutual respect of each other's interest and win-win cooperation.

Chinese and US officials lamented that despite all the talk about common interests, the two countries had only been able to achieve limited cooperation in Asia. Breakthroughs in other areas and regions, such as tackling the global problem of climate change and addressing the threat of the Ebola virus in western Africa, threw into sharp relief the inadequacy of their cooperation in Asia. Both sides lacked policy creativity and flexibility. Even cooperation on nontraditional security issues, such as humanitarian disaster relief, would have sent a positive message. Instead, because major cooperation was hard to find, negative news about strategic competition dominated headlines. The US strategy of an Asian rebalance did not provide a positive narrative. China had a positive narrative in its proposal for a new model of relationship, but that narrative was often contradicted by actual policy.[104]

A major reason behind the failure of the new model diplomacy was the contradiction between China's US strategy and its Asia strategy. This was a problem of both conception and implementation. President Xi showed a strong personal commitment to the goal of building a new model of relationship with the United States. At the same time, he outlined in October 2013 an ambitious new Asia strategy of striving for achievement. The Chinese scholar Liu Feng argues that the new strategy shifted from comprehensive reassurance toward China's neighbors to conditional reassurance, combined with selective coercion toward a small group of countries.[105] Xi's Asia strategy undercut his US strategy. It is worth noting that contradiction between bilateral policy and Asia policy due to faulty conceptions was also a problem for the United States, as noted in Chapter 3.

A significant domestic constraint on foreign policy was China's dysfunctional decision-making system. Powerful interest groups advanced parochial bureaucratic or sectoral interests at the expense of a rational protection of the national interest. The insecurity of the CCP leadership and the internal fragility of the Chinese political system amplified such dysfunction.[106] The East China Sea ADIZ and the South China Sea island-building decisions, which caused the most damage to Xi's US strategy, were both pushed by the PLA without proper consultation or deliberation with other actors and agencies, such as the Ministry of Foreign Affairs.

We highlight rampant strategic mistrust as a particularly acute problem of Sino-American relations. The US grand strategy of liberal hegemony that we critiqued in Chapter 3 is a root cause of Chinese mistrust. But Chinese mistrust also has a peculiar but extremely important domestic origin. Ever since the founding of the People's Republic of China in 1949, the CCP-led government has developed a persistent—and at times paranoid—fear of US attempts to sabotage, undermine, and even overthrow it. The US grand strategy of liberal hegemony, made more threatening by the American exceptionalism of bringing human rights and democracy to the world, not infrequently through military means, has exacerbated such anxieties. Wang Jisi observes that if there is a persistent goal in China's US policy, it is to preserve political stability centered on CCP rule by preventing the flows of American values and institutions into China.[107] The United States needs to build sensitivity to CCP political insecurity into its China policy by tempering its universalist impulses.[108] The CCP needs to cease politicizing the relationship for domestic political purposes by recognizing the limits of American influence on Chinese politics and by building up true political confidence.

Our analysis of American and Chinese mistakes in managing their relationship during the Obama years leads to an important finding. Both countries failed to develop any kind of comprehensive strategy for managing their intensifying competition. America did not have a coherent China strategy and chose to embed its China policy with its regional strategy of the Asia rebalance. But this Asia strategy undercut its declaratory goodwill toward China, deepened mistrust, and agitated China toward competition. China offered a promising start in its proposal for developing a new model of cooperative relationship, but its strategy faltered because of faulty conceptions and inadequate diplomacy. These failings point to the critical importance of finding a productive strategy for conflict management. In the next three chapters we propose precisely such a strategy. It is a tripartite, holistic strategy based on the three pillars of deterrence, reassurance, and diplomacy.

5

Deterrence

WE NOW TURN to coercive strategies of conflict management and their application—really misapplication—to Sino-American relations. We begin with a description of deterrence and compellence and how they have been theorized. We then look at how they have been applied in practice and the critique this has spawned. In Soviet-American and Sino-American relations their use has been largely counterproductive, although strategists and leaders in both countries believe otherwise. Our task in this chapter is accordingly twofold. We want to demonstrate the downside of deterrence and the psychological and political reasons why the use of threats, especially credible ones, often provokes the kind of behavior they are intended to prevent. We also want to show the ways in which these consequences of deterrence are being reflected in Sino-American strategic tensions today. The first part of the chapter is accordingly theoretical and historical. The second focuses on analyzing and critiquing the role of deterrence in Sino-American strategic relations. In addition to clarifying the nature and consequences of deterrence, this chapter also aims to pave the way for discussions in the next two chapters about the ways in which deterrence can be used more constructively in conjunction with the more productive strategies of reassurance and diplomacy.

We open with a general discussion of deterrence theory and practice. This is followed by a political and psychological critique of deterrence, focusing on its strategic pathologies. This section also identifies major dangers of immediate and general deterrence by drawing on historical lessons from the Cold War. These introductory sections create the theoretical groundwork and historical foundation for our discussion and critique of deterrence in Sino-American strategic relations.

Deterrence plays a major role in both countries' security strategies, although more so for the United States. The American strategy of hegemonic deterrence and the Chinese strategy of active defense risk mutual escalation of suspicions, increase reliance on worse-case analysis, and intensify rather than ameliorate their competition. While it is unrealistic to expect either country to abandon deterrence, it is very much in the interest of both to ease up on it and create more room for other, more constructive strategies. Less is more if the United States and China genuinely aspire to build a constructive and productive relationship.

We assume that this remains a mutual goal despite the surge in tensions since Donald Trump became president. Vice President Mike Pence excoriated China in an October 2018 speech but nevertheless declared, "[America] want[s] a constructive relationship with Beijing, where our prosperity and security grow together, not apart."[1] On the Chinese side, President Xi Jinping proposed coordination, cooperation, and stability as the tenor of the relationship during his summit with President Trump at the December 2018 G20 meeting in Argentina.[2] There are influential hawks in both countries screeching confrontation, but the ideal of a constructive relationship still remains.

Deterrence Theory and Practice

Deterrence attempts to prevent an undesired behavior by convincing the party that may be contemplating it that the cost will exceed any possible gain.[3] Deterrence presupposes decisions made in response to a rational cost-benefit calculus and that this calculus can successfully be manipulated from the outside, and most effectively, by increasing the perceived cost of noncompliance. Compellence, a related strategy, employs the same tactics to convince another party to carry out some action it otherwise would not. Deterrence has always been practiced, but the advent of nuclear weapons prompted its conscious development as a theory and strategy. The goal was to find ways of preventing catastrophically destructive wars while exploiting any strategic nuclear advantage for political gain.

Theories of deterrence must be distinguished from the strategy of deterrence. The former addresses the logical postulates of deterrence and the political and psychological assumptions on which they are based, the latter the application of the theory in practice. The theory of deterrence developed as an intended guide for the strategy of deterrence. Scholars and policymakers became interested in deterrence following the development of the atom bomb. The first wave of theorists wrote from the late 1940s until the mid-1960s. Early publications on the subject recognize that a war between states armed with atomic weapons could be so destructive as to negate Carl von Clausewitz's classic description of war as a continuation of politics by other means.[4] In 1949 the problem of deterrence gained a new urgency as the Cold War was well under way and the Soviet Union, in defiance of all US expectations, detonated its first nuclear device in August of that year. In the 1950s, often referred to as the Golden Age of deterrence, William Kaufmann, Henry Kissinger, and Bernard Brodie, among others, developed a general approach to nuclear deterrence that stressed the necessity but difficulty of imparting credibility to threats likely to constitute national suicide.[5] The 1960s witnessed an impressive theoretical treatment by Thomas Schelling that analyzed deterrence in terms of bargaining theory, based on tacit signals.[6]

The early literature began with the assumption of fully rational actors and was deductive in nature. It stipulated four conditions of successful deterrence: defining commitments, communicating them to adversaries, developing the capability to defend them, and imparting credibility to these commitments. It explored various tactics that leaders could exploit toward this end, concentrating on the problem of credibility. This was recognized as the core problem when deterrence was practiced against another nuclear adversary—and the implementation of the threats in question could entail national suicide. Schelling argued that it was rational for a leader to develop a reputation for being irrational so his threats might be believed.[7] Richard Nixon took this advice to heart in his dealings with both the Soviet Union and North Vietnam.[8]

The so-called Golden Age literature focuses almost entirely on the tactics of deterrence, as do Kaufmann and Brodie, or, like Kissinger, on the force structures most likely to make deterrence credible. Schelling fits in the former category, but unlike other students of deterrence in the 1950s and 1960s, he attempts to situate his understanding of tactics in a broader theory of bargaining that draws on economics and psychology. His *Strategy of Conflict* (1960) and *Arms and Influence* (1966) are the only works on deterrence from this era that continue to be cited regularly.

In *Arms and Influence*, Schelling makes a ritual genuflection to material capabilities on the opening page when he observes that with enough military force, a country may not need to bargain. His narrative soon makes it clear that military capability is decisive in only the most asymmetrical relationships, and even then, only when the more powerful party has little or nothing to lose from the failure to reach an accommodation. When the power balance is not so lopsided, or when both sides would lose from nonsettlement, it is necessary to bargain. Bargaining outcomes do not necessarily reflect a balance of interests or military capabilities. Three other influences are important.

First comes *context*, which for Schelling consists of the stakes, the range of possible outcomes, the salience of those outcomes, and the ability of bargainers to commit to them. In straightforward commercial bargaining, contextual considerations may not play a decisive role. In bargaining about price, there will be a range of intervals between the opening bids of buyer and seller. If there is no established market price for the commodity, no particular outcome will have special salience. Either side can try to gain an advantage by committing itself to its preferred outcomes. Strategic bargaining between states is frequently characterized by sharp discontinuities in context. There may be a small number of possible outcomes, and the canons of international practice, recognized boundaries, prominent terrain features, or the simplicity of all-or-nothing distinctions can make one solution more salient than others. Salient solutions are easier to communicate and commit to, especially when the bargaining is tacit.[9]

The second consideration is *skill*. Threats to use force lack credibility if they are costly to carry out. To circumvent this difficulty, clever leaders can feign madness, develop a reputation for heartlessness, or put themselves into a position from which they cannot retreat. Other tactics can be used to discredit adversarial commitments or minimize the cost of backing away from one's own.[10]

The third, and arguably most important, determinant of outcome is *willingness to suffer*. Paraphrasing Clausewitz, Schelling describes war as a contest of wills. Until the mid-twentieth century, force was used to bend or break an adversary's will by defeating his army and holding his population and territory hostage. Air power and nuclear weapons revolutionized warfare by allowing states to treat one another's territory, economic resources, and population as hostages from the outset of any dispute. War is no longer a contest of strength, but a contest of nerve and risk-taking, of pain and endurance. For purposes of bargaining, the ability to absorb pain counts just as much as the capability to inflict it.[11]

Schelling does not say so, but it follows from his formulation that the capacity to absorb suffering varies just as much as the capacity to deliver it. Clausewitz recognized this variation. Increases in both capabilities, he argued, made possible the nation in arms and the revolutionary character of the Napoleonic Wars.[12] By convincing peoples that they had a stake in the outcome of the wars, first the French and then their adversaries were able to field large armies, extract the resources necessary to arm and maintain them, and elicit the extraordinary level of personal sacrifice necessary to sustain the struggle.

The Clausewitz-Schelling emphasis on pain has wider implications for bargaining. The ability to suffer physical, economic, moral, or any other loss is an important source of bargaining power and can sometimes negate an adversary's power to punish. Realist approaches to bargaining tend to neglect this dimension of power and focus instead on the power to hurt and how it can be transformed into credible threats. Schelling also ignores the pain-absorption side of the power-pain equation when analyzing compellence in Vietnam, an oversight that led to his misplaced optimism that Hanoi could be coerced into recognizing the independence of South Vietnam. The power to punish derives only in part from material capabilities. Leaders must also have the will and freedom to use their power. Schelling observes that Genghis Khan was effective because he was not inhibited by the usual mercies. Modern civilization has generated expectations and norms that severely constrain the power to punish. The US bombing campaign in Vietnam, in many people's judgment the very antithesis of civilized behavior, paradoxically demonstrates this truth.

Deterrence has played a central role in the US strategy since 1945. The principal target was the Soviet Union, and the principal goal was to prevent the Red Army from overrunning Western Europe. It was also used in the Far East, initially against China with the goal of protecting Taiwan from attack. Compellence was used by the Lyndon B. Johnson and Nixon administrations in Indochina. The introduction of American forces and the bombing campaigns were never intended to defeat the National Liberation Front of South Vietnam (Viet Cong) or North Vietnam, but to compel them to stop fighting and accept the independence of South Vietnam. The Indochina intervention ended in disaster and helped to spawn a series of critiques of the theory and strategy of deterrence in the 1970s.

Vietnam paradoxically demonstrates the truth that modern civilization has generated expectations and norms that severely constrain the power to punish. The air and ground war aroused enormous opposition at home, in large part because of its barbarity, and public opinion ultimately compelled a halt to the bombing and withdrawal of US forces from Indochina. The bombing exceeded that of the Second World War in total tonnage, but was also more restricted. The United States refrained from indiscriminate bombing of civilians and made no effort to destroy North Vietnam's elaborate system of dikes. The use of nuclear weapons was not even considered. Restraint was a response to ethical and domestic political imperatives. Similar constraints limited US firepower in Iraq in the Gulf War of 1990–91 and enabled the Republican Guard and Saddam Hussein to escape destruction.

The ability to absorb punishment derives even less from material capabilities, and may even be inversely related to them. One of the reasons Vietnam was less vulnerable to bombing than Schelling and Pentagon planners supposed was its underdeveloped economy. There were fewer high-value targets to destroy or hold hostage. With fewer factories, highways, and railroads, the economy was more difficult to disrupt, and the population was less dependent on existing distribution networks for its sustenance and material support. According to the North Vietnamese strategic analyst Colonel Quach Hai Luong, "The more you bombed, the more the people wanted to fight you."[13] US Department of Defense studies confirmed that bombing "strengthened, rather than weakened, the will of the Hanoi government and its people."[14] It is apparent in retrospect that the gap between the protagonists in material and military capabilities counted for less than their differential ability to absorb punishment. The United States won every battle but lost the war because its citizens would not pay the moral, economic, and human cost of victory. Washington withdrew from Indochina after losing fifty-eight thousand American lives, a fraction of Viet Cong and North Vietnamese deaths even at conservative estimates.

A comparison between South and North Vietnam is even more revealing. The Army of the Republic of South Vietnam was larger and better equipped and trained than the Viet Cong or the North Vietnamese and had all the advantages of US airpower, communications, and logistics. Yet the Republic of South Vietnam crumbled because its forces had no stomach for a fight. The Viet Cong and North Vietnamese sustained horrendous losses whenever they came up against superior US firepower, but maintained their morale and cohesion throughout the long conflict. Unlike the South Vietnamese officers and recruits, who regularly melted away under fire, more Viet Cong and North Vietnamese internalized their cause and gave their lives for it. At the most fundamental level, the communist victory demonstrated the power of ideas and commitment. There are obvious lessons here for the American side in considering any use of force against China for purposes of compellence.

Deterrence was no more successful than compellence during the Cold War, but American academics and policymakers remain convinced of its utility. This is because they believed that the Soviet Union under Joseph Stalin or Nikita Khrushchev would have behaved far more aggressively in its absence. They further credit deterrence with resolving the Cuban missile and October 1973 Middle East crises in America's favor. And many attribute Mikhail Gorbachev's willingness to make the concessions that ended the Cold War to Soviet inability to compete with the United States in their long-standing arms race and a fear of Star Wars. There is no evidence for any of these claims; quite the reverse in fact.

The Soviet Union never intended to attack Western Europe, although it had elaborate military plans to that effect—just as the United States did to destroy the Soviet Union and China with its nuclear arsenal. Soviet leaders, moreover, never doubted American resolve but actually worried that the Americans were foolhardy and risk prone.[15] The Cuban missile crisis was resolved more by reassurance than deterrence, and the October 1973 crisis ended because the Russians belatedly recognized that Israel had halted its offensive.[16] The Cold War ended for many reasons but primarily because Gorbachev considered it wasteful and dangerous, sought to wind it down to advance his political and economic reforms, and wanted to rejoin, as he put it, the "common house of Europe." Star Wars stood in the way of these goals and the concessions they involved.[17]

Deterrence: A Political and Psychological Critique

Over the course of four decades Janice Stein and Ned Lebow have developed a critique of deterrence based on careful empirical research into conflict between conventional and nuclear powers to which the strategy has been central.[18] That critique has three interlocking components: political, psychological, and practical. Each exposes a different set of problems of deterrence in theory and practice.

The political component examines the motivations behind foreign policy challenges. Deterrence is unabashedly a theory of *opportunity*. It asserts that adversaries seek opportunities to make gains and that when they find these opportunities they pounce. It accordingly prescribes a credible capacity to inflict unacceptable costs as the best means to prevent challenges. Empirical investigations point to an alternative explanation for a resort to force, which we call a theory of *need*. The evidence indicates that strategic vulnerabilities and domestic political constraints often constitute incentives to use force. When leaders become desperate, they may resort to force even when the military balance is unfavorable and there are no grounds to doubt adversarial resolve. Deterrence may be an inappropriate and even dangerous strategy in these circumstances. If leaders are driven less by the prospect of gain than they are by the fear of loss, deterrent policies can provoke the very behavior they are designed to forestall by intensifying the pressures on an adversary to act.

The psychological component is directly related to the motivations for deterrence challenges. To the extent that leaders believe in the necessity of challenging the commitments of their adversaries, they become predisposed to see their objectives as attainable. This encourages motivated errors in the information process. Leaders can distort their assessments of threat and be insensitive to warnings that the policies to which they are committed are likely to end in disaster. They can convince themselves, despite evidence to the contrary, that they can challenge an important adversarial commitment without provoking war. Because they know the extent to which they are powerless to back down, they expect their adversaries to recognize this and be accommodating. Leaders may also seek comfort in the illusion that their country will emerge victorious at little cost if the crisis gets out of hand and leads to war. Deterrence can and has been defeated by wishful thinking.

The practical component describes some of the most important obstacles to the successful implementation of deterrence. They derive from the distorting effects of cognitive biases and heuristics, political and cultural barriers to empathy, and differing cognitive frames of reference that deterrer and would-be challengers use to frame and interpret signals. Problems of this kind are not unique to deterrence and compellence; they are embedded in the very structure of international relations. They nevertheless constitute particularly severe impediments to these strategies because of deterrer needs to understand the world as it appears to the leaders of a would-be challenger in order to manipulate effectively their cost-benefit calculus. Failure to do so correctly can result in deterrent policies that make the proscribed behavior more attractive to challengers, or the required restraint less attractive in the case of compellence.

This critique explains why deterrence is a risky and unreliable strategy. The problems associated with each component can independently confound deterrence. In practice they are often reinforcing; political and practical factors interact with psychological processes to multiply the obstacles to success. We now expand this critique to offer some observations about the conditions in which deterrence is most applicable and the foundations for more sophisticated understandings of conflict management.

Political Failings

A good strategy of conflict management should build on a good theory of the nature and causes of conflict, expansion, and aggression. Such a theory should describe the etiology of the malady it seeks to control or prevent. Theories of deterrence make no attempt to do this. They finesse the fundamental question of the causes of aggression by assuming both the existence of marked hostility between adversaries and a desire on the part of leaders of one of them to commit acts of aggression against the other. Deterrence further assumes that these leaders are under no political or strategic compunction to act aggressively but will do so if they see an opportunity in the form of a vulnerable commitment of their adversary. It accordingly prescribes defensible, credible commitments as the most important means of discouraging aggression.

Case studies of international conflict contradict this depiction of aggression in important ways. They indicate that the existence of a vulnerable commitment is neither a necessary nor a sufficient condition for a challenge. At different times in history "vulnerable" commitments have not been challenged and commitments that most observers would consider credible have. The evidence suggests, then, that deterrence theory at best identifies only one cause of aggression: outright hostility. It reflects a Cold War mentality. Deterrence theorists took for granted, like the American national security elite more generally, that Adolf Hitler was motivated by hatred of his neighbors and was intent on conquering the world. They assumed that Stalin, Khrushchev, and Mao Zedong were cut from the same mold. This homology was a matter of belief, not the product of careful analysis. They generalized from these cases to conflict in general, another unwarranted

leap. The theory and practice of deterrence are accordingly rooted in and inseparable from a view of the Cold War subsequently refuted by evidence.

Deterrence theory takes for granted that when leaders undertake a cost calculus and conclude that they confront a credible commitment by a stronger adversary to defend its commitment, they will not initiate a challenge, at least not an
irreversible one. However, there have been many conflicts wherein the weaker
side challenged the stronger one. Leaders convinced themselves that they could
design around their adversary's advantage, as the Southern Confederacy did in
1861, the Japanese in 1941, and Egypt in 1973.[19] Honor, anger, and national self-
respect routinely push leaders into starting wars they do not expect to win.[20]

Deterrence mistakes the symptoms of aggression for its causes. It ignores the
political and strategic vulnerabilities that can interact with cognitive and motivational processes to prompt leaders to choose force or challenge an adversarial
commitment. This can be attributable to hubris but is more often the result of
their perceived need to carry out a challenge in response to pressing foreign and
domestic threats. In contrast to the expectations of the theory and strategy of
deterrence, there is considerable evidence that the leaders considering challenges
or the use of force often fail to carry out any kind of serious risk assessment. In
Between Peace and War, Lebow documents the French failure to do so in 1897–
98; the Austrian, German, and Russian failure in 1914; India's failure in 1962;
and the Soviet Union's failure in 1962.[21] In *Psychology of Deterrence*, chapters
by Stein, Jack Snyder, and Lebow do the same for Russia in 1914, Israel in 1973,
and Argentina and Britain in 1981.[22] *A Cultural Theory of International Relations*
offers more evidence on 1914 and the Anglo-American decision to attack Iraq in
2003.[23]

Lebow's *Why Nations Fight* puts together an original data set of all wars since
1648 involving at least one rising or great power on each side. It reveals that initiators won slightly fewer than half the wars they began.[24] Lebow and Benjamin
Valentino found that in all wars since 1945, only 26 percent of initiators achieved
their goals in war, and if we relax the criteria of victory, only 32 percent defeated
the other side's armed forces.[25] As most initiators go to war at a time of their
choosing, a 50-50 success rate is not at all impressive. The drop to one-third in
the postwar era is compelling evidence that initiators fail to conduct a careful
assessment of risk. Rationalists might counter that the low success rate is due to
incomplete information, but in many, if not most, of these cases, evidence was
available at the time that the initiators were heading for disaster, or at best, leap-
ing into the unknown.[26]

When challengers are vulnerable or feel themselves vulnerable, deterrers'
efforts to make important commitments more defensible and credible will have
uncertain and unpredictable effects. At best, they will not dissuade. They can also

be malign in their effects by intensifying those pressures that are pushing leaders toward a choice of force. Great power interactions in the decade prior to the First World War and the US oil and scrap metals embargo against Japan in 1940–41 illustrate this dynamic.[27]

Once committed to a challenge, leaders become predisposed to see their objective as attainable. Motivated error can result in flawed assessments and unrealistic expectations; leaders may believe an adversary will back down when challenged or, alternatively, that it will fight precisely the kind of war the challenger expects. Leaders are also likely to become insensitive to warnings that their chosen course of action is likely to provoke a serious crisis or war. In these circumstances, deterrence, no matter how well practiced, can be defeated by a challenger's wishful thinking. Motivated bias blocks receptivity to signals, reducing the impact of efforts by defenders to make their commitments credible. Even the most elaborate efforts to demonstrate prowess and resolve may prove insufficient for discouraging a challenger who is convinced that a challenge or use of force is necessary to preserve vital strategic and political interests.

Deterrence is beset by a host of practical problems. It is demonstrably difficult to communicate capability and resolve to would-be challengers. Theories of deterrence assume that everyone understands, so to speak, the meaning of barking guard dogs, barbed wire, and "No Trespassing" signs. This assumption is unrealistic. Signals acquire meaning only in the context in which they are interpreted. When sender and recipient use quite different contexts to frame, communicate, or interpret signals, the opportunities for misjudgment multiply. Receivers may dismiss signals as noise or misinterpret them when they recognize that they are signals. This problem is endemic to international relations and by no means limited to deterrence because of the different historical experiences and cultural backgrounds of policymaking elites. It is, however, more likely in tense relationships, where both sides use worst-case analysis and are emotionally aroused.

If credible threats of punishment always increased the cost side of the ledger— something deterrence theory takes for granted—it would be unnecessary for would-be deterrers to replicate the value hierarchy and preferences of target leaders. This convenient assumption is belied by practice. As we have seen, leaders may be driven primarily by *vulnerability*, not by *opportunity*. When they are, raising the costs of military action may have no effect on their unwillingness to tolerate what are perceived as the higher costs of inaction. Even when motivated by opportunity, leaders may reframe their cost calculus in the opposite direction than intended in the face of threats. They may conclude that giving in to them is more costly than resistance, especially if they believe that compliance will be interpreted by their adversary as a sign of weakness and give rise to new demands.

Deterrence in the Long Term

Case evidence of deterrence failures and successes indicates that deterrence is a risky and uncertain strategy. It suggests that deterrence has a chance of success in a narrow range of conflicts: those in which adversarial leaders are motivated largely by the prospect of gain rather than by the fear of loss, have the freedom to exercise restraint, are not misled by grossly distorted assessments of the political-military situation, and are vulnerable to the kinds of threats that a would-be deterrer is capable of making credibly. Deterrence must also be practiced early on, before an adversary commits itself to a challenge and becomes correspondingly insensitive to warnings that its action is likely to meet with retaliation. Unless these conditions are met, deterrence will at best be ineffective and at worst be counterproductive.

These conditions apply only to deterrence in the short term, that is, to immediate deterrence. Proponents of deterrence generally concentrate on this kind of deterrence. However, our analysis of deterrence would be incomplete if we failed to examine its implications for the management of adversarial relationships in the longer term. Does deterrence facilitate or retard the resolution of international conflict?

Deterrence theorists maintain that it can play a positive role by convincing a challenger that its fundamental objectives cannot be met through a use of force. Alexander George and Richard Smoke contend deterrence may give the parties to a dispute time to work out an accommodation and, in so doing, reduce tensions and the potential for overt conflict.[28] However, deterrence can also retard conflict resolution by exacerbating the causes of the conflict or by creating new incentives to use force. Three different processes can contribute to this kind of negative outcome.

As noted, deterrence can intensify the pressures on adversarial leaders to resort to challenges or the use of force. American deterrence did this for Khrushchev in the Cuban missile crisis and in the second Taiwan Strait crisis. In the wake of the 1954–55 crisis, the United States reinforced deterrence in the Strait. President Dwight D. Eisenhower committed the United States to the defense of Taiwan and the offshore islands and, in 1957, authorized the deployment of nuclear-tipped surface-to-surface Matador missiles on Taiwan. To the president's annoyance, Chiang Kai-shek began a major military buildup on the islands and by 1958 had stationed 100,000 troops there, one-third of his total ground forces. To leaders in Beijing, the increased military preparedness and troop deployments indicated that Washington was preparing to "unleash" Chiang. A series of provocative speeches by Secretary of State John Foster Dulles, suggesting that Chinese Nationalist forces might invade the mainland if significant domestic unrest provided the opportunity, fueled the Chinese perception of threat. This led the Chinese leadership to demonstrate resolve with a renewed artillery assault on Jinmen and Mazu.[29]

Deterrence can also intensify conflict by encouraging defenders to develop an exaggerated concern for their bargaining reputation. Deterrence does not attach great significance to the impact of the interests at stake in influencing an adversary's judgments of a commitment's credibility. It assumes—incorrectly, according to a growing number of empirical studies—that the most important component of credibility is the defender's record in honoring past commitments.[30] Schelling emphasized the interdependent nature of commitments; failure to defend one, he argued, will make willingness to defend any commitment questionable in the eyes of an adversary. "We tell the Soviets," Schelling wrote in 1966, "that we have to react here because, if we did not, they would not believe us when we said that we will react there."[31]

Schelling and other deterrence theorists ignored the possibility of escalation inherent in the connections among commitments. More important, they ignored the likelihood that deterrence pursued this way would make the state practicing deterrence look more aggressive than defensive. We described how this happened in the Taiwan Strait crises. It was more striking in the run-up to the Cuban missile crisis, where Soviet and American efforts at deterrence convinced the other of its aggressive intentions and prompted them to take a series of reciprocal actions that culminated in the Cuban missile deployment.[32]

Schelling's fears were in any case misplaced. Ted Hopf examined Soviet reactions to thirty-eight cases of American intervention over a twenty-five-year period of the Cold War and could not discover a single Soviet document that drew negative inferences about American resolve in Europe or northeast Asia. In *We All Lost the Cold War*, Lebow and Stein demonstrated that neither Khrushchev and his advisors nor Leonid Brezhnev and his advisors ever doubted American credibility but rather considered the Americans rash, unpredictable, and aggressive.[33]

Concern for credibility gives rise to symbolic commitments like that of Dulles to defend the Taiwanese-occupied offshore islands of Jinmen and Mazu. Such commitments can easily become entangling because they tend to become at least as important to leaders as commitments made in defense of substantive interests. Their exaggerated importance is probably due in large part to the pernicious effect of postdecisional rationalization. Once a commitment is made, leaders, understandably uncomfortable about risking war for abstract, symbolic reasons, seek to justify the commitment to themselves and to others. This need motivates them to "discover" important substantive reasons for these commitments— reasons absent in and irrelevant to their original calculations.

In the case of the Taiwan Strait, top-level administration officials, who previously had questioned the importance of the offshore islands, subsequently came to see them as the linchpin of security throughout Asia. Most senior policymakers subscribed in all solemnity to an astonishing version of the domino theory. In a classified policy statement meant only for internal use, Eisenhower and Dulles both argued that loss of the islands would likely endanger not only the survival of the Nationalist regime on Taiwan but also that of pro-American governments in Japan, Korea, the Philippines, Thailand, and Vietnam, and would bring Cambodia, Laos, Burma, Malaya, and Indonesia under the control of communist forces.[34] The most far-reaching expression of this logic was Vietnam. American leaders had no substantive interests in the country but committed forces to its defense in large part because they were persuaded that failure to defend their commitment in Southeast Asia would encourage Moscow to doubt US resolve elsewhere in the world.[35]

Finally, deterrence can intensify conflict by encouraging leaders to interpret even ambiguous actions as challenges that require a response. This exaggerated sensitivity to challenge is very much a function of the heavy emphasis that deterrence places on a state's bargaining reputation. Its most paranoid formulation is Schelling's famous dictum: "If you are invited to play a game of 'chicken' and you refuse, you have just lost."[36] Invitations to play chicken in the international arena, however, are rarely direct and unambiguous. Challenges must be inferred from the context of events, and given the inherent complexity of international affairs, policymakers have considerable leeway in determining their meaning. Challenges to play chicken are particularly difficult to substantiate because they are defined in terms of the intent of an action, not its expected effect. Leaders are much more likely to perceive a challenge—and often falsely so—when they believe damage to their state's interests and reputation is the principal goal of another's actions, not just its by-product.

These three processes are important contributing causes of tension, misunderstanding, and fear between adversaries. They point to the greatest long-term danger of deterrence: its propensity to make the worst expectations about an adversary self-fulfilling. Threats and military preparations—the currency of deterrence—inevitably arouse the fear and suspicion of those they are directed against. As noted, they tend to provoke the very behavior that they are designed to prevent. Over time, military preparations, initially a consequence of tensions between or among states, can become an important cause. This kind of dynamic has operated between the United States and the Soviet Union, Israel and the Arab states, and China and the Soviet Union, and some fear it is now operating between China and the United States. In all these cases the misunderstanding and tension caused by deterrence, overlaid on substantive issues that divide protagonists, made these conflicts more acute, more difficult to manage, and less amenable to resolution.

The outlines of the policy dilemma are clear. Protagonists may need deterrence to prevent their adversaries from resorting to force, but the use of deterrence can simultaneously make the conflict more acute and more likely to erupt into war. Because deterrence can be ineffective, uncertain, and risky, it must be supplemented by other strategies of conflict management. We now examine and critique how the United States and China deploy deterrence against each other and the role deterrence plays in their strategic relations.

American Deterrence of China

"Deterrence," declared General James Mattis in his Senate confirmation hearing for secretary of defense in January 2017, "is critical and that requires the strongest military."[37] Ten years earlier, in 2007, Pacific Command commander Admiral Timothy Keating had asserted, "We must maintain the . . . powerful overmatch we currently enjoy . . . [and] the ability to dominate in any scenario, in all environments, without exception."[38] In these two statements is the essence of US security strategy toward Asia, a strategy that is central to the US grand strategy of liberal hegemony that we critiqued in Chapter 3.

A long-standing goal of American security strategy toward China is to "dissuade China from making a bid for hegemony and thereby preserve the existing power balance" in Asia.[39] The United States has been pursuing this strategy since the mid-2000s by both engaging China diplomatically and balancing against it strategically. The Obama administration's rebalance to Asia was a belated labeling as well as an extension of that George W. Bush–era strategy.[40] Combining a shifting mix of engagement and balancing, the Bush and Obama administrations sought to "preserve a balance of power favorable to U.S. interests while awaiting the eventual liberalization of China's domestic political institutions."[41]

The US Department of Defense identified three goals in its 2015 Asia-Pacific maritime security strategy document: safeguard the freedom of the seas, deter conflict and coercion, and promote adherence to international law and standards.[42] Each of these goals points toward China, especially the goal of deterrence. Prior to this historic first strategy document on the Asia-Pacific, the Pentagon had promised to deploy 60 percent of naval and air force units to the region as part of its Asia rebalance strategy, aimed—in part, according to Washington; in total, according to Beijing—at deterring Chinese assertiveness. Before the rebalance, creative minds in the US military had conceived the air-sea battle as a new operational concept directed at China. Critiqued in Chapter 3, the ASB proposes to attack Chinese defenses in full, even at the risk of nuclear escalation, and seeks to disrupt, destroy, and defeat Chinese use of force and thus deny its underlying strategic objectives. It seeks to buttress conventional deterrence by a strategy of denial.[43]

Deterrence enjoys strong support within the American academic and policy communities.[44] It is informed by two long-standing goals of America's Asia policy. The first is to prevent China from pushing the United States out of the Asia-Pacific. For well over a century, from 1899, when the William McKinley administration announced the historic Open Door policy, to the present day, a fixed objective of American policy has been to prevent a hostile power from dominating Asia.[45] A hostile Asian hegemon, it is feared, would imperil a range of US national interests, including economic access to Asian markets, technology, and resources; security access to the region's critical sea lanes and military bases; and political and ideological influence over major Asian governments.

The second goal of American policy is to prevent China's rising military capabilities from reducing US military superiority. In recent years the US defense community has developed a foreboding obsession with what it refers to as China's anti-access and area denial capabilities. The Pentagon perceives Chinese A2/AD as posing a critical challenge to America's freedom of action and its ability to project power in East Asia. It is scrambling for an effective response to ensure the US military's ability to operate effectively in A2/AD environments.[46] The ASB is a notable part of that response, as is a new determination to strengthen deterrence against China in the hope of neutralizing its new capabilities and, if necessary, defeating the PLA should deterrence fail. Ever a great spokesperson for the hardliners, Aaron Friedberg argues that Chinese A2/AD capabilities "could call American security guarantees into question, weakening the alliances on which they rest and eventually undermining the United States' place as the preponderant Asia-Pacific power."[47]

American planners worry that the purpose of China's military modernization, as seen through the lens of A2/AD, is to counter US military capabilities and preclude American forces from operating at will in the Western Pacific by attacking its forces and bases and supporting infrastructure in the region. The PLA is also seen as threatening US allies and other partners in the region, such as Japan and the Philippines, which have been at the receiving end of China's maritime assertiveness in recent years.[48] These efforts are inconsistent with China's declared policy of peaceful development, they allege, and the real intention behind them must be to deter, defeat, and expel US forces from the East Asian theater by developing new capabilities and doctrines. The United States and its allies must therefore build up their military power to deter and defeat such attempts.[49]

A central goal of American deterrence toward China is thus to counter Chinese coercion in sovereignty and maritime disputes. Toward this end the US military is developing a new generation of offensive-oriented capabilities, doctrines, and force structures. As countless analysts point out, American armed forces are wedded to offensive war-fighting operations that require preemptive or extremely rapid reaction capabilities and the early establishment of air and sea superiority throughout the theater of war. Confronting a capable adversary such as China, the United States "would place a strong emphasis on rapid, early, deep, and extensive strikes against a wide range of military targets."[50] No wonder that the ASB has appeared so appealing to American planners.

American general deterrence is intended to have a wider role than traditional general deterrence that aims only to increase the perceived cost of aggression. American deterrence certainly has this objective, but it also seeks to maintain military superiority as a means of reassuring allies. We also suspect that military superiority is pursued as an end in itself, unconnected with any broader political objectives. The goal of reassuring allies may be more of a rationalization for military superiority, as it was for the United States during the Cold War. Then, as now, American political leaders and the national security elite envisaged military superiority as a necessary condition for hegemony. This can hardly be considered a defensive goal.

Before 2010 American immediate deterrence had been focused almost exclusively on China's potential use of force to achieve reunification with Taiwan. More recently, however, the task has been broadened to include deterrence against perceived Chinese coercion or aggression in other Asian maritime territorial disputes. According to a report from the Center for Strategic and International Studies in Washington, China has been applying "gray-zone" coercion to regional disputes, especially those in the East and South China seas. Although taking place below the threshold of direct military confrontation, such coercion is nonetheless believed to destabilize the region by upsetting existing rules and norms, changing the territorial status quo, undermining the credibility of US security commitments, and increasing the risk of conflict. Deploring the Obama administration's deterrent attempts as feeble and ineffective, the study recommends a more robust deterrence posture by tailoring deterrence strategies, clarifying deterrence commitments, accepting calculated risk, tightening alliances and partnerships, and exercising restraint while demonstrating resolve.[51] All these recommendations, with the revealing exception of exercising restraint, were adopted by the Trump administration.

US analysts believe that China's maritime coercion is undermining the American interests of security, prosperity, and values in Asia. It is altering the regional territorial status quo through pressure and force. It is exacerbating the short-term risk of conflict. It is undermining the US bilateral alliance system and thus the credibility of its security commitments. It is challenging the continued viability of freedom of navigation and economic access throughout the region. Through all these actions, China is threatening the regional order and raising the specter of a hostile hegemon bent on dominating Asia. Doubting US commitments or resolve, America's regional allies may succumb to fears of alliance abandonment and bandwagon with China or develop military capabilities such as nuclear weapons that would be inimical to US interests or adopt risky strategies to entrap it in alliance commitments and possibly draw it into conflict with China. The decline of American strategic influence would mean the rise of China's leverage to dictate terms to the region. Such a zero-sum logic has led these analysts to embrace deterrence as the only viable response to rising Chinese power.[52]

China's Active Defense

Understanding Chinese deterrence must begin with an appreciation of the nature of China's military strategy.[53] This has long puzzled observers and has been described as everything from defensive in nature to hegemonic in ambition. The 2015 publication of a new Chinese defense white paper, helpfully entitled *China's Military Strategy*, provides more insight.[54] Most observers have focused on what it describes as the new naval strategy of "near-sea defense and far-sea protection." To our way of thinking, the key part of the document is the section on the "strategic guideline of active defense."

Nothing in the universe of Chinese security discourse confounds the outside world more than the idea of active defense. This is an indigenous Chinese concept informed by China's history and culture and now stated in the white paper as "the foundation of the Chinese Communist Party's military strategic thought." In Chinese thinking, the active-defense doctrine reflects the unique integration of strategic defense and operational or tactical offense. Insisting on defense as the overall strategic objective, it does not preclude operational or tactical offense that strikes hard at the enemy. The vivid Chinese phrase *hou fa zhi ren,* "gaining mastery by striking only after the enemy has struck," is often used to capture the essence of the idea.[55] China will not be "firing the first shot," as it were, but will maintain the capability to strike back in a fitting manner.[56] It is not a doctrine of preemption, which is an established part of the US doctrine, but one of durable defense by robust counterattacks. In 1950 China did not enter the Korean War until the US military began bombing Chinese border areas and pushed the front line to the Yalu River. In 1962 China dealt India a quick and devastating blow in their border clash only after India persisted with its "forward policy" in disputed areas. In 1979 China launched a one-month offensive into Vietnam after Hanoi's invasion of Cambodia revealed its hegemonic ambitions in Indochina. The Korean War ended in a stalemate. In the last two conflicts, China, having achieved strategic defense, retreated to its prior positions without seizing conquered territories or consolidating military advantages. All these conflicts are cited by Chinese strategists as salient applications of the active-defense doctrine.

What appears puzzling about this doctrine is the precise relationship between defense and offense, as well as the question of when or under what conditions defense is turned into offense and vice versa. The defense-offense relationship seems infinitely fluid. The white paper provides no precise guidance to these questions, apart from noting nine intricately worded principles for applying the doctrine under new conditions. These include, among others, first, serving national strategic goals, strengthening preparation for military struggle, and deterring war and if necessary winning wars; second, adopting a defensive national defense policy and creating a favorable strategic environment for China's peaceful development; and third, achieving a balance between safeguarding national territorial sovereignty and maritime rights and maintaining stability and security in regional relations.[57]

Chinese analysts acknowledge the difficulty in understanding the relationship between defense and offense, but they uniformly insist that the fundamental goal of China's military strategy is homeland and near-sea defense rather than overseas expansion or aggression. The outside impression of China now adopting an expansive strategy of regional domination is partly a result of the changing meaning of "active defense" and the analytical challenge in grasping it. In the 1960s and 1970s, when Sino-Soviet tensions were acute, the strategy of active defense was based on drawing the enemy deep into Chinese territory and fighting a defensive war inside China. The emphasis was placed almost entirely on the army's ability to withstand a Soviet land onslaught and achieve victory through attrition. In the 1990s, awed by US military prowess demonstrated in the Gulf War and enthralled by the "revolution in military affairs" so successfully exploited by the Pentagon, the PLA hurriedly turned its attention to information warfare. But the strategic mindset was still heavily defensive, focused as it was on coastal defense. Since about 2000 Beijing has recognized the new need to safeguard territorial interests in maritime Asia and protect overseas interests, including seaborne trade and energy supplies vital to the functioning of the Chinese economy. It accordingly began to prioritize naval and air force modernization by developing certain offensive capabilities, focusing especially on long-range precision strikes. This development coincided with the change of maritime strategy from coastal defense to near-sea defense. In 2015, with the release of the aforementioned white paper, Beijing for the first time announced "far-sea protection" as a new dimension of its naval strategy. As a result of this shift, China has embarked on building a multidimensional force structure combining both defensive and offensive capabilities.[58]

The new naval strategy of near-sea defense and far-sea protection holds the key to understanding the current emphasis of the active-defense doctrine and the nature of China's overall military strategy. Although Chinese discourse is often faulted for being opaque and elliptic, in this case the words chosen for the new naval strategy are as precise as the Chinese language can go. "Near-sea defense" signals China's intention to apply the active-defense doctrine to what it regards as the three "near seas"—the East China Sea, the Yellow Sea, and the South China Sea—separated by the First Island Chain from the far seas of the Pacific and Indian Oceans. "Far-sea protection" suggests the PLA's new mission of protecting the sea lines of communication critical to China's national well-being as well as Chinese economic, energy, and diplomatic interests in the global commons beyond the First Island Chain. On regional and global scales, China's military strategy is defensive.[59]

What role has deterrence played in the evolution of the active-defense doctrine? During the Cold War ideologically infused Chinese officials and analysts denigrated deterrence as a Western or imperialist doctrine. Since the 1990s, as they have come into contact with Western writings on deterrence, they have accepted it as an important security strategy. Deterrence now constitutes one of the twin means of realizing the goal of active defense, the other being crisis management.[60] As in general deterrence thinking, Chinese deterrence attempts to prevent undesired policies by threatening massive punishment or forestalling the success of such policies. Specifically it aims at deterring regional countries in dispute with China over territorial sovereignty and maritime interests from damaging China's interests. No less important, it intends to deter the United States from intervening in these disputes on behalf of its allies. Taiwan and maritime disputes are the two most important of these.

Taiwan stands out as a category of its own in Chinese deterrence thinking. Throughout the post–Cold War period, deterring Taiwan's independence and US intervention in a conflict in the Taiwan Strait were the sole aims of the strategy. To their dismay, Chinese planners discovered during the Taiwan Strait crisis of 1995–96 that they could not really deter the United States from such intervention and lacked good options to respond when the Pentagon dispatched two aircraft carrier battle groups to the region. A fierce determination to strengthen deterrence against both US forces and the independence movements inside Taiwan was their response to avenge this humiliation.[61]

The PLA has also been building up deterrent postures in other maritime theaters, especially the South China Sea. As Chapter 4 shows, since late 2013 China has been building a new dual-use infrastructure of island chains on existing reefs and is ready to turn the largest islands into military bases. The United States ridiculed Chinese island building as creating "a great wall of sand" at sea.[62] It is doubtful whether China is seeking a leadership contest with the United

States. The PLA has a desire to expand China's security perimeter at the cost of US military dominance. But that expansion is based on what it perceives to be China's sovereignty and maritime rights in the South China Sea. The expansion of China's military power in the region appears to be an application of the doctrine of active defense, not an offensive strategy of challenging US regional leadership. It is meant to deter or counter US intervention by imposing costs. It is not meant to end the US military presence in the region. In fact hardliners in the PLA believe that a US military intervention into South China Sea disputes, just as with intervention in the Taiwan Strait or the Diaoyu/Senkaku Islands dispute in the East China Sea, would constitute an invasion of China and thus trigger a PLA anti-invasion counterattack in the name of self-defense.[63] In such circumstances the doctrine of active defense would be fully operative.

The active-defense doctrine requires the PLA, especially its navy, to develop a modern force structure to project power into the Western Pacific. As a result, China's deterrence posture, although still moderate, has become increasingly robust and assertive since around 2010. As we will explain in the next section, the role of tactical offense in the active-defense doctrine may eclipse the primary goal of strategic defense and tempt the PLA to orient its forces toward offensive warfighting and war-winning operations, just like the US military. The result would resemble a strategy of sea control based on aggressive deterrence within the First Island Chain so as to prevent its neighboring countries and the United States from challenging its sovereignty and maritime interests within the area. Should deterrence fail, the hope is to prevail in armed conflicts. Such a strategy would make a mockery of the professed strategy of near-sea defense but might be possible if the United States persists in its goal of military predominance through its own aggressive deterrence.

Risks of General Deterrence
Exacerbating Assertiveness

America and China are adopting a mutual deterrence posture, entailing four notable risks. In the first place, it can increase threat perceptions and pressures on the other side to be more assertive. As we argued in Chapter 3, the Obama administration's Asia rebalance policy and the geopolitical setting it created served to exacerbate China's already fermenting assertive inclinations. Washington's desire to make credible its commitments to allies in their territorial and maritime disputes with China contributed to a greater Chinese resolve to face down perceived provocations from these countries. The result was both a reduction in Sino-American strategic trust and a stronger deterrence posture from China, especially in the South China Sea. Feeling threatened, Washington strengthened its own

deterrence against China by entrenching its military superiority and enhancing strategic relations with Asian countries. A vicious cycle of strategic mistrust
followed.

The US military's operational concept of the ASB is part of a more robust
deterrence strategy against China, raising Chinese fear and prompting the PLA
to strengthen its own deterrence against US forces in Asia. Other proposals of
assertive deterrence are likely to have similar effects. Andrew F. Krepinevich Jr., a
well-known defense hawk, suggests deterrence through denial so as to convince
China that it simply cannot achieve its objectives with force. He promotes a
strategy of archipelagic defense linking a series of defense points along the First
Island Chain from Japan to the Philippines, in the hope of denying China any
chance of military success.[64] Whether strategies like this can deter China in crises
is uncertain, but they are apt to "encourage China to probe these waters more
aggressively—setting up the growing possibility of an accident or misunderstanding with U.S. or allied vessels."[65] Besides, such deterrence is only going to delay,
but not prevent, China's ability to gain access to these choke points if it is resolved
to do so. Indeed two former Obama administration officials admit that American
military power and deterrence have failed to dissuade China from building a
world-class military of its own and strengthening its strategic position in Asia.[66]

Thomas Christensen argues that deterrence against China might spur Beijing
to improve relations with its neighbors. He reasons that regional tensions may
raise China's fear of US encirclement and thus motivate it to pursue cooperation
with neighboring countries as a hedge. Christensen contends that in the 1990s
America's continued military presence in Asia, a firm deterrent commitment to
the security of Taiwan, and a strengthened alliance with Japan helped channel
China's competitive energies into positive-sum areas such as regional multilater-
alism. Deterrence appears to have benefited Sino-American relations.[67]

It is doubtful whether American deterrence has produced such felicitous
outcomes. Christensen's analysis of the Chinese response to the US strategy in
the 1990s glosses over China's assertive buildup of its deterrence posture after the
1995–96 Taiwan Strait crisis. It cannot explain Chinese policy after 2010. China is
now in the grip of Xi's mission of national rejuvenation and is becoming increasingly intolerant toward perceived encroachment upon its interests from its neighbors or the United States. In any event, even in the 1990s deterrence addressed
only the symptoms, not the causes, of tensions. America's immediate deterrence
of Chinese military exercises in the Taiwan Strait crisis was successful, but it managed to suppress rather than resolve disputes. And it came at the price of accelerating Chinese deterrence efforts, thus worsening, not alleviating, tensions.

Of all Sino-American deterrence encounters, the Taiwan Strait is still the
most dangerous. The US policy of dual deterrence—deterring Beijing's use of

force and Taiwan's declaration of de jure independence—has persisted since the early 1980s. Beijing has been steadily strengthening its military capabilities vis-à-vis Taiwan and the United States since the mid-1990s. Under Xi it is growing increasingly impatient with reunification. Yet the US response is largely limited to telling Beijing that it must reduce its military buildup in order to give Taipei the confidence to engage in cross-Strait talks, while still selling arms to Taipei and increasing US surveillance and military deployments relevant to a Taiwan conflict.[68] In effect, Washington is trying to reserve the right of deterrence across the Taiwan Strait for itself while denying it to Beijing.

This is an untenable situation. Given the enormous stakes of Taiwan reunification for CCP rule in the mainland, the PLA will strengthen its capabilities to invade Taiwan and deter US intervention, even if only to prepare all the options for the future without actually launching an invasion. Rather than soothing Chinese anxiety, America's continued adherence to the policy of dual deterrence, symbolized by regular arms sales to Taipei, is likely to wear thin Chinese patience, injure its pride, and increase its assertiveness. The United States may hope that this policy's underlying strategic ambiguity—that Washington neither confirms nor denies that it would intervene in a Taiwan conflict—will continue to facilitate dual deterrence. In Chinese eyes, this ambiguity is crystallizing into the clarity of tacitly supporting Taiwan's independence, and dual deterrence increasingly looks like single-minded deterrence against Beijing.

Misjudgment and Miscalculation

General deterrence can intensify competition by encouraging the defender to develop an exaggerated concern for its bargaining reputation. Rather than examining the interests at stake, the defender may attach more significance to its record in honoring past commitments and in connecting past commitments with present and future ones. Believing in the so-called domino theory of communist expansion, the United States committed this mistake in Southeast Asia in the 1950s and 1960s, resulting in the debacle of the Vietnam War. Whether it will be trapped again by strategic commitments to its Asian allies and come into conflict with China is an open question. States, like people, do learn lessons, although not always the right ones.

Of all the areas of US anxiety toward China since the Obama years, the most significant is the South China Sea, where China is perceived to be steadily establishing strategic dominance by island building and with a mixture of inducement and coercion toward Southeast Asian countries. It is here that Washington has developed an exaggerated sensitivity and interpreted ambiguous Chinese actions as challenges to its regional supremacy. The main US response, Freedom of

Navigation Operations (FONOPs), can be seen as an attempt to buttress its strategic credibility and bargaining reputation in the face of China's challenge. Yet the very controversies these FONOPs have generated at home and abroad and the lack of other options show how difficult it is to sustain a bargaining reputation only loosely connected to intrinsic interests at stake.

FONOPs may be viewed as an instrument of deterrence against Chinese assertion of de facto control over the South China Sea. The Obama administration had been criticized for its "muddled" deterrence in the South China Sea;[69] it may have intended to use FONOPs to signal US resolve to contest China's claims, thus shoring up its strategic credibility and reassuring regional allies. But FONOPs have succeeded in neither reassuring allies nor deterring Chinese expansion. Regional countries have continued to doubt US resolve; China has pressed ahead with island building. Hugh White thus contends that FONOPs are sending "a message of weakness and timidity, not of strength and resolve."[70]

Perhaps a more useful approach is to understand FONOPs as a militarized legal instrument for challenging China's dubious legal claims, not a policy of deterrence per se, and to identify America's real deterrence in a strengthened regular military presence in the South China Sea.[71] Chinese planners, however, are not given to making such fine distinctions in American policy; they are apt to lump them together and see them as provocations and overreactions detached from the causes of tensions in the South China Sea. Until September 2018, three years after the Obama administration's first politicized FONOP in October 2015, China's reactions to US warships passing through nearby waters had been restrained. Then, on September 30, 2018, a Chinese destroyer sailed within forty-five yards of the bow of an American destroyer conducting a FONOP in the Spratlys, forcing it to maneuver to avoid a collision.[72] This incident sounded the tocsin that a stronger American deterrence posture based on more assertive FONOPs and further military buildup in the South China Sea may trigger Chinese misjudgment and overreaction. Indeed China has been enhancing its own deterrence by arming the new islands with offensive weapons and increasing military patrols and challenges in the area, heightening the risk of future incidents with the US military.

Beyond the South China Sea, US attempts to sharpen its military edge in the Western Pacific have not deterred China from developing greater capabilities in critical areas such as the Taiwan Strait and the East China Sea. Nor has it been deterred from asserting its own interpretations of international maritime law as applied to East Asian waters. On the contrary, riding on a new confidence and rising capabilities, Beijing could become more, not less, willing to use coercion and even force to defend its perceived interests, especially in the face of perceived provocations from other states.[73] Indeed if the United States continues to strengthen its deterrence and war-fighting postures and doctrines, China will in all likelihood develop an exaggerated sensitivity to the US threat. The rationale for furthering greater capabilities to reduce its still considerable vulnerability vis-à-vis the US military will become stronger. Misjudgment and miscalculation, two negative consequences of deterrence, will plague both sides.

Symbolic Commitments Become Substantive Interests

Concern for credibility is a key driving force behind deterrence by the defender. The symbolic commitments to which it gives rise may take on substantive meanings that are not part of the original calculation. Dulles's threat in the late 1950s to defend the Taiwanese-occupied offshore islands of Jinmen and Mazu with nuclear weapons, even though these islands were strategically worthless and vulnerable, is a prime example of policymakers discovering substantive interests in symbolic commitments.

It is worth asking whether the current US involvement in China's sovereignty and maritime disputes through its commitments to regional allies might generate a similar dynamic. In a Sino-American contest over these disputes, China would see itself as defending vital political and strategic interests in the near seas. But how much substantive US interests would be at stake? According to Avery Goldstein, America would seek to "preserve a regional interest in upholding its reputation as a resolute ally that cannot be intimidated . . . as well as a global interest in upholding the principle of freedom of navigation on the high seas."[74] These, he notes, are "extrinsic interests in reputation and principle, whereas China's stake reflects intrinsic interests in the territory and waters themselves."[75] Other scholars concur that the United States would be defending "nonvital" or "secondary" interests in these disputes.[76]

Such assessments may lead China to believe that its own stakes in these disputes are much higher than America's. It may expect Washington not to fight for secondary interests and thus underestimate the risk of war-threatening escalation. The temptation to demonstrate resolve by running great risks over declared vital interests to force Washington to back down may then become hard to resist. But if China miscalculates America's credibility-induced deterrence strategy, such brinkmanship may backfire and war may just be the consequence.

It will be difficult for American policymakers to mobilize domestic support and justify conflict with China for defending trivial interests in Asia. However, when they discover important substantive interests behind existing commitments, just as in the 1950s and 1960s, they may challenge China accordingly. "Strategic primacy" is a leading candidate for such interests favored by realists and liberals alike.[77] It is hard for a great power, especially one like the United

States accustomed to seventy years' regional leadership, to voluntarily cede strategic grounds. The danger is that deterrence pursued for the sake of the credibility of US strategic leadership in the region will turn it into a hegemonic strategy on a collision course with China. American preoccupation with credibility will make Washington less willing to give way and too quick to respond firmly to perceived Chinese challenges.[78] Chinese nationalism and honor, tangled with substantive interests, will make Beijing more assertive in response to perceived American affronts.

Conflict-Threatening Wishful Thinking

Deterrence can lead to conflict by generating overconfidence and wishful thinking on the part of the challenger state. This risk reflects the paradoxical and dangerous psychological consequences of deterrence. As we argued earlier, a belief in the necessity of challenging the commitments of the adversarial state may predispose the challenger state to see its objectives as attainable. This encourages motivated errors in the information process. Leaders can distort their assessments of threat and remain insensitive to warnings that their policies are likely to end in disaster. Moreover such motivated errors can be exacerbated by the belief that their deterrence against the adversarial state is succeeding and thus they will run no risk of war in a crisis that their challenge may bring about. Yet such a belief in the success of deterrence may become the very cause of its failure.

It is disturbing to consider that Chinese leaders may succumb to this belief as their country consolidates its deterrence posture in the near seas. The PLA, exhorted by Xi to fight and win wars when the moment arrives, seems supremely confident in its modernizing capabilities. Recent American assessments have done nothing to dent this confidence. A 2015 RAND study comparing US and Chinese military capabilities paints a gloomy picture of diminishing US dominance in Asia. While the United States would probably still prevail in a protracted war, PLA forces would become more capable of establishing temporary local air and naval superiority at the outset of a conflict, enabling it, under certain conditions, to achieve limited objectives without "defeating" US forces. Most troubling, "the ability to contest dominance might lead Chinese leaders to believe that they could deter U.S. intervention in a conflict between it and one or more of its neighbors. This, in turn, would undermine U.S. deterrence and could, in a crisis, tip the balance of debate in Beijing as to the advisability of using force."[79]

Other scholars have similarly argued that a belief in its ability to deter US intervention may prompt Beijing to use force in a crisis wherein its leaders perceive vital interests to be at stake.[80] Beliefs like this belong to the kind of wishful thinking that has repeatedly defeated deterrence in the past. Worryingly, they may warp Chinese calculations by virtue of the active-defense military strategy discussed earlier. Calling for tactical offense in the service of strategic defense, an active-defense strategy may be predisposed toward establishing temporary local military superiority to achieve a quick victory before the United States can bring its full strength into play—if it indeed decides to intervene. During the Cold War, Chinese counterattacks in accordance with the active-defense doctrine were usually unleashed after planners perceived diminishing strategic advantages, as in Korea, the Sino-Indian border area, and Vietnam. With the PLA now building its capabilities throughout the First Island Chain that are dwarfing those of its neighbors, and with deterrence a major strategy, neighboring countries are unlikely to erode China's military advantage. The PLA may instead seize on perceived provocations from these countries for tactical attacks, while expecting to deter US intervention or, failing that, counting on the US entry to be too late to be effective. Thus the Chinese active-defense doctrine supplies a psychological element to deterrence that may generate war-threatening overconfidence in a crisis.

A Strategy of Minimal Deterrence

We have highlighted four risks of general deterrence in the preceding section. Any one of them, and all of them collectively, should raise alarms about using deterrence as the main strategy of governing competition. Accordingly we now suggest a strategy of minimal deterrence for both countries. Abandoning deterrence in toto would be a nonstarter; it is impossible to banish deterrence from the strategic toolkit of these two countries or great powers in general. Feasibility aside, there is also an intellectual argument for practicing deterrence—where warranted—wisely and carefully. Deterrence is appropriately directed against states whose leaders harbor aggressive intentions, such as Nazi Germany. We contend that recent history offers no evidence for Chinese or American leaders harboring such intentions toward each other, nor does any alleged clash of interests between the two countries suggest an impending conflict. Aggressive deterrence would only produce the counterproductive effect of making the two countries more insecure, fearful, and convinced of each other's hostile intentions.

American officials and analysts allege that the Chinese intend to push the United States out of Asia. This supposition is based more on flimsy historical analogy, faulty realist logic, and unfounded speculation than on hard evidence. As we described in Chapter 4, the highest level of the Chinese government, including both Presidents Hu and Xi, has clarified more than once that China welcomes the United States as an Asia-Pacific nation that contributes to regional peace, stability, and prosperity. In a new formulation emanating from years of painstaking work by China's elite think tanks, Xi declared in July 2014 that "the vast Pacific Ocean must have enough space to accommodate both China and the United States."[81] Like every Chinese leader since Mao, Xi insists that "China will never seek hegemony, expansion, or spheres of influence." And like every one of his predecessors since Deng Xiaoping, he embraces peaceful development as China's international strategy.[82] These pledges of never seeking hegemony and always focusing on peaceful development are also found in the 2015 and 2019 defense white papers.[83]

The only jarring occasion when the Xi seemed to intimate an exclusivist intention was on May 21, 2014, when he called for Asian solutions to Asian problems during an international conference in Shanghai, which we also examined in Chapter 4. It is notable, however, that Xi has never again repeated the same message; indeed two months later he reassured the United States that China welcomed its presence as a Pacific power, as just noted. Feng Zhang has argued that inclusion is such a central theme of Chinese foreign policy discourse in the post–Cold War era that it is now part and parcel of contemporary Chinese exceptionalism in international relations.[84] While China disagrees with the United States on a number of issues in Asia, those disagreements have not become so serious as to amount to a wholesale rejection of America's regional role. In any case, even assuming Beijing's intention to establish military hegemony in the region, it would be an impossible goal to accomplish, as China would need to confront a string of great and middle powers—including the United States, Japan, India, Indonesia, and Australia—none of which is a pushover.

A significant number of Chinese and American scholars agree that China has not settled on a strategy of replacing the United States as the new hegemon in Asia. Beijing indeed wants Washington to accord a greater degree of respect to its international status over the long run. Nevertheless this search for respect is far from a drive for exclusive domination. Leading Chinese scholars believe that China is instead pursuing a hedging strategy aimed at minimizing strategic risks, increasing freedom of action, diversifying strategic options, and shaping US preferences and choices.[85] Michael Swaine, a prominent American China watcher, concurs that China's strategy contains both cooperative and hedging elements, but not exclusion.[86] Many other leading American analysts, including Christensen, who served as a deputy assistant secretary of state in the George W. Bush administration, find little evidence of a concerted Chinese effort to drive the U.S. military out of Asia.[87] They aver that as long as America preserves its alliances and partnerships, the prospects of China driving the United States from the Asia-Pacific are slight.[88] The Asian balance of power over the long run in fact favors the United States—hence no need for Washington to succumb to exaggerated fears.[89]

American fear of Chinese domination in Asia is thus irrational. So too is Chinese fear of American encirclement. From Washington's perspective, the United States is merely trying to preserve its postwar regional primacy by adopting a strategy of status quo defense.[90] China perceives this strategy as encirclement because it appears to erect a balancing ring across many countries on its periphery. For America, such encirclement is a response to rising Chinese capabilities and an insurance against future contingencies. It does not embody a containment strategy. At any rate, containing China in the manner of Cold War containment of the Soviet Union is implausible today. The United States, say American officials, simply wants to continue to play a key role in the region by preserving political influence over Asian governments, strategic credibility based on military presence and security commitments, and economic access to the region. Even after the election of Trump, whose much more competitive policies inflamed the containment narrative in China, his senior officials still denied containment as the US goal. James Mattis, Trump's first secretary of defense, stated in June 2018 that the United States was "prepared to support China's choice, if they promote long-term peace and prosperity for all in this dynamic [Asian] region."[91]

Both America and China are motivated by a fear of loss—loss of its postwar regional primacy in the American case, and loss of still unfulfilled sovereignty and maritime interests in the Chinese case. That they accuse each other of offensive intentions and hostile actions is attributable to psychological anxieties, cognitive errors, and motivational biases. Misperceptions of the other side's excessive or unreasonable goals and threatening capabilities are especially apt to generate misjudgment. The American strategy of sustaining a robust defensive system to preserve its preponderant position exudes a hegemonic quality. Even though American hegemony in East Asia is partial at best, China easily falls into the habit of exaggerating its potency. The Chinese strategy of building a strong near-sea defense system to realize and protect its sovereignty and maritime interests oozes an expansive quality. Even though such expansion takes place within the realm of legitimate interests as understood by China, neither the US nor regional governments have been fully persuaded thus far. The status quo bias in the US strategy has generated the Chinese fear of US attempts to prevent China from realizing the full extent of its interests. The new capabilities that China is acquiring for active defense have generated the American fear of Chinese attempts to end the status quo favoring US interests. Typical of mutual deterrence encounters, each side's fear of loss is understood by the other as a search for gain.

That both America and China are more concerned with loss than with gain has important implications for conflict management. We argued at the outset that a good strategy of conflict management should build on a good theory of the nature and causes of conflict. Theories of deterrence, however, make an arbitrary assumption: that adversaries are motivated by gains and can be restrained only by credible and defensible commitments. The assumption is unwarranted in the Sino-American case. Both countries are driven more by the fear of loss than by the prospect of gain; neither desires a conflict or would be moved to start one if they perceived a favorable balance. Assertive deterrence is apt to backfire. We should be less attentive to the need to prepare for or prevent far-fetched military confrontations and more sensitive to the negative political consequences of deterrence.

In the conventional military realm, a minimal deterrence between China and America means that neither country will be able to achieve a quick, clear, and cost-effective victory over the other within the First Island Chain. It shares the spirit of military restraint with Swaine's concept of "mutual denial": both parties possess sufficient levels of capabilities to deter each other from gaining a sustained advantage through military means over potentially volatile areas, including Taiwan, the Korean Peninsula, and Asian maritime disputes.[92] Both countries, but especially the United States, have achieved this level of capabilities. In the nuclear domain, the United States must abstain from developing offensive capabilities that threaten China's second-strike deterrent. Here again the US predilection for superiority destabilizes a largely stable strategic deterrence already in place.

What is needed is not the further augmentation of the two countries' military power but the mutual restraint of their military strategies and doctrines. America's minimal deterrence strategy would require a shift from offensive capabilities and doctrines toward a more survivable posture based on a resilient, diversified, defensive, and denial-oriented force structure. Instead of preparing for early offensive actions by itself, which would be disproportionate and escalatory, the United States should bolster the defensive capabilities of Asian countries. A survivable posture based on the aggregated capabilities of the United States and its allies "would be neither escalatory nor destabilizing."[93] Presenting China with a complex targeting challenge, it would discourage Chinese preemptive attack, obviate the need for US preemptive attack, and allow time for a crisis to be defused.[94]

China's minimal deterrence strategy would oblige it to relinquish offensive, war-winning doctrines as well as some of its long-range power projection capabilities currently under development. Capabilities to be eschewed include those designed to seize disputed maritime territories by force or to conduct penetrating conventional strikes against the territory of regional states, including Japan and other U.S. allies.[95] Instead it should focus on defending against US or allied attacks on currently occupied Chinese territories or their attempts to reestablish a position of military predominance. Some self-imposed limits on offensive doctrines and capabilities would be essential. It is worth pointing out that unlike in the US case, where a minimal deterrence strategy appears the near-opposite of the current strategy predicated on predominance, China's minimal deterrence strategy would by no means contradict its official naval strategy of near-sea defense and far-sea protection; in fact it is required by that official strategy.

A Sino-American mutual minimal deterrence strategy would reflect the US recognition that it could no longer sustain uncontested superiority over Chinese forces in the Western Pacific and must therefore accept vulnerability and compromise. It would reflect the Chinese recognition that it would be next to impossible for Beijing to establish predominance over the United States and its allies and it must therefore settle for "a decent amount of security in less confrontational ways."[96] These recognitions, as we highlight throughout this book, accord more with reality—and are thus a sounder basis for policy—than any notion of American or Chinese hegemony. It is encouraging that they are beginning to be shared by a growing number of policy elites from both countries. Kurt M. Campbell and Jake Sullivan, two senior Obama administration officials, admit that US military primacy will be difficult to restore, but deterrence does not require primacy.[97]

Is minimal deterrence sufficient for security? Deterrence, of no matter what kind, is unlikely to suffice on its own. It must combine with the strategies of reassurance and diplomacy to provide a holistic framework for conflict management. But minimal deterrence is capable of reducing the counterproductive effects of assertive deterrence while at the same time providing a basic sense of security for both countries. America and China are formidable military powers with second-strike nuclear capabilities. Minimal deterrence between them holds out the prospect of serious damage, if not mutual assured destruction. The mutual recognition of the horror of war will generate incentives to manage runaway competition. This will then create space for the more productive strategies of reassurance and diplomacy.

Summary

Deterrence aims to prevent an adversary from resorting to force, but the major policies required for its effective deployment—arms buildups, forward deployments, and threatening rhetoric—are more provocative in their consequences than they are restraining. This chapter's critique of deterrence theory and practice shows that deterrence thinking fails to grasp the causes of competition and conflict and consequently addresses only symptoms of strategic tensions. The strategy of immediate deterrence may succeed under a narrow range of conditions, while general deterrence over the long run tends to retard rather than facilitate the resolution of international tensions.

Yet despite decades of scholarly research on deterrence and plenty of alarming experiences during the Cold War, the United States and China today are pursuing deterrence strategies without much recognition, let alone concern, for their damaging consequences. The American strategy of hegemonic deterrence aims at deterring real or imagined Chinese policies, including extruding the United States from East Asia, challenging the US military's power projection capabilities in the region, and coercing its neighbors in regional sovereignty and maritime disputes. The Chinese strategy of active defense, with an ever more prominent deterrence component, in part attempts to deter regional countries from damaging China's sovereignty and maritime interests and to deter the United States from intervening on their behalf.

Such mutual deterrence has been intensifying since the Obama years. It is not an optimal strategy for managing their competition. It is inappropriate because both Chinese and American security policies are motivated more by the fear of loss than by the prospect of gain. It is counterproductive and potentially dangerous because it carries significant security risks by intensifying competition, retarding dispute resolution, and generating new conflict.

Neither Washington nor Beijing will abandon deterrence as a principal security strategy. Old habits die hard, and deterrence is still erroneously touted by many in the US strategic community—in the face of evidence to the contrary—as the reason for America's ultimate victory in the Cold War. That deterrence can prevent the other side from using force to challenge cherished interests and thus preserve a tense peace is a mesmerizing idea for both sides. It should be possible, however, for policymakers in both capitals to appreciate the multiple consequences of deterrence—including many pitfalls and risks that might lead to unwanted conflict—and to recognize the need for other, more constructive and productive strategies to manage their competition. In the strategic domain of nuclear deterrence, considerable stability has long been achieved in any case. Both countries have already been deterred by their fear of a catastrophic war escalating to the nuclear level. Yet such is the folly of aggressive conventional deterrence, as in the case of the ASB, that it may damage strategic stability at the nuclear level by blurring the line between conventional and nuclear conflict.

Less is more. Deterrence has a role to play in security policy, but overdose is likely to be dangerous. We propose a strategy of minimal deterrence for both countries to reduce the harms of aggressive deterrence and to make room for the more productive strategies of reassurance and diplomacy. These two strategies will be the subject of the next two chapters. Used skillfully, reassurance and diplomacy can dampen the fear-generating and war-threatening consequences of deterrence and thus contribute to the building of a healthier Sino-American strategic relationship.

6

Reassurance

WE NOW TURN to the strategy of reassurance, which has played an important role in easing earlier Sino-American conflict. What was called "Ping-Pong diplomacy" in the early 1970s brought about a thaw in Chinese-American relations that led to President Richard Nixon's trip to China and the Shanghai Communiqué of February 28, 1972, that committed both former adversaries to work toward normalization of their relations. Nixon and Henry Kissinger, and Mao Zedong and Zhou Enlai, were able to convince one another of their benign intentions and find common ground on issues that had previously divided them. Reassurance combined with diplomacy reset Sino-American relations. It has the potential to do so again.

Reassurance seeks to alleviate causes of competition and conflict and induce accommodation and cooperation by reducing fear, mistrust, misunderstanding, and miscalculation between adversaries. We begin by identifying six forms of reassurance that have in their own ways contributed to ameliorating conflicts in the past: reciprocity, irrevocable commitment, self-restraint, norms of competition, limited security regimes, and trade-offs. Each of these applications has distinct functions and advantages but also risks and conditions for effective implementation that must be understood and assessed. We provide historical examples to illustrate their characteristics.

We then assess the value of these applications of reassurance for managing Sino-American conflict. We select four major areas of tension and dispute in the relationship, the amelioration of which would contribute significantly to reconciliation and accommodation between the two countries. In descending order of importance, they are Taiwan, North Korea, Asian maritime tensions and disputes, and the US alliance system in Asia. These do not exhaust all areas of contention between China and the United States, but they represent the most important sources of conflict or points of tension that might escalate into war-threatening crises.

All six forms of reassurance are relevant to these four issues. For reasons we will make clear, tension reduction in Taiwan, Asian maritime tensions and disputes, and the US alliance system in Asia requires a combination of these strategies. In North Korea, reassurance based on irrevocable commitments from the United States to China and China to North Korea could be a critical step toward resolving the nuclear weapons and missile crisis. But resolution of this thorny problem requires efforts from other regional actors as well, and thus a more complex and coordinated reassurance strategy.

Our analysis of China's response to the US alliance system suggests an additional form of reassurance: authority sharing. This application is based on insights from the Greek concept of *hēgemonia* and the parallel Chinese concept of *wangdao*. It could prove especially useful for promoting accommodation between the Chinese and American security orders in Asia.

Assumptions and Strategies

Strategies of reassurance begin from a different set of assumptions than those of deterrence. They presume ongoing tensions but root them in feelings of acute vulnerability. Reassurance requires defenders to communicate to would-be challengers their benign intentions. They must attempt to reduce the fear, misunderstanding, and insecurity that can be responsible for escalation and war. Reassurance seeks to reduce the expected gains of challenges and increase those of cooperation. Even when leaders consider a conflict to be incapable of resolution, they can still practice reassurance with the goal of avoiding accidental or miscalculated war. In so doing they may simultaneously help alleviate the underlying causes of conflict.

In the most ambitious applications of reassurance, leaders attempt to shift the trajectory of the conflict and induce cooperation through reciprocal acts of de-escalation and bargaining over substantive issues. They may begin with unilateral and irrevocable concessions. If they are pessimistic about the likely success of this approach or politically constrained from attempting it, they can pursue more modest variants of reassurance. They can exercise self-restraint in the hope of not exacerbating the foreign or domestic pressures and constraints pushing an adversary to act aggressively. They can try to develop informal norms of competition to regulate their conflict and reduce the likelihood of miscalculated escalation. They can attempt through diplomacy informal or formal regimes designed to build confidence, reduce uncertainty, and diminish the probability of miscalculated war. These strategies are neither mutually exclusive nor logically exhaustive.

The strategy of reassurance, like those of deterrence and compellence, are difficult to implement successfully. They must overcome strategic, political, and psychological obstacles. Cognitive barriers to signaling, for example, can just as readily obstruct reassurance as they can deterrence.[1] Other obstacles are specific to reassurance and derive from the political and psychological constraints that leaders face when they seek to reassure an adversary. Nevertheless reassurance can be used effectively and was a significant component of all long-standing rivalries that were resolved.

Reciprocity

Reciprocity has long been a focus of sociologists, psychologists, game theorists, and analysts of the international political economy. In security, reciprocal behavior is understood to require contingent, sequential exchanges among adversaries. One variant of it has been described as graduated reciprocation in tension-reduction.[2]

Reciprocity assumes that adversaries are able to identify and distinguish effectively between policies intended to be cooperative and those that are competitive. This assumption is built into Robert Axelrod's famous tit-for-tat computer strategy but is not always warranted in the real world.[3] Students who play tit-for-tat have problems distinguishing "tits" from "tats," something more likely among adversaries. Policies—"moves," in the language of strategic bargaining—can be dismissed as noise, recognized as signals, and misinterpreted if thought to be signals. Leaders may differ in their perceptions of reciprocity and functional measures of equivalence. Such differences between the United States and the Soviet Union were starkly evident as détente unraveled. Measures of equivalence in international security are defined subjectively by leaders and are subject to cognitive and motivated bias. When opposing leaders use different measures or different assessments of the same measures, they are likely to talk past one another. In the Cuban missile crisis, the United States and the Soviet Union both valued the status quo but defined it differently. For Washington, it was a Cuba without Soviet missiles. For Moscow, it was a Cuba ruled by Fidel Castro. Each superpower accordingly saw itself on the defensive and took umbrage at the actions of the other.[4]

Policymakers and their advisors are also likely to dismiss, misunderstand, or interpret away conciliatory gestures by an adversary when such gestures clash with their beliefs about its leaders and their goals. They may attribute the cooperative actions of others to inescapable situational pressures, while believing that their cooperative behavior offers evidence of their benign disposition.[5] Israel's leaders in 1971 initially explained Anwar Sadat's cooperative overtures as a response to his political weakness at home, the growing economic crisis in Egypt, and the dearth of strategic options available to Egyptian leaders. Here the fundamental attribution error interacted with prevailing cognitive images to defeat the possibility of reciprocation. Israel's failure to respond led Sadat to embrace war. Signals can also be missed or misread due to motivational biases, as they frequently are in deterrence encounters.

The difficulty in establishing common criteria of reciprocity can be mitigated in part if leaders share social norms. This is not often the case in international conflicts, many of which have arisen in part from a clash of values and their norms. If and when values and norms converge, conflict resolution becomes easier. Anglo-French accommodation reversed six hundred years of hostility and was greatly facilitated by shared values and norms, political as well as cultural, because both countries had become democracies. The Cold War was more difficult to resolve. It began as a struggle for influence in Europe following the defeat of Germany, but it had a strong ideological component because leaders and elites on both sides believed their social systems to be incompatible. Arguably the most fundamental cause of the resolution of the Cold War was a shift in key beliefs and goals by Soviet leaders that brought their values and norms closer to those of their Western European and American counterparts.[6] This shift made reassurance an attractive strategy to Soviet leaders and helped to make it viable.

Common criteria are essential conditions for far-reaching accommodations that bring about a normalization of relations. In their absence, any accommodation is difficult, and it may not be possible to go beyond the first step that reduces the likelihood of war. This may help explain why Egyptian-Israeli relations never progressed beyond this stage and why it was so difficult to reduce Cold War tensions before Mikhail Gorbachev took power. It might also account for the failure of the brief era of détente. In the absence of shared norms, leaders must be explicit about their values and norms, come to recognize where they and their adversaries disagree and have divergent expectations, and find ways of working around or finessing these differences. By doing so they might reduce some of the tensions between them. US-Soviet arms control agreements offer a successful example. Negotiations led to several treaties that did not so much slow down the arms race as made it transparent and set limits to it. Success hinged on prior understandings of each other's strategic cultures and discourses, achieved through informal talks among scientists and the epistemic community they created.[7] This process offers a good example of how knowledge of different values, norms, and discourses can help find common ground on substantive interests.

Irrevocable Commitment

When leaders recognize that misperception and stereotyping govern their adversary's judgments as well as their own, they can try to break through this wall of mistrust by making an irrevocable commitment.[8] In effect, they attempt to change the trajectory of the conflict through learning and to make a cooperative recip- rocal process more feasible. If successful, learning about adversarial intentions reduces the cost of moves toward peace because it decreases the likelihood in the estimate of leaders that they will be exploited or misinterpreted and prompt new demands. Reassurance of this kind seeks to rectify the political-psychological damage of deterrence.

President Sadat employed irrevocable commitment to break through the prevailing images of Israel's leaders and public and to put an end to decades of Egyptian-Israeli conflict. His willingness to visit Israel—the first Arab leader to do so publicly—and make a speech before its Parliament in November 1977 was a large, dramatic, and risky concession because of its cost and irreversibility. For both reasons, he hoped it would be seen as a valid indicator of Egyptian inten- tions rather than an ambiguous signal or one whose meaning could be manipu- lated subsequently by the sender. It gained additional power by Sadat's ability to speak successfully over the heads of Israel's leadership to its public. By mobilizing support for peace among the Israeli people he removed a constraint on the coun- try's leaders and created a political inducement to reciprocate.

Gorbachev's policy was in part also one of irrevocable commitment. He pub- licly promised to withdraw Soviet forces from Afghanistan and began to do so without any prior promise from the West not to exploit this reversal. In October 1989 he made a speech in Finland that in some ways was the equivalent of Sadat's in Jerusalem. He disavowed any right of the Soviet Union to intervene militarily in other countries, a promise that rapidly accelerated political change in Eastern Europe and the end of pro-Soviet communist regimes throughout the region. He also introduced political changes within the Soviet Union, associated with his programs of *glasnost* and *perestroika*, that further demonstrated his bona fides. These actions, together with arms control agreements, broke the logjam of the Cold War.[9]

We must be very careful in extrapolating from these two cases. As appease- ment of Hitler warns, it can be very risky to design a commitment that is high in cost and irreversible. Even if concessions are not exploited to further aggressive ends, they leave one exposed to key domestic and foreign constituencies. This is why Sadat secretly sounded out the Israelis prior to announcing his intention to come to Jerusalem. The Americans and Chinese also held clandestine talks before China issued its invitation to Kissinger to come to Beijing. The success of that visit led to a subsequent invitation to President Nixon to visit China.[10] Before making any irrevocable commitments leaders must assure themselves that their adversary is likely to respond positively and has equal incentives to reach some kind of meaningful accommodation.

Self-Restraint

When leaders are pessimistic about the possibility of changing their adversary's long-term intentions, they are likely to focus on reducing the short-term likelihood of conflict. This is a valuable end in itself and also one that may help change long-term intentions. Immediate deterrence tries to do the former and general deterrence the latter. Restraint through self-restraint is a counterpart to immediate deterrence.

Self-restraint has the potential to reduce some of the obvious risks of deterrence. Because it uses the language of reassurance rather than of threat, it can allay the fears of leaders caught in a process of escalation, as it did in India and Pakistan in 1987, and reduce the likelihood of miscalculation. However, it is both demanding and dangerous for those who use it. It is demanding because it requires leaders to monitor their adversary's political pressures, strategic dilemmas, leaders' estimates of the political and strategic costs of inaction, and assessment of the alternatives. Self-restraint encourages leaders to consider their adversary's calculus within the broadest possible political and strategic context. Like deterrence, it requires leaders to view the world through the eyes of their adversaries, and as we have seen, there are formidable cognitive and motivational impediments to reconstructing the calculus of another set of leaders. Perhaps because leaders pay attention to the vulnerabilities of their adversary as well as to its opportunities when they consider self-restraint, they may be able to overcome at least some of these impediments. At a minimum they are more likely to do so than leaders who consider only deterrence.

Self-restraint can be dangerous if it culminates in miscalculated escalation. When would-be deterrers are attentive to the weaknesses of opponents, to the possibility that they may provoke adversaries who are as yet uncommitted to a use of force, they are more likely to exercise restraint. Would-be challengers may misinterpret restraint and caution as weakness and lack of resolve. Argentina's invasion of the Falkland Islands (Islas Malvinas) in 1982 is a case in point. Margaret Thatcher's diplomacy was a phony strategy of reassurance that encouraged the Argentinian junta to believe that they could gain sovereignty over the Falklands (Malvinas) through diplomacy. When the Argentines realized that Thatcher was stringing them along, they became enraged and committed to using force. Failing to recognize this shift, the Thatcher government did not practice deterrence, all but guaranteeing an Argentinian invasion.[11] The obvious lesson here is for leaders not to practice reassurance unless it is sincerely intended and they are prepared to accept its consequences.

Evidence of the use of restraint in the context of general deterrence is still fragmentary and episodic. Analysts have not yet examined the documentary record to identify the relevant universe of cases. The limited evidence that is available of the interactive use of restraint and demonstration of resolve suggests that each carries the risk of serious error. An exercise of restraint may avoid provocation of a beleaguered or frightened adversary, but it may also increase the likelihood of miscalculated escalation. The language of threat and demonstration of resolve, on the other hand, may reduce the probability that a challenger will underestimate a deterrer's response, but it may provoke a vulnerable and fearful opponent.

Norms of Competition

Adversaries can attempt mutual reassurance by developing informal, even tacit norms of competition in areas of disputed interest. Informal, shared norms among adversaries may prevent certain kinds of mutually unacceptable action and, consequently, reduce the need to manipulate the risk of war. Informal norms may also establish boundaries of behavior and reduce some of the uncertainty that can lead to miscalculated escalation.

The United States and the Soviet Union attempted to develop explicit understandings of the limits of competition when they signed the Basic Principles Agreement in 1972 and, a year later, a more specific agreement on consultation to deal with crises that threatened to escalate to nuclear war. These agreements were not a success, in part because the formal documents masked significant disagreements and differences in interpretation. If anything, the unrealistic expectations they aroused, the disputes over interpreting the agreements, the consequent allegations of cheating and defection, and the ensuing distrust and anger exacerbated the management of the conflict between the two nuclear adversaries.

The Middle East provides a better illustration of the ability of norms of competition to regulate conflict. The United States and the Soviet Union have tacitly acknowledged that each may come to the assistance of its ally if it is threatened with a catastrophic military defeat by the ally of the other. To avoid such an intervention, the superpower had to compel the regional ally who threatens to inflict such an overwhelming defeat to cease its military action.[12] The Soviet Union invoked this tacit norm in 1967 and again in 1973, and although the United States attempted to deter Soviet intervention, it simultaneously moved to compel Israel to cease its military action and to reassure the Soviet Union immediately of its intention to do so. Deterrence and reassurance worked together, and indeed it is difficult to disentangle the impact of one from the other on the effective management of that conflict.[13]

Alexander George argued that these tacit and informal norms of competition in and of themselves did not provide a sufficiently stable basis for the management of conflict between the two superpowers; they lacked both institutionalized arrangements and procedures for clarification of their ambiguities and extension to new situations. He further suggested that shared norms of competition are likely to vary in utility according to the resources and strategies the superpowers use, the domestic and international constraints they face, leaders' capacity to formulate and differentiate their own interests and evaluate the interests at stake for their adversary, the magnitude of each superpower's interest, and the symmetry of the distribution of interest.[14] Tacit norms and patterns of restraint are more likely to emerge, for example, in areas of high-interest asymmetry than in areas of disputed or uncertain symmetry.

Given these obstacles, it is surprising that, in an area of disputed symmetry like the Middle East, the United States and the Soviet Union were able to agree tacitly on a shared norm to limit the most dangerous kind of conflict. This strategy might have promising uses on the Indian subcontinent and in East Asia.

Limited Security Regimes

In an effort to reduce the likelihood of an unintended and unwanted war, adversaries have agreed, informally at times, on procedures to reduce the likelihood of accident or miscalculated war. Technically these arrangements are referred to as limited security regimes.

Adversaries may also consider participation in a limited security regime if it improves the accuracy of detection and reduces the likelihood of defection. Fear of a surprise attack can encourage leaders to try to build limited security regimes, but it can also make their attainment more difficult. Such regimes may permit adversaries to monitor each other's actions with increased confidence by providing more complete and reliable information, by increasing surveillance capabilities for all parties, or by invoking the assistance of outsiders as monitors. In the limited security regime in place between Egypt and Israel since 1974, the United States routinely circulates intelligence information about the military dispositions of one to the other. Such a regime can give leaders more leeway than they otherwise would have to meet a prospective defection by increasing available warning time. This makes estimation of capabilities and intentions less difficult and reduces the likelihood of miscalculation.

Reassurance through the creation of limited security regimes has not been restricted to Egypt and Israel. The United States and the Soviet Union agreed in 1967 to the demilitarization of outer space in an effort to limit the scope of their conflict. In 1970 they actively promoted the nonproliferation regime and in 1972 negotiated a limited regime to reduce the likelihood of accident and miscalculated conflict at sea. They also regulated their conflict in central Europe with the 1955 Austrian State Treaty, the 1971 Berlin Agreement, and the 1975 Final Act of the Conference on Security and Co-operation in Europe.

Reassurance through the creation of limited and focused security regimes can be of considerable help in the longer term in reducing fear, uncertainty, and misunderstanding between adversaries. At a minimum, adversaries gain access to more reliable and less expensive information about each other's activities, which can reduce uncertainty and the incidence of miscalculation. In a complex, information-poor international environment, valid information can be a considerable advantage in more effective management of conflict.

Trade-offs

This form of reassurance seeks to defuse conflict and reassure at the same time by means of quid pro quos. It has the short-term advantage of removing sources of conflict between adversaries and holds out the longer-term prospect of building trust and cooperation in other areas. It might be regarded as the international equivalent of David Mitrany's functionalism.[15]

The great example of reassurance by trade-offs is Anglo-French reconciliation. Anglo-French hostility had deep historical roots going back to the Hundred Years' War. In the eighteenth and nineteenth centuries their colonial rivalry was acute and an extension of their conflict in Europe. The Fashoda crisis of 1898 was the culmination of their competition for influence in Africa and nearly led to war. The coalition that came to power in France after the crisis sought an accommodation with Britain because its members regarded Germany as their principal foe. The British prime minister, Lord Salisbury, held out the prospect of British support for a French protectorate in Morocco in return for France giving up any claims to the Sudan or Egypt. This colonial quid pro quo provided the basis for cooperation on European security issues where the two countries shared common interests.

Quid pro quos also played an important part in the Egyptian-Israeli and Sino-American accommodations. The initial accord between the two countries required Israel to withdraw from the Sinai Peninsula and Egypt to recognize the state of Israel. Implementation of these commitments built the modicum of trust necessary to move on to other issues and ultimately a peace treaty.[16] Taiwan had been a principal point of contention between Beijing and Washington since the founding of the People's Republic of China (PRC) in 1949. China claimed Taiwan as a province, but the United States supported its de facto independence and provided arms and military protection to its nationalist regime. Kissinger's and Nixon's visits to China led to an agreement whereby the United States recognized Taiwan as part of China and agreed to withdraw American troops from the island. China in turn promised to use peaceful means to resolve the Taiwan question and opened diplomatic relations with the United States. This arrangement provided the basis for subsequent economic, political, and strategic cooperation.[17]

Quid pro quos are an obvious first step because they have the potential to build trust and convey commitments to seek further agreement. They also have the advantage of addressing substantive or symbolic issues that have poisoned relations in the past. Sometimes there is the possibility of a trade-off here. Israel withdrew from the Sinai, a costly substantive concession, in return for a symbolic one—recognition—that might later be withdrawn. The United States made a substantive concession to China—the promise to withdraw troops—in return for two symbolic ones: the promise not to use force against Taiwan as long as it did not declare independence, and the establishment of diplomatic relations. As with unilateral steps toward accommodation, quid pro quos are more credible if they are public, irrevocable, and costly.

Taiwan

We now turn to the four areas of tension that we identified at the beginning of this chapter. The first of these is the status of Taiwan. It has been a bone of contention between China and the United States since the end of the Chinese Civil War of 1946–49 and the proclamation of the People's Republic.

The Nature of the Dispute

The People's Republic has always insisted that Taiwan is an integral part of China. The Kuomintang, the Chinese nationalists, sought refuge in Taiwan after losing control of the mainland and carried on with the Republic of China (ROC) government. The Truman administration continued to recognize the ROC government in Taiwan. Fearful of being drawn into a protracted Chinese civil war, however, it had little intention of defending Taiwan against PRC attacks. But once the Korean War began, the Truman administration rediscovered Taiwan's strategic value, interposed the Seventh Fleet in the straits between Taiwan and the mainland, and signed a mutual defense treaty with the ROC in 1954.

Two decades later the Nixon administration, eager to end the war in Vietnam and cement a tacit alliance with the PRC against the Soviet Union, reassessed the strategic balance and improved relations with Beijing at Taipei's expense. In the famous Shanghai Communiqué of February 1972, signed at the conclusion of President Nixon's historic visit to China, the United States acknowledged the Chinese position that "there is but one China and that Taiwan is a part of China," an acknowledgment reaffirmed in the Joint Communiqué on the Establishment of Diplomatic Relations in January 1979 and the Joint Communiqué of August 1982 on the issue of US arms sales to Taiwan.[18]

Acknowledgment is not the same as endorsement, and there is a crucial difference between Washington's "one China" policy and Beijing's "one China" principle. Whereas Beijing claims Taiwan as a part of China whose sole legal government is the PRC, Washington acknowledges this position but has "*not* itself agreed to this position."[19] Believing that the sovereign status of Taiwan is yet to be determined, the United States neither confirms nor denies Taiwan's sovereignty.[20] In his 1982 "Six Reassurances" to Taiwan, President Ronald Reagan pledged that the United States would not formally recognize Chinese sovereignty over Taiwan as the sovereignty of Taiwan was a question to be decided peacefully by the Chinese themselves.[21]

Beijing insists on honoring the three PRC-US joint communiqués of 1972, 1979, and 1982 as the foundation for conducting bilateral relations and policies toward Taiwan. Washington, especially when under Republican administrations, hews more closely to the Taiwan Relations Act of 1979 and Reagan's Six Reassurances. Maintaining a continuing, if weakened and nonbinding security commitment to Taiwan as compensation for its loss of official ties, the Taiwan Relations Act requires the United States "to consider any effort to determine the future of Taiwan by other than peaceful means, including by boycotts or embargoes, a threat to the peace and security of the Western Pacific area and of grave concern to the United States."[22] It authorizes Washington "to provide Taiwan with arms of a defensive character" and "to maintain the capacity of the United States to resist any resort to force or other forms of coercion that would jeopardize the security, or the social or economic system, of the people on Taiwan."[23]

American arms sales to Taiwan have been a persistent irritant in US-China relations. So too has the prospect of US defense of Taiwan in the event of a PRC attack. China and the United States nearly came to blows in the Taiwan Strait crises of 1954–55, 1958, and 1995–96.[24] They could do so again, especially if they fail to moderate their mutual deterrence strategies by effective reassurance and clever diplomacy. Nancy Bernkopf Tucker and Bonnie Glaser rightly warn, "Taiwan remains the single issue which could spark war between the United States and the People's Republic of China, a war that might quickly go nuclear but would be devastating even were it to remain conventional."[25]

Different understandings of the nature of the Taiwan issue between Beijing and Washington affect their divergent approaches to it. Regarding Taiwan as part of its sovereign territory and asserting that it replaced the ROC as the sole legal government of China in 1949, the PRC deplores US security assistance to Taiwan as interference in its domestic affairs and a critical impediment to its goal of cross-Strait unification. China is also suspicious of the US intention of containing or at least hampering China's rise and keeping it weak and divided by supporting Taiwanese separatism.[26] The United States, on the other hand, insists on a peaceful resolution of cross-Strait hostility and fears that a reduction of its arms sales and a weakening of its security commitment to Taiwan may tempt Beijing's use of force and defeat its goal of regional peace.[27] In the mainstream US view, "arms sales help Taiwan defend itself, strengthen morale among Taiwan's population, deter Beijing, insure Taipei has the confidence to negotiate with China, and that—if talks go wrong—Taiwan could fight until US forces arrived."[28]

The Debate over Arms Sales

In the face of raucous Chinese protests and the changing balance of power moving in China's favor, some US analysts have suggested reviewing the Taiwan Relations Act, terminating the arms sales, and reducing or renouncing US security commitments to Taiwan in a unilateral concession to reassure Beijing of Washington's benign intentions and reset the US-China relationship on a heathier footing.[29] This would constitute reassurance through irrevocable commitment and would doubtless delight Beijing. However, this would not be the best kind of reassurance. Irrevocable commitment is risky because concessions may be exploited to further expansive ends—or may be perceived to be. This makes initiating leaders vulnerable to criticisms and challenges from key domestic and foreign constituencies, which in turn can ratchet up the conflict. Irrevocable commitment must be accompanied by a credible commitment from the other party not to exploit the concession, and better yet, to reciprocate in some fashion.

A US concession of ending its defense commitment to Taiwan would mean abandoning deterrence as a strategy for managing cross-Strait tensions. It is not feasible in the current environment. To make it feasible and useful, China would have to demonstrate strategic self-restraint and make a credible commitment to keep Taiwan's political system intact after unification. It has sought to convey such a commitment through the "one country, two systems" proposal since the 1980s. The implementation of this formula in Hong Kong after the former British colony's reversion to China in 1997, however, has reduced its credibility and appeal because of a widespread perception in Taiwan and the United States that it is eroding Hong Kong's autonomy.[30]

Reassurance through Trade-offs and Reciprocity

As irrevocable commitment is politically impractical and of uncertain value in Sino-American relations, the fallback policy is that of reassurance through trade-offs. In the case of Taiwan this would require a Beijing-Taipei-Washington trilateral quid pro quo. Washington has been unwilling to abandon Taiwan because it does not trust Beijing's promise to uphold Taiwan's security and autonomy, and nor does Taipei. Beijing would need to make a credible commitment to Taiwan's security and autonomy to reassure both Taipei and Washington. No such commitment would be credible if Beijing continues to subvert Hong Kong's autonomy under the "one country, two systems" formula. It needs to either shore up the viability of that formula by fixing its problems or abandon it and advance a new proposal tailored for Taiwan.

From Beijing's perspective, its great fear is Taiwan's permanent political separation from the mainland and creeping moves toward independence.[31] These prospects would defeat the PRC's goal of national unification and call into question the legitimacy of the CCP's rule of China, or at least its competence in a vital area of national policy. Taipei in turn would need to reassure Beijing by renouncing the goal of de jure independence and declaring itself amenable to unification on terms acceptable to both sides. Such cross-Strait mutual reassurance would meet the US insistence that the status of Taiwan be resolved in a peaceful manner by both sides of the Taiwan Strait.

In the interim, Washington needs a new declaratory policy to reassure Beijing that its arms sales are contingent upon the dynamics of cross-Strait relations. It should promise to reduce and eventually cease these sales to the extent that Beijing-Taipei relations improve and also declare its defense commitment conditional upon Taipei's restraint in moving toward independence. This would represent a significant elaboration of and improvement upon the US-PRC joint communiqués of August 1982, in which the United States pledges to "reduce gradually its sales of arms to Taiwan, leading over a period of time to a final resolution."[32] As every successive US administration since Jimmy Carter has sold arms to Taiwan, China has accused the United States of reneging on this pledge. Washington insists that its willingness to reduce arms sales is conditioned upon the mainland's continued commitment to a peaceful resolution of its differences with Taiwan, and since Beijing has not renounced the use of force but has increased its threat to Taiwan, the United States has no obligation to cease arms sales.[33]

Such wrangling might be reduced if Washington relaxes the condition of Beijing's continued commitment to a peaceful resolution by reframing it as "continued improvement of cross-Strait relations," including the progressive reduction of a PRC military threat to Taiwan. The current condition of a peaceful resolution is tantamount to asking for Beijing's renunciation of the use of force, a highly unlikely concession at this stage. Even if Taipei strives to reassure Beijing about not declaring independence, in the absence of a unification process, Beijing will want to keep the option of deterrence for fear that Taipei may manipulate its reassurance to serve other separatist aims.[34] Any US attempt to compel China to drop the essential elements of its long-standing policy—especially the "one China" principle and the option of force—would sound alarms in Beijing and could result in unnecessary conflict.[35]

Continued improvement of cross-Strait relations, including but not limited to the military dimension, is a more realistic and productive criterion for assessing arms sales. Washington could propose to Beijing that it will restrict its arms sales to Taipei if Beijing can place verifiable limits on its military production and deployments against Taiwan and credibly commit not to use force except in the extreme cases of Taipei's declaration of de jure independence or a significant enhancement of the US-Taiwan security relationship, such as the deployment of US forces on the island.[36] Such a move would signal a positive US intention while incentivizing Beijing to improve relations with Taipei.

A declaration linking its defense commitment to Taipei's restraint on independence would partially resolve America's long-standing "strategic ambiguity" over the prospect of its intervention in a Taiwan conflict.[37] It would reassure Beijing because it provides a new constraint on Taiwan's independence; it would not harm Taipei since Washington has long declared its opposition to Taiwan's independence.[38] Indeed Washington could go one extra step by reassuring Beijing that Taiwan's independence will not be realized without its consent and that it will welcome unification peacefully and voluntarily achieved by both sides.[39] This would not be a radical move for Washington since its Taiwan policy has always been about a peaceful process of settlement between Beijing and Taipei, not any particular outcome of that process.[40] If cross-Strait relations stabilize and improve in the longer term as a result of trilateral reassurance, political and military reconciliation between Beijing and Taipei would make it possible for Washington to reduce or discontinue arms sales, which would remove a major source of tension in Sino-American relations.

These trade-offs give some indication of how the strategy of reassurance might be used to defuse tension in the Taiwan Strait and promote a peaceful resolution. It is unlikely to result in a grand bargain given the degree of mistrust and the complexities in devising and gaining acceptance of such proposals. More feasible is a reciprocal process in the form of contingent, sequential trade-offs and agreements among the three parties through a series of interlocking agreements. Measured success could sustain the momentum of reassurance.[41]

Obstacles on All Sides

Such a process would have to overcome daunting obstacles on all sides. It would be a formidable shift for Beijing to commit itself to Taiwan's security and autonomy, and equally difficult to make such a commitment credible to Taipei and Washington. Presently China's relentless military buildup, presumably aimed at deterring Taiwan from declaring de jure independence and the United States from intervening in any attempt at forceful unification, is making Taiwan more insecure and the United States more suspicious. Even while pursuing a rapprochement with the moderate Ma Ying-jeou administration from 2008 to 2016, its missile deployments opposite Taiwan increased to more than 1,500.[42] Since the independence-leaning Tsai Ing-wen administration took office in May 2016, Beijing has ratcheted up military pressure with periodic "island-encircling" patrols.[43] China's military policy works against the peaceful attainment of goals that would make its deterrence unnecessary.

On the political side, China's offer of the "one country, two systems" formula for unification, reiterated by President Xi Jinping in a prominent January 2019 speech, has virtually no appeal to the Taiwanese.[44] It would reduce the island to the status of a province of the PRC and compromise its cherished autonomy, not to mention Taipei's claim that the ROC government is sovereign in its own right.[45] Thus a first step for reassurance on the Chinese side would be to adjust its political and military policies toward Taiwan by offering a more attractive unification proposal and by reducing its military threat to Taiwan. The latter could be accomplished through unilateral confidence-building measures or jointly negotiated arms control. Indeed reducing Taiwan's perception of the PRC military threat is the surest way to undercut the basis of US arms sales. These momentous policy shifts could be implemented only by a leadership that displayed creativity and flexibility as well as the political will to construct a new national consensus on Taiwan.

For Taiwan, a credible commitment to renounce de jure independence would be difficult. The Democratic Progressive Party (DPP), a major political party that has now governed Taiwan twice through the Chen Shui-bian administration of 2000–2008 and the Tsai administration after 2016, has long made its aspiration for independence known.[46] Tsai is more restrained and skillful in her independence agenda than was Chen, whose provocations irked not only Beijing but also Washington. She has nevertheless refused to acknowledge the so-called 1992 consensus, which Beijing has demanded as the absolute basis for cross-Strait dialogue: Taiwan must acknowledge that it and the mainland belong to a single China, even if they agree to disagree about what exactly "China" means.[47] Growing identity politics on Taiwan provide a sizable base for independence activists.[48] Both the DPP and the traditionally pro-unification Kuomintang insist on the ROC on Taiwan as an independent, sovereign country. Both would demand a more flexible unification model from the PRC than the narrow "one country, two systems" formula if unification were to ever occur.[49] Although the

Kuomintang's Ma Ying-jeou administration pledged "no independence," it was no more open to unification than the DPP.[50]

In the United States conservative strategists suspicious of China's hegemonic intentions would be loath to give up Taiwan as a strategic bulwark against China's expansion in the Western Pacific. They were influential in the Trump administration, where John Bolton, Trump's third national security advisor, and Randall Schriver, assistant secretary of defense for Asian and Pacific security affairs from 2018 to 2019, advocated a pro-Taiwan stance. Other influential voices assert that Taiwan needs to "remain in the hands of a friendly government."[51] Meanwhile the Taiwan Relations Act and Taiwan's democratization provide both legal and moral justifications for helping a democratic Taiwan against an authoritarian PRC.

These difficulties in the way of trilateral reassurance are severe but not impossible to overcome. Forgoing reassurance would mean condemning cross-Strait relations to political stalemate and military uncertainty, and with it the ever-present possibility of a catastrophic war. Economic interdependence cannot in itself overcome political deadlock. It might even create new controversies of dependency on the mainland and distribution of benefits in Taiwan. The Ma administration's economic activism but political lethargy toward Beijing have already demonstrated this possibility. It is worth bearing in mind that although China and the United States differ on many points, they share a common preference for resolving the Taiwan issue peacefully.[52] A solution will take time, but the odds of a such an outcome would increase significantly if China and the United States were able to reassure one another in other problem areas.

North Korea
The Failure of Diplomacy

The other major flashpoint in Sino-American relations is North Korea. Tensions have periodically been acute between the two Koreas and between North Korea and the United States. Tensions were heightened following North Korea's efforts to build nuclear weapons and missiles to deliver against South Korea, Japan, and the United States. In 2017 Trump threatened to "totally destroy North Korea" and its "short and fat" leader Kim Jong Un, whom he repeatedly referred to as "rocket man."[53]

North Korea's interest in nuclear weapons dates back to the Cold War. The current cycle of crisis started in 1992, when Pyongyang was caught pursuing a plutonium-based nuclear weapons program.[54] During the first crisis, 1992–94, the Clinton administration considered surgical strikes against its nuclear facilities, but tensions eased due to former president Carter's personal diplomacy in Pyongyang. In the Agreed Framework of October 1994, North Korea promised to freeze and eventually dismantle its nuclear weapons program in return for two light-water reactors, the interim supply of heavy fuel oil, some relaxation of sanctions, and progress in normalizing relations with the United States. The Agreement was never implemented because Washington suspected Pyongyang of cheating at an underground nuclear facility in 1999. For its part, the Clinton administration delayed oil delivery, easing of sanctions, and the construction of the light-water reactor. Both sides lost faith in each other and the Agreement.

The George W. Bush administration charged the Clinton administration with appeasing North Korea and, influenced by neoconservative hawks, engaged in rhetoric that aggravated tensions. President Bush was personally repelled by the North Korean leader Kim Jong-Il, whom he regarded as an evil tyrant. Bush dismissed negotiations with "rogue regimes" like North Korea as rewarding bad behavior and thus immoral. In the aftermath of the September 11, 2001, terrorist attacks, he labeled North Korea a member of the "axis of evil." This was the context in which the second nuclear crisis broke out, in October 2002. Washington confronted Pyongyang with alleged evidence of its clandestine uranium enrichment program. The Bush administration refused to engage in meaningful bilateral negotiations despite repeated North Korean appeals for talks. Instead it adopted preemption as a counterproliferation strategy and considered pressure rather than inducement the key to moderating North Korea.

China now found itself caught in the middle by Pyongyang's escalation and Washington's intransigence. In August 2003 Beijing brokered the Six Party Talks among China, South Korea, Japan, Russia, the United States, and North Korea in the hope of meaningful negotiations. The talks were beset by a coordination problem common to multilateral negotiations: everyone favored different approaches. Washington wanted to eliminate Pyongyang's nuclear weapons program and punish it for violating previous agreements. Beijing wanted to preserve peace and stability above all else and opposed unilateral US actions.[55] Two years of painstaking negotiations produced the landmark Joint Statement of September 2005. It committed the six parties to a series of quid pro quos, including a North Korean promise to dismantle the nuclear weapons program in return for security guarantees, future steps toward normalization, and economic assistance.

Now the commitment problem loomed large. Bush administration hawks added a unilateral US statement to the Joint Statement. Its strong language contravened the spirit of the Joint Statement and raised Pyongyang's doubts about US sincerity.[56] After the Six Party Talks produced a pair of implementation agreements in February and October 2007 that outlined a road map for denuclearization, North Korea experienced additional frustration with the slow pace of promised energy aid and lifting of sanctions. The United States maintained its skepticism about North Korea's commitment to full denuclearization.

Near the end of his second term, Bush had all but abandoned his earlier hawkish policy. In December 2007, in a letter to Kim, he offered full normalization of diplomatic relations in return for denuclearization.[57] By this time, however, Pyongyang had apparently decided to keep part of its nuclear weapons program whatever the outcome of the talks. To be fair, the regime may never have had an intention to denuclearize totally. If it did, its extreme mistrust of the United States, perceived lack of commitment, and the frightening lesson of the Iraq War in which America willfully invaded a country not yet possessing nuclear weapons, must also have strengthened Pyongyang's determination to maintain a nuclear deterrent. It is also possible that Kim's deteriorating health in August 2008, a crucial time when verification negotiations were under way, crippled diplomacy and set off a succession struggle that strengthened the hand of hardliners intent on keeping the weapons.[58] The Six Party Talks collapsed with the failure of verification negotiations in 2008.

The Obama administration pursued an open engagement strategy, beginning with the unprecedented appointment of ambassadorial-rank special envoys for North Korea. Seeing its goodwill snubbed by a missile test in April 2009 and a second nuclear test in May, it changed its approach to "strategic patience," combining punitive sanctions and prospective inducements. Neither deterred nor lured, North Korea accelerated its weapons program by conducting three more nuclear weapons tests and launching longer-range road-mobile and submarine-based missiles. By the end of his two terms in office, Obama realized that strategic patience had resulted in much greater North Korean capabilities, estimated at ten or more nuclear weapons. Implicitly acknowledging a colossal failure of American diplomacy across three administrations, outgoing officials advised the incoming Trump administration that North Korea represented the biggest national security threat to the United States.

President Trump took Obama's warning to heart. Throughout 2017, his first year in office, he identified North Korea as the greatest security threat and abandoned strategic patience in favor of a strategy of "maximum pressure" through diplomatic and economic sanctions. Despite his threats to destroy North Korea, Trump, like the pragmatic Obama, was open to engagement from the beginning.[59] He praised Kim as "a pretty smart cookie" and repeatedly announced his intention to make a deal.[60]

Trump's deal-making vanity helps to explain his acceptance of an invitation from Kim Jong-un, the North Korean leader since 2012, to a summit meeting. Their encounter in Singapore in June 2018 was historic in that it was the first time a sitting American president had met with a North Korean leader. Trump agreed to halt US–South Korean military exercises but refused to consider reducing the number of American troops in South Korea. The joint statement at the summit called for the "complete denuclearization" of the Korean Peninsula, without providing a timeline or details about how the North would go about relinquishing its weapons.[61] These ambiguities hampered progress, prompting two further Trump-Kim summits in February and June 2019.[62] As we write in September 2019, attention is focused on Kim's commitment to abandon completely North Korea's nuclear and missile programs. Kim demands a reciprocal, step-by-step process of mutual concessions. American officials worry that he may be using negotiation to ease sanctions in return for a freeze—not dismantlement—of his nuclear weapons programs. They demand that North Korea move quickly toward denuclearization by submitting an inventory of its nuclear weapons and fissile materials.

The Coordination Problem

Any effective strategy of reassurance must address the twin problems of coordination and commitment. The respective goals of the United States and China in resolving the crisis have not fundamentally changed in the past twenty years. Washington continues to prioritize denuclearization and nonproliferation. The Trump administration, pointing out that over 80 percent of North Korean trade goes through China, urged Beijing to curtail and cut oil and other shipments to that country. In a pithy three-sentence statement, China insists on the twin goals of denuclearization and regional peace and stability and prefers dialogue and consultation to coercion and conflict.[63] In principle, Beijing is committed to denuclearization even if it involves some destabilization of North Korea. In practice, China has valued the stability of the Korean Peninsula more than denuclearization for a multitude of historical, political, and economic reasons ranging from the profound to the parochial.[64]

China has made clear its bottom line: whatever the approach to the crisis, it should not result in major instability or military conflict. There should be no war and no chaos (*bu sheng zhan, bu sheng luan*).[65] Beijing wants to maintain a minimum degree of stability on the Korean Peninsula and keep North Korea a friend, however strained that friendship may be. In the conventional Chinese view a destabilized or hostile North Korea portends serious trouble. A desperate North Korea might initiate military action against South Korea, reigniting the Korean War. Alternatively, regime collapse could unleash a flood of refugees on the Chinese border and result in a unified Korean Peninsula under the control of the US–South Korea alliance. This is an outcome Beijing averted during the Korean War at the cost of close to one million casualties. A hostile North Korea can wreak havoc now that it has developed nuclear-capable missiles that can be trained on China. A friendly or at least deferential North Korea, the conventional wisdom goes, can serve as a strategic buffer against American forces based in South Korea. In response to the question of whether China would cut off oil supplies to North Korea under American pressure, Chinese elites uniformly answer no, for that would undermine the goal of stability.[66] The Chinese scholar Shi Yinhong warns that, pressed too hard, Beijing could flip the other way, deciding that Washington is the real threat to stability on the Peninsula, and oppose it more strongly.[67]

The only way to resolve this problem of coordination is for the United States and China to bring their goals into convergence on the basis of an enlightened understanding of their respective national interests. The two countries share the goal of denuclearization, but each attaches a different priority to it. Asking the United States to emphasize Peninsula stability over denuclearization would mean the abandonment of denuclearization as a goal altogether, with the momentous consequences for the nuclear nonproliferation regime. This is not in China's interest either and would be damaging to regional security. China needs to reassure the United States and other countries in the region that it is serious about denuclearization. To take this step it has to be convinced that denuclearization will not destabilize North Korea.

For Chinese conservatives wedded to anti-Americanism, cooperating with Washington to punish Pyongyang would amount to collaboration with a capitalist rival and betrayal of the communist cause. Internal discussions about North Korea are now among the most publicly visible, intellectually robust, politically sensitive, and strategically consequential of all Chinese policy debates. The leadership needs to rank-order its interests when it comes to North Korea.

We side with an emerging consensus among sophisticated Chinese strategists and foreign policy advisors that denuclearization serves China's fundamental interests.[68] A fully nuclear North Korea would be an even more dangerous actor. It could trigger a "nuclear domino effect" in East Asia by spooking South Korea, Japan, and even Taiwan, encouraging them to seek nuclear weapons; they are all latent nuclear powers.[69] It could also lead to a considerable tightening of the US–South Korea and US-Japan alliances, possibly their merging into a trilateral US–South Korea–Japan alliance. This could be followed by a new regional missile defense system eroding China's strategic deterrence. The costs to Chinese security, the Sino-American relationship, and regional stability would be exorbitant.

The Commitment Problem

The commitment problem is hard to overcome. Ever since the 1994 Agreed Framework, the United States has tried to reassure North Korea that it is not committed to regime change or economic strangulation. The 2005 Joint Statement of the Six Party Talks represents the climax of such reassurance: Washington promised to guarantee Pyongyang's security, normalize political relations, and provide economic assistance as long as Pyongyang demonstrated its commitment to full denuclearization. The Obama administration even offered to negotiate normalization and a peace treaty without the long-standing precondition that Pyongyang first take steps to curtail its nuclear arsenal.[70] Rex Tillerson, Trump's first secretary of state, declared that the United States does not seek regime change or an accelerated reunification of the Korean Peninsula.[71] However, twenty years of diplomatic failure and broken promises, exacerbated by periodic calls of military action from hawks, have significantly reduced the credibility of US commitments. Trump veered from military threats to diplomatic chumminess in 2018, but Kim and his advisors might well have doubted his credibility in view of his boorish impulsiveness.

North Korea is even more of a puzzle. Before 2018 it seemed all but certain that it had moved away from accommodation. Its commitment to denuclearize might have been more or less serious before the collapse of the Six Party Talks in 2008. But in 2013 it rolled out the *byungjin* line, which emphasized the simultaneous pursuit of economic development and nuclear weapons. The Kim regime enshrined the pursuit of nuclear weapons in its constitution, thus entrenching its resolve to achieving the status of a full nuclear weapons state.[72] But in April 2018 Kim Jong-un declared that *byungjin* was over and that all efforts would now go to "socialist economic construction." Perhaps he was truly different from his father, Kim Jong-il, who used negotiation to stall for time. John Delury argues that Kim Jong-un fits the model of an East Asian strongman who sets his country on the path of economic development.[73] Many Americans, recalling North Korea's failure to honor commitments in the past, remain unconvinced.

Reassurance through Irrevocable Commitment

North Korea will accept at most a freeze—not complete denuclearization.[74] How might this be achieved?

At the outset Washington needs to address relevant Chinese concerns, the two most significant being the risk of an inadvertent war and how Washington might act jointly with South Korea against the North. The United States must recognize China's concern for at least minimum stability on the Korean Peninsula and its more general interest in the strategic order in Northeast Asia. The United States needs to convince China that it will not unleash a unilateral preemptive or preventive war against North Korea.[75] It needs to make a credible commitment that can alleviate China's profound and historical concern about Korea, rooted as it is in the belief that stability on the Korean Peninsula is essential to Chinese security. An irrevocable commitment by the United States to withdraw troops from South Korea if China delivers North Korean denuclearization would go a long way to addressing its concern and making Beijing more willing to cooperate with the United States.[76]

China might offer a kind of "regime security assurance" by committing itself to protect the North Korean regime centered on the Kim family in return for denuclearization. North Korea may have wanted this type of reassurance from the United States, which, for political and ideological reasons, is very difficult for Washington to contemplate.[77] China, however, is already positioned to make such an offer by virtue of the 1961 Sino–North Korean alliance treaty. The treaty codifies a de facto Chinese security guarantee to North Korea, and Beijing can clarify the new commitment of regime security by amending its clauses. Although not essential, Chinese reassurance may go one extra step by offering extended deterrence to North Korea in the case of a US invasion or preemptive strike.[78]

North Korea is China's only treaty ally in the world today, a Cold War left-over that often embarrasses Beijing. A regime security assurance would constitute Chinese reassurance to North Korea through an irrevocable commitment and thus a tightening of the alliance. Those Chinese elites who are repelled by North Korea's past intransigence and affronts would find it objectionable. Yet a closer alliance could be a counterintuitive mechanism for controlling a recalcitrant ally if it makes possible denuclearization and stability.[79] A closer alliance has many potential advantages, among them allaying conservative grievances about abandoning North Korea, satisfying the policy bottom line of maintaining peninsular stability, avoiding the risk of turning North Korea into a hostile country, increasing Chinese influence and leverage over Pyongyang, and burnishing China's reputation as a reliable and responsible ally. The long existence of the Sino–North Korean alliance, the nature of China's authoritarian political system nominally sharing the same communist ideology with North Korea, and the Chinese fear of North Korean collapse give credibility to such a commitment—a level of credibility impossible for the United States to attain.

A parallel irrevocable commitment–based reassurance from the United States to China and from China to North Korea is an elegant, although by no means easy solution to the North Korean nuclear weapons and missile crisis. The principal obstacles are American strategic conservatism and Chinese elites' mistrust of American intentions, a mistrust now aggravated by the deployment of the Terminal High Altitude Area Defense missile defense system in South Korea. American hawks would almost certainly criticize the withdrawal of US troops from South Korea after denuclearization as too big a concession to China. Chinese conservatives may construe such an offer as an American ruse. This problem, however, can be overcome by strong and enlightened leadership on both sides.

The main obstacles China faces in adopting such a policy of reassurance are its elites' strategic conservatism and a barely concealed North Korean mistrust of Chinese intentions. The latter is exacerbated by Pyongyang's discontent with its dependence on China for survival and its perception of Chinese heavy-handedness.[80] China has developed a strong aversion to alliance in general as a result of the violent unraveling of the Sino-Soviet alliance during the Cold War. The alliance with North Korea is an anomaly in contemporary Chinese foreign policy. Beijing fears overcommitment and entrapment in a tight alliance with a willful Pyongyang. On the North Korean side, mistrust of China was transmuted, for a time, from private grumbling to public criticism. In 2017, when Beijing ratcheted up sanctions, Pyongyang accused it of "mean behavior" and "dancing to the tune of the United States" and warned it of "catastrophic consequences for their relationship."[81] Yet since March 2018, mainly because of the Trump-Kim summit, the relationship has undergone some improvement. Between March 2018 and January 2019 Kim traveled four times to China to meet with President Xi; Xi reciprocated with his first state visit to North Korea in June 2019, the first visit by a Chinese leader in fourteen years.[82] Relationship management will require Chinese strategic wisdom and diplomatic skill. And reassurance through a new commitment in a tightened alliance may paradoxically help China to ease North Korean mistrust by addressing the Kim regime's real concerns and establishing more authoritative controls over it.[83] This would then allay China's worry that an ironclad regime security guarantee might give Pyongyang a license for irresponsible behavior.

Maritime Disputes and Tensions

Maritime tensions in East Asia involving China and the United States operate at three levels: disputes about territorial sovereignty and maritime rights between China and its neighbors; disagreements over freedom of the seas, especially concerning US military activities in China's exclusive economic zones (EEZs) and the South China Sea; and geopolitical competition between an established and a rising power. Each level impinges on a core aspect of the Asian maritime order critical to the role of the United States in the region. Recent Chinese approaches to sovereignty disputes, perceived as coercive by the United States and its allies, raise the question of Beijing's commitment to their peaceful resolution in a rules-based order. They also pose challenges to the plausibility and credibility of US security commitments to its Asian allies. Disputes over freedom of military action risk upending the regional security order that the United States has dominated since the end of the Second World War. Maritime strategic competition may bring that dominance to an end. Rising tensions in these areas will harden Sino-American competition in maritime Asia, produce war-threatening incidents and miscalculations, and generate instability and turmoil in regional security.

Sovereignty Disputes

China has disputes with Japan over the sovereignty of the Diaoyu/Senkaku Islands in the East China Sea and with the Philippines, Vietnam, Malaysia, Brunei, and Taiwan over the sovereignty of South China Sea islands. Each of these sovereignty disputes in turn has significant implications for the distribution of maritime rights, including resources extraction and military activities. The US position on these disputes is principled neutrality: it takes no position on the competing claims but supports the principle that disputes should be resolved peacefully, without coercion, intimidation, threats, or the use of force, and in a manner consistent with international law.[84] China's policy, consistently maintained since the late 1970s and reiterated by a major speech that President Xi gave in July 2013, asserts Chinese sovereignty over the islands but proposes to shelve the disputes in order to pursue common development with other claimant countries.[85]

The United States and China have no territorial disputes of their own but differ in their interpretations of and approaches to disputes between China and its neighbors. Similar to its Taiwan policy, the United States stresses a peaceful process of disputes settlement without staking out a firm position on the merits of the competing claims or any particular outcome of the disputes. But just as in cross-Strait relations, Beijing accuses Washington of hypocrisy and suspects its real intention is siding with other claimant states against China. As we showed in Chapter 3, Chinese elites fault the Obama administration's intervention in the South China Sea disputes and its Asian rebalance strategy for aggravating regional territorial disputes. They attribute Asian maritime tension to the rebalance strategy while minimizing the role of Chinese policy.[86] American elites, on the other hand, criticize Chinese of coercion toward its neighbors and lack of a serious commitment to a peaceful resolution of the disputes.[87] While Beijing emphasizes its peaceful intention, as with Taiwan, it has never renounced its possible use of force to resolve the conflict to its satisfaction. China's preference for peace, says Xi, does not mean the abandonment of legitimate interests, much less the sacrifice of core interests.[88]

The possibility of China's resort to force is unsettling for Washington. Not only would this affect peace and stability in East Asia; it would also pose major strategic dilemmas for Washington. Two of its treaty allies, Japan and the Philippines, are directly, and sometimes dangerously, embroiled in disputes with China. America's security commitments to Japan are codified in the 1960 US-Japan treaty, and both the Obama and Trump administrations reaffirmed their defense commitment to the Diaoyu/Senkaku Islands. The 1951 US-Philippines treaty commits both parties to meet common dangers in case of "an armed attack in the Pacific Area on either of the Parties."[89] The Obama administration refrained from pledging defense of maritime areas disputed between the Philippines and China, such as the potentially explosive Scarborough Shoal. The Trump administration scaled up the American commitment. In March 2019 Mike Pompeo, Trump's second secretary of state, declared during a visit to the Philippines, "Any armed attack on Philippine forces, aircraft, or public vessels in the South China Sea will trigger mutual defense obligations under Article 4 of our mutual defense treaty."[90] Miscalculation by either side, not to mention by both sides, could lead them into a serious crisis, if not to war.

A no less agonizing row is over the role of international law in disputes settlement. The United States criticizes China for refusing to clarify its legal claims in the South China Sea and for failing to comply with the United Nations Convention on the Law of the Sea (UNCLOS). It supports the Philippines v. China arbitration ruling of July 2016 as the new legal framework that should govern the bilateral disputes between these two countries and should also find wider applications in the region. Contending that UNCLOS forms only part of the international maritime legal regime, Beijing argues that its claims are also based on customary international law and historic rights and practices not incorporated by UNCLOS. It vehemently opposes the July 2016 arbitration ruling, berating it as a US-backed plot to wipe out Chinese rights in the South China Sea.[91]

The satisfactory and defensible way to manage and resolve Asian maritime territorial disputes is for the states involved to clarify their claims, bring them into line with prevailing international law and norms, and work toward a negotiated settlement based on fair and reciprocal compromise. China has partially clarified its legal claims in the South China Sea but has deliberately maintained some ambiguity in order to preserve diplomatic flexibility and bargaining leverage in future negotiations.[92] In a July 2016 statement, Beijing claims sovereignty over all South China Sea islands; the internal waters, territorial seas, and contiguous zones based on these islands; any EEZ and continental shelf based on these islands; and historic rights.[93] This statement deploys internationally recognized concepts under the UNCLOS framework, suggesting an effort to enhance legal clarity. Ambiguities nevertheless remain. Does the term "islands" meet the definition of an island given in Article 121 of UNCLOS that enables claim to an EEZ and a continental shelf in addition to territorial sea and a contiguous zone? Or is the term so loosely used that it also includes "low-tide elevations," which cannot claim territorial sovereignty under UNCLOS unless they are within twelve nautical miles of an island? In claiming the various maritime rights, China leaves the geographical scope of these rights entirely undefined. And on the controversial issue of historic rights, China fails to delimit the geographical boundary of such rights or specify their content.[94]

China is both unwilling and unable to be completely clear about its claims, as a national consensus on Chinese claims to the South China Sea is still being debated inside the country.[95] Beijing should reassure regional countries and the United States by rejecting the contentious U-shaped line as a national boundary that would make the 85 percent of the South China Sea enclosed by it China's internal waters under its exclusive sovereign control and jurisdiction.[96] Even so, China's vast claims to maritime rights based on sovereignty over all of the islands would still make its neighbors nervous, fearing that a powerful but impatient China might resort to force to realize these interests.

China would still need to impart credibility to any promises of restraint in the South China Sea. This could be accomplished through an irrevocable commitment to peaceful management and settlement of disputes. It could take the form of a binding code of conduct to be negotiated between China and the ten ASEAN member states, which began a consultation process in 2017. Having long sought such a commitment from China, the United States should pledge full support for diplomatic efforts between China and its neighbors, whether bilateral or multilateral, to achieve a peaceful settlement. It should no longer take advantage of the disputes to oppose China for its own strategic purposes such as preserving maritime dominance, as Chinese elites suspect.[97]

Chinese approaches to the legal and diplomatic aspects of the East and South China seas disputes are different. In the East China Sea, China asserts its claims to the Diaoyu/Senkaku Islands and hounds Japan for refusing to even acknowledge the existence of the territorial dispute. Since 2012 Beijing has adopted a coercive strategy of asserting administrative control by dispatching coast guard and naval vessels to the area, creating risks of maritime incidents escalating into conflicts.

Peaceful resolution of the dispute requires effective reassurance and diplomacy between Beijing and Tokyo. Washington can contribute given its leverage in the US-Japan alliance relationship. Taking no position on the sovereignty of the Diaoyu/Senkaku Islands, the United States nevertheless recognizes Japan's jurisdiction over them and extends its security commitment on that basis. In 1971, when the Nixon administration was deliberating a position on the islands, Kissinger considered the State Department's recommendation that the United States remain neutral on sovereignty while returning administrative rights to Japan nonsensical and demanded a more neutral position. Even the State Department officials who made this recommendation privately recognized the superiority of Taiwan's—and thus China's—claims. They proposed the contradictory position of neutrality on sovereignty but support for Japanese jurisdiction only because of the bureaucratic need to complete the Okinawa reversion treaty then under negotiation and the strategic need to keep Japan as an ally.[98]

The United States can reassure China of its constructive role in the Sino-Japanese dispute by nudging Japan to acknowledge the existence of the sovereignty dispute and start negotiations with China. It may further propose a quid pro quo between Beijing and Tokyo to settle both the sovereignty dispute and the history issue—the other festering wound that has damaged the Sino-Japanese relationship since the 1990s.[99] Japan could offer a concession of Chinese sovereignty in return for a Chinese settlement of the history issue. To allay Japanese concerns about resources and security, China can propose to share equitably resources in the area in conjunction with their negotiation over continental shelf and maritime delimitation in the East China Sea and to impose limits on its military deployments around the islands. To ease both countries' concerns, they could include in any treaty settling the sovereignty dispute a final Japanese apology of its invasion of China in the spirit of the 1995 apology offered by Prime Minister Tomiichi Murayama. China in return could acknowledge this apology as ending their historical dispute. The resolution of these two conflicts would not only constitute a historic breakthrough in Sino-Japanese relations but herald a new era of East Asian peace and stability.

In encouraging Japan to make such concessions, the United States would be engineering its own trade-off with China: negation of its commitment to defend the Diaoyu/Senkaku Islands in return for China's strategic restraint in the East China Sea and reconciliation with the US-Japan alliance. The United States considers this alliance the cornerstone of East Asian security; China criticizes it as a destabilizing containment tool. A reconciliation between China and the US-Japan alliance through quid pro quo reassurance would remove a root cause of East Asian tension and contribute to healthy Sino-Japanese and Sino-American relations at the same time.

China's sustained commitment to peace will lessen regional countries' fear of its coercion and domination and reduce the need for the United States to bolster military deterrence. The result would be lowered tension, enhanced trust, and greater stability in the region. The disputes themselves will take a long time to resolve, necessitating careful management in the interim. But a region-wide reassurance through a commitment to peace and restraint between China and its neighbors and a US commitment to diplomacy rather than deterrence will stabilize the interim situation, creating a favorable environment for the eventual settlement of the disputes. As a salutary by-product for the United States, it would freeze the vexing question of whether its alliance commitments would help its allies deter China or encourage their risk-taking or brinksmanship in their disputes with China.

Freedom of the Seas

Freedom of the seas is defined by the Pentagon as "all of the rights, freedoms, and lawful uses of the sea and airspace, including for military ships and aircraft, recognized under international law."[100] It is the first objective of US military policy outlined in the 2015 Asia-Pacific maritime security strategy.[101] The crucial difference between this concept and the more popularly used term "freedom of navigation" reflects a major fault line between China and the United States over the lawful use of the sea. In response to increasing American calls for China to respect freedom of navigation in the South China Sea, Beijing insists that it supports this principle. However, Chinese understanding of freedom of navigation is limited to the freedom of commercial vessels transiting through international waterways. Since China relies more than the United States does on the South China Sea for maritime trade, it focuses on free civilian passage. But underpinning the US concept of freedom of the seas is a fundamental military understanding of the need to ensure free and open maritime access both to protect commercial navigation and to project US forces when necessary. This is where China and the United States are at loggerheads: American demands for access to the global commons conflict with China's search for sovereignty and security in Asia.

Before China's island construction in the South China Sea, which began in late 2013, Sino-American disputes over freedom of military action had centered on the right to conduct military activities in other countries' EEZs, based on their different interpretations of the relevant UNCLOS provisions. The United States argues that UNCLOS allows coastal states to regulate economic (such as fishing and energy exploration) but not military (such as intelligence, surveillance, and reconnaissance) activities of foreign countries in their EEZs. UNCLOS defines the EEZ as extending two hundred nautical miles outward from the twelve-nautical-mile territorial sea. The United States defines its own concept of "international waters," where freedom of the seas is supposed to dominate, as anywhere outward from the territorial sea, thus in effect asserting freedom of military action in the entire EEZs of other countries. Most countries accept the US view, while twenty-six countries—including twelve in the Indo-Pacific region—side with China's contrary position.[102] As we saw in Chapter 3, the United States asserts that it has a right to fly surveillance flights in what it defines as "international airspace" above China's EEZ. Chinese opposition has generated dangerous incidents between American and Chinese aircraft and ships, including a fatal midair collision in April 2001 that resulted in the crash of a Chinese fighter jet and the emergency landing of an American reconnaissance plane.

The United States jealously guards the right to military activities in EEZs because of its legal and military significance. Since at least the time of Hugo Grotius in the seventeenth century, freedom of the seas has been a reigning doctrine for global maritime powers. The United States has internalized it as a fundamental interest, daring to fight for it as early as the Tripolitan War of 1801–5 against "Barbary pirates."[103] Overturning this doctrine would amount to overthrowing a profound international legal tradition of four centuries.

The military implications would be even more significant. The US military relies on unfettered access to EEZs for its global operations. Large portions of the world's oceans are claimable as EEZs, including strategically critical areas in the Western Pacific, the Persian Gulf, and the Mediterranean Sea. Loss of access would hamper US ability to conduct military operations and influence events ashore and could potentially require major changes in US military strategy or foreign policy goals.[104] Giving up military rights in the EEZs of the Western Pacific would severely limit US access to its bases and allies around Asia and dramatically affect its operations in the East and South China Seas.[105] It would also set a precedent for countries around world to limit US freedom of action in other regions, crippling America's global power projection capability.

Since China began to build islands in the Spratly chain of the South China Sea, the United States has raised additional objections to what it regards as China's excessive maritime claims and an intention to constrain the US military from asserting freedom of the seas in waters surrounding the Chinese-held islands. China's refusal to clarify the legal status of the new islands further exacerbates the dispute. In July 2016 an international arbitral tribunal released its ruling of the Philippines v. China case concerning these two countries' disputes over maritime rights in the South China Sea. The United States believes that the ruling creates a vast body of "international waters" or high seas in the middle of the South China Sea and thus provides a perfect basis for it to exercise freedom of the seas.

Beijing's vitriolic attack of the ruling is met by Washington's determined, if low-key support for it. Chinese ambiguity about the legal status of the islands feeds America's suspicion that Beijing is preparing new legal grounds to limit America's freedom of action and reduce its military potency. Since 2015, with a remarkable continuity across the Obama and Trump administrations, the United States has responded by strengthening its military deterrence and by conducting regular freedom of navigation operations (FONOPs) near Chinese-held islands in both the Spratly and Paracel chains of the South China Sea. The enhanced military posture is supposed to deter Chinese assertiveness and coercion, while FONOPs, a long-standing policy now finding a prominent new mission, are meant to contest China's excessive maritime claims. Both of these approaches are interpreted by China as military challenges to its claims and positions in the South China Sea, prompting it to respond with further military buildups. This has triggered a vicious spiral of competition, escalation, and potential conflict.[106]

A strategy of reassurance over freedom of the seas in maritime Asia must address legal and strategic concerns of both countries. China can reassure the United States with a new, irrevocable commitment to the prevailing international understanding of the permissibility of military activities in EEZs. Although the treaty does not contain a clear position, Tommy Koh, a senior Singaporean diplomat who presided over the final UN debates on UNCLOS, observes, "It was the general understanding that the text we negotiated and agreed upon would permit such activities to be conducted."[107] China's new commitment would remove a thorn in the side of perennial legal wrangling. A more profound strategic argument, however, is that freedom of the seas always benefits global maritime powers. As Beijing is becoming a global maritime power in its own right, freedom of the seas is likely to benefit it just as it has benefited the Dutch Republic, Britain, and the United States over the past four centuries. Curtailing or rejecting it would ultimately affect China's freedom of action to protect its expanding overseas interests as it would America's. This kind of foresight will enable Beijing to realize that the current dispute with the United States over the latter's military activities in its EEZs is only an interim situation likely to give way to a more equitable distribution of maritime rights and military balance in the future.

In return the United States needs to reassure China through self-restraint, by considerably reducing and eventually ceasing reconnaissance flights along the Chinese coast. As we observed in Chapter 3, Chinese elites approach these flights not in terms of legal technicalities but from the strategic perspective of US-China competition. A primary objective of these flights is to collect imagery and signals intelligence of the PLA for future contingencies in the Taiwan Strait. If the trilateral Beijing-Taipei-Washington reassurance strategy over Taiwan suggested earlier can be realized, such flights will be even harder to justify. Besides, loss of intelligence through a reduction of these flights can in part be compensated by satellite reconnaissance and other, less blatant means.[108] US self-restraint in this area will enhance military trust between Washington and Beijing—an intractable problem throughout the post–Cold War period.

Reassurance over freedom of the seas in the disputed areas of the South China Sea is hampered by China's reluctance to clarify the legal status of the newly built islands and by its perception of the July 2016 arbitration ruling as politically motivated and substantively biased. Nevertheless China and the United States, along with Southeast Asian claimant states, can use a limited security regime to establish safety zones around the various land features—say, a six-nautical-mile radius—with an agreed-upon set of rules and norms to ensure navigational safety, avoid unsafe encounters, and reduce the risk of inadvertent conflict. This would at once alleviate the US concern about freedom of navigation and overflight and reduce its incentive to conduct provocative FONOPs.

Such a security regime will also complement a reassurance strategy through norms of competition already emerging between the American and Chinese militaries in confidence building. In 2014 they signed the Memorandum of Understanding regarding the Rules of Behavior for Safety of Air and Maritime Encounters and the Memorandum of Understanding on Notification of Major Military Activities Confidence-Building Measures Mechanism. In 2015 both sides expanded upon the memoranda with an air-to-air annex and a crisis com- munication annex, which enhanced efforts to reduce risk and misunderstand- ing.[109] In time, the South China Sea code of conduct consultation currently under way between China and ASEAN members is expected to produce a more comprehensive regional regime to regulate competition, reduce tension, and build trust.

Chinese reassurance through security regimes and norms of competition, designed as interim measures leading to future negotiation and reconciliation, together with its renouncement of the U-shaped line as a national boundary and its commitment to peaceful settlement of disputes through negotiated compro- mise, would credibly reassure the United States and regional countries of its stra- tegic restraint. In contrast, any attempt to establish exclusionary zones or a de facto expansion of its territorial waters in disputed areas beyond reasonable legal justifications would destroy regional confidence in Chinese restraint and bring strong American opposition, possibly including the use of force to assert freedom of the seas.[110]

Geopolitical Competition

We have repeatedly argued that alleged competition between China and the United States for hegemony or domination of East Asia is largely hype. It is prop- agated by those who innocently believe this is the case and by those who have a vested political or economic interest in fostering conflict. Such claims, along with those based on power transition theory, have the potential to be made self- fulfilling. This said, there has been a persistent US desire to preserve America's maritime strategic dominance in the Western Pacific and a new Chinese asser- tiveness in maritime Asia that poses increasing challenges to that dominance. American and Chinese naval authorities and civilian strategists have interpreted the political significance of the South China Sea in a way to reinforce their competition.[111]

How might we diminish American fixation on maritime supremacy and China's temptation to near-sea control? American strategists define US maritime supremacy in Asia in terms of the ability to defeat China on the high seas, maintain freedom of the sea lanes, and protect the insular nations in the region from Chinese coercion or attack. Such dominance is seen as essential for the United States to remain a significant political-military player in the region. America's diplomatic clout, its ability to defend Taiwan, and the credibility of its alliances and other security arrangements, so the argument goes, all hinge on it.[112]

We argued in Chapter 5 that America may maintain a military edge in sea and air power over China for some time; it is nevertheless becoming increasingly difficult for it to fight and win wars against China without horrendous costs.[113] China's military modernization has eroded America's ability to defend Taiwan and may even bring the era of US military dominance in the Western Pacific to an end in coming decades. But the result may not be a new era of Chinese regional hegemony, so feared by American analysts. The more likely outcome, conditioned by technological trends, would be competing spheres of influence rather than Chinese or US dominance.[114] Even in the Taiwan Strait—the focus of China's military modernization—a decline of relative US military superiority would not mean an easy victory for the PRC in the event of war.[115] Efforts by the United States to sustain, or by China to establish, dominance would prove equally quixotic and destabilizing over the long run.[116]

The fundamental problem with a strategy of supremacy is political. In refusing to accept a greater Chinese role in East Asia befitting its status as the region's greatest indigenous power, the United States is attempting to perpetuate a strategic status quo created in the aftermath of the Second World War, when it was the undisputed maritime hegemon and most of China and Asia lay in ruins. The Americans mistake an extraordinary and short-lived situation for a permanent one, and their definition of the status quo is accordingly highly unrealistic. They further err in thinking that the credibility of their defensive commitments in the region depends on naval dominance. Throughout the Cold War American political and military leaders and civilian strategists consistently worried—needlessly as it turned out—about their credibility. Neither the Soviet Union nor China ever questioned it, but rather interpreted American efforts to buttress it as provocative, irresponsible, and indicative of its hostile intentions.[117]

China's territorial and maritime disputes with its neighbors readily generate scenarios in which the United States might be drawn into a conflict with China. Peaceful management, and better yet settlement, of these disputes would reduce the US fear of a Chinese challenge to its alliance commitments. Reassurance should accordingly take precedence over deterrence in addressing maritime tensions. Since the Trump administration took office, however, a growing number of US analysts have instead advocated robust deterrence through cost imposition and escalation, especially in the South China Sea.[118] This can only exacerbate America's credibility worries by intensifying military competition with China.

Washington needs to reassure Beijing through self-restraint, by accepting a greater and responsible Chinese role in the region and by refraining from provocative and destabilizing attempts to preserve its military supremacy. A shift to a more survivable and less conspicuous military posture by relying on more diverse, small, long-range, and hard-to-find naval forces would be able to maintain US military competence without escalatory or destabilizing risks.[119] Some analysts suggest that both the United States and China need to adopt military doctrines and force postures that are defensive in nature, designed to deter through denial rather than control or punishment, and limit offensive capabilities in ways that would minimize escalation and reassure the other side.[120]

The Chinese are somewhat equivocal about their strategic plans for the new islands in the South China Sea. We argued in Chapter 5 that the PLA wants to expand China's security perimeter and deter US intervention. In its 2017 report to Congress on China's military power, the Pentagon observes that China wants to use these islands to bolster its de facto control of the surrounding areas by improving its military and civilian infrastructure.[121] To create a defended operating sanctuary for China's emerging sea-based strategic deterrence force of nuclear-powered ballistic missile submarines is also a motive.[122] Yet, as the islands are vulnerable to destruction by American missiles in the first hours of a high-intensity conflict, their strategic value is limited.[123] The Pentagon is correct that its value lies in enhancing China's maritime domain awareness and deterring Southeast Asian claimant states from altering the territorial status quo, not in changing the military balance with the United States. The fear that the islands will help China to create an exclusionary zone off limits to the US military and thus achieve hegemony in the region is overblown. China cannot deny access to the US military except by means of war—and then not by virtue of the islands themselves but by the integrated naval and air power of the PLA fielding from the Chinese mainland. Even then area denial will not be an assured success against a technologically superior and battle-hardened adversary.

Yet even though the main value of the islands is tactical rather than strategic in a Sino-American military contest, China needs to address the more fundamental question of the nature of its naval strategy in the Western Pacific. Is China pursuing a strategy of sea control, in addition to denial and defense? Smacking of an attempt at military hegemony, an offensive strategy of sea control would provoke the United States, long committed as it is to the goal of preventing such hegemony in Asia. Chinese control of its near-seas could greatly reduce the US ability to intervene in regional contingencies such as Taiwan and fulfill its alliance

obligations.[124] While significantly enhancing China's ability to prevent US intervention, this would destroy the regional security structure and likely compel the
United States to break Chinese control and reassert operational access through a
highly competitive and destabilizing arms race. Ultimately both countries' growing capabilities for sea denial will deprive both of assured sea control.[125] Pursuing
a sea-control strategy is thus both foolhardy and reckless. Moreover, politically
sea control would contradict Beijing's own declaratory strategy of near-sea
defense and far-sea protection outlined in its 2015 defense white paper.[126]

Self-restraint in the form of China's proclaimed doctrine of near-sea defense
constitutes a form of naval reassurance toward the United States. Defense of its
legitimate interests in maritime Asia, with a moderate dose of deterrence—not
sea control—should constitute the core of China's maritime strategy in Asia.
Honoring its claim that the new islands will have "necessary defense needs" but
no offensive functions, China could take a useful first step by limiting its military deployments to defensive weapons systems and focusing on building civilian
facilities for humanitarian assistance and disaster relief.

China's restricting itself to near-sea defense and the United States renouncing the goal of maritime supremacy would simultaneously reduce incentives for
geopolitical competition and increase those for global maritime cooperation.[127]
China's active-defense strategy, examined in Chapter 5, faithfully executed
according to its spirit of strategic defense, with its deterrent and offensive impulses
contained, would generate confidence in Chinese restraint. Beyond mutual self-
restraint, the United States and China should seek to transcend maritime rivalry
by establishing, along with other regional countries, an Asia-Pacific maritime
partnership to advance the agenda of collective maritime security. This should be
a new security regime tailored for addressing traditional and nontraditional security issues in maritime Asia. China and the United States share a major common
interest in maritime security: 95 percent of Chinese trade and 90 percent of US
trade is sea-borne. This is a powerful incentive for both countries to avoid maritime confrontation and rise above rivalries of the past—notably Anglo-German
and US-Japanese naval races—that contributed to war.[128]

The US Alliance System in Asia

The US alliance system in Asia was a product of early Cold War rivalry between
the United States and the Soviet Union. The United States negotiated four
bilateral alliances, with the Philippines (1951), Japan (1951), South Korea (1953),
and Thailand (1954). It also signed the Australia, New Zealand, United States
Security Treaty in 1951, although it suspended its treaty obligations to New
Zealand in 1985. These pacts led to the so-called hub-and-spokes bilateral alliance

system, with the United States as the hub and its regional allies as separate spokes. The system has proved remarkably resilient, able to strengthen itself in the post–Cold War era despite the disappearance of the communist threat that was its original raison d'être. American scholars argue that it reflects a bargain whereby the United States provides security protection and access to American markets, technology, and resources within an open world economy, while America's allies provide support for US leadership.[129] By providing public goods to the region in terms of military security, economic openness, and political stability, it allegedly contributes to peace and progress in East Asia.[130]

Tensions between China and the US alliance system begin with different perceptions of the purpose of these alliances. Washington touts the stabilizing benefits of its alliance system for the region. China sees it as a thinly veiled, anti-China tool of encirclement or containment and an unfortunate relic of the Cold War. The United States does indeed find value in the alliance system as a hedge against China. Perceived Chinese assertiveness in territorial disputes with Japan and the Philippines has generated a mounting sense in America of the need to buttress its strategic credibility by further strengthening the alliance system. However, untamed rivalry between China and the US alliance system risks plunging Asia into a new bipolar competition reminiscent of the Cold War. Whether reconciliation and accommodation can be achieved between the respective security orders of China and the United States will determine Asia's strategic future. Earlier we addressed the issue of a Chinese challenge to American alliance commitments by proposing a set of reassurance strategies for the peaceful management and settlement of China's territorial disputes with its neighbors. We now outline reassurance strategies to address the Chinese fear of encirclement and accommodation between Chinese and American security orders.

Minilateralizing China's Strategic Space

China maintains a principled opposition to the US alliance system in Asia, but its attitudes and strategies have undergone subtle changes. Following the end of the Cold War, some Chinese elites developed a reluctant appreciation of the system's contribution to Asian security, especially in containing the haunted specter of Japanese militarism. Watching the progressive strengthening of the US-Japan alliance, however, they have increasingly come to view it "as more of a security impediment than security facilitator."[131] At the same time Beijing has developed a sophisticated appreciation of the system's limits. The United States did not come to the aid of the Philippines during the 2012 Scarborough Shoal incident, after which China seized control of the area. Nor did it try to prevent China's island building after 2014. Beijing finds some satisfaction in its ability to withstand pressure from the US alliance system. Yao Yunzhu, a senior analyst of the PLA, recognizes that "China should be prepared to work with [it] for a long time."[132]

Having accepted coexistence with the system, China focuses on managing a tense relationship with it. Bemoaning its still limited role in regional security, Beijing hopes to create more strategic space in the institutional architecture of East Asian security. With respect to the US alliance system, its goal is to reduce its exclusivity by preventing its further tightening. The exclusivity of the system suggests a US intention to squeeze China's strategic influence. It also produces the pernicious effect of indiscriminately transforming all of China's tensions with either the United States or its separate allies into conflicts with the alliance system as a whole. The US alliance system thus risks magnifying strategic tensions in Asia by turning individual disputes between China and its neighbors into a region-wide contest between Chinese and American security orders.[133]

A US policy of giving China some institutional space in its alliance system can ease the Chinese fear of exclusion and encirclement. Such reassurance through limited security regimes could draw on Asia's burgeoning "minilateralism"—multilateral security cooperation among small groups of states informally pursuing common interests.[134] So far these institutional practices are confined to arrangements among US treaty allies and security partners, such as US-Japan-Australia, US-Japan-India, and US-Japan-Australia-India strategic dialogues. It will, however, be counterproductive to make the new minilateralism as exclusivist toward China as the US alliance system has been. In fact an opening minilateralism can usefully serve as a strategic bridge between China and the US alliance system. Bringing China in will both satisfy its desire for a greater strategic role and achieve the larger purpose of building trust and reducing tensions in the region. China, for its part, need not unduly fear exclusion, for Asia's complex security architecture means that some space can always be found to offset challenging initiatives from the US alliance system.[135]

Among the five US alliance relationships in Asia, the US-Japan alliance gnaws at China the most. A trilateral US-Japan-China minilateral strategic dialogue to address all three countries' concerns about East Asian security is thus a promising first step. Such an idea has been broached before but has never been attempted due to mistrust and tensions in both Sino-Japanese and Sino-American relations. It should be considered more seriously. The United States bears no small responsibility in promoting Japan's reconciliation with China and other Asian neighbors.[136] For seventy years its exclusive alliance with Japan and the penchant for controlling Japan's strategic choices have undercut the motivation of Japan and other states and peoples in the region to reconcile and build trust with one another.[137]

The US alliance system, with the US-Japan alliance as its cornerstone, is an organic part of Asia's security landscape. The crumbling of this alliance, with the possible consequence of an independent and assertive Japan seeking nuclear weapons, or just more capable armed forces, would not be in China's best interest.[138] But it is not in America's best interest to further strengthen this alliance. The tighter it becomes, the more expansive America's commitments, the greater the risk of entrapment, and the more dangerous its security burden. The United States needs to give more agency to regional allies and partners in providing for their own security. Capable of standing up to China collectively when necessary, Asian countries do not always need America at the forefront—quite the reverse.[139]

Reconciling the Chinese and American Security Orders

Decrying the US alliance system as an anachronistic relic offensive to contemporary realities, China proclaims an opposing approach of partnership diplomacy. President Xi announced in a 2015 speech that a new approach of "dialogue not confrontation, partnership not alliance" must be developed to build "global partnership relationships." China's new security concept of "common, comprehensive, cooperative, and sustainable security" must replace all forms of Cold War mentality.[140] In practice, China is slowly and cautiously building up a regional order conducive to its interests and centered on itself. China is now a member in a dozen regional institutions, including ASEAN+1, ASEAN+3, the ASEAN Regional Forum, the Conference on Interaction and Confidence-Building Measures in Asia (CICA), the Shanghai Cooperation Organisation (SCO), the East Asia Summit, the Regional Comprehensive Economic Partnership (RCEP), the Asian Infrastructure Investment Bank (AIIB), and the ASEAN-China Defense Ministers' Informal Meeting (ACDMIM). In the ASEAN-centered institutions of ASEAN+1, ASEAN+3, the East Asia Summit, RCEP, and the ACDMIM, China acknowledges ASEAN centrality and plays a supporting and facilitating role. In CICA, the SCO, and the AIIB, however, it seeks a central, if not dominant, role and challenges US influence accordingly. Xi's 2014 speech to CICA, in which he called for Asian approaches to Asian problems, was read by many as a call to exclude the United States and assert a greater role for China.[141] A more significant policy is the Belt and Road Initiative, a massive infrastructure-building and economic cooperation program across Eurasia and beyond. These Chinese initiatives feed the speculation about "a semi-hierarchical arrangement with individual states or subregions tied to Beijing as the central hub" in an increasingly developed and integrated Asia.[142]

America's long-standing order in Asia confronts an emerging China that also seeks to impose a kind of hierarchical order. The American order is predominantly security-focused, although economic openness is also a major aspect of it. Traditionally composed of a series of bilateral relationships centered on the United States, it is increasingly taking on networking characteristics as a result of closer security cooperation among the spokes. Having renounced alliances since the 1980s, China's order-building is predominantly economy-focused. While capitalizing on its economic strength to orient the regional agenda toward development, it nevertheless wants to expand its overall influence through partnership diplomacy, institution building, and a more proactive security policy.

We suggest two reassurance strategies to ameliorate competition and promote accommodation between the Chinese and American orders. One is based on security regimes and the other on authority sharing. Reassurance through security regimes can draw on active institutionalism that is already an integral part of the regional security architecture. China and the United States could moderate their competition in the ASEAN-centered multilateral institutional framework, credited by so many scholars and officials as a major contributor to regional stability and development in the post–Cold War era.[143] ASEAN-centered institutionalism, especially the ASEAN Regional Forum, the East Asia Summit, and the series of enlarged ASEAN foreign and defense ministers' meetings, has created an indispensable diplomatic platform that regularly brings all regional powers together. As the only party trusted by all regional countries, ASEAN is uniquely positioned to provide a neutral geopolitical platform for great power engagement, playing "a kind of 'lubricating' role by 'softening' the interactions among the great powers."[144] In helping to soothe competition and promote reconciliation, ASEAN is a felicitous strategic cushion between the Chinese and American orders.

Reassurance through authority sharing is based on insights from both Western and Chinese traditions in statecraft and is especially useful in light of the hierarchical qualities of the American and Chinese orders in Asia. A surprising parallel exists between ancient Greek and traditional Chinese conceptions of ordering relations between great and lesser political units. Drawing on Homeric portrayals of honor, Greeks developed the concept of *hēgemonia*. Our contemporary idea of hegemony derives but is different from this concept, as hegemony suggests domination through material power.[145] *Hēgemonia* describes an honorific status conferred on a leading power by others because of the services it has provided to the community. It confers a right to lead, based on the expectation that this leadership will continue to benefit the community as a whole. *Hēgemonia* represents a clientelist approach to politics: the powerful gain honor in return for providing practical benefits to the weak; the latter willingly accept their inferior status in return for economic and security benefits and the constraints such an arrangement imposes on the powerful.

Clientelist relationships are hierarchical. Their principle of fairness requires rule packages associated with different statuses in the hierarchies. The higher the status, the greater the honor and privileges, but also the more demanding the role and more restrictive its rules. Clientelist hierarchies are designed to restrain selfishness and its consequences by embedding actors with resources in a social order that requires them to protect and support those who are less advantaged and feel shame if they do not meet their responsibilities. Robust clientelist hierarchies satisfy the spirit of those with high status and the security and appetites of those with low status.[146]

Imperial China drew on Confucian ethics to develop a similar concept of *wangdao*, literally meaning "the kingly way" but more usefully translated as "humane authority," to describe clientelist relations hierarchically based on the centrality and authority of the Chinese emperor.[147] The purpose of such hierarchy was to promote a universal ethical world order based on Confucian propriety and underpinned by China's relational authority. In its ideal form it should provide political, economic, and security benefits for all units involved in such a Sinocentric order.[148] Like *hēgemonia, wangdao* confers the right to lead, but only if the powerful leads by providing benefit to the community as a whole. As the Tsinghua University scholar Yan Xuetong puts it, *wangdao* "represents a view of China as an enlightened, benevolent hegemon whose power and legitimacy derive from its ability to fulfill other countries' security and economic needs—in exchange for their acquiescence to Chinese leadership."[149]

Both the Greek concept of *hēgemonia* and the Chinese concept of *wangdao* denote legitimate leadership based on clientelist authority relationships. As such they can be shared by great powers in search of accommodation and cooperation—unlike hegemony based on material power. Both the United States and China should reject hegemony as a strategic goal and instead focus on *hēgemonia* or *wangdao*. As long as they share their *hēgemonia* or *wangdao* in Asia and maintain their respective rule packages in relationships with regional countries, no conflict should arise between the two countries or their respective networks of alliances and partnerships in the region. For the United States, this means discharging its responsibilities to its regional allies and partners while encouraging them to improve relations with China. For China, it means doubling down on its neighborhood policy by improving relations with neighboring countries without compelling them to choose between Beijing and Washington. Rather than a binary strategy dividing Asia between Chinese-led and US-led spheres of influence or opposing blocks, a common *hēgemonia/wangdao* strategy leads to an intermeshing community of regional countries friendly to both powers—or, in the words of President Xi, "a circle of friends common to both countries."[150]

Moreover, sharing authority in this way can be practiced on a global scale, with both countries seeking honor—that is, the respect of others and the influence it confers—in a cooperative, even collaborative manner. Acting this way, China and the United States would both gain influence and reduce tensions between them, while collectively contributing to global governance. Indeed that would be the ideal for the most important bilateral relationship in the twenty-first century.

Summary

Reassurance between China and the United States to manage their simmering conflict is possible but challenging. In the Taiwan Strait, reassurance would require a trilateral process of trade-offs and reciprocity from Beijing, Taipei, and Washington. Beijing needs to make a credible commitment to Taiwan's security and autonomy to reassure both Taipei and Washington; Taipei needs to reassure Beijing by renouncing the goal of de jure independence and by recommitting itself to unification; and Washington needs to reassure Beijing of the contingent nature of its defense commitment to Taiwan.

In North Korea a parallel reassurance based on irrevocable commitment from the United States to China and from China to North Korea may help resolve the nuclear weapons and missile crisis. This could come in the form of a US commitment to withdraw troops from South Korea after denuclearization and a Chinese commitment to ensure the survival of the North Korean regime in return for denuclearization.

In Asian maritime tensions, untying the three levels of disputes over sovereignty, freedom of the seas, and geopolitical competition would require reassurance through a combination of quid pro quos, irrevocable commitment, self-restraint, security regimes, and norms of competition. A region-wide reassurance through a commitment to peace and restraint between China and its neighbors in territorial disputes and a US commitment to diplomacy could pave the way for peaceful management and settlement of the disputes. A Chinese commitment to the dominant international understanding of the permissibility of military activities in EEZs, US self-restraint by reducing and eventually ceasing reconnaissance flights along the Chinese coast, Sino-American mutual reassurance through norms of competition to reduce risks of conflict, and a regional security regime to reduce tension and build trust in the South China Sea could help ensure freedom of the seas in Asia. A reciprocal reassurance strategy of self-restraint between China and the United States—one limiting China's goal to near-sea defense and the other renouncing America's goal of maritime supremacy—should dampen their geopolitical competition.

Promoting reconciliation between China and the US alliance system and accommodation between the respective Chinese and American security orders in Asia requires reassurance through security regimes and authority sharing. The United States can utilize minilateralism to give China institutional space in its alliance system, thus easing Beijing's fear of exclusion and encirclement. Both China and the United States can draw on ASEAN-centered multilateral institutionalism to moderate their competition. At the same time, in the spirit of practicing *hēgemonia* or *wangdao* statecraft, they can share their legitimate regional leadership based on their respective authority relationships with regional countries to achieve accommodation and cooperation.

Sino-American rivalry is already with us, but conflict is not inevitable. Accommodation and cooperation can be achieved through sophisticated applications of reassurance. These applications are challenging to devise and implement, however. We have suggested major steps required for reassurance without going into all the details, which would demand separate policy analyses. Our objective is to expound the plausibility and promise of the reassurance strategy while considering its challenges. The degree of challenge depends on the tenacity of deterrence and the effectiveness of diplomacy in the relationship. In Chapter 5 we examined the role of deterrence in Sino-American competition and called for reassurance and diplomacy to reduce its risks. In Chapter 7 we will assess the potential of and constraints on diplomacy to complete our discussion on a holistic, tripartite strategy for managing Sino-American conflict.

7

Diplomacy

DIPLOMACY IS THE third generic strategy of conflict management and resolution. We explore the ways in which it can serve this end, the situations in which it is most appropriate, and the important independent role that diplomats can play in clarifying objectives and proposals, feeling out the receptivity of their own governments and others to initiatives, serving as faithful go-betweens, and using their local knowledge to propose initiatives, perhaps in collaboration with their opposite numbers.

The opening section of the chapter provides a conceptual overview of the role of diplomacy and various reasons for its success or failure. We illustrate our argument with historical examples from Europe, the Middle East, and East Asia. We then explore these practices and their lessons in the context of Sino-American relations, where diplomacy has the potential to play a significant and positive role.

Conflict Management

Diplomacy is "the conduct of relationships, using peaceful means, by and among international actors, at least one of whom is usually governmental."[1] It has long been recognized as the essential mechanism of conflict management and resolution. It is impossible to reduce and resolve international conflicts without diplomacy. Even unilateral actions require explanation and interpretation to achieve their desired effects. They are at best opening moves, as they often are in the strategy of reassurance. They require follow-up and diplomacy to move from successful ice-breaking to substantive achievements.

All too often theories of foreign policy and international relations that turn to so-called structures or features of the environment for their analytical punch (for example, balance of power, changing nature of threats, and technological developments) ignore diplomacy or treat it as an unproblematic mechanism.

If conditions demand a démarche or détente, policymakers will respond as required, and diplomats will act as intended on their instructions. Political leaders and diplomats alike are treated like nonreflexive electrons transmitting charges. Rationalist approaches are just as determinist and dismissive of agency. But agency matters, and not just that of leaders. Leaders make choices, but so do diplomats. Diplomats may follow their instructions to the letter, speak, that is, to an intended audience, and advance proposals and arguments as instructed. Nevertheless where they meet, the tone they adopt, and the degree of trust between or among interlocutors may have a determining effect on how targeted leaders respond to any messages or proposals.

There are many classical works extolling diplomacy's virtues and achievements in eighteenth- and nineteenth-century Europe and globally in the twentieth century.[2] In the past few years international relations theory has become more interested in how diplomacy works.[3] The so-called practice turn emphasizes the ways in which diplomacy constitutes states and others as actors, the quasi-independent role of diplomats, and how diplomatic arguments affect and are affected by shared understandings of what kinds of means and ends are legitimate.

There is also an extensive literature on mediation, Track Two diplomacy (talks among private individuals and groups), and other forms of unofficial, people-to-people contacts.[4] We limit ourselves here to official diplomacy because we are concerned with how it can best be coordinated with other strategies, and this entails the central authority of government. States may nevertheless make use of nongovernmental organizations or private individuals for informal soundings and discussions. They can offer the advantage of trust, as did the community of Soviet and American scientists involved in decades of Pugwash talks.[5] They also allow leaders to back away and disavow them or their recommendations if they prove politically difficult or inadvisable.

The resolution of the Cold War offers a telling example of successful diplomacy in a double sense. It illustrates its important and independent contribution, but also the propensity of diplomats, like many scholars, to see foreign policy outcomes as overdetermined. Richard Herrmann and Ned Lebow interviewed some twenty-five Soviet, American, and European policymakers, intelligence officials, advisors, and diplomats who were intimately involved in terminating the Cold War. Independently of their country or ideology, they saw the end of the Cold War, the reunification of Germany, and the collapse of the Soviet Union as more or less inevitable. At the same time almost all of these officials confessed their surprise, even incredulity as these events unfolded. The contradiction in their belief systems was made even starker by the insistence of almost every official interviewed that the outcome of any decision or negotiation in which they participated was highly contingent. In conference discussions and conversations over drinks or coffee, they told amusing stories of how clever tactics, the nature of the personal relationship between themselves and their opposites, and just sheer coincidence played decisive roles in shaping the outcome of negotiations.[6]

Some policymakers interviewed maintained that the end of the Cold War, the reunification of Germany, and the dissolution of the Soviet Union were all inevitable. They were nevertheless responsive to counterfactual suggestions that process and outcome might have been different. There was widespread agreement that there was nothing foreordained about the two-plus-four format for negotiations over the future of Germany.[7] When pushed, former Soviet, American, and German policymakers agreed that a different format, perhaps one that involved more European countries as participants, might well have resulted in a different outcome given the widespread opposition to reunification by Germany's neighbors. While there was general agreement that Mikhail Gorbachev had little freedom to maneuver on the German question at the time of the two-plus-four talks (1990), several Soviet officials suggested that he might have been able to negotiate a better deal if he had broached the issue in 1987.

Some diplomats stress the importance of their profession, especially those writing memoirs about how central they were to benign outcomes.[8] It seems likely that policymakers and scholars are susceptible to what Baruch Fischhoff has called the "certainty of hindsight" bias. Experiments that he and others conducted demonstrate that outcome knowledge affects our understanding of the past by making it difficult for us to recall that we were once unsure about what was going to happen. Events deemed improbable by experts (for example, peace between Egypt and Israel or the end of the Cold War) are often considered overdetermined—indeed all but inevitable—once they have occurred.[9]

Our interest is less in the role of diplomats and more in that of diplomacy. When, how, and why is diplomacy effective in moving conflicts away from war and in resolving issues that divide adversaries? There is a large literature on the diplomacy of peacemaking. It is more historical than conceptual, but valuable for the insights it offers into particular situations. The conceptual literature in social science on conflict resolution is largely quantitative and ignores agency and diplomacy. It searches for correlations between independent and dependent variables. An important exception is the work of William Thompson and his collaborators on enduring rivalries and their resolution; they combine quantitative work with case studies and acknowledge the often determining role of agency.[10]

The qualitative literature on conflict resolution is idiosyncratic and sometimes relies on poorly specified concepts. Consider the proposition of "ripeness," as developed by I. William Zartman. It is the moment when parties in a mutually destructive stalemate recognize the destructive nature of the status quo and that they are in "a mutually hurting stalemate." Protagonists must also perceive a way out of this stalemate.[11] Zartman recognizes the entirely subjective nature of this double realization, and further recognizes that it is a necessary but insufficient condition for peace. He and his acolytes offer few guidelines about the conditions, material, psychological, or political responsible for these necessary adversarial beliefs and nothing about the other necessary conditions.

A useful analogy can be made between the causes of war and accommodation. Structural and regularity theories and, of course, rationalist accounts assume that war—or accommodation—will take place, or is highly likely to, when stipulated conditions are present. If so, an appropriate catalyst will come along or be manufactured by leaders. This assumption is sometimes warranted. In February 1965, in the aftermath of a Viet Cong attack on the American advisors' barracks at Pleiku, National Security Advisor McGeorge Bundy wrote a memorandum to President Lyndon Johnson urging the sustained bombing of North Vietnam. Bundy later acknowledged that Pleikus were like "streetcars": he could count on repeated Viet Cong attacks against South Vietnamese forces or their American advisors to provide him with the pretext he needed at the opportune moment to sell escalation to the president.[12]

Pretexts do not always resemble streetcars. They may be infrequent, inappropriate, or fail to materialize—as is, alas, true of many trams and buses—and without a catalyst the predicted behavior may not occur. In a matter of months, or years, underlying conditions may evolve to make war less likely even if an otherwise appropriate catalyst ultimately comes along. The window of opportunity for war—or for peace—may be temporally narrow or broad depending on the nature and rate of changes in the underlying conditions. War may require a *conjunction* of underlying pressures and appropriate catalysts.[13]

Catalysts are often complex causes in their own right, as Sarajevo was in 1914. The twin assassinations caused the Austrian leadership to reframe the problem of Serbia. Risks that had been unacceptable in the past now became tolerable, even welcome. The independent role of catalysts creates another problem for theories and attempts to evaluate them.[14] All the relevant underlying causes for a war or accommodation may be present, but absent a catalyst, it will not occur. The uncertain and evolving relationship between underlying and immediate causes not only makes point prediction impossible; it renders problematic more general statements about the causes of war and system transformations—and many other international phenomena—because we have no way of knowing which of these events would have occurred in the presence of appropriate catalysts, and we cannot assume that their presence or absence can be treated as random. It is thus impossible to define the universe of such events or to construct a representative sample of them.[15]

Catalysts are equally important for accommodation, and theorizing about them is just as difficult because they are so often situation-specific. In *Avoiding War, Making Peace* Ned Lebow describes three conditions he found to be critical to at least one pathway to accommodation: the belief that war, or threatening military deployments, are counterproductive; the belief that key domestic goals require a significant reduction in tensions with an adversary; and the belief that overtures toward this end are likely to be reciprocated.[16] The last two are unambiguously immediate causes as they very much depend on leaders' goals and visions of their countries and the world. All three beliefs are subjective and unlikely to be shared with other contenders for leadership. The French elite was deeply divided in 1904 as to whether Germany or Britain was the enemy. In the case of the Egyptian-Israeli and Soviet-American accommodations, it is difficult to imagine other leaders who would have pursued the conciliatory policies of Anwar Sadat or Gorbachev.[17]

Catalysts mattered in each of these accommodations, and they were largely independent of underlying causes. The Anglo-French entente required French soul-searching and hard choices, and that was encouraged by the disastrous Fashoda crisis of 1898. Along with the Dreyfus affair, it brought about a shift in power that made accommodation possible. In this instance, catalyst and confluence were critical in realigning French foreign policy. So too was agency. French and British leaders and diplomats established their credibility through repeated interactions, and the entente opened the door for further cooperation. What began as an effort to reduce the likelihood of war set in motion a full-fledged accommodation over the course of a decade. Agency was crucial at each step. Poorly considered and executed German foreign policies provided a strong incentive for Anglo-French cooperation, and clever French and British diplomacy and political and military leadership effectively capitalized on it.[18]

The Egyptian-Israeli peace treaty was equally dependent on a catalyst: the failure of Egyptian arms in a conflict where Soviet arms and new tactics had given the Egyptians an initial advantage. Egyptian defeat, and subsequent American willingness to broker a peace, convinced Sadat that he had the need and opportunity to extend the olive branch. The war was also mind-changing for Israel. It emerged victorious, but only after initial and costly defeats. Sadat was not the only critical leader. Richard Nixon and Henry Kissinger were equally essential players, setting in motion the possibility of a peace in which Egypt regained the Sinai and Israel was protected by US security guarantees. Once again diplomacy proved critical, not only during and in the immediate aftermath of the war but at the 1978 Camp David negotiations. President Jimmy Carter was masterful in his handling of Sadat and Menachem Begin, and the latter was receptive to American overtures, opposed by right-wing nationalists in Israel.[19]

The end of the Cold War was also contingent and catalyst-dependent. George Breslauer and Lebow conducted a thought experiment in which the likely inter-action of other possible Soviet and American leaders was considered.[20] None of the other combinations led to a resolution of the Cold War in the short term, and some led to its escalation. Gorbachev sought accommodation with the West to free resources and buy political room for domestic change. Contrary to the claims of some realists, Soviet leaders were not compelled to seek accommodation, and certainly not by means of unilateral concessions, one-sided agreements, and abandonment of the communist governments of Eastern Europe. No other likely Soviet leader would have acted as Gorbachev did.[21] Equally important was the degree of trust that Gorbachev established with President Ronald Reagan, which allowed both leaders to move forward and for Gorbachev to take more risks.[22]

Most important for our argument is the independence of these several cat-alysts, or immediate causes of accommodation, from underlying ones. In the Anglo-French case, the Fashoda crisis and the *faux Henri* phase of the Dreyfus affair occurred all but simultaneously, having a multiplier effect on French opin-ion, leading to an electoral victory of the *Défense Républicaine* coalition that made accommodation possible and politically advantageous. The Dreyfus affair was entirely unconnected in cause—although not in effect—from Anglo-French colonial rivalry in Africa.

For Egypt and Israel, the catalyst was not so much a war as it was the cost and outcome of that war. Arab-Israeli wars were expressions of the underlying causes of their conflict. As there had been four previous wars—in 1948, 1956, 1967, and 1970—it was not unlikely that there would be a fifth. However, it was the out-come, not the war, that mattered, and this war was unique in that the Arab side started with new weapons, an effective and coordinated two-front strategy, and the tactical advantage of surprise, and yet still lost. Defeat, and with it the encircle-ment and near destruction of their armies, convinced Sadat and his generals that they could never defeat Israel. Surprise, shock, early losses, and victory only by virtue of an American airlift bringing new weapons and ammunition convinced Israelis of the need for peace with Egypt. This outcome was entirely independent of the causes of this and previous wars.

The end of the Cold War had three principal catalysts. Gorbachev was willing to take risks in the hope of reforming and revitalizing the Soviet economy and political system. This was a response to underlying conditions that may have been inseparable from an authoritarian regime and command economy. To bring about change, Gorbachev had to overcome the opposition of much of the Communist Party, the military, and the even more conservative allied governments of Eastern Europe. The stalemated and costly war in Afghanistan, the forward American deployment of a new generation of missiles and cruise missiles in Western

Europe—which Soviet generals said would never happen—the Chernobyl disaster, and the landing of Mathias Rust's Cessna in Red Square, all made this possible.[23] Most of these catalysts had independent and largely unrelated causes but a cumulative nonlinear effect. Accommodation in all cases required committed leaders, catalysts, and good diplomacy.

What general lessons can we derive from these three cases? They suggest that neither realist nor ripeness arguments are compelling. Realists invoke shifts in the balance of power to account for accommodations, just as they do for war, but there were no notable shifts prior to the Anglo-French, Egyptian-Israeli, or Sino-American accommodations. To the extent that there was a shift in the Egyptian-Israeli power balance it was in favor of Israel, but Begin was willing to enter into negotiations with Sadat and withdraw from the strategically important Sinai as part of a peace agreement. The end of the Cold War was a clear exception as the Soviet Union had been stagnating economically since the 1970s. Three Soviet leaders before Gorbachev were aware of this situation and did nothing dramatic to address it, so at best it was a contributing condition to Gorbachev's commitment to accommodation.

Ripeness is also indeterminate as the Arab-Israeli stalemate was a mutually hurting stalemate for at least two decades prior to the Camp David Accords, and for four decades before the Oslo Accords. Nor did the latter accords lead to a peace. In contrast, the Anglo-French entente was reached in the absence of any mutually hurting stalemate. France and Britain had not been at war since 1815, and the Fashoda crisis, while it brought the two countries to the brink of war, was resolved without bloodshed.

Accommodations are most likely to be sought when new leaders come to power with strong domestic or external incentives for winding down an existing conflict. Sadat was keen to reorganize the Egyptian economy and jump-start it with Western aid, investment, and technology. For the French and Gorbachev, there were foreign as well as domestic incentives. French leaders wanted to make peace with Britain in proportion to the degree that they perceived Germany as a threat. They also wanted to do this to advance their domestic program, which involved curtailing the power of the pro-German colonial ministry and the anti-Dreyfus Catholic Church. For Nixon, Kissinger, Mao Zedong, and Zhou Enlai, the incentives were primarily external; as China's conflict with the Soviet Union became more acute, it was strategically advantageous to draw closer to the United States.[24]

Additional evidence about the importance of new leadership can be drawn from divided nations and partitioned countries. The former are once unified countries that were divided due to the Cold War. They are—or were—the two Germanies, Koreas, Chinas, and Vietnams. Partitioned countries are products of the breakup of former colonial empires and the division of disputed territory between rival ethnic groups. They include the two Irelands, Greek and Turkish Cyprus, Israel-Palestine, and India-Pakistan. Movement toward normalization of relations in West and East Germany, the People's Republic of China and the Republic of China, the two Irelands, and Cyprus could begin only when the generation of leaders and other important political and military figures associated with partition passed from the scene.[25]

Diplomacy also has the potential to be more fruitful when war, other forms of violence, or arms races and threatening deployments, have proven counterproductive—and are widely recognized as counterproductive. The Fashoda crisis drove this home to French leaders, the 1973 war to Egyptian and Israeli leaders, and NATO's forward deployment of Pershing II missiles and ground-launched cruise missiles in Western Europe to Soviet leaders. Ireland too conforms to this pattern, but in a more complicated way. The war of independence from Britain provoked an Irish civil war between moderates who were willing to settle for twenty-six of the thirty-two counties and hardliners who insisted on fighting on to gain control over the entire island. More recently the failure of either Irish nationalists or Ulster Protestant paramilitaries to impose their will in Northern Ireland, and their ultimate loss of support within their respective communities, split these groups to some degree and opened space for more moderate actors.[26]

Diplomacy is important in its own right. As noted, it played a critical role in all accommodations. The willingness of France to renounce any interest in Egypt and the Sudan, and British willingness to support France's colonial claims in Morocco, paved the way for the entente. This clever quid pro quo was not an obvious one; it required imagination and skill to implement. The entente was solidified by bad diplomacy on the part of Germany. Kaiser Wilhelm and Foreign Minister Bernhard von Bülow provoked a crisis over Morocco in 1904 that pushed France into Britain's arms, and the British backed the French, transforming their relationship from one of cautious accommodation to de facto alliance. Students of the Sino-American accommodation also credit leaders with careful, step-by-step soundings, mostly in secret, that led to trips to China by Kissinger and Nixon, followed by rapid and effective diplomacy on both sides that clarified issues and led to an understanding that each side described in its own way in separately issued communiqués.[27]

Leaders must be flexible in their thinking, as were the French foreign minister Théophile Delcassé and his British counterpart, Lord Salisbury, in the aftermath of the Fashoda crisis. Delcassé did an about-face after Fashoda, and Salisbury, who had been on the verge of going to war with France, was remarkably open to his postcrisis overtures. Nixon and Kissinger overcame their enemy images of China;

as early as the 1950s Nixon was willing to go beyond rigid Cold War thinking and explore explanations other than communist ideology for Chinese hostility.[28] When he came to office, his view of China's leaders and their motivations was primed for positive change by his desire to find a so-called honorable way out of the Indochina war with their assistance. Personal contacts led to large shifts in his and Kissinger's perceptions of Mao and Zhou.[29] We previously noted Reagan's receptiveness to Gorbachev in contrast to that of his vice president and many of his advisors. Had George H. W. Bush been president rather than Reagan, it seems unlikely that there would have been much progress toward accommodation.[30] The least flexible leader in these several accommodations was Menachem Begin, who was brought around in the end only by prodding and promises by President Carter.[31] He was nevertheless more open to the prospect of peace with Egypt than other colleagues in the Likud Party.

Finally, leaders must have the political room to extend the olive branch or grasp it when offered. Leaders may sometimes carve out room for themselves to maneuver by clever tactics such as sidetracking adversaries, positive coalition building, and masterful appeals to public opinion. Nixon benefited from being a Republican but still had Cold War opinion and right-wing opposition with which to contend. In July 1971, 56 percent of Americans branded China the world's most dangerous state.[32] Nixon and Kissinger successfully deployed realist arguments to isolate opposition from pro-Taiwan, anticommunist, and certain business interests and a pro-peace discourse to win over moderate Republicans and Democrats.[33] Following Nixon's widely televised trip to Beijing, a Gallup Poll revealed that 96 percent of the public had a favorable view of the Chinese people.[34] Gorbachev was less successful, as many elements of the Soviet military and industry and the Communist Party remained hostile to his domestic reforms and foreign policy. He set in motion a process that ultimately undermined his support.[35] Sadat faced even greater obstacles; he failed to win over much of Egypt's political-military elite or public opinion and was assassinated.

Accommodation is a reciprocal process. Following their 1959 Camp David meeting, President Dwight Eisenhower and General Secretary Nikita Khrushchev seemed on the verge of achieving major tension reduction in the Cold War. But Eisenhower's efforts came to naught because of his continued support of U-2 overflights of the Soviet Union and his need to placate a West German ally whose Christian Democratic leadership opposed accommodation. Khrushchev had gone out on a limb, and Ike in effect sawed it off. By contrast, Johnson and Khrushchev's successor, Leonid Brezhnev, negotiated a détente because both leaders had strong domestic backing, and Johnson international support as well.[36]

The Eisenhower counterexample, the seeming Johnson-Brezhnev success, and the 1993 Oslo Accords between Israel and the Palestinian Liberation

Organization reveal the downside of stalled diplomatic progress. The U-2 affair led Khrushchev to torpedo the 1960 Paris Summit, in part to protect himself against Soviet hardliners.[37] Détente raised expectations that were not fulfilled and led to an intensified Cold War.[38] The Oslo Accords unraveled for a different reason: hardliners opposed to accommodation used violence to polarize public opinion and cut the ground out from underneath moderates. The key event was the assassination of Prime Minister Yitzhak Rabin of Israel in November 1995 by a Jewish ultranationalist. Hardliners on both sides in the Northern Irish conflict periodically tried and succeeded in sabotaging any move toward peace. Violence rose in proportion to the perceived likelihood of political cooperation across sectarian lines.[39]

These failed attempts at accommodation suggest several lessons for leaders and diplomats. First and most important is the need to make hard choices about accommodation versus other goals. Leaders who express willingness to wind down tensions, or respond to adversarial overtures to do so, make themselves vulnerable to political recrimination if they fail, and possibly also if they succeed. Extending or grasping an olive branch also raises the possibility of exploitation by the other side. Eisenhower was trying to protect himself and his country against the latter threat when he authorized one final U-2 overflight because he sought reassurance that the Soviets had not deployed their first-generation intercontinental ballistic missile. He knew there was a risk because the Soviets had deployed a new surface-to-air missile, but he allowed the CIA to convince him that they could get away with it. Motivated bias can also work in favor of accommodation. In the mirror image of deterrence challenges, leaders who make peace overtures can convince themselves that they will succeed. Sadat and Gorbachev were confident beyond what the available evidence warranted and helped to make their optimism self-fulfilling.[40]

Efforts at accommodation should move both slowly and quickly. Caution and secrecy are necessary to assure leaders that they are on firm ground at home and not likely to be exploited abroad. Once overtures become known, leaders must move as quickly as possible to limit the possibility of opposing coalitions forming and mobilizing public opinion through the media or violence. The Oslo Accords were intended to be a prelude to a peace treaty that would be reached by direct negotiations between Palestinians and Israelis. Each side knew that both wanted peace and would be politically exposed if they failed to reach an agreement. Each accordingly expected the other to make additional concessions and the negotiations dragged on long enough for Israeli hardliners to derail the peace process. President Bill Clinton played a central role in bringing about the famous 1993 Rabin–Yasser Arafat televised handshake and the Oslo Accords, but the president and his diplomats failed to keep the pressure up on both sides to reach a quick agreement. The negotiations dragged on, Arafat got cold feet, and the assassination of Rabin changed the political calculus on the Israeli side. The failure of the Oslo process intensified conflict to the degree that subsequent diplomatic initiatives have had no positive effect.[41]

Peace overtures require careful assessment beforehand of their domestic and foreign risks. How will important foreign and domestic audiences respond? How much latitude will leaders have to pursue accommodation once their efforts become known? These assessments can be hit-and-miss because the goals and risk assessments of others are often opaque, and more so when based on different assumptions. As we have seen, this problem often confounds deterrence or compellence; it is an equal challenge for reassurance. Reassurance has a relative advantage in that it can often be practiced in small steps, which are reversible at low cost, and elicit some indication of how at least an adversary will respond. Cases in point are the secret consultations among diplomats prior to the Anglo-French entente and Nixon's visit to China. However, irreversible, unilateral steps toward accommodation are more credible and may be necessary to break through solid walls of distrust. They arguably served this purpose for Sadat and Gorbachev. A major strand of contemporary Russian opinion regards Gorbachev as a traitor, or at least a naïf, who was exploited by the West.[42] Even successful accommodations are reversible, and for many reasons.

Diplomacy in US-China Relations

Effective diplomacy requires committed leaders with flexibility in thinking and freedom in political maneuvering, empowered by strong incentives for conflict reduction. Leaders must often break free from conceptions of their adversary that have shaped prior policies, find ways of testing the water before committing themselves to initiatives that would be costly if unsuccessful, and devise careful plans for implementation. Diplomats, like political leaders, need what the Germans call *Spielraum*, or sufficient latitude, to exercise initiative and apply their expertise in pursuit of leader-sponsored initiatives. Novel constraints and opportunities, or crises, can be useful to leaders and diplomats alike when they generate urgency and lead to recognition that threat-based strategies such as war and deterrence are counterproductive. How do these insights shed light on diplomacy between America and China?

The Success of Mao and Deng

The rapprochement in the early 1970s engineered by Nixon and Kissinger on the American side and by Mao and Zhou on the Chinese side was motivated by external security needs. America was seeking an exit from the Vietnam War and a new strategic equation in its competition with the Soviet Union. China was exploring American support to withstand Soviet military pressure after Moscow had turned from an ally to an adversary.

The rapprochement, and the careful and far-sighted diplomacy by both countries that brought it about, is rightly celebrated as a remarkable achievement. Diplomacy of this scale, however, required more than external incentives. Chen Jian notes that although the Soviet threat necessitated strategic adjustment, it does not in itself explain how it became possible for Chinese leaders to achieve it in the late 1960s and 1970s. He argues that Mao's need to strengthen his political authority and reestablish societal order after the chaos unleashed by the Cultural Revolution led to a redefinition of China's identity from a revolutionary challenger to the existing order to a vulnerable power willing to explore coexistence with that order. Mao's famous interview with the American journalist Edgar Snow in December 1970 was a staged signal to the Chinese people—and to American leaders, who at first missed it—that the relationship with America was set for a dramatic change. Even a leader as authoritative as Mao had to lay the domestic political and psychological groundwork for the new diplomacy.[43] We argue later that such domestic political freedom remains a necessary, although not sufficient, condition for diplomatic breakthroughs today.

The establishment of a formal diplomatic relationship in January 1979 was a logical corollary of rapprochement. It nevertheless required political determination and diplomatic skill. For President Carter, the perception of a greater Soviet threat provided enough justification for normalizing relations. For Chinese leaders, the American reluctance to completely relinquish ties with Taiwan remained a thorn in its side. Nevertheless Deng Xiaoping was determined to go ahead with normalization not only because of the common interest in opposing Soviet hegemony but also because of the domestic need to spearhead his new reform and opening-up policy with American assistance. He believed that China must first open itself up to America if his reform program was to succeed. Linking diplomatic normalization to the domestic need of modernization, he emphasized cooperation with America as a strategic necessity, not a tactical expedient.[44] Diplomacy of normalization was smooth because Deng demonstrated strategic commitment to a long-term cooperative relationship, political authority in the Chinese system, and flexibility in finessing the Taiwan issue.

Crisis Diplomacy in April 2001

Since then, diplomatic breakthroughs in Sino-American conflict resolution have become harder. More common is muddling through, as in the 1990s, and struggles to contain tensions, which characterized the Barack Obama administration.

The two countries nevertheless achieved some success during the George W. Bush and Obama years. The first such success was diplomacy to resolve the aircraft collision crisis of April 2001, when an American EP-3 reconnaissance aircraft clashed with a Chinese fighter jet off the southern Chinese coast (see our discussion in Chapter 3). Upon taking office three months earlier the Bush administration had identified China as a "competitor."[45] Now it faced a crisis in which China detained the twenty-four-member crew of the damaged American plane that had landed on a Chinese airfield.

The key to diplomatic success was principled flexibility by both countries. The initial dispute following the collision centered on the US call to return the crew and the aircraft and the Chinese request for an apology from the American government. The US side would not admit any wrongdoing. It maintained that international law allows freedom of overflight over China's exclusive economic zone, which was where the collision occurred. While refusing to make a "false apology," it was nevertheless flexible in expressing regret for the incident, especially for the loss of the Chinese pilot.[46] China demanded an apology because it framed the collision and the subsequent landing of the American aircraft on Chinese soil as a threat to its security and sovereignty. But it was flexible with the American expression of apology. Diplomacy was then focused on finessing a language of apology acceptable to both sides. They found it in the expression "very sorry" after Chinese rejection of earlier American wordings of "regret" and "sorry." China translated "very sorry" to mean "expressing deep apology" in Chinese (*shen biao qian yi*).[47] This was a linguistic sleight of hand necessary to satisfy the domestic political need of demonstrating the government's success in extracting an American apology.

Leaders' commitments to a long-term, stable relationship also helped to defuse the crisis. President Bush and Secretary of State Colin Powell stressed the importance of the US-China relationship and demonstrated a commitment to prevent the incident from destabilizing relations. China initially proceeded from the premise of safeguarding sovereignty but soon realized the need to stabilize the overall relationship.[48] Although the two countries differed in their interpretations of the incident, especially the dispute over which side was responsible for the collision, both wanted a quick resolution through diplomacy.

Diplomacy nevertheless had its limits. Principled flexibility from both sides produced a diplomatic language to soothe Chinese sensibilities and negotiated an early return of the American crew and aircraft. It failed to resolve the underlying dispute: American insistence on its right to continued surveillance flights off the Chinese coast and Chinese denunciation of such flights as a threat to China's security and sovereignty. Taking continued flights as a given, the US side was willing to discuss only the technical issue of avoiding future collisions without addressing China's political and security concerns. Criticizing what it regarded as the illegality of such flights and their affronts to Chinese sovereignty, the Chinese side refused to discuss procedures for preventing future incidents for fear of legitimizing such flights.[49]

The collision cannot be said to have been a catalyst for the subsequent progress of the bilateral relationship during the Bush administration. It was nevertheless a wake-up call to both sides about the importance of improving the relationship. In his memoirs, Tang Jiaxuan, China's foreign minister at the time, recounted that the incident raised for him an urgent need to establish a close relationship with senior US officials, particularly Powell. He tried to persuade Powell that branding China a "strategic competitor" was not conducive to a constructive relationship between the two countries, and he believed that he made some progress in this regard. Meanwhile the Chinese ambassador in Washington, Yang Jiechi, seized on President Bush's offer of a telephone call with President Jiang Zemin. That conversation on July 5, 2001, two days after the return of the EP-3 plane to the United States, reaffirmed mutual interest in improving the relationship.[50]

The real catalyst for Sino-American cooperation during the Bush years was the September 11, 2001, terrorist attacks on the United States. The Bush administration reoriented its strategic focus from great power competition to counterterrorism. Assessing this to be an important opportunity for improving ties, Chinese leaders and diplomats swiftly offered support for US counterterrorism efforts. The Americans responded positively. During the October 2011 Asia-Pacific Economic Cooperation leaders' meeting in Shanghai, Jiang and Bush reached a consensus on building a constructive Sino-American relationship. Bush's state visit to China in February 2002 signaled the recovery of the relationship from the nadir of the collision crisis.[51]

The Success of Strategic Dialogue Diplomacy

The most notable success of diplomacy during the Bush administration was the Sino-American strategic dialogue pioneered by two fine diplomats: Vice Foreign Minister and subsequently State Councilor Dai Bingguo, and Deputy Secretary of State Robert Zoellick. New to the field of Sino-American relations, Dai became intrigued by the idea of a strategic dialogue after his shuttle diplomacy on North Korea and Taiwan with his American counterparts in 2003. As he relates in his memoirs, these diplomatic encounters suggested to him the potential of a regular dialogue mechanism for exploring a new cooperative relationship. The new Chinese president, Hu Jintao, supported the initiative and instructed Dai to develop it. In spring 2004 Dai visited America and consulted Zbigniew Brzezinski, former president Carter's national security advisor, who had played a supporting role in the establishment of the two countries' formal relationship in 1979. Encouraged by Brzezinski, Dai persuaded President Hu to make a formal proposal to President Bush at the November 2004 Asia-Pacific Economic Cooperation meeting. Hu suggested that the two countries each appoint a ministerial-level official to begin regular consultation over major strategic and political issues. Bush agreed. Dai was back in the United States in late November for preparatory work, consulting two other former officials, Kissinger and Brent Scowcroft.[52]

Recounting this experience, Dai stressed the importance of smart and flexible diplomacy. Although leaders were essential in providing political support and broad instructions, diplomats, exercising initiatives within the space allotted them, were indispensable in implementation. So was reciprocity from the other side. Here Dai was fortunate to have Zoellick as his American counterpart. The two senior diplomats, each entrusted with necessary freedom and authority by their respective governments, quickly forged a chemistry in their first meeting, on August 1, 2005. Initially underprepared for the talk, Zoellick was so impressed by Dai and the substance of their discussion that their conversation lasted from morning until evening. Dai demonstrated qualities of a far-sighted strategist for which some Chinese leaders and senior officials are known but which are often missing in lower-level officials.

This first encounter prompted a rethinking of the relationship by Zoellick, who delivered his famous speech one month later on China as a "responsible stakeholder" working with the United States to safeguard international order.[53] Zoellick hosted the second round of the dialogue in December 2005, spending two days with Dai in Washington. Then, amid heavy snow, he arranged a military aircraft to take Dai to the Franklin D. Roosevelt Presidential Library and Museum in New York, pointedly showing him Roosevelt's sketch of the "Four Policemen" (the United States, the Soviet Union, the United Kingdom, and China) drawn during the Teheran conference of November 1943. The two officials spent over twenty hours in this round of talks, a rarity in Sino-American high-level diplomacy before and since.[54]

In December 2006, based on a recommendation from Zoellick to Secretary of the Treasury Henry Paulson, the two countries created a new senior dialogue on economic cooperation to complement the strategic dialogue. These two dialogues played a major role in stabilizing the relationship and building bilateral trust. Despite initial turbulence from the April 2001 collision incident, the relationship during the next seven years of the Bush administration was the most stable in the post–Cold War era. Powell's September 2003 appraisal that the relationship was at its best since Nixon's first visit to China in 1972 could be applied until the end of the Bush administration.[55]

In February 2009 the new Obama administration proposed consolidating the two separate dialogues into an integrated "strategic and economic dialogue" (S&ED). For four years, the S&ED promised to elevate the relationship. Dai developed some rapport with the new secretary of state, Hillary Clinton, although not with the same degree of chemistry as with Zoellick. A new dialogue on Asia-Pacific security sprang up in 2011. At the fourth round of the S&ED, in May 2012, President Hu proposed building "a new type of major country relationship." Dai proudly claims that exploring such a relationship had been a hallmark of the strategic dialogue he initiated since 2005. At the fourth round of the S&ED, the final round for him and Clinton, Dai tried to drive home with great conviction and emotion the imperative of finding a new model of relationship. He likened himself to a "builder" and "maintenance worker" of the road leading to such a relationship, and gave Clinton his written thoughts on how to achieve it. Evidently moved, Clinton remarked that both countries must strive to build a cooperative relationship based on mutual respect and benefit by forestalling all interfering factors. One month later Dai met with President Obama's national security advisor, Tom Donilon. Having read Dai's written thoughts, Donilon assured him that the two countries had already reached an important consensus on building a new type of relationship.[56]

Dai retired in March 2013, hopeful that he had spearheaded a new Sino-American diplomacy on building a new type of relationship distinct from past, often confrontational relationships between rising and established powers. Like many others, he was buoyed by the shirtsleeve summit between Obama and the new Chinese president Xi Jinping in June 2013. He hailed the eight-hour exchanges between the two leaders as a "milestone" in the history of the relationship.[57] But such optimism was misplaced. How the "new model" diplomacy failed, after the success of the "strategic dialogue" diplomacy painstakingly built up by Dai and his American counterparts, illustrates with special clarity the requisites for effective diplomacy.

The Failure of New Model Diplomacy

That a new diplomacy for building a new model of relationship could be carried to the top leadership of both countries was itself an achievement that owed above all to leadership commitment and deft diplomats. Dai's strategic dialogue diplomacy from 2005 to 2012 laid the intellectual ground. Vice President Xi tested the idea in February 2012. Secretary of State Clinton responded positively in March. President Hu made a formal proposal in May. Momentum continued to build in 2013. In March that year Donilon called on the two countries to build a new model of relationship, noting that both Obama and Xi had endorsed it. In June,

Xi promoted it to Obama during their summit in California. A curious Obama asked Xi to elaborate further. In November, Obama's new national security advisor, Susan Rice, called for operationalizing the new model. Meanwhile Vice President Joseph Biden was preparing a visit to China for exactly this purpose (see Chapter 4). If leadership commitment was all that was required, the new model relationship would have been established.

However, effective diplomacy also requires smooth policy coordination and careful implementation that can translate ideas into practice. Sustaining the momentum from conception to implementation is crucial. Here China proved woefully inadequate. Just when Biden was about to visit China and operationalize the new model, the PLA announced a surprising decision to establish an Air Defense Identification Zone (ADIZ) for the East China Sea in November 2013. Meanwhile Xi endorsed the PLA's proposal for building islands in the South China Sea no later than September 2013. Once the full scale of island building was known after 2015, Sino-American strategic competition in maritime Asia deteriorated dramatically. In May 2014 China deployed an oil rig in waters disputed by Vietnam, triggering violent clashes between Chinese and Vietnamese vessels. The US State Department strongly criticized Chinese action. That same month Xi delivered a major speech calling on Asians to address Asian issues themselves. US elites interpreted the message as intending to exclude America from Asian affairs (see Chapter 4).

In the eyes of American officials, this unwelcome flurry of actions contradicted the premise of a new model of relationship based on mutual trust and mutual benefit. China failed to follow through on its new model diplomacy by seeking practical cooperation in hard security areas such as military confidence-building, the North Korean nuclear weapons program, and maritime tensions, as urged by US officials. Worse, it had appeared to challenge US interests in Asia. After 2014 the new model talk began to ring hollow in Washington. Suspicious analysts interpreted it as a Chinese strategic ruse to make major advances in Asia by preempting US vigilance. After 2015 the tide of US debates on China policy turned toward the necessity of competition with China.[58] In December 2017 the Trump administration designated China a "competitor" and a "revisionist power" in its first National Security Strategy, completing the transformation of the mainstream American view about China from engagement to competition.[59]

We argued in Chapter 4 that lack of policy coordination, exacerbated by competition among bureaucratic actors and interest groups, bore a heavy responsibility for the failure to carry through the new model diplomacy. The PLA, tangling its understanding of China's national interest with its organizational interest in the Chinese system, proposed both the ADIZ and island-building decisions. It did not consult with civilian agencies such as the Ministry of Foreign Affairs.

President Xi's nod to the PLA was striking in light of his enthusiasm for the new model diplomacy. He knew that President Obama had suggested military confidence-building as the first area to build a new model of relationship. If this suggestion was taken seriously, Xi should have exercised great caution, perhaps by delaying the PLA's decisions or even instructing the PLA to communicate with the American side about them. It is possible that he agreed with the PLA while giving little thought to the impact of these decisions on his new model diplomacy, in which case the problem was a faulty conception on his part. It is also possible that in 2013 he needed the PLA internally more than any foreign policy success. In that first year of his presidency, he was trying to consolidate power through an audacious anticorruption campaign and a planned, equally sweeping military reform program. He might have given in to PLA demands because he needed the military's support in his domestic political struggle. Foreign policy was a casualty of this political imperative. Or the decision might have been a result of the closed nature of the decision-making process, confined to Xi and the military top brass without inputs from the wider policy system. Regardless, a promising and potentially significant diplomacy succumbed to interest-group pressure.

It is tempting to ask whether the outcome might have been different had Dai not retired in March 2013 or had Xi consulted more widely within the government. Dai's strategic vision and diplomatic skills were universally appreciated by the Chinese and Americans alike. His successor, Yang Jiechi, was perhaps out of his depth. Moreover, unlike Dai, who was a trusted advisor to President Hu, it is not clear how much trust and confidence Xi placed in Yang. Senior Obama administration officials complained to Chinese elites that after Dai's departure they were hard-pressed to find a "point person" with comparable political authority, strategic wisdom, and tactical skills. As a result, genuine strategic discussion was left to Obama and Xi at their summit meetings.[60]

Thus another reason for the faltering new model diplomacy after 2013 appeared to be the absence of a chief diplomat like Dai. Chinese analysts refer to him as a "strategic operator."[61] Any strategic operator in the Chinese context should have political authority, a strategic vision unencumbered by bureaucratic inertia, maneuvering space entrusted by the top leader, and tactical skills to oversee and coordinate the complex and often fractured Chinese decision-making system.[62] Such an official would be able to serve as a bridge between the strategic vision of the top leadership and the operational nitty-gritty of China's vast bureaucracy.

Doubtless a strategic operator like Dai would have smoothed some of the rough edges of Chinese foreign policy after 2013. But the answer to the counterfactual question of whether such an official would have made a difference in the new model diplomacy would depend on the nature of China's domestic politics at the time. Leaders and diplomats operate under the constraints of domestic politics. If such constraints were minimal and the problem was a lack of honest and wise advice from a trusted advisor, then a strategic operator like Dai might have talked Xi out of the ADIZ and island-building decisions by pointing out their contradictions with the new model diplomacy. However, if Xi was constrained by the need to consolidate power and make concessions to interest groups such as the PLA, he could not have given much authority and freedom to his advisor for conducting strategic diplomacy unhindered by politics. Under these circumstances, even if Dai had continued to serve under Xi with the same degree of trust that he had from Hu, he would not have performed like a strategic operator as he had during the Hu years. Cooperating with the United States on North Korea, for example, could generate strong conservative resistance impossible for him—or for Xi—to break. Dai was known to have blocked the PLA's island-building proposals during the Hu years.[63] It would have been riskier for him to do so under Xi, when Xi needed the PLA's backing for political purposes.

The lesson from China's failed new model diplomacy with America is that diplomacy needs the mutual support of leadership commitment and policy implementation. In complex political systems like China's, smooth implementation depends on effective policy coordination among diverse and competing bureaucratic actors. Policy coordination in turn requires an authoritative chief diplomat with strategic insight, tactical skill, and full trust and confidence from the top leadership, or a dedicated coordination mechanism with these qualities. In the final analysis, the effectiveness of such officials and mechanisms is subject to domestic political dynamics.

American Diplomacy under the Rebalance Strategy

American diplomacy toward China during the Obama administration is also a cautionary tale. To be fair, the administration engaged China through more than sixty different kinds of dialogue under the S&ED framework. In the practical realm of meetings, negotiations, and sharing of positions across various levels of the two governments, a lot was going on. But there was no serious effort to address the balance between deterrence and reassurance, especially after the announcement of the Asia rebalance strategy in late 2011.

The principal flaws were faulty conceptions. As we described in Chapter 3, Obama and his Asia team wanted to foster cooperation and contain confrontation with China. This goal pointed out competition management and conflict reduction as central tasks of America's China policy. But there was no corresponding strategy or diplomacy to bring them about. On the contrary, administration officials eschewed the development of a China strategy in favor of an Asia regional strategy of the rebalance. They chose to embed China policy under this regional strategy, believing incorrectly that the rebalance would achieve the dual objective of improving America's relations with Asian countries as well as with China. Events have proved this premise wrong. While America indeed enhanced its relations with its Asian allies and partners, its relationship with China suffered deteriorating competition. If the rebalance strategy was meant to strengthen America's position in Asia and balance China's rise, it was arguably a measured success. But if its purpose was to improve cooperation and manage competition with China through a circuitous region-wide approach, it was a clear failure. The belief of many officials that it could do both reflected muddled thinking.

Even though faulty conceptions of the rebalance strategy made it unlikely to be a productive strategy for competition management, adroit diplomacy might have softened its sharp edges and slowed down the pace of competition. President Obama's declaration in 2009, his first year in office, that America did not seek to contain China but welcomed China's rise could have blunted Chinese criticisms about the rebalance and provided a starting point for reassurance. Kurt M. Campbell, assistant secretary of state for East Asian and Pacific affairs during the first Obama administration, and a principal architect of the rebalance, claimed in a book written after leaving the government that the rebalance toward China should be seen as a mixture of reassurance and resolve (see Chapter 3). If so, the element of reassurance, however tenuous, could create a condition for diplomacy.

In practice, diplomacy for reassurance was almost nonexistent. This was the case even before the rebalance was announced. In September 2009, when the relationship was in a brief and rare state of harmony, Deputy Secretary of State James Steinberg emphasized the need for strategic reassurance between the two countries. But this idea met with so much resistance that it was never formally accepted within the administration; it disappeared altogether after Steinberg left the State Department in March 2011.[64] Given this precedent, it is hard to believe that American officials would highlight the message of reassurance to China after the rebalance was launched in 2010, when the relationship began to go downhill. Chinese elites complained about the lack of communication about its nature when the rebalance was launched. Intentional or not, it fed Chinese suspicions and led to the judgment that it was aimed at China.[65] The overwhelming signal of the rebalance was one of deterring, not reassuring, China. This was a perception shared by all Asian countries, including China.

American officials claimed that the rebalance was a comprehensive strategy involving military, economic, diplomatic, and political efforts. Diplomacy was not absent. It was nevertheless used more to cement ties with America's Asian allies than to reassure China. Attempts to double down on America's already robust military presence in Asia and to frame the Trans-Pacific Partnership free trade agreement as competition with China for regional leadership were the most notable, and were perceived as such in Beijing. The rhetorical packaging of the new Asia strategy as a "pivot" and "rebalance" gave the impression that America was retraining its guns on China after winding down its wars in the Middle East.[66] This inevitably had unfortunate consequences for Chinese elite debates about US policy, silencing moderates and giving a voice to hardliners calling for competition. By itself the rebalance did not cause Chinese assertiveness, but it created a geopolitical setting that made domestic Chinese arguments about assertiveness more palatable. Its message of reassurance, to the extent that it existed, made no impact in China.

The absence of credible reassurance reflected the imbalance of the different components of the rebalance strategy. The military arm of the strategy was the most prominent, diplomacy of reassurance toward China the least. In addition to faulty conceptions, this imbalance was also a result of poor bureaucratic oversight and coordination. In the South China Sea, for example, the hawkish rhetoric of military officers such as Admiral Harry Harris, commander of the Pacific Command from 2015 to 2018, overshadowed the policy statements of State Department officials. A more effective approach would have been the other way around: diplomats, not officers, should have been entrusted with conveying policy messages.[67] Thus, like China in the case of the new model diplomacy, American formulation and implementation of overall policy also suffered from bureaucratic rivalry. The regrettable consequences of such rivalry were inconsistent messages and poor signaling that made misjudgment and miscalculation easier.[68]

Cognitive, psychological, and motivational limitations, notably misperception and misjudgment, inhibited diplomacy. American attitudes toward China soured after Chinese maritime assertiveness in Asia raised new regional tensions. The Obama administration determined that China was adopting a new strategy of altering the status quo and challenging US dominance. This judgment informed the rebalance strategy and marked the beginning of a new era of maritime competition in the relationship. It was an overreaction with regrettable consequences. Some hawks in China indeed entertained a vague notion of driving America out of East Asia, especially in the near-seas within the First Island Chain. But they did not command the policy mainstream. The premise of Chinese maritime policy was the protection of sovereignty and maritime interests perceived as legitimately China's. Geopolitical competition was a consequence, not a cause, of this policy. Had the Obama administration conducted a more independent, thoughtful, and balanced assessment of Chinese policy, it might have found the value of reassurance and diplomacy in managing its differences with China and finding some common ground. Instead it opted for deterrence in the name of rebalance.

These limitations were also evident on the Chinese side. They were aggravated by an ingrained mistrust of American strategic intentions. Anti-Americanism, although marginal in official thinking, has never disappeared from Chinese consciousness in the post–Cold War era. It underpins a persistent suspicion of American containment of China and a perpetual vigilance against American actions. This frame of reference provides ample grounds for misperception, misjudgment, and overreaction.[69] It is then not surprising that Chinese assessments of the rebalance were overwhelmingly negative across the policy and intellectual communities.[70] Equanimity in the face of a perceived challenge became difficult. This helps to explain the puzzle that at the same time President Xi was pushing for his new model diplomacy, parts of his government, notably the PLA, were preparing to confront America and its Asian allies. As noted, their aggressive posture torpedoed the new model diplomacy. Both the United States and China were prone to worst-case assumptions due to their cognitive, psychological, and motivational limitations. They made diplomacy difficult when both sides perceived competition to be on the rise after 2013.

We noted earlier that reciprocity is an important condition for diplomatic success. The inadequacy of diplomatic reciprocity from China was a contributing factor to the Obama administration's lack of interest in developing a China-focused, as opposed to an Asian regional, strategy. As noted in Chapter 4, President Obama began his China policy by adopting a conciliatory approach that was markedly different from approaches favored by his predecessors. In 2009, his first year in office, he set the tone of welcoming China's rise and scheduled a state visit—the first American president to do so in the history of the relationship. But Beijing gave Obama a reception that the Americans criticized as lukewarm. In international diplomacy, such as at the United Nations Climate Change Conference in Copenhagen, Chinese officials, relishing perceived American decline in the midst of a financial crisis, acted as if they could now stare down America as never before. This was a costly mistake that made 2009–10 a missed opportunity for building a cooperative relationship, just as 2012–13 was a wasted opportunity for building a new model of relationship.

Future Prospects

Our discussion of the role of diplomacy in conflict management in general, and in American-Chinese relations in particular, generates several important findings on the conditions of effective diplomacy. Leadership commitment to diplomacy in building a strong relationship is a necessary but not sufficient condition. It is a starting point for diplomacy, but never the end of it. It is nevertheless a crucial enabling condition. Crises and major policy initiatives require not only a smart and focused leadership but flexible implementation by diplomats to exploit opportunities and relationships. Diplomats must also provide useful feedback to political leaders. Major breakthroughs require recognition that threat-based approaches have been counterproductive and dangerous—as they certainly have been in Sino-American relations. Trust between political leaders is essential. No American and Chinese leaders have achieved the same kind of rapport as that between Reagan and Gorbachev, although Kissinger came close in his various interactions with Chinese leaders.

Once leadership commitment is in place, senior officials must develop a corresponding strategy based on sound assumptions. Faulty conceptions have stood in the way of diplomatic progress in Sino-American relations during the post–Cold War period. Both countries need to overcome cognitive, psychological, and motivational limitations, most notably misperception and misjudgment. A good strategy then requires careful and skillful implementation by experienced diplomats, paying particular attention to reciprocity. The differences between the Chinese and American political systems entail different domestic requirements for policy implementation. In both countries, however, leaders and diplomats must have the political room to push and implement major—and especially controversial—decisions. China, due to its fractured decision-making system, is in special need of a chief diplomat entrusted with confidence and authority from the top leader, strategic insight that rises above bureaucratic inertia, administrative competence in coordinating disparate policy preferences, and tactical skills in engaging foreign officials.

What do these conditions tell us about the future prospects of diplomacy in American-Chinese relations? We organize our thoughts according to five sets of conditions: conceptions, leadership, incentives, catalysts, and processes. As our empirical discussions in the preceding chapters are focused on the period of the Obama administration and earlier, we now draw on examples from the first three years of the Trump administration (2017–19). We also look to the future by considering the prospect of using diplomacy to support the strategy of reassurance proposed in Chapter 6.

Conceptions

The greatest danger in American-Chinese thinking about their relationship is the American inclination to engage in unbridled rivalry with China and the Chinese temptation to respond in kind. Since the Obama years American elites have increasingly come to view China as a hegemonic challenger whose rising power and influence must be resisted with America's own power and resolve. Conservative strategists portray China as an authoritarian and aggressive power bent on economic mercantilism and geopolitical revisionism.[71] We argue repeatedly throughout this book that this presumption of a hegemonic Chinese strategy to dominate East Asia is unfounded. The Obama administration's deterrence-based rebalance strategy to counter this alleged challenge was an overreaction that needlessly increased tensions. A holistic strategy through a judicious combination of deterrence, reassurance, and diplomacy, as we propose, would have been a more fruitful way to address Chinese assertiveness and enhance mutual understanding and trust.

The Chinese leadership, still regarding stability as the central goal of its US policy, wants to avoid a competitive relationship. But a growing chorus from policy hawks and nationalists calling for tit-for-tat responses to competition from America could make equanimity difficult to sustain. Moreover triumphalism was again on the rise at the end of Xi's first five-year term in office. In his report to the 19th Party Congress in October 2017, Xi announced that China "has stood up, grown rich, and is becoming strong," with "brilliant prospects of national rejuvenation." He set two cumulative goals for the current "becoming strong" stage: realizing socialist modernization in 2020–35 and developing China into "a great modern socialist country" and "a global leader in terms of composite national strength and international influence" in 2035–50.[72] Xi has made power and influence two central goals of Chinese foreign policy by 2050. Sentimentally he had announced the arrival of China as a world power in 2017. The risk for China is overconfidence and an overestimation of its power and influence. If Chinese foreign policy becomes based on hubris, a collision with an America wishing to preserve its hyped dominance in Asia could result. It would be a clash between two faulty strategic conceptions.

American analysts assert that "getting tough with China" has become the new consensus of both the left and the right and thus the strategic mainstream.[73] The Trump administration's 2017 National Security Strategy and 2018 National Defense Strategy were early reflections of this consensus, and some of its judgments were alarming. Asserting that "China seeks to displace the United States in the Indo-Pacific region, expand the reaches of its state-driven economic model, and reorder the region in its favor," the National Security Strategy framed US-China tensions as a "geopolitical competition between free and repressive visions of world order."[74] Similarly the National Defense Strategy asserted that China's military modernization "seeks Indo-Pacific regional hegemony in the near-term and displacement of the United States to achieve global preeminence in the future."[75] In contrast, we warn against imputing a hegemonic intention to China that might make it real.

The National Security Strategy urged America to integrate all elements of national power, especially military power, to "deter and if necessary, defeat aggression against US interests and increase the likelihood of managing competitions without violent conflict and preserving peace."[76] This was a strategy with military deterrence at the center, assigning only a peripheral role to diplomacy and none at all to reassurance. It gave a nod to cooperation, but only "from a position of strength."[77] It was reminiscent of the Reagan-era strategy of "peace through strength" by out-arming the Soviet Union through an aggressive military buildup.

The strategy nevertheless stopped short of calling for a return to Cold War containment. It focused its competitive instincts on the economic domain, proposing strong curbs on alleged Chinese spying, cyber-enabled economic warfare, theft of intellectual property, and forced transfers of technology. Competition, it said, "does not always mean hostility, nor does it inevitably lead to conflict."[78] Recognizing that China's intentions "are not necessarily fixed," it pledged a readiness to "cooperate across areas of mutual interest."[79] It professed no interest in imposing American values on others.[80] The National Defense Strategy claimed that its objective was to set the US-China military relationship "on a path of transparency and non-aggression."[81] The Trump administration's most hawkish position on China, delivered by Vice President Mike Pence in October 2018, still included a pledge to "a constructive relationship with Beijing."[82] Given these utterances and the factional strife and policymaking chaos of the Trump administration, Chinese observers wondered whether there was any consensus in Washington or the US strategic community about China policy.[83]

Conservative American analysts, while deeply critical of Xi's China, contend that America's policy goals toward China need not change. The United States still "wants a prosperous and secure China that acts as a responsible stakeholder in the world system and a good neighbor in Asia."[84] What needs to change is the means to achieve this goal, and that—for the first time since Nixon's visit to China in 1972—requires competition more than cooperation. Aaron Friedberg, among the most hawkish of the China analysts, exhorts America to compete with China. He nevertheless avers that engagement should not be abandoned as an objective; "the United States and its allies should continue to seek the best possible relationship with Beijing, cooperating where possible on issues of convergent interest and doing whatever they can to avoid a conflict that would be catastrophic for all concerned."[85]

In 2018–2019 a growing number of American analysts have criticized the Trump administration's overreaction, and the new Sinophobia in Washington was encountering its own backlash. Distinguished China experts such as Chas W. Freeman, Harry Harding, David Lampton, and Michael Swaine all voiced their alarm over the steady worsening of the US-China relationship, frustration with the Trump administration's casual and callous response, and policy advice that might avert a collision course.[86] A February 2019 task force report, chaired by Orville Schell and Susan L. Shirk and written by some of America's best China experts, called for restoring "equity and stability to the relationship" through "negotiated solutions." It proposed a strategy of "smart competition" instead of unbridled rivalry, involving "building on American strengths to compete effectively with China while maintaining as much cooperation as possible in areas of common interest."[87] Such a strategy does not amount to conflict management, as conceived in this book, but it is vastly superior to the hawkish chorus of a new cold war.

In July 2019 the *Washington Post* published an open letter signed by close to a hundred distinguished individuals from the scholarly, foreign policy, military, and business communities. The letter, while critical of China, declared that it is "not an enemy." It contends, in fact, that "many U.S. actions are contributing directly to the downward spiral in relations." It is significant that the letter shares our rejection of imputing a hegemonic intention to China. "The fear that Beijing will replace the United States as the global leader is exaggerated," it avows. Further, "most other countries have no interest in such an outcome, and it is not clear that Beijing itself sees this goal as necessary or feasible."[88]

Prominent former officials also highlighted the urgency of a course correction. In a December 2018 editorial for the *Washington Post*, former president Jimmy Carter criticized as equally "dangerous notions" the Chinese view of America conducting an evil conspiracy to destabilize China and the American view of China posing a threat to the American way of life. He urged American and Chinese leaders to "bring new vision, courage and ingenuity to new challenges and opportunities" in the relationship.[89] Writing in the *New York Times* in January 2019, Robert E. Rubin, a former treasury secretary in the Clinton administration, called for reversing the vicious cycle of mutual recriminations and confrontation and putting the relationship back on a constructive course. He pointed out the need for the two countries to work together on major transnational challenges, especially nuclear weapons and climate change.[90] We may expect an upswing of such constructive calls if the relationship continues to deteriorate.

Leading Chinese scholars argue that despite the Trump administration's trumpet for competition, the United States and China are unlikely to end up in a new cold war. According to Yan Xuetong, unlike US–Soviet competition for global leadership, both China and the United States today avoid undertaking excessive international responsibility. Both countries have so far constrained their rivalry from spilling over into the ideological domain. Perhaps most important, if competition is unavoidable China would prefer "peaceful competition" to outright confrontation and conflict. In particular, it would eschew a formal alliance with Russia against the United States.[91]

Both governments, to different degrees, are committed to cooperation. The Chinese commitment is strong and of long standing. Beijing redefined the relationship from no conflict and no confrontation, mutual respect, and win-win cooperation—the three pillars of "a new model of major-country relationship" proposed during the Obama years—to coordination, cooperation, and stability under Trump.[92] At times China has succumbed to hubris, as prominent Chinese scholars have warned.[93] Nevertheless hubris is not a mainstream strategic tradition in Chinese history, and the risk of China plunging into a conflict with America for vain ambitions is low.[94] Nor is China determined to or capable of spreading its model abroad, as so many Western elites fear.[95] That said, there are other pathways to violent conflict, including the nationalism that the regime has helped to stoke. The Trump administration, it is true, employed bellicose rhetoric. Its national security strategy nevertheless called for cooperation in areas of mutual interest even while highlighting a strategy of competition. How much room diplomacy will have in managing conflict will depend on how successful American and Chinese policymakers can be in containing faulty conceptions and avoiding misperception and misjudgment.

Leadership

Xi Jinping has been China's top leader since 2013, simultaneously holding three of the most powerful positions in the Chinese system: president of the Chinese state, general secretary of the Chinese Communist Party, and chairman of the Central Military Commission. In October 2017 the Party's 19th Congress enshrined "Xi Jinping Thought on Socialism with Chinese Characteristics for a New Era" in its constitution. Xi thus became the first living leader to be named as a guide for the Party since Mao died in 1976. Along with Marx, Lenin, Mao, and Deng, Xi now defines what it is to be a Chinese communist.[96] Barely five months later, in March 2018, the National People's Congress voted to abolish the two-term, ten-year limit of the presidency, theoretically paving the way for Xi to rule indefinitely.[97]

Judging from Xi's extraordinary consolidation of power, the Chinese leadership has been exceptionally stable. This provides stability for its US policy as well, in which Xi takes a strong personal interest and is committed to a stable long-term relationship. This commitment is based on the judgment that stability in Sino-American relations is a prerequisite for achieving Xi's ambitious domestic agenda of making China a world power by the mid-twenty-first century.[98] A staggering demonstration of Xi's search for stability with America was his December 2018 G20 meeting with Trump, in which he spent forty-five minutes addressing American trade concerns in the hope of reaching a deal with Trump.[99] For this extraordinary and unprecedented gesture, the American side agreed to a ninety-day window of negotiation.

In contrast, leadership change on the US side was dramatic. Not only did the administration change from Democratic to Republican, but the contrast between the cerebral Obama and the impulsive Trump is among the most striking of presidential transitions. US policy toward China became more volatile and hostile. In 2017 the relationship was still manageable, despite changes in leadership style and policy substance. One reason was the slow pace in which Trump unleashed his trade war. Another was the two countries' policy coordination toward North Korea. A third reason, more relevant to our discussion, was the ability of Trump and Xi to develop some rapport, if not trust, at a personal level through summit meetings. Trump remarked several times that he liked Xi "very much" and that they had "a great chemistry together." He was the first American president to say this about a Chinese leader. Describing his November 2017 visit to China, he was delighted that Xi had treated him "better than anybody's ever been treated in the history of China."[100] Even recognizing Trump's predilection for hyperbole, these sentiments exceeded the level of the working relationship between Obama and Xi. The two leaders also communicated frequently over the telephone—no fewer than ten times between February 2017 and March 2018, mostly over North Korea.[101]

They were also flexible in key areas. Xi went to great lengths to accommodate Trump's request for pressure over North Korea. While China eschewed the harshest measures coming out of Washington, it signed up to all the sanctions reached through the United Nations in 2017. In 2017–18 Xi tried hard to placate Trump's demands on trade, as demonstrated by his extraordinary forty-five-minute presentation to soothe Trump's trade agitations during their G20 meeting. Since 2019 Trump's impulsiveness, recklessness, and lack of credibility, in conjunction with a new assessment of China's ability to withstand the trade war, have finally prompted China to take a new approach of standing up to American demands.

Nevertheless, in view of the Trump administration's overall hawkishness, it is not clear what Beijing made of Trump's professed "chemistry" with Xi. It would not be surprising if Xi and the Chinese leadership regarded this claim as tongue-in-cheek or, worse, a malign ruse. A particularly disruptive swerve of Trump's moods in a matter of three days in late August 2019 seems more than enough to vindicate their suspicion. On August 23, 2019, in a fit of rage after hearing Chinese retaliation against his tariffs, Trump called Xi an "enemy." Three days later Xi again became "a great leader" and a "brilliant man."[102] Because the condition of leadership for diplomatic success was largely absent in the Trump era we need to look to future American leaders for leadership commitment to the long-term health of the relationship.

Incentives

Incentives were critical in the transformation of American-Chinese relations from hostility to cooperation during the Cold War. External incentives—for America, the Vietnam War and competition with the Soviet Union, and for China, conflict with the Soviet Union—were fundamental in spurring the normalization of their relationship. Domestic incentives were also critical for China. Mao needed a foreign policy breakthrough to shore up his faltering "continuous revolution" at home. Deng wanted a strategic relationship with the United States to support his nascent domestic economic reform program.

The disappearance of a common external incentive—opposing Soviet hegemony—helps to explain lackluster diplomacy in the post–Cold War period. But it is not the whole story. During the Jiang-Hu years (1989–2012), China's domestic incentive of seeking American assistance and cooperation in its economic development was still strong, even when bilateral security tensions accumulated. The culmination of Sino-American economic cooperation was China's accession to the World Trade Organization in 2001, painstakingly negotiated during the Clinton administration. For a decade thereafter Western elites believed that economic interdependence would drive economic, and eventually political, liberalization inside China. That expectation was shattered in 2012 with the ascension to power of Xi, whose rule was perceived as leaning toward repression, state control, and confrontation. As a result, as Xi started his second term in 2018 the United States and Western European countries had little appetite for deeper economic cooperation. This loss of Western interest was matched by the increase in China's confidence that, as the world's second largest economy, it no longer needed the West.

The picture on the security and political fronts was equally grim. China's military modernization and maritime policy, especially island building in the South China Sea, prompted a reassessment from American elites of China as a strategic rival. Its alleged "influence operations," using its "sharp power" to shape opinions in Western societies, raised widespread anxiety. Western elites worried about China's potential promotion of its own authoritarianism as an alternative global model to Western democracy. And Xi's scrapping of the presidential term limits at the beginning of his second term produced a disturbing perception that China had entered a new era of strongman rule or dictatorship. Believing that "the West got China wrong," as the *Economist* put it, the Western impulse was for competition, not cooperation.[103]

Nevertheless incentives for diplomacy remain. The biggest incentive, in an era when America has designated China a competitor and when China may be tempted to respond tit-for-tat, is the realization that untamed rivalry would risk making them enemies and producing a catastrophic conflict. This risk becomes greater if competition intensifies and makes preventive diplomacy to manage competition and prevent crises critical—but also more difficult.

Competition reflects the disillusionment with Xi's China of much of the American national security elite. Some American and Chinese analysts hope that competition may bring out the best sides of both countries and thus take on a benign character.[104] The Schell-Shirk report, mentioned earlier, proposes "smart competition" as a mixed strategy of competition and cooperation that does not foreclose the avenues for stability, comity, and growth.[105] Nevertheless competition can escalate into confrontation and conflict through a number of pathways, not least policymakers' misjudgment and miscalculation. The wish to avoid such consequences would give diplomacy a role in the quest for coexistence, if not accommodation. Coexistence would require successful conflict management and reduction, an important purpose of diplomacy. Accommodation would mean the winding down of competition and the resolution of conflict, a more demanding task.

For the sake of coexistence, if not accommodation, diplomacy will continue to play a central role in managing bilateral tensions over Taiwan, North Korea, Asian maritime disputes, and the Asian security architecture—key areas of reassurance that we identified in Chapter 6. US-China coordination over North Korea in 2017 was a successful example in this regard. Even if competition persists, there may come a time when threat-based strategies such as war and deterrence are recognized by both sides as counterproductive. This would then create a condition for diplomacy, as we have noted.

Catalysts

Catalysts have helped Beijing and Washington to launch creative diplomacy. Chinese-Soviet border conflicts in 1969, especially the clash in Xinjiang in August in which an entire Chinese brigade was eliminated, produced Chinese fear of a major Soviet attack.[106] That catalyst led to Chinese-American rapprochement two years later. In the case of the establishment of their official relationship in 1979, Deng was himself the decisive mover. He believed that China needed American assistance in economic reform, in addition to a common effort in opposing the Soviet Union. This belief justified normalization as a strategic decision to be made even at the cost of continued American defense ties with Taiwan through arms sales and an implicit security commitment. The biggest catalyst in the post–Cold War era was the September 11 terrorist attacks. The new terrorism triggered a reorientation of strategic priority on the American side and a recognition of this as a major opportunity to improve relations on the Chinese side. The success of Dai's strategic dialogue diplomacy is owed in no small amount to this catalyst and the new strategic environment it created.

Leaders and events can serve as catalysts. Arguably, Trump, and the priority he attached to the North Korean issue, was a critical catalyst in driving American-Chinese diplomatic cooperation in this area and in limiting the damage to their economic relationship in 2017. Trump claimed that the only thing more important to him than trade was preventing war with North Korea, and he threatened to get tough on trade if China did not help him with North Korea.[107] Chinese leaders must have found such threats credible to a certain extent. They were moreover frightened by the prospect of a war on the Korean Peninsula due to Trump's impulsiveness and the misjudgment and miscalculation it could generate in both Washington and Pyongyang. These worries prompted Beijing to placate Trump by instituting the severest sanctions against North Korea it had ever agreed to. Needless to say, Trump's impetuosity could also become a catalyst for competition and conflict, and his behavior in 2018–19 represented a catalyst of this kind.

It is impossible to predict whether comparable events like the Sino-Soviet border clash and September 11 terrorist attacks will occur in the future and will create conditions for new diplomatic breakthroughs. But a new crisis over North Korea, in the event of Pyongyang's missile launch into the vicinity of Guam, an atmospheric nuclear test, or a demonstrated nuclear intercontinental ballistic missile capability, could trigger a new round of escalation and crisis diplomacy among China, the United States, and other regional actors. So could a crisis over Taiwan or Asian maritime disputes.

Catalysts and incentives can be mutually reinforcing, in the sense that the incentives of a given situation may produce a catalyst which then strengthens the initial incentives. Nevertheless catalysts can sometimes set off more fundamental changes than incentives because of their visibility and impact over a short period of time. The Fashoda crisis of 1898 was a catalyst famous for triggering a transformation of the Anglo-French relationship from confrontation to accommodation. The German threat, an increasingly important incentive for accommodation, drove Britain and France together on continental issues. The Anglo-French entente cordiale nevertheless required the Fashoda crisis to resolve their colonial disputes. If current incentives between China and the United States are adequate only for containing competition but are insufficient for conflict resolution, a major catalyst might vault diplomacy toward the more ambitious goal of accommodation.

The value of catalysts depends on how policymakers make use of them. Agency was crucial in all the successful cases of the past, whether the Fashoda crisis of 1898, the Sino-Soviet clash of 1969, or the terrorist attacks of 2001.

Diplomatic blunders between China and the United States during the Obama administration offer a cautionary tale of both countries' competence in exploiting catalysts. At different times, Obama and Xi both served as catalysts in driving new diplomacy—Obama in 2009 and Xi in 2012–13. Obama's positive overtures were inadequately reciprocated by China, prompting his shift toward a tougher approach; Xi's new model diplomacy foundered in implementation, undermined as it was by his Asia policy. These problems, it might be noted, were equally manifest in American and Soviet leaders' search for détente during the Cold War, when they had incentives for détente but attained only short-term results.[108] The productive use of catalysts and incentives demands supportive strategic conceptions and policy processes, in addition to leadership commitment.

Processes

Once the conditions of leadership commitment, incentives, catalysts, and conceptions are in place, an effective decision-making process of coordinating and implementing corresponding policies to support diplomacy is a necessary next step. As we have seen, the absence of such a process was the main reason behind the failure of Xi's new model diplomacy toward America during the Obama administration. This in turn resulted from the outsized role of the PLA in strategic decision-making. The lack of an authoritative and trusted chief diplomat to coordinate policy, as Dai had done under Hu, might have exacerbated bureaucratic competition and policy disorder. A more fundamental reason might have been Xi's need of PLA support in consolidating power during the first year of his presidency. Domestic politics may have restricted his political space for the new model diplomacy.

At the beginning of his second term in 2018, Xi appeared to be China's strongest leader since Mao. He had waged a relentless anticorruption campaign, carried out a sweeping military reform program, enshrined his thought in the CCP charter, and abolished presidential term limits. Naming no successor at the Party's 19th Congress and spurning the norm of collective leadership instituted by Deng in the 1980s, he stood above everyone else in China's power hierarchy, with no challenger in sight. Theoretically this would give him comfortable political room to execute major strategic decisions. And indeed strengthening such authority was offered by the Party-state as a major justification for scrapping presidential term limits.[109] Xi would no longer be handicapped, as he might have been during his first term, by powerful factions and interest groups such as the PLA.

With this extraordinary concentration of power, Xi would also be in a position to tighten the foreign policy decision-making system and make it more centralized and effective. A chief diplomat in the form of a strategic operator, or a coordination mechanism to that effect, would also be easier to establish than during his first term. State Councilor Yang, his top diplomat, was promoted to the Politburo at the 19th Party Congress, although not given any government post. Yang is the first career diplomat to achieve this rank since Qian Qichen (1992–2002), enhancing the influence of the Foreign Ministry in policymaking. Foreign Minister Wang Yi, promoted to state councilor, will serve another term, from 2018 to 2023, providing stability to the foreign policy establishment. After Trump took office, Xi contemplated an even more authoritative point person, Wang Qishan, for the increasingly challenging relationship with the United States.[110] Wang was his political ally and anticorruption chief during his first term, and his intellectual gifts were much admired by foreign leaders, including senior American officials.[111] Xi appointed him vice president in March 2018, although he was not active in US policy in 2018–19. In the turbulent economic domain, Liu He, a vice premier after March 2018 and another trusted advisor, was Xi's chief trade negotiator with the United States.

Extreme concentration of power could also lead to distortion in both policy substance and the decision-making process. A weak leader, having to bow to domestic political pressures from time to time, could become incapable of making major or controversial decisions. A dictatorial ruler, facing no constraints and fearing no reprisals, could cut off the chain of decision-making and confine major decisions to a small enclave of people without consultation or input from outside. Big mistakes could result as a consequence. To some extent such a closed mode of decision-making had affected Xi's leadership during his first term. Knowledgeable observers in Beijing suggest that Xi sometimes made decisions without consulting the Politburo Standing Committee, let alone the government bureaucracies and outside experts. The South China Sea island-building decision, reached by Xi and the top leaders of the PLA navy, was such an example.[112]

In contrast to Xi's overpowering authority, Trump was an unpopular and unruly president. He failed to win the popular vote in the November 2016 presidential election and was handicapped by the investigation on Russian meddling in the election. The American policymaking process had already been beset by organizational complexity and interagency rivalry.[113] Trump made it chaotic and even conflictual. His impulsiveness distorted the policy process and damaged policy rationality. Within the first three years of his presidency, he fired or forced out three national security advisors, a secretary of defense, two chiefs of staff, a chief strategist, a press secretary, two White House communications directors, a secretary of health and human services, a secretary of state, a secretary of veterans affairs, and a director of the National Economic Council, among lesser officials. The firing of Secretary of State Rex Tillerson in March 2018, announced on Twitter before informing the incumbent, epitomized this chaos.[114]

Beginning in 2018 China was eager to appoint a point person for its US policy and wanted the Trump administration to do likewise.[115] An authoritative channel would clearly help to improve effective strategic communication between the two sides.[116] Yet nothing came from the American side. Neither the White House nor the State Department had much China expertise valued by Trump. Personnel changes were rapid, and many key positions unfilled. Cui Tiankai, China's ambassador in Washington, successfully cultivated Jared Kushner, Trump's son-in-law, in 2017, but Kushner's influence began to wane thereafter. If Xi was able to field a chief diplomat like Dai, Trump was in possession of no one like Zoellick.

The ideal condition for diplomacy in terms of the policy process is the availability of leaders and diplomats with sufficient political authority and strategic wisdom to reach the right kinds of decisions and to implement corresponding policies, on the basis of an effective decision-making system open to professional and expert input. In this regard, the Chinese system under Xi and the American system under Trump both contained promises and risks, but for different reasons. Xi's consolidation of power could generate an authoritative policymaking system conducive to diplomacy. The risk, however, was too much concentration of power in too small a circle closed off from feedback mechanisms that must be based on due process. Trump's America was beset by the president's impulsiveness and the shortage of competent officials. On the other hand, Trump's defiance of political norms and policy traditions at times created unusual, if unreliable, room for diplomatic novelty.[117]

Looking Ahead

Our discussion of the prospects of diplomacy during the Trump administration and beyond yields a mixed picture. Trump had no commitment to the long-term health of the relationship, only his daily whims and misguided beliefs. In the absence of a common adversary such as the Soviet Union during the Cold War or a domestic imperative such as China's need for economic reform, internal and external incentives have declined in both countries. The need to avoid a calamitous conflict nevertheless remains a strong incentive for diplomacy. New catalysts may create conditions for creative diplomacy, even triggering deeper changes than incentives. Both American and Chinese elites are prone to faulty conceptions about the relationship, with competitive instincts on the rise on both sides. But the relationship has not yet degenerated into a hopeless confrontation; room for diplomacy and cooperation remains. In terms of policy process, Xi's extraordinary consolidation of power in China could give rise to an effective decision-making system, although it could also cripple due process. Trump's impulsiveness, on the other hand, was a recipe for policy chaos but has also spawned diplomatic novelty. In an era of intensifying competition, diplomacy faces both opportunities and constraints. How it will perform will depend on the context of the two countries' interactions and the conditions it gives rise to.

We look ahead to American-Chinese relations after Trump with cautious optimism. Lacking any coherence or insight, Trump had made decisions based on his own nationalist and nativist instincts and a narrow, almost day-to-day appreciation of interests, chiefly his own.[118] The supposed rapport he developed with Xi was no insurance against the policy instability his impulsiveness had created. His faulty conceptions, especially the antediluvian fixation on trade deficit and the juvenile faith in military power, stood in the way of a sophisticated strategy for conflict management. His administration was marked by personnel chaos and cronyism, damaging the rationality and effectiveness of policymaking.

There is no guarantee that future American presidents will be able to escape all the ills of the Trump administration. But as long as they overcome Trump's failings in personal character and policy conceptions, more room may be found for improving the relationship. If the relationship degenerates into conflict, damaging the interests of both countries, future leaders in both countries may recognize the costs of their prior counterproductive policies and develop more constructive strategies conducive to conflict management and reduction. But our optimism is necessarily guarded because Trump was a symptom, not the cause, of the underlying changes in Sino-American relations. Across American politics and society attitudes toward China are hardening. Future American and Chinese leaders must grapple with this uncomfortable reality to create room for diplomacy in conflict management.

Summary

Diplomacy is the third leg of a holistic strategy we propose for managing conflict between America and China. Some general conditions help to make it effective, although its specific operation is always context-dependent. Leadership commitment is often necessary for launching major diplomatic initiatives. Leaders also need to be flexible in their thinking. Their motivational and cognitive qualities are best utilized in a favorable political environment, when leaders and diplomats have the necessary political freedom and policy room to exercise initiative. Rapport and trust between leaders are additional boosts to diplomacy. These conditions have helped to launch creative diplomacy in US-China relations, as they have in other historical cases. The normalization of the relationship during the 1970s, the initiation of a strategic dialogue in the 2000s, and the initial momentum to establish a new model of relationship in 2012–13, all came about because of commitment from leaders of both countries.

Leadership commitment is often the result of internal or external incentives, reinforced by catalysts that highlight pressing challenges and the imperative of diplomacy. Some of the most successful diplomatic initiatives in US-China relations were triggered by incentives and catalysts of this kind. The normalization of the relationship in the 1970s, for example, originated from the American incentive of finding a way out of the Vietnam War and strengthening its position vis-à-vis the Soviet Union, and the Chinese incentive of blunting Soviet military pressure and spearheading its domestic economic reform. In the post–Cold War period, the September 11 terrorist attacks were an important catalyst for renewing cooperation after the April 2001 aircraft collision crisis had damaged the relationship.

Effective diplomacy also requires sound strategic conceptions. A remarkable example is the transformation of American and Chinese thinking about each other in the late 1960s and early 1970s that cleared the conceptual obstacles for normalizing the relationship. A regrettable counterexample is the Obama administration's shunning of a productive strategy for managing competition with China in favor of a narrow, largely deterrence-based Asia strategy of rebalance that needlessly increased tensions.

A smooth decision-making process capable of coordinating disparate policy preferences and implementing supportive policies is also critical to effective diplomacy. In the famous example of Sino-American rapprochement during the 1970s, Nixon and Kissinger from the US side and Mao and Zhou from the Chinese side pressed their respective diplomatic machinery to serve an overriding strategic goal, at times through secrecy and manipulation. In contrast, Xi's much vaunted diplomacy for establishing a new model of relationship was undermined by policy contradictions stemming from a lack of coordination and bureaucratic rivalry.

Looking ahead, diplomacy faces both opportunities and constraints in managing Sino-American competition. The deterioration of the relationship during the Obama years and changes in the internal and external policies of Xi's China have hardened American views about China. Reflecting the new mainstream consensus, the Trump administration outlined a strategy of competition toward China. Nevertheless the need to avoid a devastating conflict between the two countries remains a powerful incentive for diplomatic management. A crisis over Taiwan, North Korea, or Asian maritime disputes could create a catalyst for ambitious diplomacy. So too could a new Democratic administration. The relationship has not degenerated into an unrelenting confrontation, and neither country is calling for a return to the Cold War.

Diplomacy has a challenging task ahead, but considerable room is still available. All the general conditions of effective diplomacy we have examined could be enabled to varying degrees. If we distinguish between the goals of managing and resolving conflict, diplomacy would need to be central in managing conflict and achieving a peaceful coexistence between America and China. For the more ambitious goal of conflict resolution, diplomacy, along with reassurance, would be indispensable in easing competition and achieving accommodation.

8

Conclusions

WE BEGAN THIS book with a critique of structural approaches to Sino-American relations. Many realists and liberals falsely assume that they have a privileged analytical perspective. They further assert that their favored perspective has predictive value. There is no historical support for either claim. There is absolutely no historical evidence for power transition theory, currently the dominant American perspective. There has never been a war of power transition. Transitions either occur peacefully or take place in the aftermath of wars fought for other reasons. Offensive realism is pure ideology, not a theory rooted in historical fact, and a dangerous ideology at that because of its propensity to be made self-fulfilling.

The balance of power and the quest for wealth demand more serious attention, but both are indeterminate. Balances fail to form about as often as they succeed; political units choose to bandwagon rather than balance or simply to ignore threats. When balances do form, they have only a so-so record in preventing war, although they have been more often successful in preventing hegemony.[1] More important, the balance of power is a Western concept that is not very helpful in explaining historical or contemporary patterns of relations among Asian political units. The search for wealth is undeniably important everywhere and has become much more so in the modern world. However, other concerns are frequently of more importance in our personal lives, let alone in interstate relations.

Any theoretical perspective is merely a starting point for a narrative that builds in context. Theories and other theoretical perspectives are frames of reference for organizing explanations or forecasts. Following Max Weber, good social scientists understand that any theory or theoretical perspective, no matter how useful, is always indeterminate.

Bipolarity is a good example. Early in the Cold War Hans Morgenthau observed that it had the potential for "unheard-of good as well as for unprecedented evil." He hypothesized that an equilibrium between two major powers should reconcile both to the status quo and thereby preserve the integrity of smaller powers. He worried that the character of modern war and nationalist universalism would prevent these advantages from being realized. The effects of bipolarity would depend entirely on the moral qualities of statesmen.[2] Similarly persuasive arguments can be made about the role of leaders in ending or not ending the Cold War, invading or not invading Iraq, or, as we have argued in this book, détente or confrontation with China.

Good analysis must meet three conditions. First, it must ask questions that have policy relevance. Ken Waltz's *Theory of International Politics* attracted much attention, but it was utterly irrelevant to the real world.[3] Even supposing that he was right in arguing that bipolar systems are more stable than multipolar systems—and there are many reasons for doubting this claim—at most it would take the form of a statistical probability. It would have told us nothing about the Cold War, a single case. And it was the Cold War that interested scholars and policymakers alike.

Second, good analysis must build on a plausible set of assumptions about how the world works. Power transition does not qualify, but most realist and liberal perspectives do. There is much historical evidence in support of security and wealth being important motives in foreign policy, just as there is evidence of their taking a backseat to other motives. Most notable in this regard is *thumos* (spirit), the drive for self-esteem, satisfied through the quest for honor and standing. Security is sometimes more important than wealth, and vice versa. *Thumos* is sometimes more important than both.

In the real world as opposed to theoretical ones, individuals and states have multiple motives that rise and fall in importance as a function of priming and context. Starting with any one motive and assuming one can explain or predict on the basis of it is a questionable enterprise. Researchers must recognize this multiplicity and attempt to ascertain which concerns are likely to be dominant under what conditions. Such an approach is one important way of bridging theory and context.

Structural theories of any kind downplay or totally ignore agency. They assume that leaders are like electrons, mere conveyors of forces. They are expected to make accurate assessments of external constraints and opportunities and to respond appropriately to them. But these assumptions fly in the face of political reality. Leaders have domestic political and personal goals, which may take primacy over foreign policy. They always make subjective assessments. Members of the same elite can, and often do, make diametrically opposed estimates of the balance of power, the direction in which it is changing, and its implications for their country or goals. Most important, these judgments rarely dictate policy because leaders have other interests and needs. To understand policy, we must reconstruct leaders' beliefs, judgments, and goals from the bottom up, not the top down.

Third, good analysis must recognize the determining nature of context. The importance of any motive or goal, the judgments leaders make of their environment and other leaders, their relative freedom of action and their assessments of this latitude are all context-dependent. The determining features of context are for the most part independent of the theories and frameworks we use to understand politics and the social world more generally. They are a product of path dependence, confluence, accident, and agency. They interact in nonlinear and, almost by definition, unpredictable ways. The effects of context can often be accounted for in retrospect, or at least a reasonable argument can be made for causal pathways. Outcome can rarely be predicted. At best, we can construct scenarios that start in the present and lead to divergent but seemingly plausible outcomes.

We believe our analysis meets these tests. They inform our proposal for a holistic strategy of conflict management and resolution based on a judicious combination of deterrence, reassurance, and diplomacy. We recognize a diversity of foreign policy motives and the difficulty of knowing beforehand—and sometimes in retrospect—which ones are, or were, dominant. This uncertainty makes analysis more difficult but also creates opportunities for policymakers. To the extent policymakers free themselves from simple mindsets regarding others' motives and recognize their complexity, they will become increasingly sensitive to the need to understand what motives are at play in any given situation. They will further recognize the possibility of influencing the motives of their adversary. This can most effectively be accomplished in a positive way by reassurance and diplomacy. They have the potential to reduce hostility and pave the way for rapprochement or accommodation.

Influencing motives is distinct from attempting to manipulate another actor's cost-calculus. The latter is the primary objective of the coercive strategies of deterrence and compellence. It is based on two false assumptions. First, that leaders considering the use of force—or provoking its use against them—are likely to undertake a thorough and rational analysis of the relative costs and gains of their contemplated behavior. Second, that the cost-calculus of leaders can be influenced from the outside in the desired direction, that is, to increase their belief in the cost of the behavior they are contemplating in the case of deterrence, or not contemplating in the case of compellence. As we have shown, the history of deterrence and compellence indicates that such efforts are hit-or-miss because the assumptions and decision-making process of target states and leaders are so often opaque. This was true of Chinese and American efforts at deterrence, which, for this reason, often had effects opposite of those intended. They tended to make each side's worst expectations of the other side self-fulfilling and served to intensify competition and retard conflict resolution. Arguably they do this today as well.

If reshaping another's cost-calculus is so problematic, what reason is there to believe that it is any easier to influence its motives in a positive way? Deterrence and compellence are threat-based strategies. They often fail, we observed, because they encourage others to reframe the issue at hand. Whatever substantive interests might have been involved take a backseat to concerns about security and standing. Leaders do not want to appear weak in the eyes of the adversary, other states, or domestic opinion by giving in to threats. They may also fear that doing so will only invite new demands. They also anger easily when they are the object of threats, and assuaging anger by not backing down, or giving the appearance of doing so, may take priority over other interests.

Reassurance and diplomacy, by contrast, encourage leaders to reframe their relationship with the initiating state in the opposite direction. They are strategies most appropriate to address *thumos*-driven tensions and conflicts. Reassurance seeks to reduce perceptions of hostility and threat, and diplomacy, to resolve outstanding substantive issues, or at least finesse the problems to which they give rise. To the extent that they arouse emotions they are positive ones, unless they are perceived as part of a nefarious policy designed to solicit restraint or concessions that are then exploited. Mikhail Gorbachev's initial overtures to the West were regarded this way by American hardliners, but those hardliners were ultimately sidelined by the favorable reaction of almost everyone else and ultimately came around themselves to taking him seriously.

Reassurance can pave the way for diplomacy and wind down tensions. Even small successes have the potential to set in motion a virtuous circle. When successful, reassurance brings about a beneficial shift in the perception of the other party's motives. The Nixon-Kissinger initiatives were motivated by security, as was Chinese receptivity to them. Sino-American cooperation reduced mutual perceptions of hostility and with it, a decline in security as the primary, if not the only, concern each state had with respect to the other. Economics entered the picture, and trade between the countries began and rapidly expanded. Trade would ultimately make appetite an important motive, but one that would generate its own conflicts.

Relaxation in tensions, increases in trade and investment, the growing presence of business people from each country in the other, exchanges of students, the opening of Western universities in China, and a huge growth in two-way tourism helped to break down mutual stereotypes. We write in September 2019, at a low point in Sino-American relations, when positive Chinese and Americans are adopting increasingly negative views of one another. This state of affairs provides a strong incentive to practice reassurance, and in the manner that we suggested in Chapter 6.

More nuanced understandings by each elite of the other and mutual restraint could act as something of a brake on further worst-case analysis and escalation. Reassurance could reverse this negative cycle if it encouraged Beijing and Washington to question its belief in the other's hostility and come to understand the extent to which both are largely motivated by the quest for status. This is asking a lot because policymakers and foreign policy analysts on both sides would have to start by recognizing this truth about themselves. Extrapolating from interpersonal relations, self-realization is almost always more difficult than reformulating insights about others and their motives. This may be particularly so in this case, where both elites and foreign policy intellectuals propagate a discourse in which pursuit of status is rarely acknowledged and almost every foreign policy is attributed to security. Honesty with oneself is the first step toward better relations with others.

Realists and power transition theorists consider the balance of power and perceptions of shifts in it as the principal determinants of foreign policy, if not of war and peace. We reject this assumption on conceptual and empirical grounds. Wars are begun just as often by those disadvantaged by the balance as by those whom it appears to favor.[4] Examples are China's entry into the Korea War and Egypt and Syria's attack on Israel in 1973. Disadvantaged states try to design around the advantages of their adversaries. As noted, determination of the balance of power is entirely subjective. Assessments often differ sharply within the same elite, and assessments of actors may bear only a passing relationship to those of analysts. Most important, the balance of power is only one factor that leaders consider in setting foreign policy goals and choosing policies to advance them.

The balance of power is not a very useful concept in analyzing Sino-American relations. What is important is the rise of China as a great power and the possibility of it becoming a superpower in the future. To be sure, this affects the relative economic and military power of the two countries, but the conflict between the United States and China is not at its core about security. There are strong incentives to portray it this way by hardliners, armed forces, and industries that supply the military. They constitute a powerful lobby and support worst-case interpretations of each other's motives and goals. Power transition theory provides an intellectual justification for American defense expenditure, alliance building in Asia, and challenges of China, and is actively supported and propagated by those who pursue these goals. It is a form of "fake" history that rivals "fake" news in its impact.

China's phenomenal rise in economic might, military power, and political influence creates a problem for the United States of a different kind. Postwar America increasingly defined itself as a superpower and, later, as a hegemon. Americans believed their country to be the City on the Hill and a society and government that others wanted, or should aspire, to emulate. They were also "the indispensable nation," whose leadership safeguarded the security and economic interests of, initially, the countries of the West and, now, of the world. Domestic and international superiority combine to make Americans feel good about themselves and buttress American self-esteem. Donald Trump's campaign slogan, "Make America Great Again," fell on receptive ears.

China has been constructed as a threat to American self-esteem. The American national security establishment portrays China's rise as a threat to American security and to America's alleged hegemony. This concern for self-esteem resonates with the population at large. Many Americans also see China as an economic threat and bully. The Chinese purchase of many flagship American enterprises also threatens American self-esteem. For all these reasons, the population generally backs confrontational measures toward China—as it did Trump's imposition of import duties on Chinese steel and other products—as long as there is no perceived risk of war.

Future American presidents nevertheless have room to maneuver. Public opinion is invariably more malleable than many analysts and talking heads think. We need only consider the turnaround on China effected by Nixon and Kissinger, the public response to US accommodation with Gorbachev's Soviet Union, and the ability of the Bush administration within a six-month period to convince a previously opposed public to support an invasion of Iraq. Trump's successor can extend the olive branch without fearing domestic loss, provided there is some reciprocation on the Chinese side. Any breakthrough on North Korea in which China plays a positive role may also be used to jump-start rapprochement. We have sought to lay out the means by which this can be accomplished.

Something of a mirror image prevails in China. America has been constructed as a threat to Chinese self-esteem. The two countries have no intrinsic conflict of interest in Asia, certainly no direct territorial disputes such as those between China and its Asian neighbors. When Chinese elites criticize American hegemony and accuse it of containing China's rise, they reveal the centrality of the search for status in China's international goals. They believe that it is only natural for China—a country with ancient history, proud traditions, and proven preeminence—to restore its rightful standing in Asia. This is why President Xi Jinping has made the "great rejuvenation of the Chinese nation" the utmost goal of China's international strategy. American efforts to maintain its alleged regional hegemony are seen as attempts to thwart this goal—an affront on Chinese *thumos* that justifies competition for honor and standing.

Chinese leaders and elites need to develop more open, confident, and balanced understandings about China's relationship with America and the Western world at large. We pointed out that American hegemony is American elites' self-serving hype divorced from reality, and one that China should not unduly fear. American containment of China is all but impossible in today's world, and Beijing can be confident that wise policy would ultimately deliver China's rise and restore its preeminence. These understandings are not difficult to acquire. A bigger challenge is to alter or reinterpret the deeply rooted frame of reference that sees China as a victim of Western powers and Japan during the "century of humiliation." This humiliation-induced frame of reference, now an integral part of the national psyche, is a deep rationale for modern Chinese foreign policy. A strenuous national effort is needed to recalibrate the frame of reference and in the process develop a new set of identities and roles for China appropriate to current realities.

Reassurance and diplomacy, and foreign policy more generally, is never divorced from domestic politics. For accommodation to be successful in the long term, the United States and China must somehow reframe their respective quests for self-esteem. As currently constructed, many leaders and much of the population regard the other as a threat to their national self-esteem. Both must disengage, find other bases for their self-esteem, and thereby remove this source of serious friction and impediment to normalized relations.

There are several possible strategies toward this end. The most obvious, and perhaps also the most difficult, is to disengage self-esteem from hegemony. This may be done by stressing the substantive accomplishments of both countries that do not involve comparison or competition with the other. The United States could emphasize wealth, science, culture, democracy—which one hopes will remain robust—and the positive role these can play in fostering development and helping to maintain international strategic and economic stability. China could do a version of the same and emphasize its phenomenal economic growth and regional and international standing, overcoming—and leaving behind—the scars of its prior humiliation by the Western powers and Japan. Both countries could also stress the ways in which an increasingly cooperative relationship—if it comes to pass—is the principal prop of international peace and stability.

Such a psychological-political arrangement becomes feasible to the extent that China seeks something other than hegemony. If instead China seeks to achieve *hēgemonia* or *wangdao,* the kind of clientelist relationship that characterized relations between China and other developed political units during its imperial past, that would be perfectly compatible with US security and economic interests in Asia.[5] Moreover *wangdao* can be made compatible with America's self-image, allowing both countries to pursue their respective interests in ways that transform from what many in both now define as a zero-sum game into one of mutual gain. The United States in return would have to recognize the nature of Chinese influence in Asia and its symbolic importance. This conception is so alien to American thinking that it would require some reeducation of the American national security elite.

If America and China were able to reconcile their respective quests for self-esteem through *hēgemonia*-based authority sharing, other contentious issues would be much easier to manage, if not resolve. Chapter 7 explored how diplomacy could be used toward this end. Leaders in both countries could assess the relative importance of these issues and the order in which they should be addressed. There is no general rule about which tension to address first. Opportunity must dictate strategy.

Our approach to Sino-American relations eschews prediction because of the all-determining role of context. Instead we support the construction of diverse story lines into the future. These narratives must start with reasonable assumptions, which include actors moved by multiple motives, framing foreign policy questions in both international and domestic terms, sensitive to constraints and opportunities but understanding them in highly subjective ways, and very much influenced by the personal relationships they develop—or do not develop—with their foreign counterparts.

Scenarios will inevitably reflect our beliefs about the world, a subjectivity that is not only unavoidable but valuable. It prompts different scholars, government and think thank analysts, journalists, and policymakers to favor different scenarios. The thoughtful way of dealing with this diversity is not to push the choice of one over another but rather to insist, in the first instance, that they are all fleshed out as fully as possible. They must make explicit their starting assumptions, and then the chain of political and economic logic that connects their starting to their end points. Better still, these scenarios should identify branching points that lead to other stories and endings, or different routes to the same endings. Most important, they should specify what information one would need in six months, two years, or whenever, that would increase or decrease confidence in any of these scenarios.

Forecasts of this kind are rarely accurate, but unlike predictions they provide early warning of when one's expectations are likely to be confounded and when the opportunity to reconsider and readjust to a different reality is present. We invite you to use our framework to construct your own scenarios about Sino-American relations and what might improve or further damage them.

Notes

CHAPTER 1

1. *Economist*, "China Is Getting Tougher on Taiwan," January 18, 2018, https://www. economist.com/china/2018/01/18/china-is-getting-tougher-on-taiwan (accessed October 1, 2018).

2. Yimou Lee, "U.S. Warships Pass through Taiwan Strait amid China Tensions," *Reuters*, January 25, 2019, https://www.reuters.com/article/us-taiwan-china-us/u-s-warships-pass-through-taiwan-strait-amid-china-tensions-idUSKCN1PJ07T?ref=hvper.com&utm_source=hvper.com&utm_medium= website (accessed February 3, 2019); Edward Wong, "Trump Administration Approves F-16 Fighter Jet Sales to Taiwan," *New York Times*, August 16, 2019, https:// www.nytimes.com/2019/08/16/world/asia/taiwan-f16.html?smid=nytcore-ios-share (accessed August 26, 2019).

3. Mark Landler, "Trump Accuses China of Undermining Diplomacy with North Korea," *New York Times*, August 29, 2018, https://www.nytimes.com/2018/08/29/ us/politics/trump-mattis-north-korea.html (accessed September 30, 2018).

4. Ana Swanson, "As Trump Escalates Trade War, U.S. and China Move Further Apart with No End in Sight," *New York Times*, September 1, 2019, https:// www.nytimes.com/2019/09/01/world/asia/trump-trade-war-china.html?action= click&module=Top%20Stories&pgtype=Homepage&utm_source=newsletter& utm_medium=email&utm_campaign=newsletter_axiossneakpeek&stream=top (accessed September 2, 2019).

5. Alan Rappeport and Keith Bradsher, "Trump Says He Will Raise Existing Tariffs on Chinese Goods to 30%," *New York Times*, August 23, 2019, https://www. nytimes.com/2019/08/23/business/china-tariffs-trump.html?module=inline (accessed August 26, 2019).

6. David E. Sanger, Katie Benner, and Matthew Goldstein, "Huawei and Top Executive Face Criminal Charges in the U.S.," *New York Times*, January 28, 2019,

https://www.nytimes.com/2019/01/28/us/politics/meng-wanzhou-huawei-iran. html (accessed February 3, 2019).

7. Timothy R. Heath and William R. Thompson, "Avoiding U.S.-China Competition Is Futile: Why the Best Option Is to Manage Strategic Rivalry," *Asia Policy* 13, no. 2 (2018), pp. 91–120.

8. Mark Landler, "Trump Accuses China of Interfering in Midterm Elections," *New York Times*, September 26, 2018, https://www.nytimes.com/2018/09/26/ world/asia/trump-china-election.html (accessed October 3, 2018).

9. Thomas G. Mahnken and Toshi Yoshihara, "Countering Comprehensive Coercion: Competitive Strategies against Authoritarian Political Warfare" (Washington, DC: Center for Strategic and Budgetary Assessments, 2018); Josh Rogin, "China's Interference in U.S. Politics Is Just Beginning," *Washington Post*, September 20, 2018, https://www.washingtonpost.com/opinions/global-opinions/chinas-interference- in-us-politics-is-just-beginning/2018/09/20/2b462558-bd0f-11e8-8792- 78719177250f_story.html?noredirect=on&utm_term=.a3471d09bb7d (accessed September 29, 2018); Larry Diamond and Orville Schell, eds., *Chinese Influence and American Interests: Promoting Constructive Vigilance* (Stanford, CA: Hoover Institution Press, 2018).

10. Hudson Institute, "Vice President Mike Pence's Remarks on the Administration's Policy Towards China," October 4, 2018, https://www.hudson.org/events/1610- vice-president-mike-pence-s-remarks-on-the-administration-s-policy-towards- china102018 (accessed February 3, 2019). A typical commentary that likens Pence's speech to the announcement of a new cold war is Walter Russell Mead, "Mike Pence Announces Cold War II," *Wall Street Journal*, October 8, 2018, https:// www.wsj.com/articles/mike-pence-announces-cold-war-ii-1539039480 (accessed February 5, 2019).

11. By contrast, some scholars outside of the United States contend that "authoritari- anism" may not be the best characterization of the nature of China's political sys- tem. See, for example, Daniel A. Bell, *The China Model: Political Meritocracy and the Limits of Democracy* (Princeton, NJ: Princeton University Press, 2016).

12. Jeffrey Bader, "U.S.-China Relations: Is It Time to End the Engagement?" (Washington, DC: Brookings Institution, 2018).

13. Aaron L. Friedberg, "Competing with China," *Survival* 60, no. 3 (2018), pp. 7–64.

14. John Pomfret, "As China-U.S. Feud Enters Uncharted Territory, Beijing Can Only Blame Itself," *Washington Post*, September 26, 2018, https://www.wash- ingtonpost.com/news/global-opinions/wp/2018/09/26/as-china-u-s-feud- enters-uncharted-territory-beijing-can-only-blame-itself/?noredirect=on&utm_ term=.423ed74fe08d (accessed September 29, 2018).

15. Orville Schell and Susan L. Shirk, "Course Correction: Toward an Effective and Sustainable China Policy" (New York: Asia Society Center on U.S.-China Relations, February 2019), p. 10.

16. Teddy Ng, "Cold War Mentality Will Harm US-China Relations, Top Diplomat Warns Kissinger," *South China Morning Post*, September 26, 2018, https://www.scmp.com/news/china/diplomacy/article/2165775/cold-war-mentality-will-harm-us-china-relations-top-diplomat (accessed September 29, 2018).

17. Kristin Huang, "China Sets Up Think Tank Alliance to Better Understand US as Trade War Continues," *South China Morning Post*, July 17, 2018, https://www.scmp.com/news/china/diplomacy-defence/article/2155678/china-sets-think-tank-alliance-better-understand-us (accessed October 1, 2018).

18. There is now a growing literature on status in Sino-American relations. See, for example, Xiaoyu Pu, *Rebranding China: Contested Status Signaling in the Changing Global Order* (Stanford, CA: Stanford University Press, 2019); Xiaoyu Pu, "One Mountain, Two Tigers: China, the United States, and the Status Dilemma in the Indo-Pacific," *Asia Policy* 14, no. 3 (2019), pp. 25–40; William Ziyuan Wang, "Destined for Misperception? Status Dilemma and the Early Origin of U.S.-China Antagonism," *Journal of Chinese Political Science* 24, no. 1 (2019), pp. 49–65.

19. Max Weber, *Economy and Society: An Outline of Interpretive Sociology*, 2 vols., Guenther Roth and Claus Wittich, eds. (Berkeley: University of California Press, 1978), I, pp. 909–11.

20. For a review of this literature, see Richard Ned Lebow, "What Can International Relations Theory Learn from the Origins of World War I?," *International Relations* 28, no. 4 (2014), pp. 387–411; Richard Ned Lebow, "World War I: Recent Historical Scholarship and IR Theory?," *International Relations* 28, no. 2 (2014), pp. 245–50.

21. Richard Ned Lebow, *A Cultural Theory of International Relations* (Cambridge, UK: Cambridge University Press, 2008), ch. 9.

22. Hans J. Morgenthau, *In Defense of the National Interest* (New York: Knopf, 1951); Richard Ned Lebow, *A Democratic Foreign Policy* (New York: Palgrave-Macmillan, 2019), pp. 173–203.

23. Steve Chan, *China, the U.S., and the Power-Transition Theory: A Critique* (London: Routledge, 2008); Richard Ned Lebow and Benjamin A. Valentino, "Lost in Transition: A Critique of Power Transition Theories," *International Relations* 23, no. 3 (2009), pp. 389–410; Richard Ned Lebow and Daniel Tompkins, "The Thucydides Claptrap," *Washington Monthly*, June 28, 2016, https://washingtonmonthly.com/thucydides-claptrap (accessed August 26, 2019).

24. Richard Ned Lebow and Janice Gross Stein, *We All Lost the Cold War* (Princeton, NJ: Princeton University Press, 1994); Jian Chen, *Mao's China and the Cold War: Beijing and the Taiwan Strait Crisis of 1958* (Chapel Hill: University of North Carolina Press, 2001), ch. 7.

25. Richard Ned Lebow, *The Tragic Vision of Politics: Ethics, Interests and Orders* (Cambridge, UK: Cambridge University Press, 2003), p. 217.

26. G. John Ikenberry, "The Rise of China and the Future of the West: Can the Liberal System Survive?," *Foreign Affairs* 87, no. 1 (2008), pp. 23–37.

27. The White House, "Remarks by Vice President Biden and Chinese Vice President Xi at the State Department Luncheon," February 14, 2012, https://obamawhitehouse.archives.gov/the-press-office/2012/02/14/remarks-vice-president-biden-and-chinese-vice-president-xi-state-departm (accessed March 15, 2018).

28. James Steinberg and Michael E. O'Hanlon, *Strategic Reassurance and Resolve: U.S.-China Relations in the Twenty-First Century* (Princeton, NJ: Princeton University Press, 2014).

29. Thomas J. Christensen, *The China Challenge: Shaping the Choice of a Rising Power* (New York: Norton, 2015).

30. Lyle J. Goldstein, *Meeting China Halfway: How to Defuse the Emerging U.S.-China Rivalry* (Washington, DC: Georgetown University Press, 2015).

31. Amitai Etzioni, *Avoiding War with China: Two Nations, One World* (Charlottesville: University of Virginia Press, 2017).

32. Bilahari Kausikan, "Asia in the Trump Era: From Pivot to Peril?," *Foreign Affairs* 96, no. 3 (2017), pp. 146–53, at p. 148.

CHAPTER 2

1. Aaron L. Friedberg, *A Contest for Supremacy: China, America, and the Struggle for Mastery in Asia* (New York: Norton, 2012); Aaron L. Friedberg, "Competing with China," *Survival* 60, no. 3 (2018), pp. 7–64; Aaron L. Friedberg, "Getting the China Challenge Right," *American Interest*, January 10, 2019, https://www.the-american-interest.com/2019/01/10/getting-the-china-challenge-right/ (accessed February 6, 2019).

2. John J. Mearsheimer, *The Tragedy of Great Power Politics* (New York: Norton, 2001), p. 400; John J. Mearsheimer, "China's Unpeaceful Rise," *Current History* 105 (April 2006), pp. 160–62; John J. Mearsheimer, "The Gathering Storm: China's Challenge to US Power in Asia," *Chinese Journal of International Politics* 3, no. 4 (2010), pp. 381–96; Christopher Layne, "The Waning of U.S. Hegemony—Myth or Reality?," *International Security* 34, no. 1 (2009), pp. 147–72; Christopher Layne, "The US-China Power Shift and the End of the Pax Americana," *International Affairs* 94, no. 1 (2018), pp. 89–111.

3. Mearsheimer, *The Tragedy of Great Power Politics*, p. 402.

4. Steven W. Mosher, *Hegemon: China's Plan to Dominate Asia and the World* (San Francisco, CA: Encounter Books, 2000); Stefan Halper, *The Beijing Consensus: How China's Authoritarian Model Will Dominate the Twenty-First Century* (New York: Basic Books, 2010).

5. For a cautious treatment, see Robert S. Ross and Zhu Feng, eds., *China's Ascent: Power, Security, and the Future of International Politics* (Ithaca, NY: Cornell University Press, 2008).

6. Paul Wolfowitz, "Remembering the Future," *National Interest* 59 (Spring 2000), pp. 35–45, at p. 42.

7. Susan Shirk, *China: Fragile Superpower* (New York: Oxford University Press, 2007), p. 4.

8. Graham Allison, *Destined for War: Can America and China Escape Thucydides's Trap?* (Boston: Houghton Mifflin Harcourt, 2017), Kindle edition.

9. Ibid., location 171.

10. Ibid., location 191.

11. Richard Ned Lebow, *The Tragic Vision of Politics: Ethics, Interests and Orders* (Cambridge, UK: Cambridge University Press, 2003); Richard Ned Lebow and Daniel Tompkins, "The Thucydides Claptrap," *Washington Monthly*, June 28, 2016, https://washingtonmonthly.com/thucydides-claptrap (accessed August 26, 2019).

12. Christopher Clark, *The Sleepwalkers: How Europe Went to War in 1914* (London: Allen Lane, 2012); Margaret MacMillan, *The War That Ended Peace: How Europe Abandoned Peace for the First World War* (London: Profile, 2013).

13. A. F. K. Organski, *World Politics* (New York: Knopf, 1958); A. F. K. Organski and Jacek Kugler, *The War Ledger* (Chicago: University of Chicago Press, 1980).

14. Robert Gilpin, *War and Change in World Politics* (Cambridge, UK: Cambridge University Press, 1981).

15. Ibid., pp. 186–87.

16. Ibid., pp. 191–93.

17. Richard Ned Lebow and Benjamin Valentino, "Lost in Transition: A Critical Analysis of Power Transition Theory," *International Relations* 23, no. 3 (2009), pp. 389–410; Jack S. Levy, "Power Transition Theory and the Rise of China," in Ross and Zhu, eds., *China's Ascent*, pp. 11–33, for another critical assessment.

18. Richard Ned Lebow, *Why Nations Fight* (Cambridge, UK: Cambridge University Press, 2011).

19. Ibid., ch. 4.

20. See, for example, Joshua R. Itzkowitz Shifrinson, *Rising Titans, Falling Giants: How Great Powers Exploit Power Shifts* (Ithaca, NY: Cornell University Press, 2018).

21. US Department of Defense, "Annual Report to Congress: Military and Security Developments Involving the People's Republic of China 2011" (Washington, DC: Office of the Secretary of Defense, 2011).

22. US Department of Defense, "Annual Report to Congress: Military and Security Developments Involving the People's Republic of China 2017" (Washington, DC: Office of the Secretary of Defense, 2017), p. ii.

23. Tai Ming Cheung, "How China Innovates in Defense Science and Technology," lecture at Centre d'Etude des Relations Internationales, Sciences Po, Paris, January 31, 2013. For further discussion, see Tai Ming Cheung, "The Chinese Defense Economy's Long March from Imitation to Innovation," *Journal of Strategic Studies* 34, no. 3 (2011), pp. 325–54; Tai Ming Cheung, *Fortifying China: The Struggle to Build a Modern Defense Economy* (Ithaca, NY: Cornell University Press, 2009), p. 2.

24. Michael Beckley, *Unrivaled: Why America Will Remain the World's Sole Superpower* (Ithaca, NY: Cornell University Press, 2018).

25. Stephen G. Brooks, "Power Transitions, Then and Now: Five New Structural Barriers That Will Constrain China's Rise," *China International Strategy Review* 1, no. 1 (2019), pp. 65–83.

26. For a recent demonstration of this effect, see Peter Gries and Yiming Jing, "Are the US and China Fated to Fight? How Narratives of 'Power Transition' Shape Great Power War or Peace," *Cambridge Review of International Affairs* 32, no. 4 (2019), pp. 456–82.

27. International Conference on East Asia Cooperation and Sino-U.S. Relations, Beijing, November 3–4, 2005, quoted in David M. Lampton, *The Three Faces of Chinese Power: Might, Money, and Minds* (Berkeley: University of California Press, 2008), p. 34.

28. Jonathan Kirshner, "Offensive Realism, Thucydides Traps, and the Tragedy of Unforced Errors: Classical Realism and US-China Relations," *China International Strategy Review* 1, no. 1 (2019), pp. 51–63, at p. 51.

29. Shivshankar Menon, "Worse China-US Relations: An Indian View," *China International Strategy Review* 1, no. 1 (2019), pp. 33–38, at p. 34.

30. Charles Glaser, "Will China's Rise Lead to War? Why Realism Does Not Mean Pessimism," *Foreign Affairs* 90, no. 2 (2011), pp. 80–91.

31. Geoffrey Garrett, "Chinese-US Economic Relations after the Global Financial Crisis," in Jane Golley and Ligang Song, eds., *Rising China: Global Challenges and Opportunities* (Canberra: ANU Press, 2011), pp. 149–72.

32. Michael A. Santoro, "Global Capitalism and the Road to Chinese Democracy," *Current History* 99, no. 638 (2000), pp. 263–67.

33. Joshua Cooper Ramo, *The Beijing Consensus: Notes on the New Physics of Chinese Power* (London: Foreign Policy Centre, 2004), p. 36; Thomas Lum and Dick K. Nanto, "China's Trade with the United States and the World," Congressional Research Service Report for Congress, January 4, 2007, especially p. 3; Garrett, "Chinese-US Economic Relations."

34. Glaser, "Will China's Rise Lead to War?"

35. Richard McGregor, *Xi Jinping: The Backlash* (Sydney: Lowy Institute, 2019); Elizabeth C. Economy, *The Third Revolution: Xi Jinping and the New Chinese State* (Oxford: Oxford University Press, 2018); Elizabeth C. Economy, "China's New Revolution: The Reign of Xi Jinping," *Foreign Affairs* 97, no. 3 (2018), pp. 60–74.

36. Kurt M. Campbell and Ely Ratner, "The China Reckoning: How Beijing Defied American Expectations," *Foreign Affairs* 97, no. 2 (2018), pp. 60–70.

37. Alastair Iain Johnston, "The Failures of the 'Failure of Engagement' with China," *Washington Quarterly* 42, no. 2 (2019), pp. 99–114.

38. Thomas Fingar, "Forty Years of Formal—But Not Yet Normal—Relations," *China International Strategy Review* 1, no. 1 (2019), pp. 11–20, at p. 14.

39. Michael Pillsbury, *The Hundred-Year Marathon: China's Secret Strategy to Replace America as the Global Superpower* (New York: Henry Holt, 2015).

40. Alastair Iain Johnston, "Shaky Foundations: The 'Intellectual Architecture' of Trump's China Policy," *Survival* 61, no. 2 (2019), pp. 189–202.

41. Alan Rappeport, "A China Hawk Gains Prominence as Trump Confronts Xi on Trade," *New York Times*, November 30, 2018, https://www.nytimes.com/2018/11/30/us/politics/trump-china-trade-xi-michael-pillsbury.html (accessed February 5, 2019).

42. Zheng Bijian, "China's Peaceful Rise to Great-Power Status," *Foreign Affairs* 84, no. 5 (2005), pp. 18–24.

43. Cited in Minxen Pei, "Playing Ball," *South China Morning Post*, December 29, 2008, p. A9.

44. Yang Jiechi, cited in "Out into the World: China Is Ready to Become a Good Citizen—But On Its Own Terms," *Newsweek*, December 31, 2008.

45. Shiping Tang, "China and the Future International Order(s)," *Ethics & International Affairs* 32, no. 1 (2018), pp. 31–43, at p. 40.

46. Suisheng Zhao, "A Revisionist Stakeholder: China and the Post–World War II World Order," *Journal of Contemporary China* 27, no. 113 (2018), pp. 643–58.

47. Wu Xinbo, "China in Search of a Liberal Partnership International Order," *International Affairs* 94, no. 5 (2018), pp. 995–1018.

48. Michael D. Swaine, "Perceptions of an Assertive China," *China Leadership Monitor* 32 (Spring 2010), pp. 1–19.

49. Alastair Iain Johnston, "How New and Assertive Is China's New Assertiveness?," *International Security* 37, no. 4 (2013), pp. 7–48.

50. Thomas J. Christensen, "The World Needs an Assertive China," *New York Times*, February 21, 2011, https://www.nytimes.com/2011/02/21/opinion/21iht-edchristensen21.html (accessed February 3, 2019).

51. Yan Xuetong, "From Keeping a Low Profile to Striving for Achievement," *Chinese Journal of International Politics* 7, no. 2 (2014), pp. 153–84.

52. Yan Xuetong, *Ancient Chinese Thought, Modern Chinese Power* (Princeton, NJ: Princeton University Press, 2011).

53. Yan Xuetong, "The Age of Uneasy Peace: Chinese Power in a Divided World," *Foreign Affairs* 98, no. 1 (2019), pp. 40–46, at p. 42.

54. Yuan Peng, "Bawo xinjieduan zhongmei guanxi de tedian he guilü" [Grasping the Characteristics and Patterns of Sino-US Relations during a New Era], *Xiandai guoji guanxi* [Contemporary International Relations], no. 6 (2018), pp. 1–3.

55. Shi Yinhong, "Zhongguo de zhoubian zhanlüe he duimei guanxi" [China's Regional Strategy and US Relations], *Xiandai guoji guanxi* [Contemporary International Relations], no. 6 (2018), pp. 3–5.

56. Chu Shulong and Zhou Lanjun, "Telangpu zhengfu waijiao texing jiqi yingxiang" [The Foreign Policy Characteristics and Impact of the Trump Administration],

Xiandai guoji guanxi [Contemporary International Relations], no. 8 (2018), pp. 23–30.

57. Liu Jianfei, "Xinshidai zhongguo waijiao zhanlüe zhong de zhongmei guanxi" [Sino-US Relations in Chinese Diplomatic Strategy during China's New Era], *Meiguo yanjiu* [Chinese Journal of American Studies] 32, no. 2 (2018), pp. 9–18

58. Evan S. Medeiros, "China Reacts: Assessing Beijing's Response to Trump's New China Strategy," *China Leadership Monitor*, no. 59 (2019), https://www.prcleader. org/medeiros (accessed September 8, 2019).

59. Zhao Minghao, "Telangpu zhizheng yu zhongmei guanxi de zhanlüe zhuanxing" [The Trump Doctrine and the Strategic Transformation of US-China Relations], *Meiguo yanjiu* [Chinese Journal of American Studies] 32, no. 5 (2018), pp. 26–48, at p. 35; Zhongguo Xiandai Guoji Guanxi Yanjiuyuan Ketizu [Project Team of the China Institutes of Contemporary International Relations], "Zhongqi xuanju hou telangpu zhengfu neiwai zhengce zouxiang" [The Trump Administration's Internal and External Policy Directions after the Midterm Elections], *Xiandai guoji guanxi* [Contemporary International Relations], no. 12 (2018), pp. 27–34, at p. 33; Zhong Feiteng, "Chaoyue baquan zhizheng: Zhongmei maoyizhan de zhengzhi jingjixue luoji" [Moving beyond Competition for Hegemony: The Political Economy Logic of the Sino-US Trade War], *Waijiao pinglun* [Foreign Affairs Review], no. 6 (2018), pp. 1–30, at p. 3; Yuan, "Bawo xinjieduan zhongmei guanxi de tedian he guilü," p. 2.

60. Yuan, "Bawo xinjieduan zhongmei guanxi de tedian he guilü," p. 2; Wei Zongyou, "Zhongmei zhanlüe jingzheng, meiguo 'diwei jiaolü' yu telangpu zhengfu duihua zhanlüe tiaozheng" [China-US Strategic Competition, the US Status Anxiety, and the Trump Administration's Strategic Adjustment toward China], *Meiguo yanjiu* [Chinese Journal of American Studies], no. 4 (2018), pp. 51–74.

61. Chu and Zhou, "Telangpu zhengfu waijiao texing jiqi yingxiang," p. 29.

62. Wei Zongyou, "Telangpu zhengfu guojia anquan zhanlüe yu zhongmei guanxi de weilai" [The National Security Strategy of the Trump Administration and the Future of Sino-US Relations], *Dangdai meiguo pinglun* [Contemporary American Review], no. 1 (2018), pp. 33–49, at p. 49.

63. Li Kaisheng, "Rongna zhongguo jueqi: Shijie zhixu shijiaoxia de meiguo zeren jiqi zhanlüe xuanze" [Accommodating China's Rise: World Order and the Responsibility and Strategic Option of the United States], *Shijie jingji yu zhengzhi* [World Economics and Politics], no. 11 (2017), pp. 89–107, at p. 106.

64. Zhao, "Telangpu zhizheng yu zhongmei guanxi de zhanlüe zhuanxing"; Liu, "Xinshidai zhongguo waijiao zhanlüe zhong de zhongmei guanxi"; Wei, "Zhongmei zhanlüe jingzheng, meiguo 'diwei jiaolü' yu telangpu zhengfu duihua zhanlüe tiaozheng"; Chu and Zhou, "Telangpu zhengfu waijiao texing jiqi yingx-iang"; Wang Yong, "Guonei jiegou bian012ge yu zhongmei guanxi de weilai zouxiang" [Domestic Structural Changes and the Future Direction of Sino-US Relations],

Xiandai guoji guanxi [Contemporary International Relations], no. 6 (2018), pp. 7–9.

65. Yan, "The Age of Uneasy Peace"; Zhao, "Telangpu zhizheng yu zhongmei guanxi de zhanlüe zhuanxing"; Liu, "Xinshidai zhongguo waijiao zhanlüe zhong de zhong-mei guanxi"; Shou Huisheng, "Zhongmei chongtu de benzhi ji qianjing" [The Nature and Prospect of Sino-US Conflict], *Xiandai guoji guanxi* [Contemporary International Relations], no. 6 (2018), pp. 9–12.

66. Zhang Tuosheng, "Zhongmei guanxi fazhan qianjing zhanwang" [Prospects of Sino-US Relations], *Dangdai meiguo pinglun* [Contemporary American Review], no. 2 (2018), pp. 1–14. For a different take on Chinese strategic culture, see Alastair Iain Johnston, *Cultural Realism: Strategic Culture and Grand Strategy in Chinese History* (Princeton, NJ: Princeton University Press, 1995).

67. Niu Jun, "Lunhui: Zhongmei guanxi yu yatai zhixu yanbian (1978–2018)" [Reborn: Sino-US Relations and the Evolution of Asia-Pacific Order], *Meiguo yanjiu* [Chinese Journal of American Studies], no. 6 (2018), pp. 9–25.

68. Wang Jisi, "The View from China," in "Did America Get China Wrong? The Engagement Debate," special issue, *Foreign Affairs* 97, no. 4 (2018), pp. 183–95, at p. 184; Zhang, "Zhongmei guanxi fazhan qianjing zhanwang," p. 13; Li, "Rongna zhongguo jueqi," p. 106.

69. Wang Yi, "Zhongmei keyi you jingzheng, bubi zuo duishou, geng xu dang huoban" [China and America May Compete, but They Need to Be Partners Rather Than Rivals], March 8, 2018, *Renminwang* (people.cn), http://world.people.com.cn/n1/2018/0308/c1002-29855973.html (accessed February 9, 2019).

70. Ren Xiao, "Guoji guanxixue de 'qu lishihua' he 'zai lishihua'—jianyi 'xiuxidide xian-jing' [The "Dehistoricization" and "Rehistoricization" in International Relations: Questioning the 'Thucydides Trap"], *Shijie jingji yu zhengzhi* [World Economics and Politics], no. 7 (2018), pp. 142–54, at pp. 152–53.

71. Li Haibo and Song Ruizhi, " 'Xiuxidide xianjing': Renshi wuqu yu zhanlüe ying-dui" [The "Thucydides' Trap": Cognitive Blind Spots and Strategic Response], *Xiandai guoji guanxi* [Contemporary International Relations], no. 9 (2017), pp. 10–17.

72. Zhang, "Zhongmei guanxi fazhan qianjing zhanwang"; Wei, "Telangpu zhengfu guojia anquan zhanlüe yu zhongmei guanxi de weilai."

73. M. Frederick Nelson, *Korea and the Old Orders in Eastern Asia* (Baton Rouge: Louisiana State University Press, 1945), pp. 11–20; James L. Hevia, *Cherishing Men from Afar: Qing Guest Ritual and the Macartney Embassy of 1793* (Durham, NC: Duke University Press, 1995), pp. 124–33; David C. Kang, *China Rising: Peace, Power, and Order in East Asia* (New York: Columbia University Press, 2007), p. 56.

74. Gregory Smits, *Visions of Ryukyu: Identity and Ideology in Early-Modern Thought and Politics* (Honolulu: University of Hawai'i Press, 1999), p. 36; Kang, *China Rising*, p. 57.

75. Donald N. Clark, "Sino-Korean Tributary Relations under the Ming," in Denis Twitchett and Frederick W. Mote, eds., *The Cambridge History of China, Volume 8: The Ming Dynasty, Part 2: 1368–1694* (Cambridge, UK: Cambridge University Press, 1998), pp. 272–300; Kang, *China Rising;* David Kang, *East Asia before the West: Five Centuries of Trade and Tribute* (New York: Columbia University Press, 2010).

76. Feng Zhang, *Chinese Hegemony: Grand Strategy and International Institutions in East Asian History* (Stanford, CA: Stanford University Press, 2015).

77. Kang, *China Rising*, pp. 82–106. For a contrary view stressing internal conflicts, see Warren I. Cohen, "China's Rise in Historical Perspective," in Quansheng Zhao and Guoli Liu, eds., *Managing the China Challenge: Global Perspectives* (London: Routledge, 2008), pp. 23–40; Andrew J. Nathan and Andrew Scobell, *China's Search for Security* (New York: Columbia University Press, 2012); Andrew Scobell, *China's Use of Military Force: Beyond the Great Wall and the Long March* (Cambridge, UK: Cambridge University Press, 2003).

78. Bilahari Kausikan, "Asia in the Trump Era: From Pivot to Peril?," *Foreign Affairs* 96, no. 3 (2017), pp. 146–53, at p. 150.

79. Morris Rossabi, "The Ming and Inner Asia," in Twitchett and Mote, eds., *Cambridge History of China*, vol. 8, pp. 221–71; John A. Mears, "Analyzing the Phenomenon of Borderlands from Comparative and Cross-Cultural Perspectives," History Cooperative, 2001, http://webdoc.sub.gwdg.de/ebook/p/2005/history_coopera-tive/www.historycooperative.org/proceedings/interactions/mears.html (accessed January 26, 2020); Peter C. Perdue, *China Marches West: The Qing Conquest of Central Eurasia* (Cambridge, MA: Harvard University Press, 2005).

80. Ronald P. Toby, *State and Diplomacy in Early Modern Japan* (Stanford, CA: Stanford University Press, 1991), pp. 170–71; Maurius B. Jansen, *Japan and Its World*, revised edition (Princeton, NJ: Princeton University Press, 1995), pp. 18–19, 24–25.

81. Kawazoe Shoji, "Japan and East Asia," in Kozo Yamamura, ed., *The Cambridge History of Japan, Volume 3: Medieval Japan* (Cambridge, UK: Cambridge University Press, 1990), pp. 396–446; Ronald P. Toby, *State and Diplomacy in Early Modern Japan: Asia in the Development of the Tokugawa Bakufu* (Stanford, CA: Stanford University Press, 1991), pp. 170–72.

82. Lampton, *Three Faces of Chinese Power*, p. 175; Kang, *China Rising*, p. 193.

83. Liu Feng, "China's Security Strategy towards East Asia," *Chinese Journal of International Politics* 9, no. 2 (2016), pp. 151–79.

84. For a comprehensive study of Chinese approaches to territorial disputes, see M. Taylor Fravel, *Strong Borders, Secure Nation: Cooperation and Conflict in China's Territorial Disputes* (Princeton, NJ: Princeton University Press, 2008).

85. Stephanie Kleine-Ahlbrandt, "Dangerous Waters," *Foreign Policy*, September 17, 2012, http://www.foreignpolicy.com/articles/2012/09/17/dangerous_waters (accessed March 5, 2013); Martine Bulard, "China: As You Were," *Le Monde*

Diplomatique, December 6, 2012, http://mondediplo.com/2012/12/06china (accessed March 5, 2013).

86. Scott L. Kastner, "Is the Taiwan Strait Still a Flash Point? Rethinking the Prospects for Armed Conflict between China and Taiwan," *International Security* 40, no. 3 (2015–16), pp. 54–92, at pp. 65–67.

87. Steve Chan, *China, the US, and the Power-Transition Theory: A Critique* (Abingdon, UK: Routledge, 2008), p. 92; Peter Hays Gries, *China's New Nationalism: Pride, Politics, and Diplomacy* (Berkeley: University of California Press, 2004), p. 11; Yong Deng, *China's Struggle for Status: The Realignment of International Relations* (New York: Cambridge University Press, 2008), pp. 257–58.

88. Neville Maxwell, *India's China War* (New York: Random House, 1970); John W. Garver, "China's Decision for War with India in 1962," in Alastair Iain Johnston and Robert S. Ross, eds., *New Directions in the Study of China's Foreign Policy* (Stanford, CA: Stanford University Press, 2006), pp. 86–130; Ramo, *Beijing Consensus*, p. 12; Thomas J. Christensen, "Windows and War: Trend Analysis and Beijing's Use of Force," in Johnston and Ross, *New Directions in the Study of China's Foreign Policy*, pp. 50–85.

89. Allen S. Whiting, *China Crosses the Yalu: The Decision to Enter the Korean War* (New York: Macmillan, 1960); Christensen, "Windows and War."

90. Rosemary Foot and Andrew Walter, *China, the United States, and the Global Order* (Cambridge, UK: Cambridge University Press, 2011).

91. For similar arguments, see Allen Carlson, "More Than Just Saying No: China's Evolving Approach to Sovereignty and Intervention since Tiananmen," in Johnston and Ross, eds., *New Directions in the Study of China's Foreign Policy*, pp. 217–41; Samuel S. Kim, "Chinese Foreign Policy Faces Globalization Challenges," in Johnston and Ross, eds., *New Directions in the Study of China's Foreign Policy*, pp. 276–308.

92. Kim Young-jin, "Chinese Leader Backs NK Denuclearization," *Korean Times*, January 28, 2013.

93. Martin K. Dimitrov, *Piracy and the State: The Politics of Intellectual Property Rights in China* (New York: Cambridge University Press, 2009).

94. Foot and Walter, *China, the United States, and the Global Order*, p. 275; Margaret M. Pearson, "China in Geneva: Lessons from China's Early Years in the World Trade Organization," in Johnston and Ross, eds., *New Directions in the Study of China's Foreign Policy*, pp. 242–75.

95. Yan, "The Age of Uneasy Peace," p. 42.

96. Johnston, "The Failures of the 'Failure of Engagement' with China."

97. Richard Fontaine and Mira Rapp-Hooper, "The China Syndrome," *National Interest* 143 (May–June 2016), pp. 10–18.

98. Foot and Walter, *China, the United States, and the Global Order*.

99. Wang, "The View from China," p. 183.

100. Ibid.

101. Lampton, *Three Faces of Chinese Power*, pp. 37–76.

102. Feng Zhang, "Chinese Thinking on the South China Sea and the Future of Regional Security," *Political Science Quarterly* 132, no. 3 (2017), pp. 435–66.

103. Eric Heginbotham, Michael S. Chase, Jacob L. Heim, Bonny Lin, Mark R. Cozad, Lyle J. Morris, Christopher P. Twomey, Forrest E. Morgan, Michael Nixon, Cristina L. Garafola, and Samuel K. Berkowitz, *China's Evolving Nuclear Deterrent: Major Drivers and Issues for the United States* (Santa Monica, CA: RAND, 2017), p. xi.

104. Arms Control Association, "Arms Control and Proliferation Profile: China," July 2017, https://www.armscontrol.org/factsheets/chinaprofile#nw (accessed September 30, 2018).

105. Arms Control Association, "US Nuclear Modernization Programs," August 2012, http://www.armscontrol.org/factsheets/USNuclearModernization (accessed February 16, 2013).

106. US Department of Defense, "Nuclear Posture Review" (Washington, DC: Office of the Secretary of Defense, 2018).

107. Stockholm International Peace Research Institute, "The Top 10 Military Spenders," in *SIPRI Yearbook 2011: Armaments, Disarmament and International Security* (Oxford: Oxford University Press, 2011), p. 9; "Military Expenditure by Country, in Constant (2015) US$m., 1988–1996, 1997–2006, 2007–2016," SIPRI Military Expenditure Database, https://www.sipri.org/sites/default/files/Milex-constant-2015-USD.pdf (accessed March 18, 2018).

108. "Military Expenditure (% of GDP)," World Bank Data, http://data.worldbank.org/indicator/MS.MIL.XPND.GD.ZS (accessed February 8, 2013).

109. "Data for All Countries from 1988–2016 as a Share of GDP," SIPRI Military Expenditure Database, https://www.sipri.org/sites/default/files/Milex-constant-2015-USD.pdf (accessed March 18, 2018).

110. Sebastien Roblin, "The Real Reason the World Needs to Pay Attention to China's Growing Aircraft Carrier Fleet," *National Interest*, May 1, 2017, http://nationalinterest.org/blog/the-buzz/the-real-reason-the-world-needs-pay-attention-chinas-growing-20406 (accessed May 8, 2017).

111. Brooks, "Power Transitions, Then and Now"; Stephen G. Brooks and William C. Wohlforth, *America Abroad: The United States' Global Role in the 21st Century* (New York: Oxford University Press, 2016); Stephen G. Brooks and William C. Wohlforth, "The Rise and Fall of Great Powers in the 21st Century: China's Rise and the Fate of America's Global Position," *International Security* 40, no. 7 (2015–16), pp. 7–48.

CHAPTER 3

1. Barack Obama, "Remarks by President Barack Obama at Suntory Hall," Tokyo, November 14, 2009, https://obamawhitehouse.archives.gov/realitycheck/the-press-office/remarks-president-barack-obama-suntory-hall (accessed March 13, 2018).

2. Kurt M. Campbell, *The Pivot: The Future of American Statecraft in Asia* (New York: Twelve, 2016).

3. Wang Dong, "Is China Trying to Push the U.S. Out of East Asia?," *China Quarterly of International Strategic Studies* 1, no. 1 (2015), pp. 59–84, at p. 60; Ruan Zongze, "Meiguo 'yatai zaipingheng' zhanlüe qianjing lunxi" [An Analysis of the Prospects of the US Asian Rebalance Strategy], *Shijie jingji yu zhengzhi* [World Economy and Politics], no. 4 (2014), pp. 4–20, at p. 10.

4. Wang Hao, "Guodu kuozhang de meiguo yatai zaipingheng zhanlüe jiqi qianjing lunxi" [America's Overexpanded Asia-Pacific Rebalance Strategy and Its Prospects], *Dangdai yatai* [Journal of Contemporary Asia-Pacific Studies], no. 2 (2015), pp. 4–37, at p. 7.

5. Wang Jisi, "An Inquiry into China-U.S. Relations: An Opinion from China," in Lindsey W. Ford, ed., *Advice for the 45th U.S. President: Opinions from Across the Pacific* (New York: Asia Society Policy Institute, 2016), pp. 24–27, at p. 25.

6. Scott W. Harold, "Optimizing the U.S.-China Military-to-Military Relationship," *Asia Policy* 14, no. 3 (2019), pp. 145–68, at p. 147; Yunzhu Yao, "Sino-American Military Relations: From Quasi-Allies to Potential Adversaries?," *China International Strategy Review* 1, no. 1 (2019), pp. 85–98, at p. 90.

7. Barry R. Posen, *Restraint: A New Foundation for U.S. Grand Strategy* (Ithaca, NY: Cornell University Press, 2014), pp. 5–6.

8. Henry Kissinger, *World Order: Reflections on the Character of Nations and the Course of History* (London: Allen Lane, 2014), p. 233; Campbell, *The Pivot*, p. 134.

9. US Department of Defense, "FY94–99 Defense Planning Guidance Sections for Comment," February 18, 1992, pp. 4, 21, http://nsarchive.gwu.edu/nukevault/ebb245/doc03_extract_nytedit.pdf (accessed October 20, 2016).

10. John J. Mearsheimer, *The Tragedy of Great Power Politics* (New York: Norton, 2001), pp. 386, 402.

11. G. John Ikenberry, *Liberal Leviathan: The Origins, Crisis, and Transformation of the American World Order* (Princeton, NJ: Princeton University Press, 2011), p. 2.

12. Michael Mastanduno, "Incomplete Hegemony: The United States and Security Order in Asia," in Muthiah Alagappa, ed., *Asian Security Order: Instrumental and Normative Features* (Stanford, CA: Stanford University Press, 2003), pp. 141–70.

13. Simon Reich and Richard Ned Lebow, *Good-Bye Hegemony! Power and Influence in the Global System* (Princeton, NJ: Princeton University Press, 2014), pp. xi, 2.

14. Barry R. Posen, "The Rise of Illiberal Hegemony: Trump's Surprising Grand Strategy," *Foreign Affairs* 97, no. 2 (2018), pp. 20–27, at p. 27.

15. Jeffrey A. Bader, *Obama and China's Rise: An Insider's Account of America's Asia Strategy* (Washington, DC: Brookings Institution Press, 2012), p. 142; James Mann, *The Obamians: The Struggle inside the White House to Redefine American Power* (New York: Viking, 2012), pp. 243–44; David E. Sanger, *Confront and Conceal: Obama's Secret Wars and Surprising Use of American Power* (New York: Crown, 2012), p. 377.

16. Bader, *Obama and China's Rise*, p. 141.

17. Ibid., p. 3.

18. Amitai Etzioni, "Who Authorized Preparations for War with China?," *Yale Journal of International Affairs* 8, no. 2 (2013), pp. 37–51, at p. 45.

19. Hillary Clinton, "America's Pacific Century," *Foreign Policy*, October 11, 2011, http://foreignpolicy.com/2011/10/11/americas-pacific-century/ (accessed October 2, 2016).

20. Barack Obama, "Remarks by President Obama to the Australian Parliament," *Canberra*, November 17, 2011, https://www.whitehouse.gov/the-press-office/2011/11/17/remarks-president-obama-australian-parliament (accessed October 2, 2016).

21. US Department of Defense, "Sustaining US Global Leadership: Priorities for 21st Century Defense" (Washington, DC: US Department of Defense, 2012), p. 2, emphasis in original.

22. Campbell, *The Pivot*, p. 7.

23. Ibid.

24. Clinton, "America's Pacific Century."

25. Obama, "Remarks by President Obama to the Australian Parliament."

26. Campbell, *The Pivot*, p. 22.

27. Ibid., p. 25.

28. Ibid., pp. 22, 26.

29. Yuan Peng, "Xunqiu zhongmei yatai liangxing hudong" [In Search of Constructive US-China Interactions in the Asia-Pacific Region], *Guoji anquan yanjiu* [Journal of International Security Studies], no. 1 (2013), pp. 55–66, at p. 58.

30. Fu Ying, "How China Sees Russia," *Foreign Affairs* 95, no. 1 (2016), pp. 96–105, at p. 104. See also Christopher P. Twomey and Xu Hui, "Military Developments," in Nina Hachigian, ed., *Debating China: The U.S.-China Relationship in Ten Conversations* (Oxford: Oxford University Press, 2014), pp. 152–75, at p. 165.

31. See, for example, Wang, "Guodu kuozhang"; Ruan, "Meiguo"; Yang Yi, "Meiguo yatai lianmeng tixi yu zhongguo zhoubian zhanlüe" [US Asia-Pacific Alliance and China's Regional Periphery Strategy], *Guoji anquan yanjiu* [Journal of International Security Studies] 31, no. 3 (2013), pp. 127–38; Lin Hongyu and Zhang Shuai, "Chaoyue kunjing: 2010 nian yilai zhongmei anquan boyi jiqi yingxiang" [Beyond Dilemma: The Security Game between China and the United States since 2010], *Guoji anquan yanjiu* [Journal of International Security Studies] 33, no. 2 (2015), pp. 61–80; Li Qingsi, "Meiguo yatai zaipingheng zhanlüe xia de dongya diqu geju" [East Asian Regional Order under America's Asian Rebalance Strategy], *Meiguo yanjiu* [Chinese Journal of American Studies], no. 3 (2014), pp. 115–17; Liu Guozhu, "Meiguo 'yatai zaipingheng' zhanlüe mianlin de tiaozhan" [The Challenges of America's "Asian Rebalance Strategy"], *Meiguo yanjiu* [Chinese Journal of American Studies], no. 3 (2014), pp. 97–102.

32. Li, "Meiguo yatai zaipingheng zhanlüe xia de dongya diqu geju," p. 117.

33. US Department of Defense, *Quadrennial Defense Review Report* (Washington, DC: Department of Defense, 2010), p. 32.

34. Etzioni, "Who Authorized Preparations for War with China?," p. 39.

35. US Department of Defense, "Joint Operational Access Concept (JOAC)" (Washington, DC: Department of Defense, 2012), p. 4.

36. According to the Pentagon, "anti-access" refers to "those actions and capabilities, usually long-range, designed to prevent an opposing force from entering an operational area." "Area denial" refers to "those actions and capabilities, usually of shorter range, designed not to keep an opposing force out, but to limit its freedom of action within the operational area." US Department of Defense, "Joint Operational Access Concept," p. i.

37. Jonathan W. Greenert and Norton A. Schwartz, "Air-Sea Battle," *American Interest*, February 20, 2012, http://www.the-american-interest.com/2012/02/20/air-sea-battle/ (accessed October 21, 2016).

38. Aaron L. Friedberg, *Beyond Air-Sea Battle: The Debate over US Military Strategy in Asia* (London: Routledge, 2014), p. 60.

39. Etzioni, "Who Authorized Preparations for War with China?" p. 41.

40. US Department of Defense, "Joint Operational Access Concept," p. 24.

41. Etzioni, "Who Authorized Preparations for War with China?" pp. 37, 40, 43.

42. US Department of Defense, "Joint Operational Access Concept," p. 38.

43. Friedberg, *Beyond Air-Sea Battle*, p. 94.

44. US Department of Defense, "Sustaining US Global Leadership," p. 5.

45. Robert Martinage, "Toward a New Offset Strategy: Exploiting U.S. Long-Term Advantages to Restore U.S. Global Power Projection Capability" (Washington, DC: Center for Strategic and Budgetary Assessments, 2014), p. v. See also Richard A. Bitzinger, "Third Offset Strategy and Chinese A2/AD Capabilities" (Washington, DC: Center for a New American Security, 2016), p. 2.

46. Martinage, "Toward a New Offset Strategy," p. v.

47. Peter Dombrowski, "America's Third Offset Strategy: New Military Technologies and Implications for the Asia Pacific" (Singapore: S. Rajaratnam School of International Studies, 2015), p. 4.

48. US Department of Defense, "Joint Operational Access Concept," p. 2; Jan van Tol, with Mark Gunzinger, Andrew Krepinevich, and Jim Thomas, *AirSea Battle: A Point-of-Departure Concept* (Washington, DC: Center for Strategic and Budgetary Assessments, 2010), p. x; Friedberg, *Beyond Air-Sea Battle*, p. 76.

49. See, for example, Andrew F. Krepinevich, "Why AirSea Battle?," (Washington, DC: Center for Strategic and Budgetary Assessments, 2010), p. 8.

50. Friedberg, *Beyond Air-Sea Battle*, pp. 12–13.

51. M. Taylor Fravel and Christopher P. Twomey, "Projecting Strategy: The Myth of Chinese Counter-Intervention," *Washington Quarterly* 37, no. 4 (Winter 2015), pp. 171–87.

52. Ji Guoxing, "Rough Waters in the South China Sea: Navigation Issues and Confidence-Building Measures," *AsiaPacific Issues* 53 (Honolulu: East-West Center, August 2001), p. 4.

53. National Institute for South China Sea Studies, *Report on the Military Presence of the United States of America in the Asia-Pacific Region* (Beijing: Current Affairs Press, 2016), p. 31; Ji You, "The Sino-US 'Cat-and-Mouse' Game concerning Freedom of Navigation and Flights: An Analysis of Chinese Perspectives," *Journal of Strategic Studies* 39, nos. 5–6 (2016), pp. 637–61, at p. 648, fn. 50.

54. Author's interview with Chinese scholar, Peking University, Beijing, September 2016.

55. Ji, "Rough Waters in the South China Sea," p. 5.

56. United Nations, *United Nations Convention on the Law of the Sea (UNCLOS)*, 1982, http://www.un.org/depts/los/convention_agreements/texts/unclos/unclos_e.pdf (accessed October 22, 2016).

57. Ji, "Rough Waters in the South China Sea," p. 4.

58. Sam Bateman, "Some Thoughts on Australia and the Freedoms of Navigation," *Security Challenges* 11, no. 2 (2015), pp. 57–66, at p. 64.

59. Dennis C. Blair and David V. Bonfili, "The April 2001 EP-3 Incident: The U.S. Point of View," in Michael D. Swaine and Zhang Tuosheng, with Danielle F. S. Cohen, eds., *Managing Sino-American Crises: Case Studies and Analysis* (Washington, DC: Carnegie Endowment for International Peace, 2006), pp. 377–90, at p. 378.

60. Shirley A. Kan et al., "China-U.S. Aircraft Collision Incident of April 2001: Assessments and Policy Implications" (Washington, DC: Congressional Research Service, 2001).

61. See Peter Hays Gries and Kaiping Peng, "Culture Clash? Apologies East and West," *Journal of Contemporary China* 11, no. 30 (2002), pp. 173–78, at p. 174.

62. Zhang Tuosheng, "The Sino-American Aircraft Collision: Lessons for Crisis Management," in Swaine, Zhang, and Cohen, eds., *Managing Sino-American Crises*, pp. 391–421; Twomey and Hui, "Military Developments." See also You, "The Sino-US 'Cat-and-Mouse' Game," p. 648; Gries and Peng, "Culture Clash?"

63. David Griffiths, *U.S.-China Maritime Confidence Building: Paradigms, Precedents, and Prospects* (Newport, RI: Naval War College, 2010), p. 17.

64. Kan et al., "China-U.S. Aircraft Collision Incident," pp. 27–30.

65. Michael Auslin, "Japan's New Realism," *Foreign Affairs* 95, no. 2 (2016), pp. 125–34, at p. 133.

66. Patrick M. Cronin, "Sustaining the Rebalance in Southeast Asia: Challenges and Opportunities Facing the Next Administration" (Washington, DC: Center for a New American Security, 2016), p. 5.

67. Hillary Rodham Clinton, "Remarks at Press Availability," National Convention Center, Hanoi, July 23, 2010, https://2009-2017.state.gov/secretary/20092013clinton/rm/2010/07/145095.htm (accessed March 13, 2018). See also Bader, *Obama and China's Rise*, p. 105; Campbell, *The Pivot*, p. 273; Mann, *The Obamians*, p. 246.

68. Clinton made these remarks in a private speech to Goldman Sachs, as published by WikiLeaks. See Mark Landler, "Philippines 'Separation' from U.S. Jilts Hillary

Clinton, Too," *New York Times*, October 21, 2016, https://www.nytimes.com/ 2016/10/22/us/politics/philippines-china-us-asia-pivot.html (accessed September 11, 2019).

69. Leszek Buszynski, "The South China Sea: Oil, Maritime Claims, and U.S.-China Strategic Rivalry," *Washington Quarterly* 35, no. 2 (2012), pp. 139–56; Alice D. Ba, "Staking Claims and Making Waves in the South China Sea: How Troubled Are the Waters?," *Contemporary Southeast Asia* 33, no. 3 (2011), pp. 269–91.

70. See You, "The Sino-US 'Cat-and-Mouse' Game."

71. Campbell, *The Pivot*, p. 180; Jane Perlez, "China Assails U.S. Pledge to Defend Disputed Islands Controlled by Japan," *New York Times*, February 4, 2017, https:// www.nytimes.com/2017/02/04/world/asia/china-us-jim-mattis-japan-islands. html (accessed September 30, 2018).

72. See influential Chinese expert Wu Xinbo's comments in Wu Xinbo and Michael Green, "Regional Security Roles and Challenges," in Hachigian, ed., *Debating China*, pp. 198–220, at pp. 201–5.

73. Fu, "How China Sees Russia," p. 104. Fu's assessment is noteworthy because of her previous policy role.

74. Lin and Zhang, "Chaoyue kunjing," p. 66.

75. Ibid., p. 70; Wang, "Guodu kuozhang," p. 14.

76. See Alastair Iain Johnston, "How New and Assertive Is China's New Assertiveness?," *International Security* 37, no. 4 (2013), pp. 7–48.

77. Wang Jisi and Lan Zhimin, "Meiguo jinru 'tao guang yang hui' shidai? Aobama zhuyi he meiguo waijiao zhuanxing" [Is America Entering an Era of "Hiding Capabilities and Biding Time"? The Obama Doctrine and the Transformation of American Foreign Policy], in Institute of Peace and Development, Chinese Academy of Social Sciences, ed., *Aobama zhengfu neiwai zhengce tiaozheng yu zhongmei guanxi* [The Adjustments of the Obama Administration's Domestic and Foreign Policies and China-US Relations] (Beijing: Zhongguo shehui kexue chu-banshe, 2015), pp. 111–31, at p. 126.

78. Wang Jisi, *Daguo guanxi* [Great Power Relations] (Beijing: China CITIC Press, 2015), p. 252.

79. Robert S. Ross, "The Problem with the Pivot: Obama's New Asia Policy Is Unnecessary and Counterproductive," *Foreign Affairs* 91, no. 6 (2012), pp. 70–82, at p. 81.

80. These criticisms are implied in a high-level American task force report on US-China relations. See Orville Schell and Susan L. Shirk (chairs), *US Policy toward China: Recommendations for a New Administration*, Task Force Report (New York: Asia Society, 2017), pp. 13, 27.

81. The twelve countries are Australia, Brunei, Canada, Chile, Japan, Malaysia, Mexico, New Zealand, Peru, Singapore, the United States, and Vietnam. Together they comprise 40 percent of the world's gross domestic product.

82. Ian F. Fergusson and Brock R. Williams, "The Trans-Pacific Partnership (TPP): Key Provisions and Issues for Congress" (Washington, DC: Congressional Research Service, 2016).

83. Campbell, *The Pivot*, p. 266.

84. James Stavridis, "The American Brexit Is Coming," *Foreign Policy*, October 2, 2016, http://foreignpolicy.com/2016/10/06/the-american-brexit-is-coming-tpp-trade-trans-pacific-partnership/ (accessed October 28, 2016).

85. Cronin, "Sustaining the Rebalance in Southeast Asia," p. 8.

86. See Jamil Anderlini, "A Shaky Trade Pact That Signals American Decline," *Financial Times*, October 5, 2016, https://www.ft.com/content/6f14756c-8a1e-11e6-8aa5-f79f5696c731 (accessed September 11, 2019).

87. Barack Obama, "The TPP Would Let America, Not China, Lead the Way on Global Trade," *Washington Post*, May 2, 2016, https://www.washingtonpost.com/opinions/president-obama-the-tpp-would-let-america-not-china-lead-the-way-on-global-trade/2016/05/02/680540e4-0fd0-11e6-93ae-50921721165d_story.html (accessed September 11, 2019). See also Barack Obama, "Statement by the President on the Trans-Pacific Partnership," White House, October 5, 2015, https://www.whitehouse.gov/the-press-office/2015/10/05/statement-president-trans-pacific-partnership (accessed October 28, 2016).

88. Fergusson and Williams, "The Trans-Pacific Partnership," p. 4.

89. Geoff Dyer and George Parker, "US Attacks UK's 'Constant Accommodation' with China," *Financial Times*, March 12, 2015, https://www.ft.com/content/31c4880a-c8d2-11e4-bc64-00144feab7de (accessed September 11, 2019).

90. Campbell, *The Pivot*, p. 276.

91. Yuan, "Xunqiu zhongmei yatai liangxing hudong," p. 58.

92. Susan E. Rice, "Remarks as Prepared for Delivery by National Security Advisor Susan E. Rice," Georgetown University, Washington, DC, November 21, 2013, https://www.whitehouse.gov/the-press-office/2013/11/21/remarks-prepared-delivery-national-security-advisor-susan-e-rice (accessed October 28,2016).

93. Nina Silove, "The Pivot before the Pivot: U.S. Strategy to Preserve the Power Balance in Asia," *International Security* 40, no. 4 (2016), pp. 45–88, at p. 84.

94. Peter Baker, "Trump Abandons Trans-Pacific Partnership, Obama's Signature Trade Deal," *New York Times*, January 23, 2017, https://www.nytimes.com/2017/01/23/us/politics/tpp-trump-trade-nafta.html (accessed August 29, 2019).

95. Brian Montopoli, "In Full: U.S.-China Joint Statement," CBS News, November 17, 2009, https://www.cbsnews.com/news/in-full-us-china-joint-statement/ (accessed March 13, 2018).

96. Wu Xinbo, "China and the United States: Core Interests, Common Interests, and Partnership" (Washington, DC: US Institute of Peace, 2011), p. 2.

97. Da Wei, "Zhongmei xinxing daguo guanxi: Gainianhua yu caozuohua" [A New Type of Great Power Relationship between China and the United States: Conceptualization and Operationalization], *Guoji zhengzhi kexue* [Quarterly Journal of International Politics], no. 1 (2015), pp. 4–24, at pp. 4–5.

98. James B. Steinberg, "China's Arrival: The Long March to Global Power," keynote address to the Center for a New American Security, Washington, DC, September 24, 2009.

99. Josh Rogin, "The End of the Concept of 'Strategic Reassurance'?" *Foreign Policy*, November 6, 2009, http://foreignpolicy.com/2009/11/06/the-end-of-the-concept-of-strategic-reassurance/ (accessed October 28, 2016).

100. Dai Bingguo, "Persisting with Taking the Path of Peaceful Development," *China News*, December 7, 2010, http://www.chinanews.com/gn/2010/12-07/2704984.shtml (accessed March 13, 2018).

101. Wu, "China and the United States," p. 2.

102. Thomas J. Christensen, *The China Challenge: Shaping the Choices of a Rising Power* (New York: Norton, 2015), p. 254.

103. Thomas J. Christensen, "The Need to Pursue Mutual Interests in U.S.-PRC Relations" (Washington, DC: US Institute of Peace, 2011), p. 2, emphasis in original.

104. Ibid., p. 5.

105. Wang Jisi, ed., "Separate or Similar Goals? On Building a New Type of Great Power Relations between China and the United States," in *International and Strategic Studies Report* (Beijing: Institute of International and Strategic Studies, Peking University, 2014), p. 6.

106. Bilahari Kausikan, "The Roots of Strategic Distrust: The US, China, Japan and ASEAN in East Asia," *Straits Times*, November 18, 2014, https://www.strait-stimes.com/opinion/the-roots-of-strategic-distrust-the-us-china-japan-and-asean-in-east-asia (accessed September 11, 2019).

107. Wang, "Separate or Similar Goals?," p. 7.

108. Larry Diamond, "Democracy Demotion: How the Freedom Agenda Fell Apart," *Foreign Affairs* 98, no. 4 (2019), pp. 17–25.

109. Kurt M. Campbell and Ely Ratner, "The China Reckoning: How Beijing Defied American Expectations," *Foreign Affairs* 97, no. 2 (2018), pp. 60–70, at p. 61.

110. Posen, "The Rise of Illiberal Hegemony," p. 26.

111. Campbell and Ratner, "The China Reckoning," p. 70.

112. Wang Jisi, "The View from China," in "Did America Get China Wrong? The Engagement Debate," special issue, *Foreign Affairs* 97, no. 4 (2018), pp. 183–95, at p. 183.

113. Nicholas Borroz and Hunter Marston, "Washington Should Stop Militarizing the Pacific," *New York Times*, October 9, 2016, https://www.nytimes.com/2016/10/10/opinion/washington-should-stop-militarizing-the-pacific.html (accessed September 11, 2019).

114. Clinton, "America's Pacific Century."

115. Campbell, *The Pivot*, p. 198.

116. Ibid., p. 7.

117. Simon Denyer, "Don't Let Beijing Push Us Around, Warns 'Frustrated' Former Ambassador to China," *Washington Post*, February 26, 2017, https://

www.washingtonpost.com/world/dont-let-beijing-push-us-around-warns-frustrated-former-ambassador-to-china/2017/02/24/f1eb41a0-fa71-11e6-9b3e-ed886f4f4825_story.html (accessed September 11, 2019).

118. Campbell, *The Pivot*, p. 232.

119. Yuan Peng, "Zhongguo wei lishi nanti xunzhao xin da'an" [China Is Seeking a New Answer to a Historically Difficult Question], *Caokao Xiaoxi* [Reference News], http://www.guancha.cn/YuanPeng/2016_08_31_372956_s.shtml (accessed March 29, 2018).

120. Da Wei and Zhang Zhaoxi, "Zhongmei guanxi xinjieduan zhong de zhanlüe shiyu yu zhanlüe wending tansuo" [The "Loss of Language" in Strategy in a New Era of China-US Relations and an Exploration of Strategic Stability], *Guoji anquan yanjiu* [Journal of International Security Studies], no. 5 (2016), pp. 39–59, at p. 50. See also Liu, "Meiguo 'yatai zaipingheng' zhanlüe mianlin de tiaozhan," p. 99.

121. Cronin, "Sustaining the Rebalance in Southeast Asia," p. 2.

122. Ruan, "Meiguo," p. 12.

123. Author's interview with Ministry of Foreign Affairs official, Beijing, September 9, 2016.

124. Wang, "Guodu kuozhang," p. 17.

125. Feng Zhang, "Challenge Accepted: China's Response to the US Rebalance to the Asia-Pacific," *Security Challenges* 12, no. 3 (2016), pp. 45–60.

126. Yuan, "Zhongguo wei lishi nanti xunzhao xin da'an."

127. Yang Jiemian, "US Rebalance to Asia-Pacific and Sino-US Relations," speech to the Boao Forum for Asia's Strategic Planning Workshop, October 15, 2016, http://mp.weixin.qq.com/s?__biz=MzAwODc2MDY2Nw==&mid=224748 4038&idx=2&sn=277c9f5425b8da0afaadbb5dbfeeea37&chksm=9b68beb2ac 1f37a4caf5360bbcf802494432ad2b451c49e3e4fbe007bca556f21b440d10bca8 &scene=0&from=groupmessage&isappinstalled=0#wechat_redirect (accessed October 26, 2016).

128. Silove, "The Pivot before the Pivot."

129. Campbell, *The Pivot*, p. 150.

130. Ibid., p. 206.

131. Thomas J. Christensen, "Obama and Asia: Confronting the China Challenge," *Foreign Affairs* 94, no. 5 (2015), pp. 28–36, at p. 29; Christensen, *The China Challenge*, pp. 250–51.

132. Ross, "The Problem with the Pivot," p. 72.

133. Xue Li, "Meiguo zaipingheng zhanlüe yu zhongguo 'yidai yilu'" [America's Rebalance Strategy and China's "One Belt, One Road"], *Shijie jingji yu zhengzhi* [World Economy and Politics], no. 5 (2016), pp. 56–73, at pp. 62, 65.

134. Liu, "Meiguo 'yatai zaipingheng' zhanlüe mianlin de tiaozhan," p. 98.

135. Campbell, *The Pivot*, p. 150, emphasis in original.

CHAPTER 4

1. Colin Dueck, *Reluctant Crusaders: Power, Culture, and Change in American Grand Strategy* (Princeton, NJ: Princeton University Press, 2006), p. 11; Paul Kennedy, "Grand Strategy in War and Peace: Toward a Broader Definition," in Paul Kennedy, ed., *Grand Strategies in War and Peace* (New Haven, CT: Yale University Press, 1991), pp. 1–7; Feng Zhang, "Rethinking China's Grand Strategy: Beijing's Evolving National Interests and Strategic Ideas in the Reform Era," *International Politics* 49, no. 3 (2012), pp. 318–45.

2. Richard Ned Lebow, *The Tragic Vision of Politics: Ethics, Interests and Orders* (Cambridge, UK: Cambridge University Press, 2003).

3. Barack Obama, "Remarks by President Barack Obama at Suntory Hall," Tokyo, November 14, 2009, https://obamawhitehouse.archives.gov/realitycheck/the-press-office/remarks-president-barack-obama-suntory-hall (accessed February 12, 2017); Barack Obama, "Remarks by President Barack Obama at Town Hall Meeting with Future Chinese Leaders," Museum of Science and Technology, Shanghai, November 16, 2009, https://obamawhitehouse.archives.gov/realitycheck/the-press-office/remarks-president-barack-obama-town-hall-meeting-with-future-chinese-leaders (accessed March 15, 2018).

4. Barack Obama and Hu Jintao, "Joint Press Statement by President Obama and China's President Hu, November 2009," Beijing, November 17, 2009, https://obamawhitehouse.archives.gov/realitycheck/the-press-office/us-china-joint-statement (accessed March 29, 2018).

5. James B. Steinberg, "China's Arrival: The Long March to Global Power," keynote address to the Center for a New American Security, Washington, DC, September 24, 2009.

6. Zbigniew Brzezinski, "The Group of Two That Could Change the World," *Financial Times*, January 14, 2009, https://www.ft.com/content/d99369b8-e178-11dd-afa0-0000779fd2ac (accessed September 11, 2019).

7. Susan Shirk, "The Domestic Context of Chinese Foreign Security Policies," in Saadia M. Pekkanen, John Ravenhill, and Rosemary Foot, eds., *The Oxford Handbook of the International Relations of Asia* (Oxford: Oxford University Press, 2014), pp. 391–410, at p. 398.

8. Jeffrey A. Bader, *Obama and China's Rise: An Insider's Account of America's Asia Strategy* (Washington, DC: Brookings Institution Press, 2012), p. 66.

9. James Mann, *The Obamians: The Struggle inside the White House to Redefine American Power* (New York: Viking, 2012), p. 244.

10. Helene Cooper, "Obama Meets Dalai Lama, and China Is Quick to Protest," *New York Times*, February 18, 2010, https://www.nytimes.com/2010/02/19/world/asia/19prexy.html (accessed September 11, 2019).

11. US-Taiwan Business Council and Project 2049 Institute, "Chinese Reactions to Taiwan Arms Sales" (Arlington, VA: US-Taiwan Business Council and Project 2049 Institute, 2012), p. 96.

12. Michael D. Swaine, "Perceptions of an Assertive China," *China Leadership Monitor* 32 (Spring 2010), pp. 1–19.

13. Edward Wong, "Chinese Military Seeks to Extend Its Naval Power," *New York Times*, April 23, 2010, https://www.nytimes.com/2010/04/24/world/asia/24navy. html (accessed September 11, 2019).

14. Bader, *Obama and China's Rise*, p. 76.

15. Phuong Nguyen, "Deciphering the Shift in America's South China Sea Policy," *Contemporary Southeast Asia* 38, no. 3 (2016), pp. 389–421, at p. 397.

16. See, for example, Thomas J. Christensen, *The China Challenge: Shaping the Choices of a Rising Power* (New York: Norton, 2015), pp. 252–53.

17. Yuan Peng, "Dui zhongmei guanxi weilai fazhan de zhanlüe sikao" [Strategic Thoughts on the Future Development of China-US Relations], *Xiandai guoji guanxi* [Contemporary International Relations], supplementary issue (2010), pp. 65–70, at p. 69.

18. Yuan Peng, "Guanyu goujian zhongmei xinxing daguo guanxi de" [Strategic Thought on Building a New Model of Great Power Relationship], *Xiandai guoji guanxi* [Contemporary International Relations], no. 5 (2012), pp. 1–8, at p. 4.

19. Shi Yinhong, "Zhongguo zhoubian xingwei zhong ceng you de 'shengli zhuyi': Dongneng he juece fuzaixing" [The "Triumphalism" in China's Regional Behavior: Motivations and Policymaking Complexities], *Xiandai guoji guanxi* [Contemporary International Relations], no. 10 (2013), pp. 3–5.

20. In reality, however, China's stimulus package, though designed to blunt the impact of the financial crisis, contributed to a serious debt problem in the Chinese economy, with long-term consequences on economic performance.

21. Thomas J. Christensen, "Obama and Asia: Confronting the China Challenge," *Foreign Affairs* 94, no. 5 (2015), pp. 28–36, at p. 28.

22. Alastair Iain Johnston, "Is Chinese Nationalism Rising? Evidence from Beijing," *International Security* 41, no. 3 (2016–17), pp. 7–43.

23. Christensen, *The China Challenge*, p. 255.

24. Yuan Peng, "Zhongguo waijiao xu jinfang dazhanlüe shiwu" [Chinese Foreign Policy Must Guard Against Grand Strategy Mistake], *Xiandai guoji guanxi* [Contemporary International Relations], no. 11 (2010), pp. 12–14, at p. 13.

25. Bader, *Obama and China's Rise*, p. 79.

26. Alastair Iain Johnston, "How New and Assertive Is China's New Assertiveness?," *International Security* 37, no. 4 (2013), pp. 7–48.

27. Robert S. Ross, "The Problem with the Pivot: Obama's New Asia Policy Is Unnecessary and Counterproductive," *Foreign Affairs* 91, no. 6 (2012), pp. 70–82, at p. 76.

28. Bader, *Obama and China's Rise*, p. 60.

29. For an overview of this debate, see Swaine, "Perceptions of an Assertive China," pp. 7–8.

30. Wang Jisi, "Shijie zhengzhi bianqian yu zhongguo duiwai zhanlüe sikao" [Transformations in World Politics and Thoughts on China's Foreign Strategy], in Wang Jisi, ed., *Zhongguo guoji zhanlüe pinglun 2011* [China Strategy Review 2011] (Beijing: Shijie zhishi chubanshe, 2011), pp. 1–12, at p. 10.

31. Ibid., p. 11; Zhang Tuosheng, "Xinxingshi xia dui zhongguo duiwai zhengce de ruogan sikao" [Thoughts on Chinese Foreign Policy under New Circumstances], in Wang, ed., *Zhongguo guoji zhanlüe pinglun 2011*, pp. 61–69, at p. 62; Yuan, "Dui zhongmei guanxi weilai fazhan de zhanlüe sikao," p. 70.

32. Yuan, "Zhongguo waijiao xu jinfang dazhanlüe shiwu," p. 13.

33. Dai Bingguo, "Persisting with Taking the Path of Peaceful Development," *China News*, December 7, 2010, http://www.chinanews.com/gn/2010/12-07/2704984.shtml (accessed February 14, 2017).

34. The White House, "U.S.-China Joint Statement," January 19, 2011, https://obamawhitehouse.archives.gov/the-press-office/2011/01/19/us-china-joint-statement (accessed February 14, 2017).

35. The White House, "Remarks by Vice President Biden and Chinese Vice President Xi at the State Department Luncheon," February 14, 2012, https://obamawhitehouse.archives.gov/the-press-office/2012/02/14/remarks-vice-president-biden-and-chinese-vice-president-xi-state-departm (accessed March 15, 2018).

36. Hillary Clinton, "Secretary Clinton on 40 Years of U.S.-China Relations," The World and Japan Database, March 7, 2012, http://worldjpn.grips.ac.jp/documents/texts/USC/20120307.S1E.html (accessed March 15, 2018).

37. "Hu Jintao: Tuijin huli gongying hezuo, fazhan xinxing daguo guanxi" [Hu Jintao: Facilitate Mutually Beneficial Cooperation and Build a New Model of Great Power Relationship], Xinhuanet, May 3, 2012, http://news.xinhuanet.com/world/2012-05/03/c_111882964.htm (accessed February 14, 2017).

38. Graham Allison, "The Thucydides Trap: Are the U.S. and China Headed for War?," *The Atlantic*, September 24, 2015, https://www.theatlantic.com/international/archive/2015/09/united-states-china-war-thucydides-trap/406756/ (accessed February 24, 2017).

39. Tom Donilon, "Remarks by Tom Donilon, National Security Advisor to the President: 'The United States and the Asia-Pacific in 2013,'" The Asia Society, New York, March 11, 2013, https://obamawhitehouse.archives.gov/the-press-office/2013/03/11/remarks-tom-donilon-national-security-advisor-president-united-states-an (accessed February 23, 2017).

40. Ibid.

41. "Yang Jiechi tan Xi Jinping zhuxi yu aobama annaboge zhuangyuan huiwu chengguo" [Yang Jiechi on the Outcomes of President Xi Jinping's Meeting with Obama

at Sunnylands], Xinhuanet, June 9, 2013, http://news.xinhuanet.com/world/2013-06/09/c_116102752.htm (accessed February 22, 2017).

42. Barack Obama and Xi Jinping, "Remarks by President Obama and President Xi Jinping of the People's Republic of China after Bilateral Meeting," Sunnylands Retreat, Rancho Mirage, June 8, 2013, https://obamawhitehouse.archives.gov/the-press-office/2013/06/08/remarks-president-obama-and-president-xi-jinping-peoples-republic-china- (accessed February 23, 2017).

43. Susan E. Rice, "Remarks as Prepared for Delivery by National Security Advisor Susan E. Rice," Georgetown University, Washington, DC, November 21, 2013, https://www.whitehouse.gov/the-press-office/2013/11/21/remarks-prepared-delivery-national-security-advisor-susan-e-rice (accessed October 28, 2016).

44. Ibid.

45. Feng Zhang interview with an analyst at the China Institutes of Contemporary International Relations, Beijing, June 2016.

46. Ian E. Rinehart and Bart Elias, "China's Air Defense Identification Zone (ADIZ)" (Washington, DC: Congressional Research Service, 2015), p. 15.

47. Jane Morse, "Vice President Biden Urges 'Practical Cooperation' in U.S.-China Relations," *American News & Views*, December 6, 2013, https://photos.state.gov/libraries/burma/895/pdf/ANV20131206.pdf (accessed March 15, 2018).

48. Joe Biden and Xi Jinping, "Remarks by Vice President Joe Biden and President Xi Jinping of the People's Republic of China," Great Hall of the People, Beijing, December 4, 2013, https://obamawhitehouse.archives.gov/the-press-office/2013/12/04/remarks-vice-president-joe-biden-and-president-xi-jinping-peoples-republ (accessed March 15, 2018).

49. Da Wei, "Zhongmei xinxing daguo guanxi: Gainianhua yu caozuohua" [A New Model of China-US Great Power Relationship: Conceptualization and Operationalization], *Guoji zhengzhi kexue* [Quarterly Journal of International Politics], no. 1 (2015), pp. 4–24, at p. 7.

50. Ibid.

51. John J. Mearsheimer, *The Tragedy of Great Power Politics* (New York: Norton, 2001).

52. "Xi Jinping zai xiyatushi huanying yanhui shang fabiao yanjiang (quanwen)" [Xi Jinping's Speech to the Welcome Dinner in Seattle (Full Text)], Xinhua News Agency, September 23, 2015, http://www.china.com.cn/cppcc/2015-09/23/content_36662360_4.htm (accessed March 9, 2017).

53. Quoted in Da, "Zhongmei xinxing daguo guanxi," p. 11.

54. On the Scarborough Shoal incident, see International Crisis Group, "Stirring up the South China Sea (III): A Fleeting Opportunity for Calm," Asia Report No. 267 (Brussels: International Crisis Group, 2015).

55. Nguyen, "Deciphering the Shift," p. 398.

56. See Feng Zhang, "Assessing China's South China Sea Policy, 2009–2015," *East Asian Policy* 8, no. 3 (2016), pp. 100–109.

57. "Vietnam/China: Chinese Oil Rig Operations Near the Paracel Islands," US Embassy & Consulate in Vietnam, May 7, 2014, https://vn.usembassy.gov/vietnamchina-chinese-oil-rig-operations-near-the-paracel-islands/ (accessed March 4, 2017).

58. Jane Perlez, "American and Chinese Navy Ships Nearly Collided in South China Sea," *New York Times*, December 14, 2013, https://www.nytimes.com/2013/12/15/world/asia/chinese-and-american-ships-nearly-collide-in-south-china-sea.html (accessed September 11, 2019).

59. Yan Xuetong, "From Keeping a Low Profile to Striving for Achievement," *Chinese Journal of International Politics* 7, no. 2 (2014), pp. 153–84.

60. Christensen, *The China Challenge*, p. 263.

61. Ji You, "The Sino-US 'Cat-and-Mouse' Game concerning Freedom of Navigation and Flights: An Analysis of Chinese Perspectives," *Journal of Strategic Studies* 39, nos. 5–6 (2016), pp. 637–61.

62. Christensen, *The China Challenge*, p. 263.

63. Kurt M. Campbell, *The Pivot: The Future of American Statecraft in Asia* (New York: Twelve, 2016), p. 180; Paul Eckert, "Treaty with Japan Covers Islets in China Spat: U.S. Official," Reuters, September 21, 2012, http://www.reuters.com/article/us-china-japan-usa-idUSBRE88J1HJ20120920 (accessed March 9, 2017).

64. Juliet Eilperin, "Obama Reassures Japan as He Begins Asian Visit," *Washington Post*, April 24, 2014.

65. You, "The Sino-US 'Cat-and-Mouse' Game," pp. 655–56.

66. David E. Sanger and Julie Hirschfeld Davis, "Conflict Flavors Obama's Meeting with Chinese Leader," *New York Times*, September 22, 2015, https://www.nytimes.com/2015/09/23/world/asia/conflict-flavors-obamas-meeting-with-chinese-leader.html (accessed September 11, 2019).

67. Feng Zhang interview with a Chinese official involved in relevant policymaking, Beijing, September 2016. See also Lyle J. Morris, "The New 'Normal' in the East China Sea," *The Diplomat*, February 24, 2017, http://thediplomat.com/2017/02/the-new-normal-in-the-east-china-sea/ (accessed March 18, 2017).

68. US Department of Defense, "The Asia-Pacific Maritime Security Strategy: Achieving U.S. National Security Objectives in a Changing Environment" (Washington, DC: US Department of Defense, 2015), p. 16. See also John Grady, "PACOM CO Harris: More U.S. South China Sea Freedom of Navigation Missions Are Coming," *USNI News*, January 27, 2016, https://news.usni.org/2016/01/27/pacom-co-harris-more-u-s-south-china-sea-freedom-of-navigation-missions-are-coming (accessed September 23, 2016).

69. US Department of Defense, *Annual Report to Congress: Military and Security Developments Involving the People's Republic of China 2016* (Washington, DC: Office of the Secretary of Defense, 2016), pp. 13–20.

70. "Build It and They Will Come," Asia Maritime Transparency Initiative, August 1, 2016, https://amti.csis.org/build-it-and-they-will-come/ (accessed March 5, 2017);

"A Look at China's SAM Shelters in the Spratlys," Asia Maritime Transparency Initiative, February 23, 2017, https://amti.csis.org/chinas-sam-shelters-spratlys/ (accessed March 5, 2017).

71. Hannah Beech, "China's Sea Control Is a Done Deal, 'Short of War with the U.S.,'" *New York Times*, September 20, 2018, https://www.nytimes.com/2018/09/20/world/asia/south-china-sea-navy.html (accessed September 30, 2018).

72. "China's New Spratly Island Defenses," Asia Maritime Transparency Initiative, December 13, 2016, https://amti.csis.org/chinas-new-spratly-island-defenses/ (accessed March 5, 2017).

73. Asia Maritime Security Initiative, "China Lands First Bomber on South China Sea Island," May 18, 2018, https://amti.csis.org/china-lands-first-bomber-south-china-sea-island/ (accessed October 1, 2018).

74. "Update: China's Continuing Reclamation in the Paracels," Asia Maritime Transparency Initiative, August 9, 2017, https://amti.csis.org/paracels-beijings-other-buildup/ (accessed March 15, 2018).

75. Quoted in Nguyen, "Deciphering the Shift," p. 401.

76. US Department of Defense, "The Asia-Pacific Maritime Security Strategy," p. 17.

77. Lynn Kuok, "The U.S. FON Program in the South China Sea: A Lawful and Necessary Response to China's Strategic Ambiguity," East Asia Policy Paper 9 (Washington, DC: Brookings Institution, 2016).

78. Ankit Panda, "What ARIA Will and Won't Do for the US in Asia," *Diplomat*, January 14, 2019, https://thediplomat.com/2019/01/what-aria-will-and-wont-do-for-the-us-in-asia/ (accessed August 29, 2019).

79. Ministry of Foreign Affairs of the People's Republic of China, "Ministry of Foreign Affairs Spokesman Lu Kang's Press Briefing on China's Island Building in the Spratlys," June 16, 2015, http://www.fmprc.gov.cn/web/ziliao_674904/zt_674979/dnzt_674981/qtzt/nhwt_685150/zxxx_685152/t1273364.shtml (accessed March 6, 2017).

80. Feng Zhang interview with a Ministry of Foreign Affairs official, Beijing, September 2016.

81. Feng Zhang, "Chinese Thinking on the South China Sea and the Future of Regional Security," *Political Science Quarterly* 132, no. 3 (2017), pp. 435–66.

82. See Feng Zhang, "Challenge Accepted: China's Response to the US Rebalance to the Asia-Pacific," *Security Challenges* 12, no. 3 (2016), pp. 45–60.

83. Feng Zhang interview with an influential Chinese expert privy to this process, Beijing, December 2016.

84. Feng Zhang interview with an influential Chinese foreign policy expert, Beijing, December 2016.

85. "Xi Jinping zai yaxin huiyi zuo zhuzhi fayan (quanwen)" [Xi Jinping Delivers Keynote Speech to CICA Conference (Full Text)], People Net, May 21, 2014, http://world.people.com.cn/n/2014/0521/c1002-25046183.html (accessed March 4, 2017).

86. "Xi Jinping zai yaxin diwuci waizhang huiyi kaimushi shang de jianghua" [Xi Jinping's Speech at the Opening Ceremony of Fifth Foreign Ministers' Meeting of the Conference on Interaction and Confidence-Building Measures in Asia], Xinhua News Agency, April 28, 2016, http://news.xinhuanet.com/2016-04/28/ c_1118761158.htm (accessed March 4, 2017).

87. "Barack Obama's Asian Tour: So Long, and Thanks for All the Naval Bases," *Economist*, April 28, 2014, http://www.economist.com/blogs/banyan/2014/04/ barack-obama-s-asian-tour (accessed March 6, 2017).

88. Barack Obama, "Remarks by President Obama to Filipino and U.S. Armed Forces," Fort Bonifacio, Manila, April 29, 2014, https://ph.usembassy.gov/remarks-by-president-obama-to-filipino-and-u-s-armed-forces/ (accessed March 6, 2017).

89. Feng Zhang interview with a Ministry of Foreign Affairs official, Beijing, September 2016.

90. "Xi Jinping zai diliulun zhongmei zhanlüe yu jingji duihua he diwulun zhong-mei renwen jiaoliu gaoceng cuoshang lianhe kaimushi shang de zhici (quanwen)" [Remarks by Xi Jinping to the Joint Opening Ceremony of the 6th Round of China-US Strategic and Economic Dialogue and the 5th Round of China-US High-Level Consultation on People-to-People and Cultural Exchange], Xinhua News Net, July 9, 2014, http://news.xinhuanet.com/world/2014-07/09/c_ 1111530987.htm (accessed March 6, 2017).

91. Mark Landler, "U.S. and China Reach Climate Accord after Months of Talks," *New York Times*, November 11, 2014, https://www.nytimes.com/2014/11/12/ world/asia/china-us-xi-obama-apec.html (accessed September 11, 2019).

92. Michael S. Schmidt and David E. Sanger, "5 in China Army Face U.S. Charges of Cyberattacks," *New York Times*, May 19, 2014, https://www.nytimes.com/ 2014/05/20/us/us-to-charge-chinese-workers-with-cyberspying.html (accessed September 11, 2019).

93. Sanger and Davis, "Conflict Flavors Obama's Meeting with Chinese Leader."

94. Julie Hirschfeld Davis and David E. Sanger, "Obama and Xi Jinping of China Agree to Steps on Cybertheft," *New York Times*, September 25, 2015, https://www. nytimes.com/2015/09/26/world/asia/xi-jinping-white-house.html (accessed September 11, 2019).

95. Barack Obama and Xi Jinping, "Remarks by President Obama and President Xi of the People's Republic of China in Joint Press Conference," White House, Washington, DC, September 25, 2015, https://obamawhitehouse.archives. gov/the-press-office/2015/09/25/remarks-president-obama-and-president-xi-peoples-republic-china-joint (accessed March 6, 2017).

96. Ibid.

97. Feng Zhang interview with an influential Chinese expert, Beijing, November 2015.

98. Feng Zhang, "Assessing China's Response to the South China Sea Arbitration Ruling," *Australian Journal of International Affairs* 71, no. 4 (2017), pp. 440–59.

99. Dai, "Persisting with Taking the Path of Peaceful Development."

100. Le Yucheng, "Zhongguo yu shijie guanxi de xinshidai" [A New Era in China's Relationship with the World], in Wang Jisi, ed., *Zhongguo guoji zhanlüe pinglun 2010* [China Strategy Review 2010] (Beijing: Shijie zhishi chubanshe, 2010), pp. 1–9, at p. 7.

101. Zhang Tuosheng, "Tiaozhan, jiyu yu duice" [Challenges, Opportunities and Responses], in Wang Jisi, ed., *Zhongguo guoji zhanlüe pinglun 2013* [China Strategy Review 2013] (Beijing: Shijie zhishi chubanshe, 2013), pp. 31–41, at p. 37.

102. Yuan Peng, "Jiegouxing maodun yu zhanlüexing jiaolü—Zhongmei guanxi de zhongda fengxian jiqi pojie zhidao" [Structural Contradictions and Strategic Anxieties: Major Risks in Sino-US Relations and Ways to Handle Them], in Wang, ed., *Zhongguo guoji zhanlüe pinglun 2011*, pp. 99–107, at p. 103.

103. Wang Jisi, "An Inquiry into China-U.S. Relations: An Opinion from China," in Lindsey W. Ford, ed., *Advice for the 45th U.S. President: Opinions from across the Pacific* (New York: Asia Society Policy Institute, 2016), pp. 24–27, at p. 26.

104. Feng Zhang interview with Chinese Ministry of Foreign Affairs officials, Beijing, December 2016. For similar views from the US side, see Michael Green's comments in Wu Xinbo and Michael Green, "Regional Security Roles and Challenges," in Nina Hachigian, ed., *Debating China: The U.S.-China Relationship in Ten Conversations* (Oxford: Oxford University Press, 2014), pp. 198–220, at p. 220.

105. Liu Feng, "China's Security Strategy towards East Asia," *Chinese Journal of International Politics* 9, no. 2 (2016), pp. 151–79. See also Oriana Skylar Mastro, "Why Chinese Assertiveness Is Here to Stay," *Washington Quarterly* 37, no. 4 (2015), pp. 151–70.

106. Shirk, "The Domestic Context," p. 401.

107. Wang Jisi, "Women jianxin, zhongmei guanxi zhonggui yao haoqilai caixing" [We Firmly Believe That Sino-US Relations Must Eventually Improve], *China Newsweek*, January 11, 2017, http://pit.ifeng.com/a/20170111/50556708_0.shtml (accessed March 10, 2017).

108. Yuan Peng, "Zhongmei zhanlüe huxin: Weilai daguo guanxi de fengxiangbiao" [Sino-US Strategic Trust: The Weathervane of Major Country Relations in the Future], in Wang Jisi, ed., *Zhongguo guoji zhanlüe pinglun 2008* [China Strategy Review 2008] (Beijing: Shijie zhishi chubanshe, 2008), pp. 47–55, at p. 51.

CHAPTER 5

1. Mike Pence, "Vice President Mike Pence's Remarks on the Administration's Policy towards China," Hudson Institute, October 4, 2018, https://www.hudson.org/events/1610-vice-president-mike-pence-s-remarks-on-the-administration-s-policy-towards-china102018 (accessed February 3, 2019).

2. Zhao Jiaming and Du Shangze, "Xi Jinping tong meiguo zongtong telangpu juxing huiwu" [Xi Jinping Meets with American President Trump], *People's Daily*,

December 3, 2018, http://cpc.people.com.cn/n1/2018/1203/c64094-30437336. html (accessed February 9, 2019).

3. Richard Ned Lebow, *Between Peace and War: The Nature of International Crisis* (Baltimore, MD: Johns Hopkins University Press, 1981), p. 83.

4. Bernard Brodie, "The Absolute Weapon: Atomic Power and World Order," *Bulletin of the Atomic Scientists* 3, no. 6 (1947), pp. 150–55; Carl von Clausewitz, *On War*, trans. M. Howard and P. Paret (Princeton, NJ: Princeton University Press, 1976), pp. 75–89.

5. William W. Kaufmann, "The Requirements of Deterrence" (Princeton, NJ: Center of International Studies, Princeton University, 1954); Henry Kissinger, *Nuclear Weapons and Foreign Policy* (New York: Harper, 1957); Bernard B. Brodie, "The Anatomy of Deterrence," *World Politics* 11, no. 2 (1959), pp. 173–91; Morton A. Kaplan, "The Calculus of Nuclear Deterrence," *World Politics* 11, no. 1 (1958), pp. 20–43.

6. Thomas C. Schelling, *The Strategy of Conflict* (Cambridge, MA: Harvard University Press, 1960); Thomas C. Schelling, *Arms and Influence* (New Haven, CT: Yale University Press, 1966).

7. Schelling, *Arms and Influence*.

8. Jeffrey Kimball, *Nixon's Vietnam War* (Lawrence: University Press of Kansas, 1998), pp. 76–86.

9. Schelling, *Arms and Influence*, pp. 6–16.

10. Ibid.

11. Ibid.; Clausewitz, *On War*, pp. 479–83.

12. Clausewitz, *On War*, pp. 585–94.

13. Robert S. McNamara, James G. Blight, and Robert K. Brigham, with Thomas J. Biersteker and Herbert Y. Schandler, *Argument without End: In Search of Answers to the Vietnam Tragedy* (New York: Public Affairs, 1999), p. 194.

14. Ibid., pp. 191, 341–45.

15. Ted Hopf, *Peripheral Visions: Deterrence Theory and American Foreign Policy in the Third World, 1965–1990* (Ann Arbor: University of Michigan Press, 1994); Richard Ned Lebow and Janice Gross Stein, *We All Lost the Cold War* (Princeton, NJ: Princeton University Press, 1994).

16. Lebow and Stein, *We All Lost the Cold War*, chs. 5, 11, 12–13; Raymond L. Garthoff, *Reflections on the Cuban Missile Crisis* (Washington, DC: Brookings Institution, 1989).

17. Lebow and Stein, *We All Lost the Cold War*, postscript; Archie Brown, *The Gorbachev Factor* (Oxford: Oxford University Press, 1996); Robert D. English, *Russia and the Idea of the West: Gorbachev, Intellectuals and the End of the Cold War* (New York: Columbia University Press, 2001); Richard K. Herrmann and Richard Ned Lebow, eds., *Ending the Cold War: Interpretations, Causation, and the Study of International Relations* (New York: Palgrave Macmillan, 2004).

18. For the most recent and comprehensive summations of this critique, see Lebow and Stein, *We All Lost the Cold War*; Richard Ned Lebow, *Avoiding War, Making Peace* (London: Palgrave Macmillan, 2017).

19. Michael A. Barnhart, *Japan Prepares for Total War: The Search for Economic Security, 1919–1941* (Ithaca, NY: Cornell University Press, 1987); Gerhard L. Weinberg, *A World at Arms: A Global History of World War II* (Cambridge, UK: Cambridge University Press 1994), pp. 260, 323, 329–30; Janice Gross Stein, "Calculation, Miscalculation, and Conventional Deterrence I: The View from Cairo," in Robert Jervis, Richard Ned Lebow, and Janice Gross Stein, *Psychology and Deterrence* (Baltimore, MD: Johns Hopkins University Press, 1985), pp. 34–59.

20. Richard Ned Lebow, *A Cultural Theory of International Relations* (Cambridge, UK: Cambridge University Press, 2008); Richard Ned Lebow, *Why Nations Fight: Past and Future Motives for War* (Cambridge, UK: Cambridge University Press, 2010).

21. Lebow, *Between Peace and War*, chs. 4–5.

22. Jervis, Lebow, and Stein, *Psychology and Deterrence*, chs. 4–5, 7.

23. Lebow, *Cultural Theory of International Relations*, chs. 7–9.

24. Lebow, *Why Nations Fight*, ch. 4.

25. Richard Ned Lebow and Benjamin Valentino, "Lost in Transition: A Critical Analysis of Power Transition Theory," *International Relations* 23, no. 3 (2009), pp. 389–410.

26. See Lebow, *Why Nations Fight*, ch. 4, for elaboration.

27. Barnhart, *Japan Prepares for Total War*; Weinberg, *A World at Arms*, pp. 260, 323, 329–30.

28. Alexander L. George and Richard Smoke, *Deterrence in American Foreign Policy: Theory and Practice* (New York: Columbia University Press, 1974), p. 5.

29. Melvin Gurtov and Byong-Moo Hwang, *China under Threat: The Politics of Strategy and Diplomacy* (Baltimore, MD: Johns Hopkins University Press, 1980), pp. 63–98; Jian Chen, *Mao's China and the Cold War: Beijing and the Taiwan Strait Crisis of 1958* (Chapel Hill: University of North Carolina Press, 2001), ch. 7.

30. Glenn H. Snyder and Paul Diesing, *Conflict Among Nations: Bargaining, Decision Making, and System Structure in International Crises* (Princeton, NJ: Princeton University Press, 1977), pp. 183–84; George and Smoke, *Deterrence in American Foreign Policy*, pp. 550–61.

31. Schelling, *Arms and Influence*, p. 55.

32. Lebow and Stein, *We All Lost the Cold War*, ch. 2.

33. Hopf, *Peripheral Visions*; Daryl G. Press, *Calculating Credibility: How Leaders Assess Military Threats* (Ithaca, NY: Cornell University Press, 2007); Lebow and Stein, *We All Lost the Cold War*, chs. 2, 10–11.

34. Morton H. Halperin and Tang Tsou, "The 1958 Quemoy Crisis," in Morton H. Halperin, ed., *Sino-Soviet Relations and Arms Control* (Cambridge, MA: MIT Press, 1967), pp. 265–304; George and Smoke, *Deterrence in American Foreign Policy*, pp. 386, 578.

35. Fredrik Logevall, *The Origins of the Vietnam War* (London: Routledge, 2001), ch. 4; Brian VanDeMark, *Into the Quagmire: Lyndon Johnson and the Escalation of the Vietnam War* (New York: Oxford University Press, 1995).

36. Schelling, *Arms and Influence*, p. 118.

37. Quoted in Patrick M. Cronin, Mira Rapp-Hooper, Harry Krejsa, Alex Sullivan, and Rush Doshi, "Beyond the *San Hai*: The Challenge of China's Blue-Water Navy" (Washington, DC: Center for a New American Security, 2017), p. 31.

38. Quoted in Aaron L. Friedberg, *A Contest for Supremacy: China, America, and the Struggle for Mastery in Asia* (New York: Norton, 2012), p. 103.

39. Nina Silove, "The Pivot before the Pivot: US Strategy to Preserve the Power Balance in Asia," *International Security* 40, no. 4 (2016), pp. 45–88, at p. 46.

40. Ibid.

41. Friedberg, *A Contest for Supremacy*, p. 252.

42. US Department of Defense, "The Asia-Pacific Maritime Security Strategy: Achieving US National Security Objectives in a Changing Environment" (Washington, DC US Department of Defense, 2015), p. 1.

43. Dan Blumenthal, "The US Response to China's Military Modernization," in Ashley J. Tellis and Travis Tanner, eds., *Strategic Asia 2012–13: China's Military Challenge* (Seattle, WA: National Bureau of Asian Research, 2012), pp. 309–40.

44. Friedberg, *A Contest for Supremacy*, p. 278; Andrew F. Krepinevich Jr., "How to Deter China: The Case for Archipelagic Defense," *Foreign Affairs* 94, no. 2 (2015), pp. 78–86.

45. Henry Kissinger, *World Order: Reflections on the Character of Nations and the Course of History* (London: Allen Lane, 2014), p. 233; Friedberg, *A Contest for Supremacy*, p. 252; Robert S. Ross, "US Grand Strategy, the Rise of China, and US National Security Strategy for East Asia," *Strategic Studies Quarterly* 7, no. 2 (2013), pp. 20–40.

46. US Department of Defense, "Sustaining US Global Leadership: Priorities for 21st Century Defense" (Washington, DC: US Department of Defense, 2012), p. 5.

47. Aaron L. Friedberg, *Beyond Air-Sea Battle: The Debate over US Military Strategy in Asia* (London: Routledge, 2014), pp. 12–13.

48. David M. Finkelstein, Philip C. Saunders, and Randall G. Schriver, "The Military and Defense Dimensions of United States Relations with China," in *Joint US-China Think Tank Project on the Future of US-China Relations: An American Perspective* (Washington, DC: Center for Strategic and International Studies, 2017), pp. 26–44, at p. 33.

49. Cronin et al., "Beyond the *San Hai*," p. 31.

50. Michael D. Swaine, with Wenyan Deng and Aube Rey Lescure, *Creating a Stable Asia: An Agenda for U.S.-China Balance of Power* (Washington, DC: Carnegie Endowment for International Peace, 2016), p. 65.

51. Michael Green, Kathleen Hicks, Zack Cooper, John Schaus, and Jake Douglas, *Countering Coercion in Maritime Asia: The Theory and Practice of Gray Zone Deterrence* (Washington, DC: Center for Strategic and International Studies, 2017).

52. Ibid., p. 15.

53. For recent research, see M. Taylor Fravel, *Active Defense: China's Military Strategy since 1949* (Princeton, NJ: Princeton University Press, 2019); M. Taylor Fravel, "Shifts in Warfare and Party Unity: Explaining China's Changes in Military Strategy," *International Security* 42, no. 3 (2017–18), pp. 37–83.

54. State Council Information Office of the People's Republic of China, *Zhongguo de junshi zhanlüe* [China's Military Strategy], May 2015, http://www.mod.gov.cn/auth/2015-05/26/content_4586723.htm (accessed October 1, 2017).

55. Ibid.

56. Christopher P. Twomey and Xu Hui, "Military Developments," in Nina Hachigian, ed., *Debating China: The US-China Relationship in Ten Conversations* (Oxford: Oxford University Press, 2014), pp. 152–75, at p. 164.

57. State Council Information Office, *Zhongguo de junshi zhanlüe.*

58. Author's interview with a scholar, Academy of Military Sciences, Beijing, June 2017.

59. Author's interview with a scholar, Renmin University, Beijing, June 2017.

60. Ibid. See also Xiao Tianliang, ed., *Zhanlüe Xue* [Strategic Studies] (Beijing: National Defense University Press, 2015), p. 29.

61. Robert S. Ross, "The 1995–96 Taiwan Strait Confrontation: Coercion, Credibility, and the Use of Force," *International Security* 25, no. 2 (2000), pp. 87–123.

62. Associated Press, "US Admiral: China 'Creating a Great Wall of Sand' in Sea," VOA, March 31, 2015, https://www.voanews.com/a/us-adminral-china-creating-a-great-wall-of-sand-in-sea/2700920.html (accessed October 1, 2017).

63. Feng Zhang, "Chinese Thinking on the South China Sea and the Future of Regional Security," *Political Science Quarterly* 132, no. 3 (2017), pp. 435–66, at p. 455.

64. Krepinevich, "How to Deter China."

65. Cronin et al., "Beyond the *San Hai*," p. 21.

66. Kurt M. Campbell and Ely Ratner, "The China Reckoning: How Beijing Defied American Expectations," *Foreign Affairs* 97, no. 2 (2018), pp. 60–70, at p. 67.

67. Thomas J. Christensen, "Fostering Stability or Creating a Monster? The Rise of China and US Policy toward East Asia," *International Security* 31, no. 1 (2006), pp. 81–126.

68. Swaine, *America's Challenge*, p. 359.

69. Richard K. Betts, "The Lost Logic of Deterrence: What the Strategy That Won the Cold War Can—and Can't—Do Now," *Foreign Affairs* 92, no. 2 (2013), pp. 87–99, at pp. 96–97.

70. Hugh White, "America Is Navigating Freely to Nowhere in the South China Sea," *War on the Rocks*, June 2, 2017, https://warontherocks.com/2017/06/america-is-navigating-freely-to-nowhere-in-the-south-china-sea/ (accessed October 21, 2017).

71. Peter A. Dutton and Isaac B. Kardon, "Forget the FONOPs—Just Fly, Sail and Operate Wherever International Law Allows," *Lawfare*, June 10, 2017, https://www.lawfareblog.com/forget-fonops-—-just-fly-sail-and-operate-wherever-international-law-allows (accessed October 21, 2017).

72. Steven Lee Myers, "American and Chinese Warships Narrowly Avoid High-Seas Collision," *New York Times*, October 2, 2018, https://www.nytimes.com/2018/10/02/world/asia/china-us-warships-south-china-sea.html (accessed February 10, 2019).

73. Swaine, *America's Challenge*, p. 164.

74. Avery Goldstein, "First Things First: The Pressing Danger of Crisis Instability in US-China Relations," *International Security* 37, no. 4 (2013), pp. 49–89, at p. 77.

75. Ibid.

76. Campbell Craig, Benjamin H. Friedman, Brendan Rittenhouse Green, Justin Logan, Stephen G. Brooks, G. John Ikenberry, and William C. Wohlforth, "Debating American Engagement: The Future of US Grand Strategy," *International Security* 38, no. 2 (2013), pp. 181–99, at pp. 185, 186.

77. Stephen G. Brooks, G. John Ikenberry, and William C. Wohlforth, "Don't Come Home, America: The Case against Retrenchment," *International Security* 37, no. 3 (2012–13), pp. 7–51.

78. Robert J. Art, "The United States and the Rise of China: Implications for the Long Haul," *Political Science Quarterly* 125, no. 3 (2010), pp. 359–391.

79. Eric Heginbotham, Michael Nixon, Forrest E. Morgan, et al., *The US-China Military Scorecard: Forces, Geography, and the Evolving Balance of Power, 1996–2017* (Santa Monica, CA: RAND, 2015), p. xxxi.

80. Thomas J. Christensen, "Posing Problems without Catching Up: China's Rise and Challenges for US Security Policy," *International Security* 25, no. 4 (2001), pp. 5–40, at p. 14; Ross, "US Grand Strategy," p. 26.

81. Xi Jinping, "Nuli goujian zhongmei xinxing daguo guanxi" [Striving to Build a New Model of Sino-US Major Country Relationship], July 9, 2014, Beijing, http://cpc.people.com.cn/n/2014/0710/c64094-25261696.html (accessed September 30, 2017).

82. Xi Jinping, "Remarks at the Seventieth United Nations General Assembly," New York, September 28, 2015, http://news.xinhuanet.com/world/2015-09/29/c_1116703645.htm (accessed October 8, 2017).

83. State Council Information Office, *Zhongguo de junshi zhanlüe*; State Council Information Office of the People's Republic of China, *China's National Defense in the New Era* (Beijing: Foreign Languages Press, 2019).

84. Feng Zhang, "The Rise of Chinese Exceptionalism in International Relations," *European Journal of International Relations* 19, no. 2 (2013), pp. 305–28.

85. Wang Dong, "Is China Trying to Push the US out of East Asia?," *China Quarterly of International Strategic Studies* 1, no. 1 (2015), pp. 59–84.

86. Michael D. Swaine, *America's Challenge: Engaging a Rising China in the Twenty-First Century* (Washington, DC: Carnegie Endowment for International Peace, 2011), p. 42.

87. Thomas Christensen and Patricia Kim, "Don't Abandon Ship," in "Did America Get China Wrong? The Engagement Debate," special issue, *Foreign Affairs* 97, no. 4 (2018), pp. 183–95, at p. 189.

88. Orville Schell and Susan L. Shirk, "Course Correction: Toward an Effective and Sustainable China Policy" (New York: Asia Society Center on U.S.-China Relations, February 2019), p. 8.

89. Joseph S. Nye Jr., "Time Will Tell," in "Did America Get China Wrong? The Engagement Debate," special issue, *Foreign Affairs* 97, no. 4 (2018), pp. 183–95, at p. 191.

90. Charles L. Glaser, "A US-China Grand Bargain? The Hard Choice between Military Competition and Accommodation," *International Security* 39, no. 4 (2015), pp. 49–90, at p. 49.

91. US Department of Defense, "Remarks by Secretary Mattis at Plenary Session of the 2018 Shangri-La Dialogue," June 2, 2018, https://dod.defense.gov/News/Transcripts/Transcript-View/Article/1538599/remarks-by-secretary-mattis-at-plenary-session-of-the-2018-shangri-la-dialogue/ (accessed 1 October 2018).

92. Michael D. Swaine, "The Real Challenge in the Pacific: A Response to 'How to Deter China,'" *Foreign Affairs* 94, no. 3 (2015), pp. 145–53, at pp. 150–51.

93. David C. Gompert, *Sea Power and American Interests in the Western Pacific* (Santa Monica, CA: RAND, 2013), p. xv. See also Eric Heginbotham and Jacob L. Heim, "Deterring without Dominance: Discouraging Chinese Adventurism under Austerity," *Washington Quarterly* 38, no. 1 (2015), pp. 185–99.

94. Gompert, *Sea Power and American Interests in the Western Pacific*, p. xv.

95. Swaine, *Creating a Stable Asia*, p. 68.

96. Ibid, p. 148.

97. Kurt M. Campbell and Jake Sullivan, "Competition without Catastrophe: How America Can Both Challenge and Coexist with China," *Foreign Affairs* 98, no. 5 (2019), pp. 96–110, at pp. 101–3.

CHAPTER 6

1. Robert Jervis, *Perception and Misperception in International Politics* (Princeton, NJ: Princeton University Press, 1976), pp. 58–113; Richard Ned Lebow, *Between Peace and War: The Nature of International Crisis* (Baltimore, MD: Johns Hopkins University Press, 1981), chs. 4–5.

2. Louis Kreisberg and Bruce W. Dayton, *Constructive Conflicts: From Escalation to Resolution* (Lanham, MD: Rowman & Littlefield, 2011), ch. 8.

3. Robert Axelrod, *The Evolution of Cooperation* (New York: Basic Books, 1984); Robert Axelrod, "An Evolutionary Approach to Norms," *American Political*

Science Review 80, no. 4 (1986), pp. 1095–111; Robert Axelrod and Robert O. Keohane, "Achieving Cooperation under Anarchy," *World Politics* 38, no. 1 (1985), pp. 226–54.

4. Richard Ned Lebow and Janice Gross Stein, *We All Lost the Cold War* (Princeton, NJ: Princeton University Press, 1994), ch. 5.

5. Robert E. Nisbett and Lee Ross, *Human Inference: Strategies and Shortcomings of Social Judgment* (Englewood Cliffs, NJ: Prentice-Hall, 1980); Lee Ross, "The Intuitive Psychologist and His Shortcomings: Distortions in the Attribution Process," in Leonard Berkowitz, ed., *Advances in Experimental Social Psychology*, vol. 10 (New York: Academic Press, 1977), pp. 174–220.

6. Archie Brown, *The Gorbachev Factor* (Oxford: Oxford University Press, 1996); Jacques Lévesque, *The Enigma of 1989: The USSR and the Liberation of Eastern Europe* (Berkeley: University of California Press, 1997); Robert D. English, *Russia and the Idea of the West: Gorbachev, Intellectuals and the End of the Cold War* (New York: Columbia University Press, 2000); Robert D. English, "Power, Ideas, and New Evidence on the Cold War's End: A Reply to Brooks and Wohlforth," *International Security* 26, no. 4 (2002), pp. 70–92.

7. Matthew Evangelista, *Unarmed Forces: The Transnational Movement to End the Cold War* (Ithaca, NY: Cornell University Press, 1999).

8. Thomas C. Schelling, *The Strategy of Conflict* (Cambridge, MA: Harvard University Press, 1960), pp. 131–37.

9. Robert Service, *The End of the Cold War 1985–1991* (London: Macmillan, 2016), pp. 143–48, 202, 329–38, 400–415.

10. Evelyn Goh, *Constructing the US Rapprochement with China, 1961–1974: From Red Menace to Tacit Ally* (Cambridge, UK: Cambridge University Press, 2005), pp. 153–83; Margaret MacMillan, *Nixon and Mao: The Week That Changed the World* (New York: Random House, 2006).

11. Richard Ned Lebow, "Miscalculation in the South Atlantic: The Origins of the Falkland War," *Journal of Strategic Studies* 6, no. 1 (1983), pp. 5–35.

12. Bradford Dismukes and James M. McConnell, eds., *Soviet Naval Diplomacy* (New York: Pergamon Press, 1979); Alexander L. George, "US-Soviet Global Rivalry: Norms of Competition," *Journal of Peace Research* 23, no. 3 (1986), pp. 247–62.

13. Janice Gross Stein, "Extended Deterrence in the Middle East: American Strategy Reconsidered." *World Politics* 39, no. 3 (1987), pp. 326–52.

14. George, "US-Soviet Global Rivalry."

15. Jens Steffek, "The Cosmopolitanism of David Mitrany: Equality, Devolution and Functional Democracy beyond the State," *International Relations* 29, no. 1 (2015), pp. 23–44.

16. Shibley Telhami, *Power and Leadership in International Bargaining: The Path to the Camp David Accords* (New York: Columbia University Press, 1992); Yaacov Bar-Siman-Tov, *Israel and the Peace Process 1977–1982: In Search of Legitimacy for Peace* (Albany: State University of New York Press, 1994).

17. Raymond L. Garthoff, *Détente and Confrontation: American-Soviet Relations from Nixon to Reagan* (Washington, DC: Brookings Institution Press, 1994), chs. 6–8; Goh, *Constructing the US Rapprochement with China*.

18. For the text of the document, see Kerry Dumbaugh, "Taiwan: Texts of the Taiwan Relations Act, the U.S.-China Communiques, and the 'Six Assurances'" (Washington, DC: Congressional Research Service, 1998).

19. John J. Tkacik, "Donald Trump Has Disrupted Years of Broken Taiwan Policy," *National Interest*, December 5, 2016, emphasis in original, http://nationalinterest.org/feature/donald-trump-has-disrupted-years-broken-taiwan-policy-18609 (accessed January 3, 2018). See also Nancy Bernkopf Tucker, "Strategic Ambiguity or Strategic Clarity?," in Nancy Bernkopf Tucker, ed., *Dangerous Strait: The U.S.-Taiwan-China Crisis* (New York: Columbia University Press, 2005), pp. 186–211, at p. 209; Richard C. Bush, *Untying the Knot: Making Peace in the Taiwan Strait* (Washington, DC: Brookings Institution Press, 2005), p. 90; Shelley Rigger, *Why Taiwan Matters: Small Island, Global Powerhouse* (Lanham, MD: Rowman & Littlefield, 2011), p. 180.

20. Bush, *Untying the Knot*, p. 254.

21. The text is in Dumbaugh, "Taiwan."

22. On the Taiwan Relations Act's defense comment as modest and nonbinding, see Bush, *Untying the Knot*, pp. 22, 110.

23. Dumbaugh, "Taiwan," p. 2.

24. Allen S. Whiting, "China's Use of Force, 1950–96, and Taiwan," *International Security* 26, no. 2 (2001), pp. 103–31.

25. Nancy Bernkopf Tucker and Bonnie Glaser, "Should the United States Abandon Taiwan?," *Washington Quarterly* 34, no. 4 (2011), pp. 23–37, at p. 23.

26. Zhu Feng, Huang Renwei, and Hu Bo, "Competing Perspectives between China and the United States in the Asia-Pacific and the Path for Mitigation," in Fu Ying and Wang Jisi, eds., *China-US Relations: Exploring a New Pathway to a Win-Win Partnership* (Beijing: National Institute of Global Strategy, Chinese Academy of Social Sciences, 2017), pp. 72–121, at p. 81.

27. Tucker and Glaser, "Should the United States Abandon Taiwan?," p. 23.

28. Ibid., p. 26.

29. Charles Glaser, "Will China's Rise Lead to War? Why Realism Does Not Mean Pessimism," *Foreign Affairs* 90, no. 2 (2011), pp. 80–91; Charles L. Glaser, "A U.S.-China Grand Bargain? The Hard Choice between Military Competition and Accommodation," *International Security* 39, no. 4 (2015), pp. 49–90; Bruce Gilley, "Not So Dire Straits: How the Finlandization of Taiwan Benefits U.S. Security," *Foreign Affairs* 89, no. 1 (2010), pp. 44–60; Bill Owens, "America Must Start Treating China as a Friend," *Financial Times*, November 18, 2009.

30. Joseph Bosco, "China's Crackdown on Hong Kong Slams the Door on Peaceful Unification with Taiwan," *The Hill*, August 6, 2018, https://thehill.com/opinion/international/400315-chinas-crackdown-on-hong-kong-slams-the-door-on-peaceful-unification-with-Taiwan (accessed February 10, 2019).

31. Bush, *Uncharted Strait*, p. 7.
32. Dumbaugh, "Taiwan," p. 17.
33. Bush, *Uncharted Strait*, p. 237; Tkacik, "Donald Trump Has Disrupted Years."
34. Bush, *Uncharted Strait*, p. 101.
35. Michael D. Swaine, "Trouble in Taiwan," *Foreign Affairs* 83, no. 2 (2004), pp. 39–49, at p. 44.
36. Michael D. Swaine, "The Real Challenge in the Pacific: A Response to 'How to Deter China,'" *Foreign Affairs* 94, no. 3 (2015), pp. 145–53, at p. 150.
37. On "strategic ambiguity," see Tucker, "Strategic Ambiguity or Strategic Clarity?"; Bush, *Untying the Knot*, pp. 255–56; Rigger, *Why Taiwan Matters*, p. 181.
38. Bush, *Uncharted Strait*, p. 18.
39. Swaine, "Trouble in Taiwan," p. 43.
40. On the process-centered nature of US policy, see Bush, *Uncharted Strait*, p. 214; Rigger, *Why Taiwan Matters*, p. 193.
41. Bush, *Untying the Knot*, p. 10; Bush, *Uncharted Strait*, p. 72.
42. Tucker and Glaser, "Should the United States Abandon Taiwan?," p. 30.
43. *Economist*, "China Is Getting Tougher on Taiwan," January 18, 2018, https://www.economist.com/china/2018/01/18/china-is-getting-tougher-on-taiwan (accessed October 1, 2018).
44. Chris Buckley and Chris Horton, "Xi Jinping Warns Taiwan That Unification Is the Goal and Force Is an Option," *New York Times*, January 1, 2019, https://www.nytimes.com/2019/01/01/world/asia/xi-jinping-taiwan-china.html?module=inline (accessed February 10, 2019).
45. See Bush, *Untying the Knot*.
46. Rigger, *Why Taiwan Matters*, p. 152.
47. *Economist*, "China Is Getting Tougher on Taiwan."
48. Bush, *Uncharted Strait*, p. 25.
49. Ibid., p. 33.
50. Ibid., p. 84; Rigger, *Why Taiwan Matters*, p. 6.
51. Ian Easton, *The Chinese Invasion Threat: Taiwan's Defense and American Strategy in Asia* (Arlington, VA: Project 2049 Institute, 2017), p. 241.
52. Michael D. Swaine, *America's Challenge: Engaging a Rising China in the Twenty-First Century* (Washington, DC: Carnegie Endowment for International Peace, 2011), p. 37.
53. Peter Baker and Rick Gladstone, "With Combative Style and Epithets, Trump Takes America First to the U.N.," *New York Times*, September 19, 2017, https://www.nytimes.com/2017/09/19/world/trump-un-north-korea-iran.html (accessed October 1, 2018).
54. The account of the North Korean nuclear crisis draws on the following works: Leon V. Sigal, *Disarming Strangers: Nuclear Diplomacy with North Korea* (Princeton, NJ: Princeton University Press, 1999); Charles L. Pritchard, *Failed Diplomacy: The Tragic Story of How North Korea Got the Bomb* (Washington, DC: Brookings Institution Press, 2007); Mike Chinoy, *Meltdown: The Inside Story of the North*

Korean Nuclear Crisis (New York: St. Martin's, 2009); Victor Cha, *The Impossible State: North Korea, Past and Future* (New York: Vintage, 2012).

55. Pritchard, *Failed Diplomacy*, p. 97.

56. Ibid., p. 131.

57. Chinoy, *Meltdown*, p. xviiii.

58. Cha, *The Impossible State*, p. 271; Stephan Haggard and Marcus Noland, *Hard Target Sanctions, Inducements, and the Case of North Korea* (Stanford, CA: Stanford University Press, 2017), p. 197.

59. Baker and Gladstone, "With Combative Style and Epithets."

60. Josh Mitchell and Eric Morath, "Trump Leaves Open Possibility of Military Action against North Korea," *Wall Street Journal*, April 30, 2017, https://www.wsj.com/articles/trump-leaves-open-possibility-of-military-action-against-north-korea-1493561694 (accessed September 11, 2019).

61. Mark Landler, "The Trump-Kim Summit Was Unprecedented, but the Statement Was Vague," *New York Times*, June 12, 2018, https://www.nytimes.com/2018/06/12/world/asia/north-korea-summit.html (accessed October 1, 2018).

62. Choe Sang-Hun, "U.S. Envoy Arrives in North Korea to Prepare for 2nd Trump-Kim Summit," *New York Times*, February 6, 2019, https://www.nytimes.com/2019/02/06/world/asia/trump-kim-north-korea-summit.html (accessed February 10, 2019).

63. Wang Yi, "Xiwang gefang lengjing panduan xingshi, zuochu mingzhi xuanze" [I Hope All Parties Judge the Situation Coolly and Make Wise Choices], March 18, 2017, http://www.fmprc.gov.cn/web/zyxw/t1446819.shtml (accessed January 9, 2018); see also Fu Ying, "The Korean Nuclear Issue: Past, Present, and Future: A Chinese Perspective" (Washington, DC: John L. Thornton China Center at Brookings, 2017), p. 23.

64. Cha, *The Impossible State*, pp. 342–45.

65. Yao Yunzhu, Zhang Tuosheng, Zhao Xiaozhuo, Lyu Jinghua, and Li Chen, "China-US Military Relations: Evolution, Prospect, and Recommendations," in Fu and Wang, eds., *China-US Relations*, pp. 122–80, at p. 136.

66. Author's interview with Chinese officials and scholars, Beijing, December 2017.

67. Simon Denyer, "China's Korea Policy 'in Tatters' as Both North and South Defy Sanctions," *Washington Post*, April 17, 2017, https://www.washington-post.com/world/chinas-korea-policy-in-tatters-as-both-north-and-south-defy-sanctions/2017/04/17/50da5e28-22f2-11e7-928e-3624539060e8_story.html (accessed September 11, 2019).

68. See, for example, Zhu Feng, "China's North Korean Liability: How Washington Can Get Beijing to Rein in Pyongyang," *Foreign Affairs*, July 11, 2017, https://www.foreignaffairs.com/articles/china/2017-07-11/chinas-north-korean-liability (accessed January 14, 2018).

69. Mark Fitzpatrick, *Asia's Latent Nuclear Powers: Japan, South Korea and Taiwan* (London: Routledge, 2016).

70. Alastair Gale and Carol E. Lee, "U.S. Agreed to North Korea Peace Talks before Latest Nuclear Test," *Wall Street Journal*, February 21, 2016, https://www.wsj.com/articles/u-s-agreed-to-north-korea-peace-talks-1456076019 (accessed September 11, 2019).

71. David E. Sanger, "Trump on North Korea: Tactic? 'Madman Theory'? Or Just Mixed Messages," *New York Times*, April 28, 2017, https://www.nytimes.com/2017/04/28/world/asia/trump-kim-jong-un-north-korean.html (accessed September 11, 2019).

72. Haggard and Noland, *Hard Target*, p. 7.

73. John Delury, "Kim Jong-un Has a Dream. The U.S. Should Help Him Realize It," *New York Times*, September 21, 2018, https://www.nytimes.com/2018/09/21/opinion/kim-jong-un-moon-economic-development-north-korea-denuclearization.html (accessed October 1, 2018).

74. Henry A. Kissinger, "How to Resolve the North Korea Crisis," *Wall Street Journal*, August 11, 2017; Stephen Krasner, "A Least Worst Option on North Korea," *Lawfare*, May 15, 2017, https://lawfareblog.com/least-worst-option-north-korea (accessed January 12, 2018).

75. On the danger of war as a result of the Trump administration's combative rhetoric, see Scott D. Sagan, "The Korean Missile Crisis: Why Deterrence is Still the Best Option," *Foreign Affairs* 96, no. 6 (2017), pp. 72–78.

76. As the crisis escalated in 2017, more analysts called on the United States to make such an offer. See, for example, Yasuhiro Izumikawa, "Acting on the North Korea Playbook: Japan's Responses to North Korea's Provocations," *Asia Policy* 23 (January 2017), pp. 90–96, at p. 96; Krasner, "A Least Worst Option on North Korea."

77. Cha, *The Impossible State*, p. 304.

78. Philip Bobbitt, "What to Do about North Korea," *Lawfare*, December 18, 2017, https://www.lawfareblog.com/what-do-about-north-korea (accessed January 12, 2018).

79. Victor Cha argues that an alliance potentially becomes a powerful instrument for a great power to control its smaller ally if the alliance relationship is asymmetrical and unequal. Victor D. Cha, *Powerplay: The Origins of the American Alliance System in Asia* (Princeton, NJ: Princeton University Press, 2016), p. 30.

80. Cha, *The Impossible State*, p. 338.

81. Choe Sang-hun, "North Korea Accuses China of 'Mean Behavior' after It Tightens Sanctions," *New York Times*, February 23, 2017, https://www.nytimes.com/2017/02/23/world/asia/north-korea-china.html (accessed September 11, 2019); Chris Buckley, "China's Leader Urges Restraint on North Korea in Call with Trump," *New York Times*, April 24, 2017, https://www.nytimes.com/2017/04/24/world/asia/north-korea-trump-china-xi-jinping.html (accessed September 11, 2019).

82. Keith Bradsher and Choe Sang-Hun, "With Kim's Visit, China Shows U.S. It Has Leverage on Trade," *New York Times*, January 8, 2019, https://www.nytimes.com/2019/01/08/business/china-north-korea-kim-trade.html (accessed February 10, 2019).

83. For a theoretical argument along this line, see Cha, *Powerplay*, p. 34.

84. Ronald O'Rourke, "Maritime Territorial and Exclusive Economic Zone (EEZ) Disputes Involving China: Issues for Congress" (Washington, DC: Congressional Research Service, 2017).

85. Xi Jinping, "Tuidong haiyang qiangguo jianshe" [Building a Maritime Great Power], July 30, 2013, http://jhsjk.people.cn/article/22402107 (accessed January 15, 2018).

86. Zhu, Huang, and Hu, "Competing Perspectives between China and the United States," p. 79.

87. Michael J. Green, Kathleen H. Hicks, Zack Cooper, John Schaus, and Jake Douglas, *Countering Coercion in Maritime Asia: The Theory and Practice of Gray Zone Deterrence* (Washington, DC: Center for Strategic and International Studies, 2017).

88. Xi, "Building a Maritime Great Power."

89. For the text of these treaties concerning the US defense commitments, see O'Rourke, "Maritime Territorial and Exclusive Economic Zone (EEZ) Disputes," pp. 61–62.

90. John Reed, "Pompeo Assures Philippines of Mutual Defence in South China Sea," *Financial Times*, March 1, 2019, https://www.ft.com/content/d7bee564-3bf8-11e9-b72b-2c7f526ca5d0 (accessed September 2, 2019).

91. Feng Zhang, "Assessing China's Response to the South China Sea Arbitration Ruling," *Australian Journal of International Affairs* 71, no. 4 (2017), pp. 440–59.

92. Ibid., p. 450.

93. Government of the People's Republic of China, "Zhonghua renmin gongheguo zhengfu guanyu zai nanhai de lingtu zhuquan he haiyang quanyi de shengming" [Statement of the Government of the People's Republic of China on China's Territorial Sovereignty and Maritime Rights and Interests in the South China Sea], July 12, 2016, http://www.mfa.gov.cn/nanhai/chn/snhwtlcwj/t1380021.htm (accessed January 16, 2018).

94. Zhang, "Assessing China's Response," p. 450.

95. Feng Zhang, "Chinese Thinking on the South China Sea and the Future of Regional Security," *Political Science Quarterly* 132, no. 3 (2017), pp. 435–66.

96. On the U-shaped line, see Zhiguo Gao and Bing Bing Jia, "The Nine-Dash Line in the South China Sea: History, Status, and Implications," *American Journal of International Law* 107, no. 1 (2013), pp. 98–123; Chris P. C. Chung, "Drawing the U-Shaped Line: China's Claim in the South China Sea, 1946–1974," *Modern China* 42, no. 1 (2016), pp. 38–72.

97. Wu Xinbo and Michael Green, "Regional Security Roles and Challenges," in Nina Hachigian, ed., *Debating China: The US-China Relationship in Ten Conversations* (Oxford: Oxford University Press, 2014), pp. 198–220, at p. 204.

98. Richard McGregor, *Asia's Reckoning: The Struggle for Global Dominance* (London: Allen Lane, 2017), pp. 67–68.

99. Ibid.

100. US Department of Defense, "The Asia-Pacific Maritime Security Strategy: Achieving US National Security Objectives in a Changing Environment" (Washington, DC: US Department of Defense, 2015), pp. 1–2.

101. Ibid.

102. O'Rourke, "Maritime Territorial and Exclusive Economic Zone (EEZ) Disputes," p. 9.

103. George C. Herring, *From Colony to Superpower: U.S. Foreign Relations since 1776* (Oxford: Oxford University Press, 2008), pp. 99–100.

104. O'Rourke, "Maritime Territorial and Exclusive Economic Zone (EEZ) Disputes," p. 5.

105. Bill Hayton, *The South China Sea: The Struggle for Power in Asia* (New Haven, CT: Yale University Press, 2014), p. 213.

106. Zhu, Huang, and Hu, "Competing Perspectives between China and the United States," p. 83.

107. Hayton, *The South China Sea*, p. 212.

108. Lyle J. Goldstein, *Meeting China Halfway: How to Defuse the Emerging US-China Rivalry* (Washington, DC: Georgetown University Press, 2015), p. 287.

109. US Department of Defense, "Annual Report to Congress: Military and Security Developments Involving the People's Republic of China 2016" (Washington, DC: Office of the Secretary of Defense, 2017), p. 96.

110. Swaine, "The Real Challenge in the Pacific," p. 150.

111. Robert D. Kaplan, *Asia's Cauldron: The South China Sea and the End of a Stable Pacific* (New York: Random House, 2015); Patrick M. Cronin, "Power and Order in the South China Sea: A Strategic Framework for U.S. Policy" (Washington, DC: Center for a New American Security, 2016).

112. See, for example, Robert J. Art, "The United States and the Rise of China: Implications for the Long Haul," *Political Science Quarterly* 125, no. 3 (2010), pp. 359–91, at p. 386.

113. Michael D. Swaine, with Wenyan Deng and Aube Rey Lescure, *Creating a Stable Asia: An Agenda for U.S.-China Balance of Power* (Washington, DC: Carnegie Endowment for International Peace, 2016), p. 47; James Dobbins, Andrew Scobell, Edmund J. Burke, David C. Gompert, Derek Grossman, Eric Heginbotham, and Howard J. Shatz, "Conflict with China Revisited: Prospects, Consequences, and Strategies for Deterrence" (Santa Monica, CA: RAND, 2017).

114. Stephen Biddle and Ivan Oelrich, "Future Warfare in the Western Pacific: Chinese Antiaccess/Area Denial, U.S. AirSea Battle, and Command of the Commons in East Asia," *International Security* 41, no. 1 (2016), pp. 7–48.

115. Easton, *The Chinese Invasion Threat*; Denny Roy, "Prospects for Taiwan Maintaining Its Autonomy under Chinese Pressure," *Asian Survey* 57, no. 6 (2017), pp. 1135–58.

116. Swaine, Deng, and Lescure, *Creating a Stable Asia*, p. 61.

117. Lebow and Stein, *We All Lost the Cold War*; Ted Hopf, *Peripheral Visions: Deterrence Theory and American Foreign Policy in the Third World, 1965–1990* (Ann Arbor: University of Michigan Press, 1994).

118. Ely Ratner, "Course Correction: How to Stop China's Maritime Advance," *Foreign Affairs* 96, no. 4 (2017), pp. 64–72; James R. Holmes and Toshi Yoshihara, "Deterring China in the 'Gray Zone': Lessons of the South China Sea for U.S. Alliances," *Orbis* 61, no. 3 (2017), pp. 322–39; Green et al., *Countering Coercion in Maritime Asia*.

119. David C. Gompert, *Sea Power and American Interests in the Western Pacific* (Santa Monica, CA: RAND, 2013), p. xv.

120. Swaine, Deng, and Lescure, *Creating a Stable Asia*, p. 73.

121. US Department of Defense, "Annual Report to Congress: Military and Security Developments Involving the People's Republic of China 2017" (Washington, DC: Office of the Secretary of Defense, 2017), p. 12.

122. O'Rourke, "Maritime Territorial and Exclusive Economic Zone (EEZ) Disputes," p. 3.

123. Eric Heginbotham, Michael Nixon, Forrest E. Morgan, et al., *The US-China Military Scorecard: Forces, Geography, and the Evolving Balance of Power, 1996–2017* (Santa Monica, CA: RAND, 2015), p. 89.

124. O'Rourke, "Maritime Territorial and Exclusive Economic Zone (EEZ) Disputes," p. 6.

125. Gompert, *Sea Power and American Interests*, p. xvii.

126. See Chapter 4.

127. David M. Finkelstein, Phillip C. Saunders, and Randall G. Schriver, "The Military and Defense Dimensions of United States Relations with China," in "Joint US-China Think Tank Project on the Future of US-China Relations: An American Perspective" (Washington, DC: Center for Strategic and International Studies, 2017), pp. 26–44, at p. 41.

128. Gompert, *Sea Power and American Interests*, p. xiii.

129. G. John Ikenberry, *Liberal Leviathan: The Origins, Crisis, and Transformation of the American World Order* (Princeton, NJ: Princeton University Press, 2011), pp. 208–9.

130. Victor D. Cha, "Complex Patchworks: US Alliances as Part of Asia's Regional Architecture," *Asia Policy* 11 (January 2011), pp. 27–50, at p. 41.

131. Zhou Fangyin, "The U.S. Alliance System in Asia: A Chinese Perspective," *Asian Politics & Policy* 8, no. 1 (2016), pp. 207–18, at p. 208.

132. Yunzhu Yao, "Sino-American Military Relations: From Quasi-Allies to Potential Adversaries?," *China International Strategy Review* 1, no. 1 (2019), pp. 85–98, at p. 97.

133. Author interview, Beijing, June 2017.

134. William T. Tow, "The Trilateral Strategic Dialogue, Minilateralism, and Asia-Pacific Order Building," in Yuki Tatsumi, ed., *US-Japan-Australia Security Cooperation: Prospects and Challenges* (Washington, DC: Stimson Center, 2015), pp. 23–36.

135. Cha, *Powerplay*, p. 216.

136. Goldstein, *Meeting China Halfway*, pp. 226–27.

137. Cha, *Powerplay*, p. 204.

138. Art, "The United States and the Rise of China," p. 385.

139. Michael Beckley, "The Emerging Military Balance in East Asia: How China's Neighbors Can Check Chinese Naval Expansion," *International Security* 42, no. 2 (2017), pp. 78–119.

140. Xi Jinping, "Xi Jinping zai di qishijie lianheguo dahui yibanxing bianlun shi de jianghua" [Remarks at the Seventieth United Nations General Assembly], New York, September 28, 2015, http://news.xinhuanet.com/world/2015-09/29/c_1116703645.htm (accessed January 20, 2018).

141. See Chapter 4.

142. Cha, *Powerplay*, p. 204.

143. Amitav Acharya, *Constructing a Security Community in Southeast Asia: ASEAN and the Problem of Regional Order,* 2nd edition (London: Routledge, 2009).

144. Kishore Mahbubani and Jeffery Sng, *The ASEAN Miracle: A Catalyst for Peace* (Singapore: NUS Press, 2017), p. 101.

145. Simon Reich and Richard Ned Lebow, *Good-Bye Hegemony! Power and Influence in the Global System* (Princeton, NJ: Princeton University Press, 2014); Richard Ned Lebow and Robert Kelly, "Thucydides and Hegemony: Athens and the United States," *Review of International Studies* 27, no. 4 (2001), pp. 593–609.

146. Richard Ned Lebow, *A Cultural Theory of International Relations* (Cambridge, UK: Cambridge University Press, 2008), pp. 64, 84.

147. Yan Xuetong, *Ancient Chinese Thought, Modern Chinese Power*, ed. Daniel A. Bell and Sun Zhe, trans. Edmund Ryden (Princeton, NJ: Princeton University Press, 2011).

148. Feng Zhang, *Chinese Hegemony: Grand Strategy and International Institutions in East Asian History* (Stanford, CA: Stanford University Press, 2015).

149. Yan Xuetong, "The Age of Uneasy Peace: Chinese Power in a Divided World," *Foreign Affairs* 98, no. 1 (2019), pp. 40–46, at p. 44.

150. Xi Jinping, "Wei goujian zhongmei xinxing daguo guanxi er buxie nuli" [Persistently Working toward a New Model of Sino-US Major Country Relationship], Beijing, June 6, 2016, http://jhsjk.people.cn/article/28416143 (accessed January 22, 2018).

CHAPTER 7

1. Andrew F. Cooper, Jorge Heine, and Ramesh Thakur, "Introduction: The Challenges of 21st-Century Diplomacy," in Cooper, Heine, and Thakur, eds., *The Oxford Handbook of Modern Diplomacy* (Oxford: Oxford University Press, 2013), pp. 1–34, at p. 2.

2. Henry Kissinger, *Diplomacy* (New York: Simon & Schuster, 1994); G. R. Berridge, *Diplomacy: Theory and Practice*, 5th edition (London: Palgrave Macmillan, 2015); Jean-Robert Leguey-Feilleux, *The Dynamics of Diplomacy* (Boulder, CO: Lynne Rienner, 2009); Cooper, Heine, and Thakur, *The Oxford Handbook of Modern Diplomacy*.

3. Paul Sharp, *Diplomatic Theory of International Relations* (Cambridge, UK: Cambridge University Press, 2009); Ole Jacob Sending, Vincent Pouliot, and Iver B. Neumann, eds., *Diplomacy and the Making of World Politics* (Cambridge, UK: Cambridge University Press, 2015); Silviya Lechner and Mervyn Frost, *Practice Theory and International Relations* (Cambridge, UK: Cambridge University Press, 2018).

4. William D. Davidson and Joseph V. Montville, "Foreign Policy According to Freud," *Foreign Policy* 45 (Winter 1981–82), pp. 145–57; Louise Diamond and John McDonald, *Multi-Track Diplomacy: A Systems Approach to Peace* (West Hartford, CT: Kumarian Press, 2006); Joseph V. Montville, "The Arrow and the Olive Branch: A Case for Track Two Diplomacy," in Vamik D. Volkan, Joseph V. Montville, and Demetrios A. Julius, eds., *The Psychodynamics of International Relationships, Volume 2: Unofficial Diplomacy at Work* (Lanham, MD: Lexington Books, 2003), pp. 161–75; Hussein Agha, Shai Feldman, Ahmad Khalidi, and Zeev Schiff, *Track-II Diplomacy: Lessons from the Middle East* (Cambridge, MA: MIT Press, 2003).

5. Matthew Evangelista, *Unarmed Forces: The Transnational Movement to End the Cold War* (Ithaca, NY: Cornell University Press, 1999), pp. 144–46.

6. Richard K. Herrmann, "Learning from the End of the Cold War," in Richard K. Herrmann and Richard Ned Lebow, eds., *Ending the Cold War: Interpretations, Causation, and the Study of International Relations* (New York: Palgrave Macmillan, 2004), pp. 219–38.

7. The "two" were the two Germanies, and the "four" the occupying powers at the end of World War II (The USSR, US, United Kingdom, and France).

8. A particularly egregious example is Jack F. Matlock, *Autopsy on an Empire: The American Ambassador's Account of the Collapse of the Soviet Union* (New York: Random House, 1995).

9. Baruch Fischhoff, "Hindsight Is Not Equal to Foresight: The Effect of Outcome Knowledge on Judgment under Uncertainty," *Journal of Experimental Psychology: Human Perception and Performance* 1, no. 3 (1975), pp. 288–99; S. A. Hawkins and R. Hastie, "Hindsight: Biased Judgments of Past Events after the Outcomes Are Known," *Psychological Bulletin* 107, no. 3 (1990), pp. 311–27.

10. William R. Thompson, ed., *Great Power Rivalries* (Columbia: University of South Carolina Press, 1999); Jack S. Levy and William R. Thompson, *Causes of War* (New York: Wiley-Blackwell, 2010); Sumit Ganguly and William R. Thompson, eds., *Asian Rivalries: Conflict, Escalation, and Limitations on Two-Level Games* (Stanford, CA: Stanford University Press, 2011).

11. I. William Zartman and Maureen R. Berman, *The Practical Negotiator* (New Haven, CT: Yale University Press, 1982); I. William Zartman, "The Strategy of Preventive Diplomacy in Third World Conflicts," in Alexander L. George, ed., *Managing US-Soviet Rivalry: Problems of Crisis Prevention* (Boulder, CO: Westview Press, 1983), pp. 341–63; Saadia Touval and I. William Zartman, eds., *International Mediation in Theory and Practice* (Boulder, CO: Westview Press, 1985); I. William Zartman, *Ripe for Resolution: Conflict and Intervention in Africa*, updated edition (New York: Oxford University Press, 1989); I. William Zartman, "Ripeness," in Guy Burgess and Heidi Burgess, eds., *Beyond Intractability* (Boulder, CO: Conflict Information Consortium, University of Colorado, June 2013).

12. *The Pentagon Papers: The Defense Department History of United States Decisionmaking on Vietnam*, Volume 3, Senator Gravel edition (Boston: Beacon Press, 1971), pp. 687–91; Townsend Hoopes, *The Limits of Intervention: An Inside Account of How the Johnson Policy of Escalation Was Reversed* (New York: David McKay, 1969), p. 30.

13. Richard Ned Lebow, *Forbidden Fruit: Counterfactuals and International Relations* (Princeton, NJ: Princeton University Press, 2010), chs. 1, 3–4.

14. Ibid., ch. 3 for documentation.

15. Richard Ned Lebow, "Contingency, Catalysts, and International System Change," *Political Science Quarterly* 115, no. 4 (2000–2001), pp. 591–616; William R. Thompson, "A Streetcar Named Sarajevo: Catalysts, Multiple Causation Chains, and Rivalry Structures," *International Studies Quarterly* 47, no. 3 (2003), pp. 453–74; Richard Ned Lebow, "A Data Set Named Desire: A Reply to William P. Thompson," *International Studies Quarterly* 47, no. 3 (2003), pp. 475–78.

16. Richard Ned Lebow, *Avoiding War, Making Peace* (London: Palgrave Macmillan, 2017), ch. 6.

17. On the latter accommodation, see George W. Breslauer and Richard Ned Lebow, "Leadership and the End of the Cold War: Did It Have to End This Way?," in Lebow, *Forbidden Fruit*, pp. 103–36.

18. On the Anglo-French accommodation, see Richard Ned Lebow, "The Search for Accommodation: Gorbachev in Comparative Perspective," in Richard Ned Lebow and Thomas Risse-Kappen, eds., *International Relations Theory and the End of the Cold War* (New York: Columbia University Press, 1995), pp. 167–86.

19. Shibley Telhami, *Power and Leadership in International Bargaining: The Path to the Camp David Accords* (New York: Columbia University Press, 1990); Yaacov Bar-Simon-Tov, *Israel and the Peace Process, 1977–1982: In Search of Legitimacy for Peace* (Albany: State University of New York Press, 1994).

20. The following also stress the importance of agency, and of leaders in particular: George W. Breslauer and Richard Ned Lebow, "Leadership and the End of the Cold War: A Counterfactual Thought Experiment," in Herrmann and Lebow, eds., *Ending the Cold War*, 161–88. Archie Brown, *The Gorbachev Factor* (Oxford: Oxford University Press, 1996); Raymond L. Garthoff, *The Great*

Transition: American-Soviet Relations and the End of the Cold War (Washington, DC: Brookings Institution Press, 1994); Robert Service, *The End of the Cold War, 1985–1991* (New York: Public Affairs, 2015); Hal Brands, *Making the Unipolar Moment: US Foreign Policy and the Rise of the Post–Cold War Order* (Ithaca, NY: Cornell University Press, 2016).

21. For the most intelligent statement of structural argument and critique, see William C. Wohlforth, ed., *Cold War Endgame: Oral History, Analysis, Debates* (University Park: Pennsylvania State University Press, 2003).

22. Martin Klimke, Reinhold Kreis, and Christian F. Ostermann, eds., *Trust, but Verify: The Politics of Uncertainty and the Transformation of the Cold War Order, 1969–1991* (Stanford, CA: Stanford University Press, 2016); Brown, *The Gorbachev Factor*; Service, *The End of the Cold War*, p. 250.

23. Service, *The End of the Cold War*, pp. 150–61, 185–86, 245.

24. John W. Garver, *China's Decision for Rapprochement with the United States, 1968–1971* (Boulder, CO: Westview Press, 1982), ch. 2; Robert S. Ross, *China, the United States, and the Soviet Union: Tripolarity and Policy Making in the Cold War* (Armonk, NY: M. E. Sharpe, 1993), pp. 1–2; Evelyn Goh, *Constructing the US Rapprochement with China, 1961–1974: From "Red Menace" to "Tacit Ally"* (Cambridge, UK: Cambridge University Press, 2005), pp. 2–4, 171–75, 222–25.

25. Gregory Henderson, Richard Ned Lebow, and John G. Stoessinger, eds., *Divided Nations in a Divided World* (New York: David A. Mackay, 1974), ch. 11.

26. Feargal Cochrane, *Northern Ireland: The Reluctant Peace* (New Haven, CT: Yale University Press, 2013), pp. 254–81.

27. Robert S. Ross, *Negotiating Cooperation: The United States and China, 1969–1989* (Stanford, CA: Stanford University Press, 1995), pp. 1–2; Goh, *Constructing the US Rapprochement with China*, pp. 4–5, 133–36, 143–47, 153–81, 192–204.

28. Goh, *Constructing the US Rapprochement with China*, pp. 121–22.

29. Ibid., pp. 4–5, 101–23.

30. Breslauer and Lebow, "Leadership and the End of the Cold War"; Service, *The End of the Cold War*, pp. 364–66 on Bush's caution.

31. Telhami, *Power and Leadership in International Bargaining*; Bar-Simon-Tov, *Israel and the Peace Process*.

32. Leonard A. Kusnitz, *Public Opinion and Foreign Policy: America's China Policy, 1949–1979* (Westport, CT: Greenwood Press, 1984), p. 138.

33. Goh, *Constructing the US Rapprochement with China*, pp. 6, 206–18.

34. Kusnitz, *Public Opinion and Foreign Policy*, pp. 138–39.

35. Brown, *The Gorbachev Factor*; Garthoff, *The Great Transition*, chs. 6–8; Service, *The End of the Cold War*, pp. 482–95.

36. Richard Ned Lebow and Janice Gross Stein, *We All Lost the Cold War* (Princeton, NJ: Princeton University Press, 1994), chs. 3–5; Raymond L. Garthoff, *Détente and Confrontation: American-Soviet Relations from Nixon to Reagan*, revised edition (Washington, DC: Brookings Institution Press, 1994), chs. 2–4.

37. Lebow and Stein, *We All Lost the Cold War*, pp. 55–58; William Taubman, *Khrushchev: The Man and His Era* (New York: Norton, 2003), pp. 442–79.

38. Garthoff, *Détente and Confrontation*, pp. 1125–46.

39. Cochrane, *Northern Ireland*, pp. 31–66; Richard English, *Armed Struggle: The History of the IRA* (Oxford: Oxford University Press, 2003), pp. 148–227.

40. On Gorbachev versus other possible leaders, see Richard Ned Lebow and Janice Gross Stein, "Understanding the End of the Cold War as a Non-Linear Confluence," in Herrmann and Lebow, eds., *Ending the Cold War*, pp. 189–218.

41. Ofira Seliktar, *Doomed to Failure? The Politics and Intelligence of the Oslo Peace Process* (Boulder, CO: Praeger, 2009); Robert L. Rothstein, Moshe Ma'oz, and Khalil Shikaki, eds., *The Israeli-Palestinian Peace Process: Oslo and the Lessons of Failure. Perspectives, Predicaments, and Prospects* (Brighton, UK: Sussex Academic Press, 2002).

42. "Russians Name Brezhnev Best 20th-Century Leader, Gorbachev Worst," *RT*, May 22, 2013, https://www.rt.com/politics/brezhnev-stalin-gorbachev-soviet-638/ (accessed November 15, 2016); "What Do Russian People Think of Gorbachev?," *Quora*, November 7, 2015, https://www.quora.com/What-do-Russian-people-think-of-Gorbachev (accessed November 15, 2016).

43. Chen Jian, *Mao's China and the Cold War* (Chapel Hill: University of North Carolina Press, 2001), ch. 9.

44. Niu Jun, "Yu meiguo hezuo shi zhanlüe, bushi celüe he quanyi zhiji" [Cooperation with America Is Strategy, Not a Tactic or Temporary Expedient], *Meiguo Yanjiu* [Journal of American Studies], no. 6 (2015), pp. 114–18, at p. 116.

45. Zhang Tuosheng, "The Sino-American Aircraft Collision: Lessons for Crisis Management," in Michael D. Swaine and Zhang Tuosheng, with Danielle F. S. Cohen, eds., *Managing Sino-American Crises: Case Studies and Analysis* (Washington, DC: Carnegie Endowment for International Peace, 2006), pp. 391–421, at p. 392.

46. Dennis C. Blair and David B. Bonfili, "The April 2001 EP-3 Incident: The U.S. Point of View," in Swaine, Zhang, and Cohen, eds., *Managing Sino-American Crises*, pp. 377–90, at p. 381.

47. Zhang, "The Sino-American Aircraft Collision," p. 400; Blair and Bonfili, "The April 2001 EP-3 Incident," p. 383.

48. Zhang, "The Sino-American Aircraft Collision," p. 401.

49. Blair and Bonfili, "The April 2001 EP-3 Incident," p. 387.

50. Tang Jiaxuan, *Jin Yu Xu Feng* [Strong Rain and Warm Wind] (Beijing: Shijie zhishi chubanshe, 2009), pp. 289–95.

51. Ibid., p. 297.

52. Dai Bingguo, *Zhanlüe duihua* [Strategic Dialogues] (Beijing: Renmin chubanshe, 2016), pp. 115–18.

53. Robert B. Zoellick, "Whither China: From Membership to Responsibility?," remarks to National Committee on US-China Relations, New York, September 21, 2005, https://2001-2009.state.gov/s/d/former/zoellick/rem/53682.htm (accessed March 12, 2018).

54. Dai, *Zhanlüe duihua*, pp. 125–31.

55. For Powell's sentiments, see Kai He, "Explaining United States–China Relations: Neoclassical Realism and the Nexus of Threat-Interest Perceptions," *Pacific Review* 30, no. 2 (2017), pp. 133–51, at p. 145.

56. Dai, *Zhanlüe duihua*, pp. 149–77.

57. Ibid., p. 113.

58. An important indicator is Robert D. Blackwill and Ashely J. Tellis, "Revising U.S. Grand Strategy toward China," Council Special Report No. 72 (New York: Council on Foreign Relations, 2015).

59. President of the United States, "National Security Strategy of the United States of America" (Washington, DC: White House, 2017).

60. Author interview, Beijing, June 2016.

61. Ibid.

62. On China's fractured foreign policy decision-making system, see Linda Jakobson and Dean Knox, "New Foreign Policy Actors in China," SIPRI Policy Paper No. 26 (Stockholm: Stockholm International Peace Research Institute, 2010).

63. Feng Zhang, "Assessing China's South China Sea Policy, 2009–2015," *East Asian Policy* 8, no. 3 (2016), pp. 100–109, at p. 104.

64. See Chapter 3 for discussion.

65. Author interview, Beijing, March 2016.

66. Thomas J. Christensen, *The China Challenge: Shaping the Choices of a Rising Power* (New York: Norton, 2015), pp. 250–51.

67. Susan Shirk, "Trump and China: Getting to Yes with Beijing," *Foreign Affairs* 96, no. 2 (2017), pp. 20–27, at p. 22.

68. Michael D. Swaine, *America's Challenge: Engaging a Rising China in the Twenty-First Century* (Washington, DC: Carnegie Endowment for International Peace, 2011), p. 310.

69. On the causal significance of the frame of reference in international relations, see Richard Ned Lebow, *Constructing Cause in International Relations* (Cambridge, UK: Cambridge University Press, 2014).

70. Feng Zhang, "Challenge Accepted: China's Response to the US Rebalance to the Asia-Pacific," *Security Challenges* 12, no. 3 (2016), pp. 45–60.

71. Walter Russell Mead, "Left and Right Agree: Get Tough on China," *Wall Street Journal*, January 8, 2018.

72. Xi Jinping, "Report to the 19th Congress of the Chinese Communist Party," October 18, 2017, Beijing, http://jhsjk.people.cn/article/29613458 (accessed March 13, 2018).

73. Mead, "Left and Right Agree."

74. President of the United States, "National Security Strategy," pp. 25, 45.

75. US Department of Defense, "Summary of the 2018 National Defense Strategy of the United States of America: Sharpening the American Military's Competitive Edge" (Washington, DC: Office of the Secretary of Defense, 2018), p. 2.

76. President of the United States, "National Security Strategy," p. 26.

77. Ibid.

78. Ibid., p. 3.

79. Ibid., p. 25.

80. Ibid., p. 37.

81. US Department of Defense, "Summary," p. 2.

82. Hudson Institute, "Vice President Mike Pence's Remarks on the Administration's Policy towards China," October 4, 2018, https://www.hudson.org/events/1610-vice-president-mike-pence-s-remarks-on-the-administration-s-policy-towards-china102018 (accessed 3 February 2019).

83. Da Wei, "A Restructuring International Order and the Paradigm Shift in China-U.S. Relations," *China International Strategy Review* 1, no. 1 (2019), pp. 21–32, at p. 31.

84. Mead, "Left and Right Agree."

85. Aaron L. Friedberg, "Competing with China," *Survival* 60, no. 3 (2018), pp. 7–64, p. 27.

86. Harry Harding, "The U.S. and China from Partners to Competitors," paper presented to the workshop marking the fortieth anniversary of the normalization of US-China diplomatic relations, January 2019, pp. 1–17; Chas W. Freeman Jr., "Sino-American Interactions, Past and Future," paper presented to the workshop marking the fortieth anniversary of the normalization of US-China diplomatic relations, January 2019, pp. 1–11; David Lampton, "U.S.-China Relations: Revisionist History Needs Revision," paper presented to the workshop marking the fortieth anniversary of the normalization of US-China diplomatic relations, January 2019, pp. 1–24; Michael D. Swaine, "A Relationship under Extreme Duress," paper presented to the workshop marking the fortieth anniversary of the normalization of US-China diplomatic relations, January 2019, pp. 1–28.

87. Orville Schell and Susan L. Shirk, "Course Correction: Toward an Effective and Sustainable China Policy" (New York: Asia Society Center on U.S.-China Relations, February 2019).

88. M. Taylor Fravel, J. Stapleton Roy, Michael D. Swaine, Susan A. Thornton, and Ezra Vogel, "China Is Not an Enemy," *Washington Post*, July 3, 2019, https://www.washingtonpost.com/opinions/making-china-a-us-enemy-is-counterproductive/2019/07/02/647d49d0-9bfa-11e9-b27f-ed2942f73d70_story.html?noredirect=on (accessed September 3, 2019).

89. Jimmy Carter, "How to Repair the U.S.-China Relationship—and Prevent a Modern Cold War," *Washington Post*, December 31, 2018, https://www.washingtonpost.com/opinions/jimmy-carter-how-to-repair-the-us-china-relationship--and-prevent-a-modern-cold-war/2018/12/31/cc1d6b94-0927-11e9-85b6-41c0feoc5b8f_story.html?noredirect=on (accessed February 11, 2019).

90. Robert E. Rubin, "Why the World Needs America and China to Get Along," *New York Times*, January 2, 2019, https://www.nytimes.com/2019/01/02/opinion/america-china-climate-change-nuclear-weapons.html (accessed February 11, 2019).

91. Yan Xuetong, "Trump Can't Start a Cold War with China, Even If He Wants to," *Washington Post*, February 6, 2018.

92. Zhao Jiaming and Du Shangze, "Xi Jinping tong meiguo zongtong telangpu juxing huiwu" [Xi Jinping Meets with American President Trump], *People's Daily*, December 3, 2018, http://cpc.people.com.cn/n1/2018/1203/c64094-30437336.html (accessed February 9, 2019).

93. Shi Yinhong, for example, has been cautioning against strategic overstretch since 2015. Shi Yinhong, "Guanyu zhongguo duiwai zhanlüe youhua he zhanlüe shenshen wenti de sikao" [Reflections on China's Strategy in Foreign Relations: Issues of Improvement and Prudence], *Taipingyang xuebao* [Pacific Journal] 23, no. 6 (2015), pp. 1–5. See also Xiaoyu Pu and Chengli Wang, "Rethinking China's Rise: Chinese Scholars Debate Strategic Overstretch," *International Affairs* 94, no. 5 (2018), pp. 1019–35.

94. For a discussion on Chinese strategic traditions from a cultural perspective, see Feng Zhang, "Confucian Foreign Policy Traditions in Chinese History," *Chinese Journal of International Politics* 8, no. 2 (2015), pp. 197–218.

95. Jessica Chen Weiss, "A World Safe for Autocracy? China's Rise and the Future of Global Politics," *Foreign Affairs* 98, no. 1 (2019), pp. 92–102.

96. "China's Communist Party Has Blessed the Power of Its Leader," *Economist*, October 26, 2017, https://www.economist.com/news/china/21730741-it-his-wield-life-chinas-communist-party-has-blessed-power-its-leader (accessed March 12, 2018).

97. Chris Buckley and Steven Lee Myers, "China's Legislature Blesses Xi's Indefinite Rule. It Was 2,958 to 2," *New York Times*, March 11, 2018, https://www.nytimes.com/2018/03/11/world/asia/china-xi-constitution-term-limits.html (accessed September 11, 2019).

98. Author interview, Beijing, December 2017.

99. *VOA News*, "Interview Transcript: Peter Navarro on US-China Talks, Trade," December 6, 2018, https://www.voanews.com/a/transcript-peter-navarro-us-china-talks-trade/4689880.html (accessed February 10, 2019).

100. "Excerpts from Trump's Interview with the Times," *New York Times*, December 28, 2017, https://www.nytimes.com/2017/12/28/us/politics/trump-interview-excerpts.html (accessed September 11, 2019).

101. See Ministry of Foreign Affairs of the People's Republic of China, www.fmprc.gov.cn.

102. Peter Baker, "As Trump Swerves on Trade War, It's Whiplash for the Rest of the World," *New York Times*, August 26, 2019, https://www.nytimes.com/2019/08/26/world/asia/trump-g7-meeting.html (accessed September 3, 2019).

103. *Economist*, "How the West Got China Wrong," March 1, 2018, https://www.economist.com/news/leaders/21737517-it-bet-china-would-head-towards-democracy-and-market-economy-gamble-has-failed-how (accessed March 13, 2018).

104. Harding, "The U.S. and China from Partners to Competitors," p. 16; Wang Jisi, "The View from China," in "Did America Get China Wrong? The Engagement Debate," special issue, *Foreign Affairs* 97, no. 4 (2018), pp. 183–95, at p. 184; Zhang

Tuosheng, "Zhongmei guanxi fazhan qianjing zhanwang" [Prospects of Sino-US Relations], *Dangdai meiguo pinglun* [Contemporary American Review], no. 2 (2018), pp. 1–14, at p. 13; Li Kaisheng, "Rongna zhongguo jueqi: Shijie zhixu shijia-oxia de meiguo zeren jiqi zhanlüe xuanze" [Accommodating China's Rise: World Order and the Responsibility and Strategic Option of the US], *Shijie jingji yu zhengzhi* [World Economics and Politics], no. 11 (2017), pp. 89–107, at p. 106.

105. Schell and Shirk, "Course Correction," p. 8.

106. Chen, *Mao's China and the Cold War*, p. 248.

107. See "Excerpts from Trump's Interview with the Times."

108. See Melvyn P. Leffler, *For the Soul of Mankind: The United States, the Soviet Union, and the Cold War* (New York: Hill and Wang, 2008).

109. Associated Press, "China Defends Planned Scrapping of Presidential Term Limits," March 4, 2018, https://www.voanews.com/a/china-defends-planned-scrapping-of-presidential-term-limits/4279593.html (accessed March 27, 2018).

110. Lucy Hornby, "China Searches for Point Person to Manage Relationship with Trump," *Financial Times*, March 8, 2018, https://www.ft.com/content/92481cea-21fe-11e8-add1-0e8958b189ea (accessed September 11, 2019).

111. Henry M. Paulson, *Dealing with China: An Insider Unmasks the New Economic Superpower* (New York: Twelve, 2016).

112. Author interview, Beijing, September 2016.

113. Swaine, *America's Challenge*, p. 309.

114. Peter Baker, Gardiner Harris, and Mark Landler, "Trump Fires Rex Tillerson and Will Replace Him with C.I.A. Chief Pompeo," *New York Times*, March 13, 2018, https://www.nytimes.com/2018/03/13/us/politics/trump-tillerson-pompeo.html (accessed September 11, 2019).

115. Hornby, "China Searches for Point Person."

116. Shirk, "Trump and China," p. 22.

117. On Trump's foreign policy during his first year in office, see Hal Brands, "The Unexceptional Superpower: American Grand Strategy in the Age of Trump," *Survival* 59, no. 6 (2017), pp. 7–40; Reinhard Wolf, "Donald Trump's Status-Driven Foreign Policy," *Survival* 59, no. 5 (2017), pp. 99–116.

118. Rebecca Friedman Lissner and Mira Rapp-Hooper, "The Day after Trump: American Strategy for a New International Order," *Washington Quarterly* 41, no. 1 (2018), pp. 7–25, at p. 17; *Economist*, "Why Donald Trump Is Unlikely to Start a Catastrophic Conflict," March 31, 2018, https://www.economist.com/news/united-states/21739772-war-games-why-donald-trump-unlikely-start-catastrophic-conflict (accessed March 30, 2018).

CHAPTER 8

1. Richard Ned Lebow, *Why Nations Fight: Past and Future Motives for War* (Cambridge, UK: Cambridge University Press, 2010), ch. 4 for evidence.

2. Hans J. Morgenthau, *In Defense of the National Interest: A Critical Examination of American Foreign Policy* (Lanham, MD: University Press of America, [1951] 1982), pp. 285–86; Hans J. Morgenthau, "World Politics in the Mid-Twentieth Century," *Review of Politics* 19 (April 1948), pp. 154–73.

3. Kenneth N. Waltz, *Theory of International Politics* (Reading, MA: Addison-Wesley, 1979).

4. Lebow, *Why Nations Fight*, ch. 4.

5. David C. Kang, *East Asia before the West: Five Centuries of Trade and Tribute* (New York: Columbia University Press, 2010); Feng Zhang, *Chinese Hegemony: Grand Strategy and International Institutions in East Asian History* (Stanford, CA: Stanford University Press, 2015).

Index